AND ALL SAINTS' COLL

THE
SOCIOLOGY
OF
DEVIANCE

THE SOCIOLOGY OF DEVIANCE

edited by

M. Michael Rosenberg
DAWSON COLLEGE

Robert A. Stebbins
UNIVERSITY OF CALGARY

Allan Turowetz
DAWSON COLLEGE

St. Martin's Press
NEW YORK

Library of Congress Catalog Card Number: 81-51864
Copyright © 1982 by St. Martin's Press, Inc.
All Rights Reserved.
Manufactured in the United States of America.
65432
fedcba
For information, write St. Martin's Press, Inc.,
175 Fifth Avenue, New York, N.Y. 10010

cover design: Myrna Sharp
typography: Judith Woracek

ISBN: 0-312-74064-6

Acknowledgment

Walter R. Gove would like to express his appreciation to Mayer Zald, Nina Gove, Lisa Heinrich, and Michael Hughes for their helpful comments on Chapter 7.

CONTENTS

PREFACE

The study of deviance is always popular with students and demanding on teachers. In no other area of sociological research does the full range of sociological concepts and concerns come so clearly into play. For students, the study of deviance forces a reevaluation of their assumptions about how and why people do what they do. It is a sometimes unsettling, but always exciting, experience.

In the past, anthologies in the sociology of deviance have described and explained a broad range of topics, including such issues as the labeling approach, the vested interests of moral entrepreneurs, and the careerlike activities of such persons as Skid Row alcoholics, nudists, and safecrackers. Often narrowly focused, these studies put the burden of integration on the teacher while creating for the student the impression that the study of deviance is a disjointed mixture of topics ranging from school skipping to ritual murder.

The essays in *The Sociology of Deviance* are original; they were specifically commissioned and organized for the teaching of a first course in deviance. Each contributor was guided by two central concerns: first, that the book contain all of the fundamental concepts in the field and, second, that it include some of the newer conceptual approaches and report some of the recent research on social deviance. The introductions to each of the four parts reinforce key ideas and provide connections between the individual chapters.

Part I, "Deviance and Identity," examines the microsociological level of individual experience. Its main concern is studying deviants from their own point of view. Barry Glassner's chapter on labeling theory sets forth the basic principles of the labeling perspective and analyzes its three central components: the people-processing institutions, the people being processed, and the negotiation process between them. Prue Rains's chapter on deviant careers analyzes the processes of socialization into deviant behavior and its implications for the everyday life of the deviant. Earl Rubington's work on deviant subcultures presents the functionalist perspective on deviant groups in which such groups are understood to be responding to group values in ways that others may find deviant.

Part II, "Deviance, Power, and Conflict," consists of three chapters that deal with the *macrosociological* context essential for understanding deviance as a social phenomenon. Since deviance is perceived as deviation from "something," it is important to examine the socially approved system of norms and expectations with which deviant behavior is contrasted. Arnold Birenbaum and Henry Lesieur's treatment of social values and expectations considers this concept of deviance as a departure from "normal" behavior. Ian Taylor's chapter on moral entrepreneurs approaches this topic from the perspective of power. What are the processes whereby individuals, groups, or governments create deviance? This chapter, then, is concerned with the dynamic of changes in the definition of deviance and normality and with the interests behind such changes. Charles E. Reasons's work deals with crime in high places—in government and corporations—away from public view. This phenomenon has become one of great concern in recent years, and a good deal of research is being done on it.

Part III, "Social Control and Social Change," examines the significance of social control at the macrosociological level. Walter R. Gove's chapter on the formal reshaping of deviance examines the operation of the criminal justice system and develops a distinction between criminal and noncriminal deviance. Changes in the definition of *criminal* have enormous implications for those perceived as deviant. The chapter by Edward Sagarin and Robert J. Kelly on the collective and formal promotion of deviance looks at the emergence of organizations through which groups defined as deviant try either to decriminalize their behavior or to change public opinion concerning that behavior.

Part IV presents new directions in deviance research. D. Lawrence Wieder and Charles W. Wright's treatment of deviant realities presents the ethnomethodological questioning of the concept of deviance and undertakes to determine the grounds on which people are able to define each other as deviant or normal in everyday life. Edwin M. Lemert's chapter deals with those issues that are central to an understanding of the sociology of deviance. It reviews controversial issues and raises new questions for debate. Jim Thomas's work briefly describes the approaches and research that are currently developing in the field of deviance and their implications.

The Sociology of Deviance is a text of eleven contributed readings written by noteworthy sociologists. It deals with conceptual problems in the theoretical depth they require, illustrates the significance of these issues by use of empirical data, and provides diverse approaches. We believe that this book will provide both students and teachers with a much-needed tool for the creative study of deviance.

M. MICHAEL ROSENBERG

ROBERT A. STEBBINS

ALLAN TUROWETZ

THE
SOCIOLOGY
OF
DEVIANCE

INTRODUCTION

To study deviance is to study the creation, structure, and change of *morally condemned* differences in a society. And, unlike many other areas of social science, the study of deviance poses a major philosophical question—the one of what is right and wrong among a group of people. Morally condemned differences—differences that are perceived as wrong—are a smaller, albeit especially significant, subclass of the larger category of aberrant behavior or norm violation. Moral aberrations evoke emotional responses in those who witness them and in those who have a stake in the maintenance of virtuous conduct. Such transgressions are more than merely disgusting (e.g., belching at the dinner table), annoying (e.g., tailgating by motorists), or eccentric (e.g., wearing an overcoat on a hot day). The last three behaviors are *improprieties*. They stir our sensibilities, but seldom to the degree that morally condemned behavior does. Rarely does an impropriety become a moral problem.

Differentness becomes a moral problem when it is seen as violating long-standing and at times carefully worked out solutions to the recurrent problems of everyday living. These problems include sexual expression, use of power (politics), relating to the supernatural, exposure of the human body, ownership of property, treatment of the individual, use of mind- and mood-altering substances, and leisure behavior (when it is proper not to work and what one does during this time). When institutionalized solutions to these problems are rejected by members of the community who find them unsatisfactory, other members who prefer the status quo are threatened. Improprieties can never have this sort of impact,

1

which is why they are of little concern to the student of deviant conduct.

Even within the subclass of moral differentness, some forms are more threatening than others (Stebbins, 1980). They provoke active opposition in an attempt to eliminate them. Among such forms in North America, as well as in many other parts of the world, are the "crimes of predation" (Glaser, 1974: 60): theft, burglary, murder, forgery, rape, assault, embezzlement, confidence games, and many types of fraud. Some sociologists would add certain personality defects to this list; namely, addictive drug use, compulsive gambling, alcoholism, suicide, and acute mental disorder. These threatening forms of differentness violate one of two sets of mores: (1) natural law (in the sense intended by Hobbes and Locke) and, quite likely, criminal law, or (2) moral precept, in that most people assume we ought to be in control of our behavior and emotions, especially in connection with the hedonistic pleasures of life. Because these forms are threatening, they are *intolerable*.

Other forms of moral differentness in our society are substantially less menacing than the intolerable forms, but substantially more so than life's improprieties. Nondeviant members of the community for all sorts of reasons cannot bring themselves to engage in such acts. Yet, so long as other members who do cross the threshold and become "willing" (Matza, 1969) remain within bounds (i.e., discreetly enact their deviance and confine it to a small minority of uninfluential people), their behavior is unthreatening enough to ignore. Their deviant ways are *tolerable*, with little or no effort made to eradicate them. Depending on the political jurisdiction and, to some extent, on the sociologist doing the classifying, the following behaviors are generally considered tolerable in present-day North America: eccentric behavior, occultism, heavy drinking and drunkenness, transsexualism, transvestism, deviant politics, deviant religion, striptease acts, nudism, pornography, "swinging" or group sex, gambling, marijuana use, vagrancy, and recreational pill taking.

Moral differentness, whether tolerable or intolerable, contains the seeds for a potential new solution to a recurrent problem of social life, a solution threatening to replace the existing institutionalized one. So there is always a degree of threat to those who value the status quo, even if they are sufficiently unthreatened at the moment by the tolerable forms to refrain from taking action against them.[1] In other words, deviance becomes still another community problem demanding a solution.

Seen in this light, it is no wonder that a number of social scientists, particularly sociologists, have developed a lasting research interest in deviance. Like other members of their society, sociologists have learned its commonsensical meaning of morally condemned differentness through their childhood socialization. But today's sociologists have also learned through their professional training and research to suspend common sense in this area of life, for it too often provides a seriously misleading version of everyday events. To make matters worse, the differences between scientific and lay knowledge of deviance are frequently blurred. The strong moral underpinnings of common sense have influenced the scientific work of the past and, to some extent, even that of the present. Sociologists have found it difficult to place themselves at a distance from the influences of their society sufficient to achieve an accurate and objective assessment of it.

Today, for example, there is widespread agreement among students of deviance that the definition of differentness is by no means absolute. Some groups in the community are powerful enough to make their definitions official or legal, while other groups who find the officially censured behavior attractive (or at least tolerable) are, nevertheless, forced to live by those rules. It is also generally accepted by contemporary social scientists, though the observation is an old one, that deviance is actually irradicable. Durkheim (1951: 1362) writes: "Now there is no society known where a more or less developed criminality is not found under different forms. No people exists whose morality is not daily infringed upon. We must therefore call crime necessary and declare that it cannot be nonexistent, that the fundamental conditions of social organization, as they are understood, logically imply it. Consequently, it is normal."

It took years for ideas such as these to germinate and grow, because students of deviance were disposed toward a different (commonsensical) conception of the world. Indeed, the history of deviance theory and research is, in no small part, a history of coming to grips with the fact that, when it comes to moral issues, common sense plays tricks on the scientific mind.

DEVIANCE THEORY PAST AND PRESENT

Our first task is to set the stage for the chapters in this book, most of which provide their own detailed histories of the concepts with which they deal. This introduction complements those efforts by offering a broad history of the study of deviance, dwelling on the rise and fall of its various theoretical positions. George Vold and Thomas J. Bernard (1979), David Matza (1969), and Nanette Davis (1975) have all written extensive accounts of the fads and fashions of deviance through the years. Their works form the basis for much of this short review of the various approaches to the subject, which, since the eighteenth century, have come and (usually) gone in response to society's definition of certain forms of differentness as objectionable.

Understandably, the earliest social scientific concern with deviance centered on its intolerable forms. The name most frequently associated with the first, or "classical," school of criminology is that of Cesare Bonesana, marchese di Beccaria (1738–1794), an Italian criminologist, economist, and jurist. Today his ideas would be considered part of the branch of criminology known as criminal justice. He argued against capital punishment and the inhuman treatment of offenders, urging instead the adoption of an exact scale of penalties, which could be applied to particular deviant acts without reference to their perpetrators. Certainty and swiftness of punishment, he believed, are more important in preventing crime than severity.

Constitutional Approaches

A century intervened between the classical period and the rise of positivism in criminology. Perhaps the best known criminological positivist was another Italian, Cesare Lombroso, who with his two students, Enrico Ferri and Raffaele Garofalo, strove to develop a multiple causation theory of crime. They argued that the behavior of human beings is caused by natural biological and environmental forces to so great an extent that their actions are determined by these forces. The appropriate program for criminology in the middle of the nineteenth century was to construct typologies of offenders and to examine the biological and environmental factors leading them into a life of crime. This required studying criminals directly, with the intention of amassing suitable statistical data on them.

The biological underpinnings of the positive school eventually led to several individualized, constitutionally based attempts to explain crime. Viewed from the perspective of modern deviance theory, these now amount to a scientific dead end, inasmuch as criminality and most other forms of differentness are currently viewed as products of the deviant's social environment. The search in the late nineteenth and early twentieth centuries for, first, a physical and, later, a mental explanation of crime is briefly summarized here.

Lombroso's work on physical types became the foundation for several typologies, each purporting to classify criminals and distinguish them from respectable folk. The early typologies, including Lombroso's, depicted criminals as degenerate or atavistic creatures, as a lower or more primitive evolutionary form of human development. As these efforts at classification progressed and the use of data became more sophisticated, the number of traits convincingly identifiable as criminalistic dropped markedly. By 1913 Charles Goring could point only to inferiority in stature and body weight as valid differentiae, which hardly constitute a physical type. Even these differences are rejected now.

Interest in the physical traits of criminals waned sharply at this point in the face of a convincing newcomer to the explanatory scene—subnormal intelligence. But as we shall see shortly, mental ability as a possible factor in the etiology of crime was quickly shown to be a false lead. Consequently, classification of physical traits was resumed with E. A. Hooton's (1939) publication of an elaborate study proclaiming new evidence for the proposition that such traits do separate the criminal from the noncriminal. Unfortunately, his work was beset with serious validity and reliability problems. Methodological flaws also tainted the research of Ernst Kretschmer (Vold and Bernard, 1979) and William H. Sheldon (1949). Sheldon tried during the late 1940s and early 1950s to adapt the typology of mental disorders developed by Emil Kraepelin, a psychiatrist, to the physiques of adult and juvenile offenders. Sheldon studied three types: the endomorph, who is small boned, soft skinned, fat, and round; the mesomorph, who is hard, muscled, and heavy chested; and the ectomorph, who is lean, fragile, delicate boned, and small faced.

While physical type theories slowly lost their appeal through a failure to marshal adequate empirical support, one of their central propositions briefly managed to retain its popularity: the concept of low intelligence or feeblemindedness as a cause of criminality. Alfred Binet's development of the intelligence test in the late nineteenth century stimulated this interest, and comparisons of various populations began to appear shortly thereafter. In 1914 H. H. Goddard (Vold and Bernard, 1979) reported several studies of inmates in prisons, hospitals, and other public institutions, with the median study for prisoners claiming a feeblemindedness rate of 70 percent. Nevertheless, it soon became obvious, from research on the World

War I draft army in the United States, that the cutoff point between normal and subnormal intelligence had been set far too high in the early investigations. Research on these draftees also provided the first procedurally correct sampling of the intelligence of the general population. When their test scores were compared with those of criminals, it was clear no mental differences of any significance existed between the two groups.

With social scientists' eyes at the turn of the century trained almost hypnotically on potential constitutional causes of crime, it is to be expected that the possibility of the inheritance of criminal tendencies should sooner or later catch their fancy. Goring (1913), for example, held that father-son similarities in deviance could be accounted for by heredity rather than imitation. Glandular malfunctioning was another attractive explanation for criminality, though it was subsequently found to be no more prevalent in criminals than in the general population. The most recent attempt to link crime with the criminal's heredity is the XYY chromosome hypothesis: Men cursed with this rare cellular structure are predisposed to violent, antisocial acts. While research is still being conducted on this assertion, it is generally conceded that such a genetic link with criminality is, at best, tenuous (Fox, 1971; Owen, 1972).

As the preceding paragraphs indicate, the biological or constitutional explanations of crime and deviance have borne little fruit. What is disconcerting from a scientific standpoint is their enduring attraction for some scientists and many lay people, despite their procedural flaws. Nassi and Abramowitz (1976: 591) point out that "contemporary studies of the biological correlates of criminality reveal the same basic assumptions and methodological drawbacks as their historical counterparts." They go on to describe the substantial political appeal inherent in a simple, measurable explanation of crime, which is the hope held out by the biological theories.

Psychopathology is a calling for both psychiatrists and clinical psychologists, one where a link between the biological factors in crime (to the extent they exist) and the social factors is most likely to be forged. Psychopathological interest in certain forms of deviance, including crime, date from Sigmund Freud. Since then, in-depth interviews and personality tests have become standard tools for these practitioners as they attempt to isolate personal peculiarities and abnormalities correlating with both intolerable and tolerable kinds of deviance. Still, carefully controlled comparisons indicate that the personality tests have yet to gain the precision needed to separate deviant traits from normal ones as found in the general population. To some extent, this field suffers from the same methodological short-comings as the purely biological approaches: It relies heavily on case studies of small numbers of subjects or of people already suspected of being deviant, neither of which is an adequate basis for generalization to the overall population of a society.

Social Pathology and Disorganization

Nearly as lengthy a sequence of sociological attempts to explain crime and deviance parallels the ones in biology and psychopathology. The view that deviance is a type of *social* pathology was expressed as early as the middle of the nineteenth century by Auguste Comte (Davis, 1975). Comte was followed by the social Darwinists. Both he and they defined deviance as individual maladjustment, a pathological response to the stresses of urban living in industrial society. Some members of this type of society were seen as better able to survive these rigors than others; they are the fittest. The state should refrain from intervening in this process of natural selection. In harmony with the prevailing biological theories of the day, the social scientists also viewed individual maladjustment as ultimately due to inherited physical and mental defects. Later sociologists added their own propositions to this model: Deviance is a departure from the norms of an organized society, where organization rests on a consensus among its middle class on major values. Deviance is personal disorganization in this organized community, the remedy for which is change of the offending person.

The ideas of the social pathologists, who were ruralists at heart, were eventually superseded by those of a group of sociologists more in tune with the trends of twentieth-century urban America. Like Durkheim, members of the Chicago school (many were professors at the University of Chicago) looked upon deviance as a natural phenomenon. Thus, it was to be "appreciated" rather than "corrected" (Matza, 1969). Participant observer research by field workers, such as Nels Anderson (1923), Harvey Zorbaugh (1929), and Louis Wirth (1928), brought social scientists into direct contact with their subjects and the lives they led. Members of the Chicago school were interested in the situations in which deviant behavior is enacted and the social worlds deviants create because of their differentness. Their further tendency to try to explain deviance with rates of deviant behavior and its geographical distribution, as Robert Park (Davis, 1980) did, sometimes failed to square with the accounts given by the deviants themselves. The Chicago school also had its theoretical difficulties. For instance, these sociologists held that the social integration of a community is occasionally shattered by larger uncontrollable forces, which results in crisis and deviant behavior. Though they believed that reintegration is eventually achieved, when and how this happens was left unsaid. And they appear to have been unaware of Durkheim's observation that deviance is inevitable. Theoretically, at any rate, they expected deviance to disappear in the long run.

Functionalism

The reigning approach to deviance from the late 1940s to the early 1960s was that of the functionalists. It complemented the work of the Chicago school. Talcott Parsons (1951) paved the way with his systemic conception of social life in general. He conceived of deviance as dysfunctional, as a force endangering the system's stability. But a true social system weathers these minor storms, since its component parts adjust to them in such a way as to preserve equilibrium. In Robert Merton's (1957) famous theory of anomie, temporary disjunction in the means-ends nexus of a society (anomie) sometimes fosters deviant adaptations which, in the end, pose no threat to the overall working of the system. There are five modes of personal adaptation to the societal condition of anomie.

Even under conditions of anomie, some members of society continue to conform to its rules, which they do by accepting its goals and the means for reaching them. A significant minority, however, choose to innovate. This they do by retaining their allegiance to the goals while finding deviant means to achieve them (e.g., theft). Others adapt by ritualizing, by employing institutionalized or acceptable means to given deviant ends (such as the bureaucrat who, when threatened with demotion, responds by following to the letter organizational rules). The retreatist rejects both the conventional goals and the conventional means. Retreatists may be, among others, alcoholics, heavy drinkers, vagrants, or drug addicts. Those who rebel substitute new goals and means of reaching them for the old ones. Those who strive to establish new political or religious sytems exemplify this mode of adaptation.

In opposition to Parsons and Merton, other functionalists theorized that deviance has salutary, albeit unintended, consequences. Some of these are listed by Kingsley Davis (1971) in a study of prostitution and by Kai Erikson (1964, 1966) in his studies of the Puritans and of deviants in general. Davis, for example, argues that

A Typology of Modes of Individual Adaptation

Modes of Adaptation	Culture Goals	Institutionalized Means
I. Conformity	+	+
II. Innovation	+	−
III. Ritualism	−	+
IV. Retreatism	−	−
V. Rebellion	±	±

(+) = acceptance, (−) = rejection, (±) = rejection of prevailing values and substitution of new ones.

prostitution protects the purity of the family by channeling irregular sexual expression away from respected wives and daughters, and that it provides a sexual outlet for those otherwise lacking sexual privilege (e.g., soldiers, strangers, perverts, repulsive individuals). In short, functionalism sees deviants as both good and bad for a society, but certainly not bad enough to bring about its decline.

Though these two functional models bear some resemblance to the organization-disorganization-reorganization sequence of the Chicago school, they are based on the assumption that social systems maintain themselves. This was never part of the thinking of the earlier group. Moreover, the functionalists' methods of data collection are different. Because their models pertain to an entire society or community, those models discourage direct observation of their predictions. After all, it is difficult to observe an entire society. The functionalists worked from their armchairs (and those in the university library) to develop explanations of deviance testable only by means of archival data. To this day, the theory has also been dogged by the question of how one determines what is good and bad for society, what is right and wrong, what is functional and dysfunctional.

Labeling

While the functional school of thought dominated the study of deviance, its eventual successor, the labeling approach, was quietly forming in the background. The origin of the latter can be traced to a statement by Frank Tannenbaum (1938: 19–20) in which he notes that "the process of making the criminal . . . is a process of tagging, defining, identifying, segregating, describing, emphasizing, making conscious and self-conscious; it becomes a way of stimulating, suggesting, emphasizing, and evoking the very traits that are complained of."

This passage contains the germ of many of the ideas more fully developed later by Edwin Lemert (1951, 1967), Howard S. Becker (1963), and David Matza (1969), the three main thinkers whose theorizing became the foundation of this school of thought. Moral entrepreneurs create rules in their own interest, the violation of which results in some cases (depending on personal influence and police concern) in the violator being officially labeled as deviant. The societal reaction to this deviance is such that people so identified, or "tagged" in Tannenbaum's terminology, are often forced into a deviant career in which their fate hinges on the nature of their interaction with agents of social control, nondeviant members of the community, and other deviants. The labeling theorists returned to the open-ended, qualitative methodology of the Chicago school, especially participant observation, and to its focus on first-hand accounts by the deviants themselves of their problems and life-styles. Labeling's dramatic rise to ascendancy in the 1960s came as a response to the cumulative failure of functionalism to come to grips with the interactive side of becoming deviant and its failure, along with that of mainstream criminology, to recognize the arbitrariness of formal and informal norms.

Conflict Theory

The labeling approach shares with the group conflict approach the assumption that the laws of the state are framed and enforced by those groups with the power to control other groups who threaten them. In the study of deviance, however, the application of conflict theory went in a different direction from labeling theory. The latter's ancestors were social psychologists, while today's conflict specialists have descended from scholars interested in organizational and societal questions; chiefly, Simmel, Marx, and Dahrendorf. These men contended that a society is composed of a shifting equilibrium of opposing groups, all of whom are jockeying for enough control of the state to defend and further their interests. The conflict approach reinstates politics as a central thesis in deviance theory. For instance, law is seen by many of these theorists as a means for protecting group rights, privileges, and interests. With such ends in mind, groups strive to control society's lawmaking and enforcing procedures. At its extreme, conflict theory argues for a fundamental reorganization of society (see Chapter 5). Although isolated strands of the conflict orientation appeared in the writings of some of the Chicago sociologists, credit must go to Vold and Bernard (1979) for first identifying clearly its main tenets and applying them to deviance. They indicate how particular forms of crime flow from the power struggle between opposing groups. At the present time, the theory of deviance-based group conflict continues to be shaped under the banners of *new criminology* and *radical criminology* by men such as Richard Quinney (1970), Austin Turk (1969), and Ian Taylor et al. (1973).

"Controlology"

"Controlology" is the latest chapter in this continuing narrative of the study of deviance, and, like most of the preceding chapters, it is one that rests on a dissatisfaction with the prevailing theories. It is Jason Ditton's (1979) term for the study of the wavelike nature of crime rates, which, as he demonstrates, result from the vicissitudes of law enforcement. In Ditton's (1979: 100) words: "Control rather than 'crime' is the vital element . . . explanations of the rise or fall in crime rates have to be sought elsewhere than in the motives and intentions of those eventually called 'criminal.' "

His crime wave model is based on a modification of Leslie Wilkins's (1964) deviance-amplification hypothesis and an expansion of Becker's (1963) classification of secret, falsely accused, and pure deviants, the latter being those who have actually broken a rule and are apprehended for it. The pure and falsely accused deviants officially come to our attention through *control*, which happens in wavelike fashion. Ditton describes how a combination of such processes as hardening judicial attitudes, increased police detection, and legislative redefinition of behavior as deviant can eventuate in a larger known criminal population. As these processes continue, however, the actual number of criminals at large necessarily begins to decline. A decelerating rate of arrest and conviction is the only possible outcome now. This, in turn, diminishes judicial and legislative concern with the problem. Moreover, a falling crime rate is of little news value, which pushes the problem even further from public and official attention and contributes to further deceleration. But this condition increases the actual number of criminals on the street, ultimately causing the crime rate to recover from the bottom of its cycle.

THE STUDY OF DEVIANCE TODAY

One inescapable conclusion from the foregoing review is that the field is currently in a state of intellectual disarray. That state is the legacy of over two hundred years of mixing science with morals. No less than four theoretical approaches have been in vogue at one time or another during the past twenty years.[2] And, as we shall soon see, a fifth—ethnomethodology—may be forming on the horizon. Of the four, controlology is the most recent arrival and must therefore establish itself in competition with the new criminology and labeling theory, which continue to dominate over a now largely outmoded functional theory of deviance. The subjects of the chapters in this book reflect the confused state of this art, while the chapters themselves attempt to remedy the situation.

Part I concentrates on the persistent issue of deviance and personal identity—a central theme in the labeling perspective. This perspective is taken up first in this book, because most contemporary research and theorizing in the study of deviance use it as a major point of reference. Since the Chicago school, students of deviance have shown an unflagging interest in such questions as these: How do deviants justify their actions to themselves and to nondeviant others? Are they proud or ashamed of their imputed status of gay, nudist, gambler, communist, tramp, and the like? In what ways does the deviant subculture help shape the deviants' views of themselves? How do these views change over time and over the deviants' moral careers? These are largely, though not entirely, social psychological questions. They have intrigued sociologists for more than fifty years. For example, Thrasher (1963: 230) wrote:

> Internally the gang may be viewed as a struggle for recognition. It offers the underprivileged boy probably the best opportunity to acquire status and hence it plays an essential part in the development of his personality. . . . For this reason the gang boy's conception of his role is more vivid with reference to his gang than to other social groups.

And Zorbaugh (1929: 108–109) commented:

> They [hobos] are mostly the misfits of society. They can't or won't fit it. And however much they may boast of their freedom, they are always on the defensive against the condemnation of a larger society, sensitive to the opinion of a larger world.

Questions of the sort just mentioned continue to interest the labeling theorists. Today, their concept of career is so important that separate treatment of it is in order. In Chapter 1, Rains examines this notion, which has actually been present in deviance research longer than the term *career* itself (for a history of it, see Petersilia et al., 1978). Although Shaw (1930) and Sutherland (1937) dealt with the special turning points and contingencies of the criminals whose biographies they annotated, and Glueck and Glueck (1937) used the term in the title of their famous book, it remained for Erving Goffman (1959) and Howard S. Becker (1963) to popularize it by formally extending this term from occupations to moral behavior.

The same happened with the concept of subculture. According to Arnold (1970), the term was first systematically considered by Gordon (1947) with reference to racial and religious groups. More than twenty years earlier, however, Sutherland (1924) had discussed the subculture of criminals without referring to it as such. Rubington's review of the concept in Chapter 2 demonstrates its inherent appeal for functionalists and labeling theorists alike, who, when studying it empirically, usually take an ethnographic approach.

Labeling theory's immense popularity in sociological circles from the early 1960s to the present has also encouraged some scholars to assess carefully its strengths and weaknesses. Glassner mounts such a review in Chapter 3, thereby setting the stage for discussion in Parts II and III of subsequent theoretical and empirical developments in the study of deviance.

Part II centers on another core issue in the study of deviance, that is, deviance as a product of the capacity of certain powerful groups to impose their will on other groups and the conflict resulting from this relationship. This is a macrosociological topic. It is one of great importance for the new criminologists and of only somewhat lesser importance for many labeling theorists. Underlying this issue is the question, addressed in Chapter 4 by Birenbaum and Lesieur, of whose values and their more specific normative manifestations will triumph to rule the community. Concern with moral norms, though not with their arbitrariness, stretches back to the social pathologists who, it appears, judged all deviance from the only perspective they knew; namely, the middle class one in which they were raised. Recognition of the arbitrariness of these norms came much later. The seed for this idea was first planted by Tannenbaum (1938) in his discussion of "tagging" deviants, but it remained dormant until Becker's (1963) essay on "moral entrepreneurs."

Taylor's chapter describes how the new criminologists have developed the idea from there. Reasons, in Chapter 6, takes the arbitrariness theme in another direction. His thesis is that formal moral norms are not only enacted in accordance with the interests of powerful groups, but also enforced in sympathy with those same interests. In corporate crime, secret deviants are allowed to remain at large. The study of this type of deviance is not traditionally attached to any particular school of thought. It has been pursued, often under the heading of "white-collar crime," since Sutherland's (1940) initial statement over forty years ago.[3]

Social control and social change are treated in Part III. Gove's chapter on the formal reshaping of deviants deals with issues broached by Beccaria in the eighteenth century. Reshaping deviants is probably the oldest concern in the scientific study of deviance and was a popular concern long before the rise of social science. Since present ways of reshaping deviants are as controversial as ever, it may come as a surprise for some to learn that this subject is of only peripheral interest in the labeling and new criminology approaches. Today, only the criminal justice wing of mainstream criminology consistently addresses this problem. Labeling theory, nonetheless, shares with the field of criminal justice an interest in the day-to-day social life in institutions constructed and operated for (it is hoped) the betterment of various kinds of deviants.

For their part, the deviants often have a different opinion of society's favorite methods of social control; they believe these methods operate against their best interests. Many of them prefer that society change the institutionalized solutions it has worked up in response to their behavior. Sagarin and Kelly (Chapter 8) tell us how different groups of deviants organize to promote their own causes by advocating formal social and political modification of the social structure or, failing that, at least an understanding attitude. Sociological interest in self-help groups of deviants appears to be approximately three decades old, even though some of these groups have a much longer history (Sagarin, 1969).[4] Studies of the formal promotion of deviance have no special theoretical affiliation, although their largely enthnographic orientation places them in the same methodological camp with the labeling theorists and members of the Chicago school.

Part IV looks to the future of the sociological study of deviance. It opens with Lemert's discussion of the many issues still outstanding in this field. Some of these issues are addressed by Wieder and Wright (in Chapter 10) and Thomas (in Chapter 11) as they prescribe new theoretical goals for it. Wieder and Wright call attention to the failure of the study of deviance to examine the culturally structured "methods" people use when perceiving and applying moral norms, which, when violated, lead to deviance. Their chapter indicates that sporadic ethnomethodological examinations of deviance have been going on for roughly twenty years, even though this branch of sociology has yet to develop a self-conscious approach to the subject of deviance.[5] To date, ethnomethodologists seem to prefer working from a general theoretical level to specific examples in many different spheres of social life, including deviant behavior. But that may change. Thomas takes a different tack by arguing for the program of research suggested by Marxist and neo-Marxist writings.

To conclude, the study of deviance bears a strong family resemblance to one of its parents, the discipline of sociology—for the parent of this unruly child is exhibiting many of the same behavioral problems as the child itself: proliferating theories, diverse methodologies, and ideological cross-currents (e.g., Gordon, 1980). Yet such ferment is anything but dull. The reader who relishes the stimulation of scientific change and intellectual uncertainty will find this critique of the contemporary study of deviance too absorbing to put down.

NOTES

[1]The reasons why members of our society might tolerate some forms of deviance even though they stand as *potential* threats to their way of life have never been systematically explored. Future research in this area could well disclose the presence of a "live and let live" attitude; a sort of democratic acknowledgment of a person's right to be different, as long as we can think of no pressing grounds for opposing the difference. Furthermore, daily life has enough immediate threats, both social and personal, to keep us occupied. Their sheer weight may force us to leave the more remote ones uncontested.

[2]This statement pertains to sociology only and not to developments in psychiatry and psychology.

[3]Vold and Bernard (1979: 359) refer to white-collar crime as a "specialized aspect of social and economic conflict," which is how one would have to classify contemporary research on the related subject of corporate crime.

[4]Alcoholics Anonymous is possibly North America's oldest self-help group for deviants. Sociological research on it appears to date to no earlier than 1949 (Sagarin, 1969).

[5]Garfinkle's (1956) study of degradation ceremonies as used in courtrooms and similar situations is perhaps the first ethnomethodological study of deviance.

Part I

Deviance and Identity

Since Howard Becker's seminal contribution, *Outsiders* (1963), the labeling approach has succeeded in becoming the dominant paradigm in the sociology of deviance. This perspective has sponsored research in such diverse areas as the management and transformation of deviant identities, the social organization of deviant lifestyles, and the dynamic of people-processing institutions. Even its many critics tend to agree that the labeling perspective has provided at the very least a point of departure for the understanding of social deviance.

Labeling theory is derived from the symbolic interactionist perspective contending that identity, meaning, and society are situationally created phenomena. Applied to deviance, this perspective generates the recognition that "deviance is not the quality of the act the person commits but rather a consequence of the application of rules and sanctions applied to an offender. The deviant is one to whom that label has successfully been applied; deviant behaviour is behaviour that people so label (Becker, 1963:9). That is, it is the interpretation of, and response to, a specific form of behavior on the part of the social audience that subsequently determines its deviant nature.

Labeling theory's impact was a consequence of its successful integration of two preexisting traditions in the sociology of deviance that had previously seemed incompatible. Research on *subcultures* was an attempt to generate a structural theory that would account for processes of social differentiation that were at the core of deviance. Research on deviant *careers* attempted to grasp those social experiences in terms of which persons organize their lives around deviant behaviors. As with so much of sociology, these separate approaches split the study of deviance into an objective and subjective component seemingly beyond synthesis.

As Prudence Rains demonstrates (Chapter 1), the career concept was one that provided a convenient sociological approach to the study of commitment and identification among deviants. Drawing on the work of Hughes (1958), the study of career provided a framework for detailed ethnographic studies of those persons engaged in deviant activities. For Hughes, an individual's work identity is the most important part of that person's social identity. In an effort to understand the emergence of that occupational identity as it comes to be experienced during career socialization, he searched for a set of commonalities and uniformities linking all kinds of occupations and professions. Hughes suggested that the process of identification with, and commitment to, an occupational culture, is, to a large degree, the consequence of moving through a sequence of phases— that is, experiences of occupational socialization, which include occupational selection, apprenticeship and training, maintenance, and the development of a consistent understanding of both the native language and the subtle nuances of that particular occupational culture.

The concept of career, then, became useful to labeling theorists insofar as stigmatized persons tend to pass through a similar sequence of phases and share a common set of experiences during the process of coming to terms with their deviant identities. At the same time, however, labeling theorists recognized that members of the deviant community, unlike those persons involved in "normative" occupational cultures, are *provided* with a common set of experiences which may well have certain character-defining and identity-building implications; for example, as a result of being sorted through a processing system, the person who steals "from time to time" is transformed into a thief.

Lindesmith's (1940) study of opium addiction went one step further by emphasizing that deviant motivation and deviant commitment are built into the course of involvement in deviant activities as a result of interaction with others. Lemert (1967a) generalized on Lindesmith's framework to produce the notion of secondary deviation.

Cohen's (1955) theory of subcultures was an attempt to free sociologists from a concern with deviant motivation toward a focus on the structural features within which deviant activities emerged. Although Cohen did discuss in detail the social psychological problems that motivate the delinquents, he emphasized the structural features that determine the direction their behavior takes. Students facing similar problems form groups as they try to solve their problems; they form subcultures when their solutions reverse the values and norms of middle class culture.

Although Becker's research on jazz musicians and marijuana users was directly derived from the career tradition, he did not limit himself to ethnographic studies; rather, he emphasized the transactions between deviants and others that determine the course of the deviant's life. In doing so, Becker also recognized the importance of structural features, such as the differential distribution of power and the manipulation of public opinion on the part of moral entrepreneurs. In this way, he succeeded in combining the interactionist focus on experience within a structuralist account.

Since the development of labeling theory, neither the notion of careers nor that of subcultures has been dropped, but both have been profoundly altered. Career continues to be a useful notion, but the interest has now shifted to one of *moral* careers. Moreover, the individual is no longer treated as the master of his own fate; instead, it is recognized that institutions such as prisons and mental hospitals (Goffman, 1961) both shape the person's perception of self and determine the course of his life.

Rubington points out that one weakness of Cohen's concept of subcultures was its assumption of the total separation between subculture and the normative group. Using a more situational approach to subcultures, Rubington suggests that there are different degrees and forms of participation in conventional and deviant cultures. The form of participation in turn has a profound effect on the deviant's moral career as commitment and identification vary.

Barry Glassner sums up some of the main tenets of the labeling approach to deviance and articulates some of the more significant and serious objections to which it has given rise. One of labeling theory's initial strengths was that it provided a simple, yet seemingly powerful, model for the understanding of deviance. As time has passed, and research has continued, however, deviance has come to be seen as a far more complex phenomenon than it appeared. While Glassner sees labeling as still relevant, he suggests a number of directions in which the approach might expand in order to address some of the new critiques that have been lodged against it. Others, rejecting the labeling approach as inherently *oversimplified*, suggest that it be discarded. The remainder of this text displays both options and gives an indication of the dynamism and intellectual excitement generated by the contemporary study of deviance.

1 DEVIANT CAREERS

PRUE RAINS

The terms sociologists have devised to talk about people's experiences at work have for some time now been used by sociologists to talk about people's experiences at deviance. The term *career* is perhaps the most familiar and central of these terms, having made its entrance into discourse about deviance in Erving Goffman's (1961) essay about the "moral careers" of mental patients and in Howard Becker's subsequent discussion of "deviant careers" in his widely read book, *Outsiders* (1963).

This chapter describes how this work terminology, and the term *career* in particular, has served to transform studies of deviant activity. In the first section, the sense in which deviant worlds are sometimes literally work worlds is explored; in the second section, it is explained how the notion of "deviant career" has been employed more generally to look at what happens after people get involved with deviance rather than at what happens before they do; and in the third section, the "moral' aspects of deviant careers are discussed, and we examine how sociologists of deviance have frequently (but not always) organized their discussions of these aspects of career in relation to the practices of social control agencies. The chapter concludes with a few observations about what we know and do not know about deviant careers.

DEVIANCE AND CRIME AS WORK

Sometimes work and deviance have something in common in the literal sense that deviance or crime can be what people do for a living. In other words, some people have deviant careers in the quite straightforward sense that deviance or crime is their work. And there are now quite a few sociological studies that present the activities of prostitutes, burglars, strippers, fences, card hustlers, and bank robbers in occupational terms and that describe their worlds as work worlds.

While studies such as these are still far from commonplace, they were at one time downright startling because they represented so marked a departure from the approach more customarily taken toward deviance. Deviance was for some time rather automatically viewed from what David Matza (1969) has called a "correctional perspective"—a perspective that, because it assumed that deviant behavior was pathological and because it focused so relentlessly on finding its causes, left very little room for looking at the actual activities in which deviants were engaged. As Howard Becker (1963: 166) observed, many studies of juvenile delinquency had been undertaken, yet "very few [have told] us in detail what a juvenile delinquent does in his daily round of activity and what he thinks about himself, society, and his activities." Thus, when Edwin Sutherland, in one of the earliest and best known presentations of crime as work (The Professional Thief, 1937, written in collaboration with Chic Conwell, a thief), proceeded not only to tell us what thieves do but also that thievery was a profession, he was advancing an orientation toward crime that was genuinely surprising and that has only recently become a fully familiar feature of the literature about deviance and crime. And his intention to "reveal to the person in middle class society the details of a profession with which he has had little contact and which he has probably not even recognized as a profession" (Sutherland, 1937: 229) is still a useful one.

The presentation of deviance and crime as work serves to recognize the truth about some kinds of deviant and criminal activities from the point of view of those who engage in them (it was, after all, Chic Conwell who defined himself as a "professional"), and has restored what is therefore a rightful occupational frame of reference to activities that, simply because they were illegal or dishonorable, had been either ignored or "pathologized." A number of interesting and effective accounts now exist in which sociologists explore deviant and criminal activity using this occupational frame of reference and the conceptual equipment that goes with it: recruitment, apprenticeship, the nature and organization of work skills, activities, and roles, and, of course, career patterns.

In a study based on interviews with call girls in Los Angeles, for example, James Bryan (1965) describes how call girls begin their careers with a period of apprenticeship to another "working girl"; during this period of apprenticeship, the novice works under the supervision of the trainer, in the trainer's apartment, and with clients referred to her by the trainer. While some training does go on during this period, Bryan suggests that the apprenticeship period is not primarily a way for the novice to acquire skills (it is, he observes, essentially an unskilled job) but is instead a way for the novice to acquire clients. As the following quote from one of his informants illustrates, it is not as easy to become a call girl as it might seem.

> I met this guy at a bar and I tried to make him pay me, but the thing is, you can't do it that way because they are romantically interested in you, and they don't think that it is on that kind of basis. You can't all of a sudden come up and want money for it, you have to be known beforehand. . . . I think that is what holds a lot of girls back who might work. . . . You can't just, say, get an apartment and get a phone in and everything and say, "Well, I'm gonna start business," because you gotta get clients from somewhere. There has to be a contact (Bryan, 1965: 289).

The apprenticeship period exists, therefore, because it solves the novice's problem of getting clients while providing the "trainer" with a way to make a profit (the trainer gets a 40 to 50 percent kickback for each new referral) and a way to regulate the demand for her own services. Like a number of other would-be professionals (although for different reasons), call girls cannot advertise their services and have to rely at the beginning of their careers on referrals from a mentor or colleagues.[1]

As a second and rather different example of this occupational approach toward deviance and crime, Peter Letkemann (1973), in a study based on prison interviews with experienced criminals, compares the occupational skills required for cracking safes with those required for robbing banks. In a discussion so detailed it could be read as a recipe for cracking safes, he describes the technical expertise safecrackers have and the sense of craftsmanship they experience in bringing off a "beautiful job." He then contrasts the technical skills required for these surreptitious crimes with the social skills required for overt crimes, such as bank robbery, in which victims must be directly confronted and managed and in which, Letkemann suggests, violence may be staged in order to avoid violence.

Experienced bank robbers feel their work is made more difficult, and the victim's situation more dangerous, by the tendency of the mass media to depict bank robberies as phony, "toy gun stuff." Robbers feel they are now constrained first of all to convince their victims the event is "not a joke." This may require more brutal action on their part than they would otherwise need to use. . . . The establishment of authority is no doubt enhanced by the display and use of weapons . . . [but] the gun is only one of various persuasive devices used by robbers. This is not to deny that the successful use of other resources such as loud commands and physical violence is possible only because he has a gun. Nevertheless, much of the robber's activity during a robbery is necessitated only because he does not want to use his gun. He is, therefore, rightly dismayed at the condescension of those who fail to appreciate that his techniques revolve around the nonuse, rather than the use of guns (Letkemann, 1973: 114).

Letkemann uses the contrast he has drawn between the work skills of a safecracker and those of a bank robber to point out that criminal activity is by no means a unitary phenomenon, but includes working skills as diverse as those that distinguish a mechanic from a psychiatrist. And, in fact, various types of deviant and criminal activity have been described as profession (but see Klein, 1974, on the overextended application of this term to criminal activity), as business (see Moore, 1978), as family business (Ianni, 1972), and as show business (Newton, 1972). There even exists now an integrated presentation of a number of these studies of deviance and crime as work in the suitably titled book *Odd Jobs: The World of Deviant Work* (Miller, 1978).

While these numerous accounts have usefully restored a rightful occupational frame of reference to activities that were once ignored or "pathologized," it may be that the view of deviance and crime as work has become overly appealing to sociologists of deviance. It is a viewpoint that has, after all, the double allure of being both utterly noncorrectional in its assumptions about deviant activity, and nicely complete in its conceptual equipment for looking at that activity. And this very theoretical convenience may have had two effects: the effect of steering sociologists toward studying the kinds of deviant and criminal activity that can most easily be treated as work, and the effect of producing overly neutral and occupationalized accounts of forms of activity that, from the point of view of those who engage in them, are not always simply or merely their way of making a living. As a female impersonator observes:

If you have messed up your life so much by, uh . . . growing your own hair and making yourself too obvious, so that your job . . . so that you're holding your job by being feminine . . . and if you're too feminine on the street, then the only thing you can do is go up and down the street camping, or saying, "I don't care," when in reality you really *do* care. And it's not a beautiful life at all. There's nothing really pretty about it . . . it's like Outward Bound. You're going to have to ride this ship the rest of . . . eternity. Just back and forth, back and forth. Uh . . . I think this is the saddest I've ever talked to you about it, but it *isn't* a nice way of life, simply because of the fact it isn't an acceptable way of life (Newton, 1972: 130–1).

In other words, occupationalized accounts of deviant activity may, to employ David Matza's (1969) more general reservation about modern studies of deviance, "romanticize diversity," and they may also tend to present an overorganized picture of deviant activity (see also Millman, 1975, on these tendencies as expressions of a male-oriented sociology of deviance).

Not all deviant activities are, in any case, easily construed as work, and it is not clear even that most forms of crime are forms of work for those who engage in them; for many, their criminal activities appear to be intermittent, sideline, and only quasi-committed forms of activity. While the term *career* has sometimes been used in the study of deviance in the straightforward sense that deviance is sometimes work and might therefore by something someone could have a career doing, the term has more often been used in a more general sense, one that includes, but is not restricted to, the phenomenon of deviant or criminal work.

SIGNIFICANCE OF *DEVIANT CAREER*

In choosing to formulate a person's involvement in deviance as a "deviant career," Howard Becker, whose discussion in *Outsiders* (1963) did most to popularize the term, was explicitly altering discourse about deviance. In its emphasis on sequence and process, the term *career* calls for explanations of *how* people move from one step of a sequence to another; and the term *deviant career* points specifically to a process of involvement that *begins* rather than ends with a person's first deviant experience. And in these ways, the use of the term *deviant career* has been instrumental in shifting discourse about deviance away from its more traditional focus on the causes of deviant behavior and its traditional location of these causes in the deviant person's past (the individual's social and personal background and characteristics).

As an illustration of the enormous difference it makes to look at what happens after rather than before the point at which a person first becomes involved with deviance, I will refer to the work I did some years ago on the experiences of teenage girls who were then labeled "unwed mothers."[2] The literature about unwed mothers at that time described their personalities, their social characteristics, and their early family lives—aspects of girls' pasts that were understood as possible causes of the deviant behavior. This was typically conceived of as being the sexual activity that produced the pregnancy, rather than the pregnancy itself or the decisions made about the pregnancy once it became known. Virtually no attention was paid in this literature to girls' sexual activities or contraceptive practices, and no attention at all was paid to what happened after girls discovered they were pregnant.

My own research dealt entirely with girls' experiences after they discovered they were pregnant (Rains, 1971). As it turned out, there were many such experiences, and all of these had implications for a girl's sense of her situation and self as deviant. These experiences included the revelation of her predicament to her parents; the considerations and discussions she had about abortion and marriage as possible solutions, and sometimes the steps she took toward these alternative solutions; her expectations about what a maternity home would be like; her encounters at the maternity home with a psychiatric view of her situation; her considerations about whether to place her baby for adoption or keep it; her experience of labor, birth, and (often) separation (for those who chose adoption); her return home and the complications of lying to some while telling the truth to others about where she had been; and, finally, her considerations about dating again. As it turned out, much of the girls' experience with becoming deviant had to do not so much with how or why they came to find themselves in this situation, but with the sequence of experiences that then ensued; that is, it was at the point where they discovered they were pregnant that they began to anticipate and encounter the morally relevant reactions of others to their current situation, with all of its possible implications for a revised interpretation of their past. As this brief illustration may suggest, the shift from looking for the causes of illegitimate pregnancy or illegitimacy to looking at the career of the unwed mother opens up an entirely different empirical turf.

The most productive aspect of this shift has been the assertion that deviant motivations and deviant commitments are built over the course of involvement in deviant activity rather than existing in the form of predispositions that persons may have toward deviance prior to engaging in it. As Becker (1963: 42) put it, "To put a complex argument in a few words: instead of the deviant motives leading to the deviant behavior, it is the other way around; the deviant behavior in time produces the deviant motivation."

A number of studies of deviant careers describe how actual experience with deviant activity can supply conceptions and definitions of that activity that facilitate further involvement with it. The essay, "Becoming a Marihuana User," which supplied the model for such descriptions, describes how, in the course of their first actual experiences of smoking marijuana, novice smokers learn to recognize the effects of the drug and to define these as pleasurable, conceptions which then facilitate and become the motive for further use (Becker, 1963). Martin Weinberg's (1978) articles on nudists and nudist camps describe how further involvement with nudism is facilitated for the curious but nervous novice by the effectiveness with which the camps maintain and convey a definition of being nude as essentially nonsexual and health-oriented. Most of the camps Weinberg studied, for example, discouraged the presence of single men (through higher rates, quotas, or direct exclusion) because "they suspect that singles may indeed see nudity as something sexual" (Weinberg, 1978: 343), and prohibitions against staring, sex talk, and body contact also served to support a nonsexual definition of the situation. For the apprehensive couple making their first visit to a camp, these practices not only pacify their initial apprehensions, but also supply them with a new and positive motive for coming back. That is, they have made their first visit out of curiosity; their later visits are made out of their gathering definition of nudism as wholesome.

In an even more striking analysis of how conventional people become involved in and then committed to activities they once would have regarded as deviant, Richard Stephenson (1973) describes how conventional couples come to consider, try out, and take up group sex—how, in the course of their first and experimental forays into "swinging," they not only discover that the other participants are couples like themselves (and not hippies or kinks), but also acquire a conception of group sex as an activity that will support and enrich rather than threaten their marriage. As Stephenson observes:

> Just as nudists divorce nudity from sexuality, swingers separate
> marriage from group sex. Support and enrichment are seen in
> terms of the value of mutual involvement in social activities;
> avoidance of the hypocrisy, exclusiveness, and threat of infidel-
> ity; revitalization of flagging interests; improvement of sexual
> performance . . . and overcoming sexual inhibitions that cause
> marital difficulties; controlling jealousy and possessiveness; pro-
> viding a spouse with gratifications where the sexual needs are
> unequal or extending to both inclusive rather than exclusive
> rights and, thereby, validating the norms of personal autonomy;
> extending the openness and communication necessary for in-
> volvement in swinging to the marital relationship generally; and
> other similar linkages of means to acceptable ends (Stephenson,
> 1973: 181).

In other words, the actual experiences people have in taking up
these forms of deviant activity supply them with what David Matza
(1969) has called the "terms and issues" that will facilitate or impede their further involvement.

The observation that motives and dispositions emerge in the
course of experience with deviance is not unique to deviant activities or deviant involvements. That is, it is no different to observe
that deviant motives and dispositions emerge in the course of a
person's experience with deviant activity than it is to say that occupational motives and dispositions emerge in the course of experience with a given occupation, or that athletic motives and dispositions emerge in the course of a person's experiences with athletic
activities. The symbolic interactionist orientation toward how
people become involved in deviant activity is not in principle different from the symbolic interactionist orientation toward how
people become involved in any kind of activity.

The term *career* has, in other words, supplied a general framework within which it is possible to look at involvement with any
line of activity in terms of the considerations and issues that arise
in the course of experience with the activity; the novelty of this
framework as it is applied to the study of deviance has been its
orientation toward what happens *after* a person tries out deviance
rather than toward what happened before.

One of the most surprising discoveries that was made possible
when sociologists of deviance began to look at what happened after
a person got involved with deviance was that the experiences of
deviants included their contacts with agents and agencies of social
control. Perhaps the most dramatic and compelling illustration of

this is provided in Jacqueline Wiseman's (1970) research on Skid Row alcoholics. The lives of Skid Row alcoholics, she discovered, were extensively organized around the rehabilitation agencies that were presumably designed to contain, control, fix, or save them; men organized their lives in a way they referred to as "making the loop"—making the rounds among these agencies.

> Although the world of the urban male alcoholic appears to close down as his continued consumption of alcohol increases and he loses such conventional ties as family, friends, employers, and co-workers, a new environment of rehabilitation agencies, serving the same clientele in rotation, opens up to him. If the Row man is adroit, he is not limited to just one of these agencies for sustenance, but can travel from control agencies to therapeutic agencies, to spiritual renewal agencies, returning to Skid Row in between institutional sojourns (Wiseman, 1970: 62).

Wiseman's data and analysis provide a striking illustration of the extent to which deviant careers can include, as an important feature of their social and not just moral organization, contacts with agents and agencies of social control as well as an illustration of the irony that these agencies, organized to control, cure, contain, fix, or save the Skid Row alcoholic and to keep him from his way of life, in fact make that way of life viable. In their more recent evaluation of the newly created public detoxification centers in Seattle (designed to medicalize and decriminalize responses to public drunkenness), Fagan and Mauss (1978: 244), along similar (although less sympathetic) lines, observe that the new arrangements

> may simply be facilitating the perpetuation of a skid-row lifestyle for clients. There is nothing to stop the chronic inebriate from self-referral to the detox center (with its comfortable accommodations and friendly staff) two or three times in a given week. A few days of drunkenness can be interspersed with a few days in detox, and this round of life can continue indefinitely, at public expense if the client is indigent. Such subversion of the function of detox is not likely to be changed without some kind of coercion against the client, a procedure which would compromise the medical model on which the new Uniform Act [Uniform Alcoholism and Intoxication Treatment Act] is mainly based.

Contacts with social control agencies thus have relevance for the shape deviant careers can take; but they have been most frequently regarded by sociologists as having relevance for the "moral aspects" of deviant careers, and it is to those aspects that I shall now turn.

"MORAL" ASPECTS

While the term *deviant career* points generally to a framework within which it becomes possible to look at a person's gathering (or loosening) involvement with deviant activity, the term *moral career* points to the particular aspects of career that have to do with self-conception and identity.

The term *moral career* first entered discourse about deviance in Erving Goffman's (1961) essay, "The Moral Career of the Mental Patient." There Goffman used the term *career* to point to the sequence of experiences that mental patients have in common by virtue of the common path they travel in getting to and through the mental hospital. As he observed then:

> Traditionally the term *career* has been reserved for those who expect to enjoy the rises laid out within a respectable profession. The term is coming to be used, however, in a broadened sense to refer to any social strand of any person's course through life. The perspective of natural history is taken: unique outcomes are neglected in favor of such changes over time as are basic and common to the members of a social category, although occurring independently to each of them (Goffman, 1961: 127).

Not only do mental patients, like college students or unwed mothers, share a common career—a common set and sequence of experiences by virtue of the common social path they travel, but they share as well the more specific implications that the steps of this career have for their conceptions of self. These are the "moral" aspects of career. As Goffman (1961: 168) writes: "The moral career of a person of a given social category involves a standard sequence of changes in his way of conceiving of selves, including, importantly, his own."

One "moral" aspect of the career of the mental patient, for example, has to do with the practices and arrangements of mental hospitals: the case record, the ward system, the case conference, and, above all, the fact that patients are available to observation around the clock and in every arena of activity. These make it difficult for patients to protect the version of self that they, like all of us, put forward to others. "In general . . . mental hospitals systematically provide for circulation about each patient the kind of information that the patient is likely to try to hide. And in various degrees of detail this information is used daily to puncture his claims" (Goffman, 1961: 161–162). Not only may the patient's claims about himself get punctured, but his own response to that

experience (for example, withdrawal or argument) may itself become part of what's used to discredit him; Goffman (1961) calls this
process "looping" and explains that "an agency that creates a defensive response on the part of the inmate takes this very response
as the target of its next attack. The individual finds that his protective response to an assault upon self is collapsed into the situation;
he cannot defend himself in the usual way by establishing distance
between the mortifying situation and himself." The moral career of
the mental patient includes, then, a set of experiences of self that
are importantly linked to the arrangements and practices of mental
hospitals.

Although Goffman's analysis of the situation of the mental patient was grounded in his more general and radically sociological
view of the self ("the self is not a property of the person to whom it
is attributed, but dwells rather in the pattern of social control that
is exerted in connection with the person by himself and those
around him" [1961: 168]), it became the model for numerous
studies that describe the degrading conceptions of social control
agencies.

Social control agencies in fact proved to be spectacularly suitable for this kind of analysis. As Wolfensberger's (1975) description
of institutions for the mentally retarded illustrates, degrading conceptions of the deviant "client" can be embedded in even the most
mundane physical aspects of the institution:

> The atmosphere and design of a residential facility can very
> clearly express an expectancy that the resident will behave in a
> subhuman fashion—no matter how vociferously the staff may
> deny adherence to dehumanizing attitudes. Such expectancies
> are implicit in any of virtually hundreds of dehumanizing prac-
> tices encountered in institutions. . . .

> The perception of the retarded as animals usually implies an
> expectation that they behave in a primitive, uncontrolled fash-
> ion. Thus the environment is designed to be "abuse-resistant,"
> which implies measure such as . . . walls, floors, etc. made of
> material that is indestructible . . . unbreakable, shatterproof or
> wire-enmeshed glass in windows and partitions . . . installation
> of the sturdiest, most heavy-duty furniture and equipment . . .
> [and] soundproofing to muffle the sounds residents are expected
> to emit. . . .

> Since the perceived subhuman is not believed to be capable of
> meaningful controlled choice behavior, he is permitted minimal
> control over his environment. This typically implies the follow-

> ing: (a) Switches controlling the lights of resident areas . . . are
> made inaccessible to residents by placement in staff control
> areas . . . (b) Water temperature in lavatories, showers, etc., is
> controlled by thermostats . . . (Wolfensberger, 1975: 8, 9).

The very success of Goffman's model has created an emphasis, however, on the extent to which the moral aspects of career are simply provided in the fateful conceptions of self supplied in so many ways by social control agencies to their clients. It will be useful, therefore, to observe in some detail that the moral aspects of deviant careers can also be linked to the workings of social control agencies *in more general ways, in less dramatic ways,* and *in more positive ways,* and that *sometimes the moral aspects of deviant careers may have little, if anything, to do with the operation of social control.*

General Impact of "Ban" on Moral Careers

There are, first of all, moral or self-definitional aspects of deviant careers that arise not out of direct encounters with agents or agencies of social control, but out of the more general effects of doing things that are disapproved of by others.

In his brilliant rumination on the process of becoming deviant, David Matza (1969: 143–155) discusses these as the effects of "ban." People who take up activities that are disapproved of by others will, for reasons of either practical or moral self-protection, find themselves more deeply involved with deviance than they might at first have bargained for. The boy who skips school, for example, gets involved not just in skipping school but in a variety of other deviant activities: lying convincingly about it to teachers and parents; forging notes to cover his absence; being careful about his presence in public places during school hours; and staging an anonymous and inconspicuous self at school. (The irony of this last tactic is that, by not participating in class and by avoiding contact with the teacher, the school skipper may seem to be, and may actually become, a poorer student than he might otherwise be.[3])

In taking up an activity that is disapproved of by others, people are likely to find themselves involved in a variety of other activities that amplify the extent of their deviant involvement, and that increase their experience of the distance that now seems to lie between themselves and conventional others. Thus, school skippers not only add lying to skipping, but may come to see their parents as gullible and themselves as accomplished at deception. Deviation is compounded, as Matza puts it, and it is compounded in the moral or self-definitional realm.

Sometimes, of course, it is this very experience that will lead people to disengage themselves from deviant activity. In a class I teach about deviance, my students write an essay describing a deviant career they have had; they describe the process through which they came to consider and try out some activity they had considered deviant at the time they had engaged in it—an activity about which they'd had some reservations. Their essays, which illustrate again and again how the dynamics of becoming deviant do not depend on the "seriousness" or illegality of the act in question, have described their involvement with such varied "deviant" acts as having an affair with a married woman or man, breaking the kosher dietary laws, trying cocaine, having sex for the first time, not going to mass, barhopping while underage, going to see a pornographic movie, stealing, smuggling, driving their parents' car without permission, breaking and entering, and trying out a dating bureau. These accounts supply an interesting supplement to the kinds of studies of deviance to which I have been referring. For one thing, they illustrate the effectiveness of ban in producing disengagement from deviant activity; that is, many of the students' accounts are about trying out an activity and experiencing the undesired compounding of their sense of deviation. So, for example, a student reports on her considerations after visiting a bar illegally when she was sixteen:

> There were some good points like learning how to order drinks, trying different drinks, meeting new people, learning how many drinks I could handle, learning how to converse with older men, and engaging in new experiences in a "grown-up" place. But there were also several negative things like using a false I.D., having to pretend to be older, having to lie continually, spending a good deal of money and traveling a long distance. . . . In order to get a false I.D. I would have to borrow one from an older person or have one made illegally. To get to the bar I would have to find a person I could trust with a car and driver's license willing to take me. To look more mature I would have to borrow or buy older-looking clothes. Paying for drinks meant I would have to keep borrowing money from my parents and lying about what I was doing with the money or I would have to find a job. . . . I would have to lie to my parents about where I was going. . . . It would mean concealing the fact that I had been drinking from them by never getting drunk and buying rolls of life-savers. I would have to be careful in school that none of my

> friends said anything in front of my sisters. Because it is illegal, I
> would have to be very careful and think up explanations in case
> we were caught. I also would have to live with the fear of being
> caught or meeting some of my parents' friends in the bar, and the
> guilt I would feel about lying and sneaking around. After con-
> sidering the "terms and issues" involved with bar-hopping
> underage, I decided that once was enough. . . . I found that I dis-
> liked the lying and sneaking around that were necessary to en-
> gage in this activity. Correlation between myself as a bar-hopper
> and myself as a daughter and good person produced too great a
> conflict for this behavior to survive reconsideration.

Thus, one effect that "ban" can have on a deviant career is to
curtail it.

For those who continue along a deviant path, however, the
effect of "ban" will be to amplify both the extent of their deviation
and its significance as something that sets them apart from conventional others. In this way, "ban" provides the circumstance that
strengthens association with like-minded others, weakens association with conventional others, and helps to create progressive commitment to a life and a self organized around deviance. As Stephenson (1973: 182) observes about swingers:

> While social interaction is not exclusively devoted to other
> swingers, establishing contacts and preliminaries to their con-
> summation tend to diminish other possible social relations. Fur-
> thermore, *fear of being found out* and perhaps plain boredom
> with non-swingers tend to restrict interaction. The search for
> new participants often increases spatial distance necessary for
> engagement; and weekends and vacations may be given to swing-
> ing activities. *This is likely to isolate swingers from non-
> swingers and to insulate them from the impact of more conven-
> tional others, while lending support for the preferred activity.*
> [Emphasis added.]

To summarize, there are moral or self-definitional aspects to
deviant careers that arise as a consequence of doing things that are
disapproved of by others whether or not this disapproval is actually
encountered in either an official or unofficial way.

Secondary Deviation

The moral aspects of deviant careers may also have to do with
reactions to deviance (whether the formal reactions of social control agencies or the less formal reactions of others) in ways that are
more subtle and less dramatic than the simple imposition of deval-

ued identities. Edwin Lemert (1951; 1967a), in this respect, proposed the term *secondary deviation* for the symbolic reorganization
that reactions to deviance can bring about in a person's relationship
to his or her own deviant activity. That is, the reactions of others
can create for the deviant the experience of seeing the self (most
likely a devalued one) that is reflected in other people's view of his
or her activities, and the experience of then becoming unable to act
except in relation to that imputed self.

> The child begins to fear stuttering. These fears are attached to
> certain words, persons, and situations. Finally the fears become
> generalized in the sense that the stutterer symbolically visual-
> izes situations in which the stuttering appears, together with
> the anticipated social penalties. This is the cause of rather com-
> plex anticipatory behavior in which the stutterer plans his
> speech far in advance in order to avoid spasms on feared
> words. Other more immediate anticipatory behavior takes shape
> in postponement of words, avoidance, substitution, release de-
> vices, pitch and attitudinal disguises. . . . The anticipatory fears
> create tensions and the greater likelihood of stuttering in each
> new situation he enters. . . . The predominant self of which he
> is conscious at these times is that of a "stutterer." . . . When this
> point is reached, the speech deviation has become secondary,
> and it may correctly be said that the person now stutters be-
> cause he stutters (Lemert, 1951: 164).

Secondary deviance is therefore deviance that "emerges as an
artifact of its control" (Lemert, 1967a: 70) that is produced as a
response to the attempts of others to "do something" about some
initial, or primary, deviance. Secondary deviation is a concept that
contains sociologists' skepticism about organized programs for "re-
habilitating" deviants. Because Lemert's conception has been
widely used, and sometimes abused, in sociological writing about
deviance, it is worth emphasizing that reactions to deviance—even
degrading and official ones—do not *necessarily* produce secondary
deviance; that is, it must be shown specifically how control *produces* deviance as a response. As Lemert (1967a: 77) observes about
the impact of narcotics laws on addiction:

> A good deal has been written on the contribution which repres-
> sive laws make to the "problem" of narcotics in the United
> States, especially as sources of illegal traffic in drugs and the
> commission of crimes by addicts in order to supply themselves
> with drugs. Yet *it remains to be shown that the laws themselves
> cause addiction:* more plausible are the assertions that laws and

policy determine access to drugs, their forms of use, the attributes of the addict population, their degree of contact with criminals and other deviants, their involvement in other deviance, and the particular kinds of self-conception held by addicts. *From these must be teased out the more generic factors which underlie or sustain addiction.* Needless to say, after this has been done, it would be totally unrealistic to ignore the peculiar physiological effects of the drugs in the making of an addict. [Emphasis added.]

While the concept of secondary deviation focuses attention on the practices of social control agencies (and on social control policies), the implications of those practices for the deviant's conception of self and *further involvement with deviance that is reactive to those practices* is a subtle and still relatively unexamined process.

Moral Reinstatement

The practices of social control agencies do not necessarily (although they may primarily) express a discrediting conception of the deviant client. In the study previously mentioned of teenage girls' experiences in maternity homes (Rains, 1971), I found that maternity homes have traditionally been characterized by practices that not only sustained but in fact insisted on a definition of their clients as essentially morally respectable girls whose current situation was out of character and represented, in this sense, a "mistake." In the more traditional home I studied, for example, girls were required to dress in a "ladylike" manner (no shorts or pants), were not allowed to receive male visitors (except for their fathers or clergymen), and were expected to conduct themselves so as not to call attention to their situation (girls were not allowed to leave the home in groups of more than two and were expected to wear false wedding rings). Girls pregnant for a second time were not accepted as residents. And traditional maternity homes provided their clients with various protections for their "original" respectable identities: the non-use of last names in the home, the use of phony mailing addresses and sometimes phony medical records to support a girl's cover story, and so forth.

In the newer and more professionally staffed maternity homes, these practices and points of view have been called into question and replaced by a more psychologically oriented and sophisticated version of the girls' situation. In the professionally staffed home I studied, a girl's pregnancy was regarded as an emotional symptom, an expression of psychological troubles with which the girl would have to come to terms lest the same situation recur.

The two types of maternity homes, in other words, operated with rather different conceptions of their clientele. They put forward to their clients rather different definitions of their past and current situations and selves—the good girl who made a mistake that is essentially out of character, or the emotionally troubled girl whose situation is essentially in character. For the girls who came to these homes, however, these two different versions held much the same appeal: Both versions of a girl's situation and self shifted attention away from what the girls themselves worried about—namely, the troublesome, self-definitional implications of their newly approved sexual activity. The typical client at either type of home had been shocked to discover her pregnancy, and dismayed and upset that she might now be seen as "that kind of girl," which is to say sexually promiscuous. For most girls, the experience of arriving at either type of home was one of surprised relief—first, at encountering other girls like herself, and second, at encountering a version of her situation that did not focus attention on her sexual activity per se.

Thus, social control agencies may engage both intentionally and unintentionally in moral rescue rather than in moral degradation—although, of course, the first depends on the possibility of the second. The fact that maternity homes depend on voluntary clients and can count on their clients to bring with them a ready sense of their own moral failing is perhaps not a coincidence. A final irony is worth mentioning: The moral career of the unwed mother (only partly described here) can be described as a career of moral reinstatement; to the extent that this moral reinstatement is accomplished without rendering sexual activity acceptable, it may well be that the effort to rehabilitate "produces deviance as an artifact." That is, the morally reinstated and newly respectable girl may find herself embarking upon future sexual activity with the same hesitancy (expressed, for example, in the nonuse of contraceptive methods) that resulted in her first pregnancy.

Moral Aspects Unrelated to Social Control

I have been discussing the "moral" aspects of deviant careers and their connection to the practices of social control agencies at some length because these aspects are usually thought to distinguish deviant careers from other, more conventional kinds of careers a person might have (for example, one's career as a parent). That is, what generally distinguishes deviant careers from other kinds of careers is that they must be pursued in a context of potential and often actual disapproval and social control.

There are, however, moral aspects of deviant careers that have little or nothing to do with the context of social control. In the same way that involvement with other kinds of activities (for example, occupations) may supply conceptions of self and possibilities for identity, so involvement with deviant activity can in the same way supply a version of self and possibilities for identity. To speak about the "moral" aspects of deviant careers is not different in principle from speaking about the "moral" aspects of other careers that people have, or other activities and organizations in which they are involved. The term *moral* is simply a way of pointing to the implications that involvements with others in a common line of activity can have for one's conception of self. As a rather round-about illustration of this observation, I will call upon Lemert's (1967b) intriguing consideration of the unusual moral aspects of the career of the systematic check forger.

Like other criminals, the person who engages in systematically passing bad checks goes about it in a way that will reduce the likelihood of getting caught. To effectively pass bad checks, one must live a life that is seclusive, highly mobile, and organized around one's skill at adopting and shifting among a variety of shallow and conventionalized "identities":

> In a very literal sense the check forger becomes a real life actor, deliberately assuming a variety of roles and identities which both facilitate the cashing of checks and conceal his former or, if preferred, his "real" identity. Thus he may become a spurious customer in a supermarket, a guilty husband purportedly buying his wife a gift, an out-of-town real estate buyer, a corporation executive seeking to set up a branch office . . . (Lemert, 1967b: 166).

Unlike other forms of criminal work, then, the practices involved in successful bad-check passing rule out the kinds of genuine interaction with others that provides support for a sense of self. The check forger cannot particularize his interaction and has no way of getting appreciation as a separate person. And because the check forger is a lone criminal operator, he does not find this support for a sense of self in associations with other criminals. The systematic check forger has a gathering problem with identity, that is, who he is for others. As Lemert (1967b: 180–181) observes:

Systematic check forgery comes closest to being a way of life which contains the seeds of its own destruction. . . . In a sense the forger fails because he succeeds; he is able to fend off or evade self-degradative consequences of his actions but in so doing he rejects forms of interaction necessary to convert his rewards into positive, status-specific self-evaluations. In time he reaches a point at which he can no longer define himself in relation to others on any basis. The self becomes amorphous, without boundaries; the identity substructure is lost. Apathy replaces motivation, and in phenomenological terms, "life" or "this way of life" is no longer worth living. This is the common prelude to the forger's arrest.

Lemert's presentation is a fascinating and unorthodox demonstration of how issues for the self can arise in the course of deviant activity that do not have to do with the deviance of the activity per se or with the negative impact on self-conception of getting caught. The moral aspects of the career of the systematic check forger illuminate less about *deviant* careers than about how identities and selves are kept together and on what they depend.

SUMMARY

There are no hypotheses in the notions of either *deviant career* or *moral career*; the terms are recommendations about what to look *at* rather than about what to look *for*. The term *deviant career* implies nothing about how involvements in deviant activity are organized, and nothing about the necessary shape or outcomes of such careers. And the "moral" aspects of these deviant careers might likewise take a variety of forms. As Becker (1963: 24–25) observed: "We should not confine our interest to those who follow a career that leads them into ever-increasing deviance, to those who ultimately take on an extremely deviant identity and way of life. We should also consider those who have a more fleeting contact with deviance, whose careers lead them away from it into conventional ways of life."

Even with so open a mandate, however, it would be fair to say that some aspects and some types of deviant careers have been more fully described and analyzed than others. Like the beginnings of piano pieces, the beginnings of deviant careers are most fully rehearsed; the concept of "career" more or less requires starting at the beginning of a person's involvement with some particular form of deviance. As a result, we know a great deal about the considerations of a person embarking on a path about which he or she has some initial reservations. We know a lot, for example, about "techniques of neutralization" (Sykes and Matza, 1957)—ways that "nervous novices" have of defining and going about their activities so as to evade or "neutralize" their moral misgivings. And we have become highly attentive to the beginnings of a person's career as an officially designated deviant, to the "contingencies" (Goffman, 1961: 135–136) that call one person and not another to official attention.

Despite Becker's recommendation, we have been more interested in how people move into deviance than in how they may move out of it; we have paid more attention to the process of becoming deviant than to several other possible variants. As brief illustrations, I will point to the process of self-acceptance, on the one hand, and to the process of going straight, on the other.

In the student accounts mentioned earlier, many students described taking up "deviant" activities that they had since come to experience as normal and acceptable activities (various kinds of sexual activity and the nonobservance of religious customs are apt examples). These were activities, in other words, that lost their negative implications as people continued to be involved in them, and that did not, for the most part, provide grounds for a restructured association with others (although an association with like-minded others was helpful in supporting initial experimentation).

In a presidential address to the Society for the Study of Social Problems, John Kitsuse (1980: 9) describes, on a much larger plane, the vigorous and organized movement toward self-affirmation on the part of deviant groups whose activist stance he calls "tertiary deviance":

> Our theoretical formulations of the social or the social psychological situation of deviants do not provide an adequate framework for the investigation of the developing politics of deviance. If secondary deviation is instituted when deviants "react symbolically to their own behavior aberrations and fix them in their socio-psychological patterns" [Lemert, 1951: 75], then we might propose the concept of "tertiary deviation" to refer to the deviant's confrontation, assessment, and rejection of the negative identity imbedded in secondary deviation, and the transformation of that identity into a positive and viable self-conception. As an extension of the natural history of deviant lives outlined by Lemert, the concept of tertiary deviance would direct us to investigate questions of how it is possible for the stigmatized, ridi-

culed and despised to confront their own complicity in the maintenance of their degraded status, to recover and accept the suppressed anger and rage as their own, to transform shame into guilt, guilt into moral indignation, and victim into activist.

These two rather different paths toward self-acceptance may be contrasted with another, less well-described career path—that of "going straight." The literature about deviance has tended to be highly sensitive to the process whereby deviants get committed to, and locked into, a pattern of activity or a way of life from which there appear to be few real or attractive exits. Sometimes this way of life is portrayed as chosen, sometimes as compelled. Neither rendition leaves much room for looking at the process whereby people come to reconsider their involvement with deviance, and to consider, try out, and take up a more conventional way of life. Yet "going straight" is not only a path that deviants are likely to encounter in the recommendations of outsiders, but also one whose occasional lure they may be in the best position to appreciate.

As applied to the study of deviance, the concept of career has made it possible to look at deviant activity and people's involvement in it in much the same way that sociologists have looked at other kinds of social activity and involvement. The concept of career has served as a central device for "de-pathologizing" the sociological study of deviance. At the same time, the special emphasis on the "moral" aspects of deviant careers has made it possible, *where relevant*, to look at and talk about what might be distinctive about deviant careers—namely, that they occur in, and are affected by, a context of disapproval. It is not clear whether the term *deviant career* is useful as much more than a general guide to looking at sequence and process; it may well be that it has now served the purpose for which it was generally proposed in the early sixties.

NOTES

[1]The interested reader should see Barbara Sherman Heyl's (1977) discussion of the rather different function that is served by the training of house prostitutes.
[2]I will not use the currently preferred term *single mother* because the girls I talked with and the girls that the literature was typically about did not, in fact, remain mothers long. These girls were unmarried, pregnant girls who were residents in maternity homes, where they lived until the birth and placement for adoption of their babies. The old term *unwed mother* is, of course, equally inaccurate, but at least it tends to summon up the proper image.
[3]I am indebted, throughout this discussion of the school skipper, to Manuel Crespo's excellent rendition of the career of the school skipper (Crespo, 1973, 1974).

2 DEVIANT SUBCULTURES

EARL RUBINGTON

Sociologists postulate that group membership influences conduct. To know the kind of groups to which people belong, the type of members they are, and the nature of these group influences is to understand, if not actually explain, regularities of social behavior. Similarly, there is reason to believe that what is true for conformists may be as true (if not more true) for deviant people. This chapter therefore seeks to indicate the significance and power of the group postulate for an understanding and explanation of deviant behavior.

To develop the argument, an elementary episode of social deviance is described. Then we examine why the behavior reported is deviant. Next, after contrasting this variety of *social deviance* with its partner, *solitary deviance*, it is indicated why the episode of social deviance denotes the presence of a deviant subculture, and the minimal elements to be found in such subcultures are listed. Then we consider briefly the varieties of deviant subcultures. The chapter then takes up subcultural theory, looking first at its history and development and then at its current state. We close with a glimpse of participation in deviant subcultures and some of the social and psychological consequences of variations in subcultural participation.

AN EPISODE OF SOCIAL DEVIANCE: THE BOTTLE GANG

It is noon on a midsummer day in a large city. Four men meet in a large common just off the central business district. All are hatless and tieless. Their clothes are old, rumpled, and ill-fitting. All are middle-aged or older, unshaven, somewhat red-faced, and a little unsteady on their feet. They huddle together as if they might be plotting something. One of them—the "leader"—asks the other three if they have any money. They all reach into their pockets and hand some coins over to him. The leader counts out a certain amount, points to one of the men, and hands him the money. That man then heads for a store located three blocks away. He walks quickly, in a very determined, businesslike manner. The other three men amble over to a bench, where they sit down, light up cigarettes, talk, and await his return.

After fifteen minutes, the man comes back. He reaches into his pocket and pulls out a small bag containing a pint of inexpensive wine, which he hands over to the leader very quickly, looking over his shoulder all the while to see if anyone sees what he is doing. The leader unscrews the bottle's white plastic cap and discards it. Leaving the bottle in its bag, he takes a drink from it, then passes it to the man on his left. This man takes the bottle, still in the bag, looks quickly to his right and left, takes a fast drink, then hands it to the man on his left. He, in turn, looks about while drinking rapidly from the bottle. Done, he hands the bottle back to the leader, who tucks the bottle between his belt and his shirt. The four stand around in a small circle and talk for a few minutes. Then the leader takes the bottle out of his belt, drinks from it, and passes it around until all have drunk from the bottle and there is no wine left. One man empties the bottle, then walks over to a nearby trash can and drops it in.

When he comes back, the little circle breaks up. The leader and the man who went to get the bottle of wine walk off together, heading south. The other two men go their separate ways, one going east, the other west. Before the sun goes down, all of these men will have taken part in several similar kinds of drinking groups. Often the people will be the same; at other times, many new faces will appear. Nevertheless, whether the drinking place is an alley, a street corner, another section of the park, or an abandoned car, the actions of all the participants will generally follow the format just described—for this is an example of the bottle gang, the typical transitory drinking relationship that indigent alcoholics enter into regularly. This particular drinking episode (Rubington, 1968) raises two questions: Why is this an episode of social deviance, and how do we know that members participating in the episode share in a deviant subculture?

Any instance of social deviance contains the following elements: a pattern of deviant behavior, rules that have been broken, persons said to be responsible for the violations, persons who take action against the rule-breaker, and interested parties who side either with the controllers (those taking action against the rule-breakers) or with the rule-breakers. Participants in the bottle gang are defined by others as deviants because their appearance, their behavior, their condition, and their doctrine all combine to violate several social, moral, and legal norms. Their attire and grooming all offend against the implicit rule that people should "make a good appearance" when in public places. Drinking in public, being drunk in public, loitering, obstructing a public way, and being a disorderly person are only some of the municipal ordinances that bottle gang participants violate. Drinking when most other people are busy with their work constitutes still another violation of an implicit social rule. Being intoxicated violates the moral imperative that people control themselves. Drinking inexpensive fortified wine from a bottle diverges from several drinking customs. Most participants in bottle gangs are in the condition of, or have the status of, public drunk, a basic deviant social category. And the public behavior of the bottle gang implies that all participants subscribe to a doctrine that turns conventional values upside down.

Essentially, the behavior of bottle gang participants constitutes deviance because their definition of the situation varies so markedly from the conventional definition of how people ought to comport themselves when in public places such as streets and parks. Already deviant by repute, as well as by their actions, they engage in inappropriate actions in general, and, in particular, with the strange ways they make use of beverage alcohol. They, as well as other people, are well aware of the meaning of their actions. Passersby, for example, frown or laugh at them, make flippant remarks to them, or quicken their paces and avert their eyes so as to avoid any "pollution" that might come from being in the same vicinity as bottle drinkers. The participants, for their part, show their awareness of the social meaning of their actions by their feeble attempts to conceal their activity. In huddling together as they do, they try not to be seen doing what they're doing. They act as if they are not doing what they're doing, but they, and everybody else, know otherwise. Most of all, they fear police responses to their conduct. Should any police officer suddenly happen to come upon them, the chances are very good that they will be arrested for violation of one of several municipal ordinances. They are marked men—marked by police, citizens, and themselves. And, through their joint actions in public, they seek to deal as best they can with the consequences of these several social markings.

Viewed from the outside, their actions appear to be those of people who have either been cast out of conventional groups, who have voluntarily fled from such groups, or who have never known the ways of group membership. Frequently, they are referred to as derelicts in the double sense of having no duties and being unable to discharge any. Such people are aimless, not responsible for themselves, unpredictable, at a loss, disorganized, and so on. But viewed from the inside, they appear to feel some obligation toward people like themselves. As a result, there are a degree of regularity in their behavior and a patterning to their actions that belie social dislocation. They are, then, members of groups, however transitory, and their membership appears to exercise some influence upon their conduct (and these influences, as we shall see, derive from the fact that they share in the subculture of street drinkers).

How do we know that they are participants in a deviant subculture? Because they are not alone in their actions but rather come into contact with a circle of street-drinking acquaintances, because they share a number of actions, because they seek to bring these actions (as do all people in groups) under some social regulation, because they use in common a set of shared ideas to define and interpret their experiences with deviant alcohol use and its consequences, because they look upon themselves differently than do most people, and finally, because they do not drink the way most people do.

Of the one hundred million Americans over the age of fifteen who drink alcoholic beverages, probably one-tenth of that number are problem drinkers. They are problem drinkers because their drinking brings trouble to them and to a lot of other people, because they can't or won't control their drinking, and because none of their primary groups can control their drinking either. Most problem drinkers deviate from conventional group drinking norms, just as public drunks do. The main difference between these two varieties of deviants is that most problem drinkers, unlike public drunks, do their uncontrolled drinking in private. Problem drinkers avoid drinking with people like themselves and deny their alcoholism. Public drunks seek out people like themselves to drink with for social as well as financial reasons. Drinking in bottle gangs allows participants to get the maximum amount of absolute alcohol for the minimum amount of money. In turn, they have the benefits of one another's company during the life of the bottle. Similarly, public drunks find themselves thrust into one another's company when they are sentenced to jail or are sent to alcoholism treatment centers. It is through the frequent involuntary contacts in agencies of social control that the street drinkers' subculture emerges and is sustained. Most alcoholics, because they drink alone, do not interact with others like themselves. Most are solitary deviants. Only a small percentage—those who become involved with public drinking—come to share in a deviant subculture, and they are social deviants.

Alcoholics, including public drunks, share in common the fact that they do not drink like most other people do. Beyond that, they have very little in common. Whereas most solitary alcoholics have become estranged from significant others and themselves because of their alcohol drinking, bottle gang drinkers link up with an extended circle of drinking acquaintances. Their deviant use of alcoholic beverages, along with the punitive social reaction, brings public drinkers into frequent and regular contact. Out of this sustained contact, a deviant subculture emerges. It has six elements as described below.

1. *Patterns of behavior.* A pattern of acts centers around the bottle gang's interest in, and dependence upon, alcohol. The need for alcohol makes the gang look for a supply to drink. In contrast to solitary alcoholics, bottle gang drinkers have evolved a simple group structure for obtaining and consuming alcoholic beverages. Since no one person can afford to buy a bottle himself, he needs the cooperation and the contributions of the others. The one who initiates the gang is its leader; the one who is sent off with the money to get the bottle of wine is the "runner."

2. *Artifacts.* The main object of the bottle gang's joint action is alcohol. Some package stores stock inexpensive fortified wines. Homeless men's quarters in many large cities develop a set of establishments that cater to the needs of unattached street drinkers. When liquor stores are closed, bootleggers appear on Sunday morning to sell wine at twice the usual price (however, street information passed on makes it possible to obtain alcohol from nonbeverage sources such as canned heat, vanilla extract, shoe polish, paint thinner, and other industrial products).

3. *Norms.* The men pool their money and come together so they can share a few drinks from the bottle and in one another's company. When people associate regularly, they usually try to

bring conduct under a set of rules. Hence, even bottle gang drinkers make rules. The leader takes the first drink, holds the bottle between rounds, and decides what the group will talk about. Since he contributes the most toward the purchase of the bottle, he calls the tune. The leader generally selects the best dressed and least intoxicated man to buy the bottle, and he expects him to return with the bottle rather than to abscond and drink it all by himself. The leader expects all members of the gang, while together, to be as discreet as possible while in public and to avoid calling unnecessary attention to their drinking.

4. *Argot.* Men involved in the street-drinking life communicate with one another by means of argot. This language distinguishes veterans from newcomers and insiders from outsiders (outsiders can't have a very good idea of what is being talked about). More important, it prescribes symbols for talking and thinking about matters of common interest to all present in the immediate drinking occasion. Thus, "making the run" means going off to the package store to get a bottle for the group, and the "runner" is the one who performs this duty. All drinking groups make moral evaluations of their members' performances, hoping thereby to guarantee cooperation and to fend off conflict. Hence, from time to time, while drinking in such groups, drinkers will talk about so-and-so who "pulled a Dick Smith" or "went South." These terms refer to a runner who violated the group's trust and failed to return with the bottle. Or they will talk about "wacks," "performers," "jail bait," or "chiselers," in referring to those who call attention to the gang or who violate its simple code.

5. *Ideology.* Bottle gang drinkers know full well the legal, moral, and social norms they have violated in the past, those they are violating in the present, and those they are likely to violate in the near future. As a result, they devise ideas that suit their interests and justify their actions. This ideology mitigates their blameworthiness and calls attention to the deviance of seemingly "respectable" people. These drinkers need not subscribe privately to any of these ideas, nor is there any obligation that they be brought together in a systematic fashion. All that is required is that, from time to time, particularly when in the presence of one another, they make pronouncements about the hidden alcoholism of this judge or that police officer. Or, as sometimes happens, one of them may call a person not present a drunk. Or they can point to illustrious people who have been forced into the streets because of their alcoholic drinking.

6. *Self-image.* Bottle gang drinkers are well aware of the stigma attached to alcoholism in general and to its public varieties in particular. Consequently, when in one another's company, bottle gang drinkers make it possible for all members to achieve a measure of self-respect, if only in terms of the present and its demands. Thus, no one talks about what he was or what he used to do in the past. By avoiding any reference to past attainments, no one claims to be better than any of the others. Similarly, members lavish praise on one another for meeting minimal expected requirements, actions which in other groups would be taken for granted and not mentioned at all. Complimenting the runner for returning quickly, for instance, rewards a member for immediate, observable performance. And members can, if they so desire, contrast themselves with alcoholics who have broken bottle gang norms in the past.

VARIETIES OF DEVIANT SUBCULTURES

Deviant subcultures differ among themselves according to the number, variety, and complexity of the patterns of behavior they prescribe; the number and kinds of artifacts these patterns require; the number, strength, and extent to which their norms conflict with those of the wider society; the number, diversity, and complexity of their argot; the systematic nature of their ideology; and the extent to which their self-image is reactive or proactive. Three major factors influencing variation include the number of persons included in the deviant social circle, the frequency and patterning of interaction within that social circle, and the definitions and responses of the wider society to the deviant pattern of social behavior. We take up first, briefly, the kinds of variation between deviant subcultures; next, we look at the three main sources of variation.

At one extreme, as far as behavior patterns go, would be the bottle gang itself; at the other, would be the communes of the 1960s (Zablocki, 1971). In between on the continuum would be the hippie subculture of the 1960s and the gay culture, with its many satellites, of the 1980s (Partridge, 1973; Humphreys and Miller, 1980). The bottle gang concentrates interest, attention, and activity on the act of drinking. But since the gang focuses on a transitory episode lasting only as long as the bottle does, ideas and actions can only be generalized to similarly time-bound and simple social ventures. The commune, by contrast, centers attention, interest, and activity on the instrumentation and expression of an alternate way of life. The sheer number of behavior patterns, which encompass so many different aspects of social life, will likewise necessarily be much greater and more diverse, if only because of the difference in the time-commitments members make to communes as opposed to the time-commitments members make to bottle gangs. Hippie time-commitments, along with the number and the variety of deviant behavior patterns, stand midway between bottle gang members and commune members. As the tolerance for homosexuality increases, signs of homosexual behavior patterns giving rise to more variety, diversity, and depth of involvement in homosexual sociality have recently appeared (Humphreys and Miller, 1980). Acceptance of the homosexual family, should it ever come, would probably signify the height of social tolerance.

Artifacts exist in the world as cultural objects and, accordingly, gain a set of conventional definitions. Again, deviant subcultures differ according to the kinds of symbolic definitions of existing artifacts they make, the extent to which they use conventional artifacts in illicit or unconventional ways, and the extent and degree to which they make use of illegal artifacts. The sadomasochistic wing of male homosexuality, for instance, looks upon leather goods and chains in a different way than do most people (Plummer, 1975). Participants in bottle gangs, as noted previously, create drinking places out of the natural and built environments that have other and more conventional definitions and uses. In addition, also as noted previously, bottle gangs define, interpret, and respond to alcoholic beverages in the most unconventional ways possible. Drug addicts use illegal drugs, and to inject drugs, they fashion hypodermic needles, syringes, and ancillary equipment from eyedroppers, rubber bands, bent spoons, matches, and the like. Possession of these homemade artifacts (called "the works" by addicts) is grounds for arrest.

All groups develop norms, and deviant groups are no exceptions. Variations in subcultural norms depend on the amount of interdependence and cooperation required in deviant transactions, as well as the need and capacity to sanction those who breach these norms. Participants in criminal subcultures who work together in executing joint illegal acts of force, fraud, or stealth set down a few clear working rules and strictly enforce them. Homosexuals cannot set down an exhaustive set of norms intended to regulate their sexual and other conduct and be assured of swift, speedy, and severe enforcement if one of the parties should violate these norms. Since they are parties to an illicit social contract, aggrieved partners cannot seek redress from impartial third parties such as the state and its legal apparatus for resolving disputes. Because of the inter-dependent and recurrent patterns of their interaction, bottle gangs may well formulate a greater number of rules regarding the getting and consuming of alcoholic beverages. However, because of their own indigency and need for partners, they are often in no position to sanction bottle gang norms when they are broken.

Deviant subcultures vary according to the number, variety, and speed with which its sharers manufacture new terms and expres-sions. Again, those subcultures that engage in a fairly large number of behavior patterns are more apt to fashion a distinctive deviant vocabulary or argot than those who confine themselves to a deviant act of relatively simple social construction. In turn, those persons—who, as members of deviant groups, have deviant experiences that diverge more markedly from social and cultural norms than do other social deviants—are much more likely to fashion a special set of terms and categories for defining, interpreting, and responding to their extremely deviant experiences.

Deviant ideologies are much more apt to be systematic, inter-nally coherent, and comprehensive to the extent that they comprise a world view. Such ideologies are more likely to appear among deviant groups that either seek to withdraw from the conventional world, such as Utopian communities, or religious sects that vigor-ously proselytize for converts, as does the Unification Church (Mel-ville, 1972; Lofland, 1966). In both instances, the groups do not so much seek to justify their conduct (as prostitutes do when they claim everyone is crooked or all women are whores) because they have developed a pattern of beliefs in a totally different and alter-native life-style (Bryan, 1966).

This helps to account for the kinds of self-images that exist among deviant subcultures. Reactive self-imagery adopts a justifica-tory stance and argues that the particular deviants in question are no worse than all those people who do similar things in secret or who have yet to get caught (Sykes and Matza, 1957). On the other hand, a proactive self-imagery defines the deviant constituency as being a nobler variety of human being simply because of their iden-tity (Humphreys and Miller, 1980).

Three factors influencing varieties of subcultures include (1) the number and kinds of persons within the deviant social circle, (2) the frequency and kinds of contacts they sustain among them-selves, and (3) the changing definitions and responses of the wider society to their particular pattern of social behavior. The two polar type include, at one end of the continuum, the case of a small number of persons who make sporadic contact with one another for the purposes of engaging in a deviant act that requires two people (e.g., secret homosexuality). Ranged at the opposite end is the group that consists of an extended circle of deviant associates who engage one another in frequent and diverse kinds of social contacts, not all of which are deviant in character (for example, the religious cult). The first is more like a roving band, furtive and coming together in brief, expedient encounters. Furtive expediency is the way of stealthy deviants who seek to remain as ostensible conventional participants in the dominant culture (Merton, 1976). By contrast, the other types are overt deviants who are not only principled in their deviant behavior but seek, as sects have always done, to secede from society.

A deviant social act can become integrated into an elementary kind of subculture, as the bottle gang exemplifies so well. On the other hand, a series of such acts become part of some more complex and interrelated patterns of social behavior. The original "flower children," for instance, had merged variant patterns of social interaction, drug use, permissive sexuality, and Eastern religions as a step toward the development of a new social movement (Yablonsky, 1968). Those early adherents, who seceded and took followers with them to develop communes, indicate that, when supported by a growing and extended circle of deviant people, the spread and diversification of deviant behaviors can lead to a new and different kind of community (Davis, 1967).

Central to all of these possibilities, of course, is the pattern of changing cultural definitions and social responses to deviant acts and deviant persons (Becker, 1963). The interaction between powerful interest groups and their agents and deviant social types goes a long way toward explaining whether the roving band continues to support furtive expediency, whether diversity in deviance results in a new version of community, or whether a particular deviant social act almost becomes assimilated into the conventional cultural tradition. Public drunkenness, marijuana-smoking, and homosexuality afford three different examples of the consequences of changing cultural definitions and social responses to deviant behavior. All three also indicate that as the costs of the punitive societal reaction rise and its benefits drop accordingly, a different pattern of relations between deviant groups and control agents develops. Under differing social circumstances, this pattern can lead to a continuance of the roving band, assimilation, and the emergence of a deviant community.

Decriminalization of public drunkenness in many (though not all) jurisdictions has made possible a de facto social contract between police and bottle gang members (Rubington, 1975). Social contacts have both decreased and taken a different form; as a result, more bottle gang participants, if they so choose, can adopt the illness definition of their personal situation—for police, in some jurisdictions, can now transport public drunks to voluntary treatment agencies, such as detoxification centers, rather than arrest them for public drunkenness. These developments amount to a greater tolerance of the roving band.

Marijuana-smoking formerly was an integral pattern of a deviant subculture. But, with the spread of the practice, the frequency of its use, and the elevation of the social rank of smokers, the costs of marijuana policing suddenly rose relative to benefits it conferred on individual agents of criminal justice, such as police officers, prosecuting attorneys, and judges. The first indication of the increasing and growing de facto decriminalization of marijuana was the shift in the arrest-conviction ratio (National Commission on Marihuana and Drug Abuse, 1972). Today, although possession of more than an ounce of marijuana is a criminal act, marijuana-smoking has become assimilated into the routines of a variety of groups in the United States. Adoption of marijuana by large segments of the middle class has taken the act out of the realm of social deviance and into the area of acceptable recreational behavior for many people. Formal and informal social controls have correspondingly diminished and the oppositional basis for the emergence and maintenance of a marijuana-smoking counterculture has declined appreciably (Goode, 1970).

The number of people who engage in discreet homosexuality is not likely to ever be known with complete accuracy and confidence. Conservative estimates, however, suggest that there are about as many homosexuals as there are problem drinkers—approximately ten million (Marmor, 1980). Again, with the increased tolerance of homosexuality and the dissemination of the idea that it constitutes an alternative sexual orientation, the costs of policing homosexuality are also beginning to mount relative to the benefits. In addition, as noted earlier, the proactive positive identity has spread. What this means is that in large, metropolitan areas, acceptance of homosexuality has grown, and will continue to grow, among several segments of the population, heterosexual as well as homosexual. This can only lead, as some observers have pointed out, to diversification, integration, and the spread of several interrelated homosexual worlds (Humphreys and Miller, 1980). In large metropolitan areas, many of these already exist and have become communities in their own right.

SUBCULTURAL THEORY

Subcultural theory began in Chicago in the 1930s. Sociologists focused on behavior patterns the law defined as juvenile delinquency and asked a number of questions about these patterns. Why was delinquent behavior more apt to appear in working class neighborhoods than in middle class residential areas? Why did rates of delinquency remain very high despite changes in the ethnic composition of these neighborhoods? Why did some persons become delinquents while others did not? To what kinds of social and cultural stimuli was delinquent behavior a response? Why did the pattern of delinquent behavior exist in the first place?

As subcultural theory became more complex, three developments followed. First, several theories were synthesized into one comprehensive theory. Second, subcultural theory was subjected to criticism and rigorous testing in empirical research. Third, the idea of a subculture was extended to account for other varieties of deviant behavior, besides juvenile delinquency. Let us now briefly consider these points.

Sociologists at the University of Chicago began to study sections of Chicago that seemed to have high rates of social problems. One of these problems was juvenile delinquency. Shaw and McKay (1931), for example, studied a number of urban areas over a period of years and reported two important findings. First, they noted that rates of juvenile delinquency were higher in working class than in middle class residential areas; and, second, they pointed out that despite several changes in the ethnic composition of these working class areas, the rates of juvenile delinquency remained as high as ever. Shaw (1930, 1931, 1938) linked his quantitative work with the three juvenile-delinquent life-histories he had collected. He advanced a theory of cultural transmission to account for both the maintenance and the spread of delinquency in these areas. Social disorganization in these urban neighborhoods weakened both community and parental controls on male teenagers. As a consequence, they were free to indulge in several varieties of behavior, all of which violated legal, moral, and social norms. These deviant acts included truancy, vandalism, fighting, and stealing. Thrasher, in his study *The Gang* (1963), produced additional support, both quantitative and qualitative, for Shaw's theories.

Sutherland, a criminologist, had first set forth his theory of differential association in 1924. He revised it later, and then set forth its most complete statement in 1939. He was largely concerned with developing a general theory of criminal behavior. His theory of differential association, essentially an interactionist account, seeks to explain why some people become criminals while others do not. He argued that those people who came into early, frequent, and intensive contacts of long duration with people who were favorably disposed toward breaking the law were much more apt to become criminals. People would acquire these favorable views on their own through interaction with criminals and, in the process, would come to adopt the behavior system of crime. The behavior system, a precursor of the concept of subculture, includes the techniques, attitudes, and rationalizations that mark the "professional thief."

Merton published his classic paper, "Social Structure and Anomie," in 1938. In this paper, he set forth the view that deviant behavior is an adaptation to social strain. Using the United States as his case, Merton argued that the emphasis upon the success goal in the United States is one clear instance of strain and inconsistency between culture and society. The culture prescribes pursuit of success for all persons, no matter where they are situated in the social structure. The strain results from the fact that although all people are exposed to the cultural imperative to strive for economic success, the chances to compete are not distributed equally in the society. Merton argued that there were several ways of adapting to this sociocultural strain, one of them being to engage in criminal behavior in order to achieve economic success. His theory accounts for why property crime is concentrated in the lower and working class segments of American society. Another adaptation to the disjunction between institutionalized means and cultural goals is to give both of them up—what he called *retreatism*. He included in this type of adaptive response drug addiction, vagrancy, alcoholism, and psychosis.

In 1955 Cohen synthesized these three theories and formed his theory of the delinquent subculture. According to Cohen, working class boys first confront strains when they enter high school. The social structure of the high school creates and perpetuates an anomic situation for the working class boy. Middle class teachers sanction success-striving in all areas of academic life for all of their students, but they only encourage, assist, and reward students who can and do respond to their exhortations, students who are for the most part from a middle class background themselves. The working class boys face a crisis of self-esteem and status. On the one hand, they are encouraged to have ambition and to seek status, yet, on the other hand, they find all avenues to successful striving blocked. This only induces a chronic situation of status-frustration. As they come to see that the system rejects them, they in turn reject the social system of the high school. They turn middle class values upside down and become negativistic, nonutilitarian, and malicious. Denied status in terms of high school cultural values, they create an alternate social system within which they can hold their heads up high and have some sense of self-esteem and status in the eyes of their peers. Their adaptation to high school social structure and anomie is juvenile delinquency. But in order for all of this to come about, the working class students must talk with other students in order to find out if they also feel abused and rejected by the system and have hostile feelings as a result—for without talking with others who feel the same way, without sharing their problems with others, they cannot find a solution to their acute problems of social-psychological adjustment.

Cohen's synthesis indicates why delinquency rates have been, and continue to remain, high in working class residential areas. It is working class, not middle class, students who confront anomie in high school. This anomie creates and perpetuates the social and cultural strain to which juvenile delinquency becomes the adaptive response. This portion of the theory accounts for the situation that confronts the working class boy. But unless he enters into communicative interaction with others similarly situated who feel much the same way, a delinquent solution cannot emerge. Cohen makes it plain that the answer to the questions the school raises for these working class boys can only come out of social interaction. Finally, because all remain in the working class situation, all pass on the shared and collective solution to their personal status problems. Thus, Cohen joins Merton, Sutherland, and McKay in a creative synthesis to form his theory of the delinquent subculture—one that explains why working class boys are overexposed to strains, why some but not all of them adopt the delinquent solution, and how they share and pass it on to their peers.

Cloward and Ohlin in 1961 joined Merton and Cohen and derived from this combination a theory that posited, not one, but three delinquent subcultures. According to Cloward and Ohlin, anomie could also come into being if people were denied access to illegitimate as well as legitimate opportunities. In either case, the gap between aspirations and opportunities, which young men might feel in their particular situation, constituted a problem. Three kinds of delinquent gangs, as collective solutions, emerge as adaptive responses to gaps between aspirations and opportunities.

Criminal gangs—those specializing in stealing, for example— come into being when working class teenagers are denied access to legitimate opportunities but do have access to opportunities in the criminal underworld in their neighborhoods. Consequently, they engage in criminal activities while in school only to literally graduate into better positions in the world of organized crime. *Conflict* gangs, on the other hand, come into existence when access to both illegitimate and legitimate opportunities are restricted. In these circumstances, few community controls on the expressions of violence exist, and, consequently, gangs organize to fight each other. *Retreatist* gangs form when there are neither legitimate nor illegitimate opportunities. Under these social and cultural conditions, gangs turn their attention to such retreatist activities as drugs, alcohol, and "kicks."

Short and Strodtbeck carried out extensive studies of delinquent gangs in Chicago in 1965. Their work cast considerable doubt on the systematic formulations on delinquent subcultures. Their findings refuted both Cohen's and Cloward and Ohlin's on three major points. They did not find the specialization in delinquent behavior patterns that Cloward and Ohlin's opportunity theory had predicted; they did not find the massive rejection of middle class values that Cohen's theory had predicted; and they did not find the cohesive social organization among gangs that both theories had predicted. On this last point, their findings supported the work of both Yablonsky and Matza. Yablonsky, in his 1959 study of New York City gangs, found a tendency for newspaper people, social workers, police, and sociologists alike to attribute a degree of cohesion and organization to delinquent gangs. Yablonsky, however, found that so-called members were unclear on the actual number of members of gangs, as well as being uncertain about what rules and roles were supposed to regulate their behavior. Similarly, Matza (1964) found that juvenile delinquents were not as committed to their deviant acts as sociological theories would have predicted.

Though research may have failed to provide sufficient empirical support for subcultural theories of delinquency, the notion that subcultures come into being as collective solutions to problems that persons face in specific kinds of situations spread. More and more writers began looking at several varieties of deviant behavior as if they were, in fact, instances of deviant subcultures. The impetus for this extension of the idea of subcultures, of course, came from the chapter in Cohen's book in which he specifically set forth a general theory of deviant subcultures. We turn now to a brief discussion of this seminal idea.

THEORY OF DEVIANT SUBCULTURES

Cohen says that all behavior is problem-solving. The genesis of deviant subcultures follows from that general principle; that is, people in a given social situation face social-psychological problems of adjustment. Given an appropriate sequence of events, a subculture can emerge. The result of its emergence, of course, is that it provides a solution to the common problem experienced by all people in the situation. The reason why there aren't more subcultures, conventional or deviant, follows from a natural history model of how subcultures emerge.

As Cohen sees it, there are five stages in the development of a subculture: (1) experiencing a problem, (2) communicating about it with someone else in the same situation, (3) interacting on the basis of the problem, (4) developing a solution, and (5) sustaining and passing on the tradition.

Experiencing a problem is a necessary but not sufficient condition for the development of a subculture. Although people without problems are not likely to create and sustain a special subculture, experiencing a problem cannot lead to the emergence of a subculture if people do not talk about their common problem. If they do communicate with one another about their shared problem, then the chances of the next step (namely, that they will come to interact with one another on the basis of their shared problem) being taken become that much better. Out of this focused interaction, they come to forge a solution to their common problem. They apply their solution, it works, and soon a few others in the same situation join up with them. The last stage comes when they practice and pass on the tradition they have just developed.

According to Cohen (1955), the delinquent subculture emerged in the following way. First, working class youth came to sense difficulties in their competition for status in school. Their parents could not train them as well to compete for the middle class values the school distributed. A few of them began talking about the way they felt. Soon others came to express similar feelings. In the course of subsequent meetings, they focused in their interaction on their common fate. Unable to compete successfully for these values, they rejected them, turned them around, and became malicious, negativistic, and nonutilitarian. A few of them hit upon some joint activities that captured their imagination, such as breaking school windows after school was out. This activity only led to similar kinds of negativistic acts. It soon became a pattern, and after a while they found a number of recruits who wanted to join up with them and engage in similar activities. In effect, they invented a new game—juvenile delinquency—in which they were able to achieve status.

Critics argue that Cohen's theory requires all gang participants to respond to the same set of unconscious motives when they form a delinquent gang. Kitsuse and Dietrick (1959), for example, argue that a reactive theory of delinquent subculture formation is more plausible; that is, when working class youths engage in delinquent behavior, they are responding to an almost infinite variety of motives for participation. The sense of rejection and alienation from middle class values, they say, happens after these youths have been caught, punished, and stigmatized as gang delinquents. The common fate they experience is that of being singled out and treated as deviants by their teachers and classmates. According to Kitsuse and Dietrick, the punitive reaction isolates them from middle-class values and their representatives in schools and thrusts them into the company of all the others who have been tarred with the same brush. The rejection of middle class values follows from sharing the common fate of social punishment and becomes the basis for delinquent gang formation. Unlike Cohen, Kitsuse and Dietrick argue that the shared status problem has little to do with failure to compete for success and status in the school's social system. Rather, having now been defined as outsiders by the authorities, they react with group vengeance against their social punishment. These actions only trigger another acting out–social punishment cycle. In the interaction between authorities and youth, the delinquent subculture is born.

Whether the deviant subculture arises out of deviant motivation or in response to a process of social differentiation, Cohen's main point still holds. In either case, people who feel rejected, as well as people who have actually experienced rejection, have an acute problem of social-psychological adjustment. Under whatever conditions the deviant subculture emerges, people who share in it sustain it and live by it so long as it helps them to manage these problems.

A deviant subculture, then, consists of a body of shared solutions to the problems of social deviance. Three areas in which a variety of problems may develop include the act, partners, and the consequences of the act. A subculture of deviants of whatever kind will make available to its constituents ways of organizing and executing the deviant act, a set of rules of associating with one's partners in deviance, and some means for either avoiding or managing the consequences of deviance. The subculture of drug addicts provides a useful example (Rubington, 1967).

Once addicted, drug users require another shot some four hours after their last injection, if they are to avoid severe withdrawal symptoms. Awareness of this necessity generates a set of fairly regular activities. The cycle of activities the addict engages in includes obtaining a supply of drugs, having the drug experience, managing the aftermath, and then starting the cycle all over again. The cycle begins with a "hustle." This includes selling drugs, engaging in prostitution, and stealing goods and then fencing them for money. Once the addict has the price, the next step is to "cop" (obtain a supply of drugs). The third step is to find a "shooting gallery" (a place where one can take drugs in safety) and then "fix" (inject the dose). The fourth step is either "going on the nod" (falling asleep) or just "feeling normal." After a few hours, the cycle is reactivated, and the addict goes out to "hustle," "cop," and "fix" all over again.

At each juncture of the cycle, addicts go through all of the steps required before they can administer the needed dosage. In the process, there are always problems connected with obtaining drugs, interacting with an assortment of role-partners, and avoiding capture. Through the process of interaction with other addicts, they learn, share, and employ a set of collective and rather personal solutions to every one of these problems, all of which are contingent on their status as drug addicts.

Addict subculture, learned in intimate interaction with other addicts, provides solutions to problems that arise at any of the phases of the addict's cycle of activities. Thus the behavior patterns center on the administration of drugs in order to obtain the desired drug experience. The norms specify rules for how to conduct oneself when in the company of other addicts, dealers, undercover agents, the police, and so on. The self-image consists of ideas about the addict's self and moral character that refute the beliefs about drug addicts held by participants in conventional culture. And the ideology contains justifications for the drug experience, along with a body of ideas about the social world of nonusers. In addition, it is the main repository of collective definitions of the range of situations in which addicts may expect to find themselves. In summary, then, the beliefs, values, and norms of the addict subculture provide information on how to think, feel, and act like an addict. This subculture affords to each of its participants answers to the central question of drug addiction: what to think, feel, say, and do while having drug experiences and coping with their social and psychological consequences.

Culture for deviants such as drug addicts is essentially the same as it is for conventional people. The main difference, of course, is that the content of deviant subcultures is illegal, immoral, or both. The content provides knowledge and skills on how to execute deviant activities and further the interests of those who engage in such activities. Because the activities are stigmatized, those who engage in them place themselves in opposition to the dominant culture. Their resistance to conventionality requires them to develop justifications for their activities. The ideology of the deviant subculture supplies these justifications. Without them, it is questionable whether these actions could continue, given the necessity that people understand the meaning of their own conduct.

The major difference between social deviants and solitary deviants is that social deviants draw upon a stock of collective solutions to the problems their deviance creates for them. By contrast, solitary deviants proceed by trial-and-error and fashion private solutions to the problems of deviance. Being a member of a group, albeit a deviant one, the social deviant experiences the benefits as well as the costs of group membership. As with all groups, however, the benefits of membership are contingent on the members paying the price of conformity. Considering the hazards attached to the situation of most social deviants, they are usually more than willing to pay this price. The group, as is the case with any group, prescribes norms for its members to follow. By adhering to the group's code of conduct, members satisfy their deviant motives.

Solitary deviants lack guidelines, not to mention social support. Lacking both a membership and a reference group of similarly situated other people, they also lack a set of consistent definitions for the range of unpredictable and hazardous situations in which they may become implicated. In these isolated circumstances, solitary deviants cannot achieve consensus about the meaning of their activities and how best to pursue their interest in deviance.

GETTING INTO DEVIANT GROUPS

Through a combination of socialization and social control, most people acquire conventional culture and perform legitimate social roles. Few engage in deviant behavior on a systematic or career basis. Those who do, of course, go on to become secondary or career deviants. Some perform deviant roles as members of deviant groups; others do not, preferring social isolation and anonymity. In either case, it is necessary to explain how both categories of deviants come to persist in their deviant careers. It is also important to establish whether both have dropped out of conformist groups. Finally, it is important to find out how social deviants gain admission to deviant groups.

Answers to the three questions of persistence in deviance, dropping out of conformist groups, and affiliation with deviant groups come from an analysis of the social bond, those ties that bind people to one another and emerge in the process of social interaction. The bond has a circular character, based on the changing interrelationships of attachments and commitments. The ties to people are attachments, the ties to culture are commitments. Attachment is a measure of the extent and degree to which one person continues to associate with a person or group in the face of competing attractions. Commitment is a measure of the extent and degree to which a person subscribes to the tenets of a given culture in the face of strong resistance or opposition. If attachment refers to the strength of one's ties to specific people, then commitment is the strength of ties to a culture, to its beliefs, values, and norms.

Attachments and commitments have a mutually reinforcing character. Each feeds, sustains, and replenishes the other. Social interaction in primary groups leads to an enactment of one's attachments and a profession of one's commitments. The recurrent processes of everyday behavior guarantee these outcomes. A circular process is at work, whereby binding or renewing the ties to persons simultaneously evokes the need for the expression of a renewed commitment to the culture of the group, its beliefs, its values, and its norms. The relations between attachment and commitment are those of a virtuous circle.

Entry into deviant groups, then, requires the disruption or reversal of the virtuous circle of attachments and commitments. In the case of conformity, attachments strengthen commitments and vice versa. In the case of deviance, detachment strengthens decommitment. Regardless of the point at which the vicious circle begins, whether it is weakening ties to people or weakening ties to culture, the end result remains the same. The ties that were supposed to bind have been cut. Both detachment and decommitment arise in the course of social interaction and become an interactive process in their own right.

People can persist in deviance and yet remain in primary groups as long as members achieve a working stalemate between attachment and commitment on the one hand, and detachment and decommitment on the other. The tolerance for deviance in many primary groups is predicated on this kind of social equilibrium. Alcoholism in the family is one very good case in point (Jackson, 1954). Mental illness is another (Yarrow, Schwartz, Murphy, and Deasy, 1955). In general, primary groups tend to overlook behavior that other groups would never tolerate. Attachment to the deviant person or commitment to family norms generally suffices to account for the well-known tolerance primary groups extend to their members.

By the same token, in some groups or families, a mutual process of detachment and decommitment gets under way. In these instances, the ties are not so much cut as they are withered away. A person can easily drift out of this group and further the deviant career upon which he or she has already embarked. The group's definition of the situation and its social ties can no longer exercise any controls on the person's conduct. On departure from the group, the person persists in deviance.

Whether the person who has dropped out of a conventional group enters a deviant group or not depends upon the workings of the attachment-commitment cycle. Thus, for most people, the drifting out of conformist groups is matched by the drifting into deviant groups. Entry into the Skid Row way of life, for example, seems to follow a series of stages wherein the newcomer first becomes slowly detached from conventional people (usually through geographic isolation) and, in consequence, from their conventional norms. In time, through a process of slow drift, the newcomer becomes committed to Skid Row people and their norms.

SOCIALIZATION INTO DEVIANT SUBCULTURE

Through the workings of the attachment-commitment or detachment-decommitment interactive process, deviants become grouped or ungrouped. The nature and kind of influence that deviant groups can have upon their members' conduct depends greatly on, among other things, the kind of group it is, the deviant activities and values it prescribes, and the duration of contact among members.

A study of socialization in correctional communities shows the relationship of primary group membership to commitment to deviant or conventional values. Wheeler (1961) carried out this study in a Western reformatory and found a U-shaped curve in the commitment of inmates to either conventional or deviant values. He interviewed prisoners three times: shortly after they became inmates, at the midpoint of their inmate careers, and shortly before they completed sentence and were discharged. He also measured involvement in inmate primary groups and commitment to the inmate code as well as to conventional values during each interview.

When Wheeler first contacted them, inmates were new, not yet integrated in prison primary groups; as a result, they got high scores on conventional values and low scores on inmate values. At the midpoint of their inmate careers, he found that inmates who had become integrated into inmate primary groups scored high on inmate values and got extremely low scores on conventional values.

At the end of their inmate careers, Wheeler found scores similar to those he had obtained at the beginning of the inmates' careers; that is, high scores on conventional values, low scores on deviant values. As membership in inmate primary groups is about to end, anticipatory socialization comes into play. As the prisoners look forward to freedom, they think ahead to the kinds of values most people share in the conventional world. As they mentally prepare for conventional roles, they begin to decommit themselves from the inmate code and those groups that uphold that deviant subculture.

The prison is an abnormal social situation, and the inmate culture constitutes the shared problem-solving device prisoners use to try to deal with the acute social and psychological problems imprisonment creates for all of them. But Wheeler's time-bound analysis of the influence of primary inmate groups on conduct and commitment calls attention to two important truisms: (1) most prisoners ultimately return to society, and (2) most people, conformists and deviants alike, belong to a plurality of groups, most of which are conformist in nature. The nature of society and culture is such that people have membership in a number of groups, few of which are deviant, and that people also share in a plurality of subcultures rather than only one. Thus, even so-called deviant people are conformist most of the time. They are members of a wide variety of groups, and their behavior is largely influenced by the groups to which they belong, the situations in which they customarily find themselves, and the definitions they construct for these situations.

PARTICIPATION IN CULTURE: CONVENTIONAL AND DEVIANT

When we extend the notion of multiple group membership to the understanding of deviant behavior, we expect that those who are members of deviant groups and who participate to some degree in a deviant subculture ought to behave differently from those people who are solitary deviants, who are not members of a deviant group, and who do not participate (or only marginally) in a deviant subculture. Thus, conformity, as well as deviance, will be spread out across a range. And this range encompasses behavior, groups, and culture. The hypothetical extremes include, at one end, complete conformists, and, at the other end, complete deviants. Similarly, persons can belong to conformist groups only, to deviant groups only, or to a mixture of the two. Finally, as with groups, so with culture. Thus there can be complete immersion in conventional culture at one extreme, complete immersion in deviant subculture at the other extreme, and a range of possibilities in between. These several variations show, once again, how deviance, at least for most of its varieties, is integrated in a number of ways with the conformist world.

Naturally, the kinds of groups, the nature of the behavior, and the variety of deviance must be taken into account. The extreme case of Joey (1973), a "hit man," for example, gives some clues about the frequency of behavior, the gravity of the deviance, and the extent of participation in conventional and deviant culture. Joey murdered 33 persons for money. Other than this extreme and invisible deviance, Joey lived a life of superconventionality. His case suggests that an examination of the relationship between behavior, group, and culture may shed light on how deviant subcultures prescribe ways of organizing and executing the deviant act, and avoiding or managing the consequences of deviant behavior.

The extent and degree of participation in both deviant and conventional cultures may afford some answers to these questions. The typology of participation in conventional and deviant subcultures in Table 2.1 lists some of the logical possibilities.

Table 2.1.   Types of Participation in Culture.

	Conventional	Deviant
1. Two-worlder	+	+
2. Secret	+	−
3. Public	−	+
4. Marginal	−	−

(+) = participation, (−) = nonparticipation.

Two-Worlder

The two-worlder leads a double life, living in two different social worlds and managing to keep these worlds apart. The nature of the deviant activity in which he or she is involved requires concealing information about it from family, friends, authorities, and the general public. As long as the person keeps these separate lives apart, participation in both worlds can be full, and commitment and involvement in deviant values can exist without reservation and without being of two minds about the situation. Stimson (1973), in his study of English drug addicts, coined the term *two-worlder* to describe those addicts who participated in both the drug world and the conventional world. Another example of social deviants who manage to exist rather well in two different social worlds is the ambisexuals about whom Humphreys (1970) has written in his study of homosexuality in public places.

Secret Deviant

All deviants fear exposure, albeit in varying degrees. Secret deviants fear exposure in direct proportion to their lessened capacity or abilities to conceal their activities from the view of others. These fears, of course, have their subjective as well as objective components. As a result, secret deviants experience considerably more tension when it comes to thinking about or actually organizing and executing the deviant act. In some instances, their fear of getting caught may well be way out of proportion to the actual chances of getting caught. Given this state of tension, the actual number of times they engage in deviance is inversely related to the frequency with which they contemplate such activities. "Closet" homosexuals (Humphreys, 1970) and solitary drug addicts (such as the physician narcotic addicts described by Winick [1961]) are two examples of the secret deviant.

Public or Overt Deviant

There are, of course, degrees of visibility. Nonetheless, the overt deviant is considerably more involved with the deviant subculture than with the conventional culture. Again, social visibility is proportional to the depth of involvement in deviant subculture. The extent of their involvement in deviant life relieves overt deviants of the necessity of concealing their identity. In contrast with the tension-ridden existence of the secret deviant, their activities and relationships with fellow deviants (and sometimes with conventional others) is extremely relaxed, easygoing, and matter-of-fact. Their relative absence of deviant status anxiety comes from the fact that they largely know who they are, always a dependable consequence of stable group memberships. Street "junkies" and members of Hell's Angels are two examples of overt social deviants (Waldorf, 1973; Thompson, 1966).

Marginal Deviant

Marginal deviants have minimal involvements with both the conventional and the deviant world. If a two-worlder has one foot solidly planted in each world, then a marginal can be said to be on tiptoes in both of these worlds. Both their attachments and commitments to both of these worlds is relatively weak. When it comes to the performance of the deviant activity in which they have a fleeting interest, they are mainly concerned with an expedient, quick performance. This stands to reason. For just as most of their conformist acts are poorly integrated in an ongoing network of social activities, so also are their deviant acts. "Trade" (heterosexual males whose marriages are failing and who infrequently visit public toilets for sexual contact with homosexuals) are outstanding examples of marginal deviants (Humphreys, 1970).

SOME CONSEQUENCES OF PARTICIPATION IN DEVIANT SUBCULTURE

The typology of participation in deviant and conventional culture accomplishes four objectives: it offers a multidimensional perspective on deviant behavior, it recognizes the dynamic nature of deviant behavior, it orders research findings on effects of participation in deviant subcultures, and it makes predictions about the relative probabilities of resocialization for social and solitary deviants alike.

Although a one-dimensional view of deviance has its social

uses, a typology of differential participation does more justice to the complexity of deviant subcultures. Explication of the typology makes it clear that deviants participate in several social worlds. Thus, before safe generalizations about the behavior of deviants can be made, it becomes necessary to measure the extent of their attachments and commitments to conventional people and their norms as well as the extent of their attachments and commitments to deviant people and their norms. Yablonsky's (1959) study of delinquent gangs, for example, reveals how conventional stereotypes about delinquent behavior impute a greater degree of organization to delinquent gangs than is actually the case. He describes three kinds of involvement in gangs: hard-core, occasional, and peripheral. Only hard-core members are attached and committed to delinquent peers and their norms.

The typology of participation reveals the dynamic aspects of deviant behavior. Without a multidimensional focus on norms and group membership, it is quite easy to adopt a deterministic attitude toward deviance. This is most unfortunate and untrue to the realities of deviant behavior. Contrary to the views of the conformist world, participation in deviant subcultures is not all that attached and committed. Because of shifting alignments with a variety of groups, deviant as well as conventional, many would-be deviants have two minds about their status. To the extent that they are ambivalent about their situation, their memberships are fluid rather than fixed. Thus, multiple-group membership refutes determinism. In a multigroup society, people retain some alliances, make new ones, and drop others. As a result, there is a good deal of traffic across the boundaries of many groups, whether conventional or deviant. Fluidity rather than fixity characterizes relations between the two. This is largely because deviance is more often integrated into society rather than the reverse.

The role, self, and status of deviant persons depend on how frequently they engage in deviant behavior, how visible their behavior is, and how severely people punish them (Lemert, 1951). The organization and execution of the deviant act constitutes the role of the deviant. The self-definition arises out of interaction with significant others. And the status of the deviant follows from the interaction with conventional others. Solitary deviants handle these career problems differently than social deviants.

Membership in deviant groups, the source of deviant subculture, makes for variations in deviant role-performance. Research suggests that social deviants engage in their particular variety of deviant behavior much more frequently than solitary deviants, with more rewards, and, very often, with more fun (Weinberg and Williams, 1974). Having several deviant role-partners expands the range of deviant acquaintances and increases the chances of integration into deviant primary groups. A presumable consequence of integration in such deviant groups would seem to be a greater degree of self-acceptance. Finally, conflict with conventional norms invites the negative reaction. But when deviants experience social punishment as a group, they gain mutual respect in one another's eyes, particularly if they unite in rejecting their rejectors (McCorkle and Korn, 1954). In so doing, in coming together against those who punish them, they become more tightly knit. Thus, social punishment, particularly when it is given to people in groups, may unite deviants against conformists and stabilize their deviant careers.

Deviants, social or solitary participants in deviant subculture of whatever degree, risk social punishment. They also run risks of self-punishment. Research suggests that social deviants manage these risks as members of social groups, whereas solitary deviants manage them as individuals. Solitary deviants seem to be somewhat better at avoiding social punishment than social deviants. The converse, however, is also true. Namely, solitary deviants experience considerably more self-punishment than do social deviants. Social deviants (that is, those who engage in deviant activity as part of a group) run greater social risks (the larger the group, the greater the risk of capture). But, similarly, the larger the company, the lesser the amount of misery to be shared. Solitary deviants have better chances of not getting caught, but if they are caught, they have to suffer the consequences alone.

Research support for these theoretical speculations exists. Studies of prisoner subcultures suggest that the more involved prisoners are in inmate subcultures, the more frequent their deviant behavior while in prison, particularly during the middle stages of their inmate careers (Irwin, 1980). Similarly, the greater their involvement with the prisoner subculture, the greater the frequency of violation of prison norms coupled with lesser exposure to sanctions. Put otherwise, seasoned prisoners know how to break the rules without getting caught. Knowledge of these skills comes from their greater involvement with the prisoner subculture, along with greater experience with breaking rules and avoiding sanctions.

Research on addicts, Skid Row alcoholics, and juvenile delinquents points to the general proposition that the greater the involvement with the deviant subculture, the greater the self-acceptance. Hall (1966), for example, has shown that delinquents most involved in the delinquent subculture manifest the greatest degree of self-acceptance. Weinberg and Williams (1974), comparing overt with secret homosexuals, report similar findings. Stimson (1973) also found the same relationships between degree of self-acceptance and involvement in the addict subculture. Denial is much more likely the stock in trade of the solitary deviant. Whereas there is congruence between the self and the deviant role for the social deviant, discrepancy between the self and the deviant role is much more frequently the case for the solitary deviant. As Schur (1965) has pointed out, the physician addict does not define himself as a criminal. But most people see street addicts as criminals, which is exactly how addicts see themselves.

Resocialization combines resumption of legitimate social roles with renunciation of deviant roles. Research suggests that both the chances and modes of reentry into society vary with levels of involvement in deviant subcultures. For example, the great bulk of alcoholics who join Alcoholics Anonymous have been solitary drinkers. If solitary drinking is coupled with attachment to primary groups in which sharing personal troubles is common, then affiliation with Alcoholics Anonymous is even more likely (Trice, 1957). By contrast, immersion in Skid Row subculture turns out to be the most significant barrier against those who seek to make a return to society by way of group therapy (Wiseman, 1970).

High involvement in the addict subculture, by way of contrast, seems related to a greater percentage of treatment successes when ex-addicts conduct the therapy of primary group authoritarianism, as in Synanon (Volkman and Gressey, 1963). Similarly, when addicts with considerable prior involvement in the addict subculture form close primary group relations in a prison hospital, higher rates of meaningful participation in group therapy result (Tittle, 1972).

SUMMARY

Deviant subculture refers to the shared ways of thinking, feeling, and acting that members of a deviant group have developed for engaging in deviant behavior, organizing relations among themselves, and defending themselves against social punishment. They use these ways to adapt to situations in groups, settings, or institutions. The idea of a deviant subculture grew out of the researches of the Chicago school of sociology on crime and delinquency. But it was not until Cohen synthesized these views with Merton's anomie theory that a general theory of deviant subcultures came into being. Stripped to its essentials, the theory says that people experiencing a common situational fate, such as status-frustration, will hit upon a collective solution to their problems if they communicate and interact with one another on the basis of their shared problems of adjustment.

Getting into deviant groups depends on the opposite process of getting out of conformist groups. Consequently, there are at least three types of deviants: those who are solitary and integrated to some extent into conformist groups, those who are solitary and marginal to both conformist and deviant groups, and those who are social and integrated into deviant groups. There is a history to the socialization process in deviant groups; just as some become more deeply involved in the beliefs and practices of a deviant way of life, others become disaffected with those same beliefs and practices. These changing patterns of participation in deviant subcultures chart stages in deviant careers. In turn, they give a clue to the chances of terminating these careers. "Burning one's bridges" to the conventional world does happen. But it is most likely to be the result of a long interactive process in which people have cut themselves off from (or have been cut off from) conformist groups and have become committed to a deviant life-style. For solitary deviants, who have not become so involved in a deviant subculture, the chances of effecting a return to legitimate society seem somewhat better.

3 LABELING THEORY

BARRY GLASSNER

We view ourselves in part through the eyes of others, and when others see us in a certain way, at least for long enough or sufficiently powerfully, their views are sure to have some effect. This is a core notion of labeling theorists, who see deviance in the way defined by one of their leading proponents, Howard S. Becker:

> Social groups create deviance by making the rules whose infraction constitutes deviance and by applying these rules to particular people and labeling them as outsiders. From this point of view, deviance is not a quality of the act the person commits, but rather a consequence of the application by others of rules and sanctions to an "offender." The deviant is one to whom that label has successfully been applied; deviant behavior is behavior that people so label (Becker, 1963: 9).

This perspective is sometimes called the societal reaction theory of deviance because, as Becker's definition illustrates, it emphasizes the importance of the response to behavior that violates social rules or customs, rather than the behavior itself. Unlike other sociological interpretations of deviance, it does not take as most important the basic actions of persons considered deviant—such as whether a person has delusions, steals cars, or engages in sexual activities with someone of the same sex. Instead, labeling theorists consider the responses of others in society as keys to understanding deviance. Labeling theory is thus an interactionist perspective: It emphasizes the actions and reactions of deviants *and* of other persons who deal with these deviants. Labeling theorists explain de-

71

viance as the ongoing outcomes of interactions between persons labeled deviant and those who label them.

Thus, the labeling approach concentrates upon social processes rather than upon social causes of deviance. As Becker suggests in response to some of the empiricalist critics (discussed later in this chapter):

> It recognizes the making of official diagnoses and statistics as part of the process of meaning construction and so takes the statistics . . . as something to be studied rather than used uncritically. It further deals with the meaning attached to deviant activity by those who engage in it and so studies the organization of social worlds and careers within them, as well as the organization of those professional worlds that intersect them, and the intersection itself—thus, the world of the drug user, of the narcotics police, and the events that involve both. . . . Researchers who use the labeling paradigm don't worry about testing causal theories rigorously. . . . They are more likely to "explore" and "discover" variations in the ways meanings are constructed. They want to understand a process rather than verify a causal connection. They insist on the rigor of detailed, comprehensive description rather than of measurement. . . . They differ from those of the more traditional view in ways that are difficult, perhaps impossible to reconcile. Its theories of etiology are about "becoming," not about variables that discriminate between groups and thus demonstrate causality (Becker, 1981).

"Labeling theory" is actually a misnomer because it does not constitute a theory in the formal sense of a body of well-confirmed and logically related hypotheses (Gibbs, 1966, 1972; Scheff, 1974), or, as Becker notes, a causal explanation. Rather, what is called labeling theory is a particular group of applications to the field of deviance of the symbolic interactionist model of social life.

Built upon the works of George Herbert Mead, a philosopher of social psychology, symbolic interactionism explains particular phenomena and events in social life as produced primarily by the participants themselves, through the symbols people use in interactions with one another. Everything in the social world—from the economy of nations to your own view of yourself—emerges through people interacting with one another, using and creating their symbols. In the case at hand, this means that deviance is not simply "out in the world," but persons are *creating* deviants through interactional processes. In other chapters of this book, a variety of such processes will be considered, but the one of interest at present is the interactions in which one group of persons identifies another person, or group of persons, by way of a word or phrase. The word or phrase then becomes the basis of further interactions of a special nature.

Consider a story told to me during the course of some research with persons diagnosed manic-depressive (Glassner et al., 1979; Glassner, 1980b). A women in her sixties, who had been under psychiatric care for about twenty years, was talking about her life.

> The first time I was taken to a psychiatrist for help was when I was getting depressed over a miscarriage. I had tried for many years to have that baby, and finally I was pregnant and planning to be a mother and all, and then I lost it. Anyhow, they told me I was "deeply depressed," but it didn't really mean much to me. I figured I'd get over it once I got pregnant again or something. But when I went home, everybody treated me differently. My husband and my mother had met with the social worker, who explained that I had this problem, with depression and all. From then on I was a depressive. I mean, that's the way everyone treated me, and I thought of myself in the same way after a while. Maybe I am that way, maybe I was born that way or grew up like that, but anyhow, that's what I am now.

In this short passage we find a good bit of what labeling theorists consider important about the process of deviance. Most centrally, the woman says that not until significant other persons labeled her as a depressive did she consider herself to be a depressive. In her full story, it turns out that she had never been severely depressed before this point, but that she frequently became depressed thereafter. The *meaning* (a key term for symbolic interactionism) of her depressed feelings, and of her own identity in general, changed. She *became* a depressive, both in the minds of others and to herself. As one of the earliest symbolic interactionists, Charles Horton Cooley (1902), expressed the matter, how we feel about ourselves depends upon how we imagine we appear to others and how we imagine they judge, or feel about, us.

Probably the first proponent of a labeling perspective on deviance was Frank Tannenbaum (1938), who wrote that juvenile delinquents start thinking of themselves as different, rather than as simply naughty, when the community around them characterizes them in such ways (e.g., by calling them juvenile delinquents). Tannenbaum claimed that the community's reaction to the boys is more important than the boys' own behaviors in establishing them as deviants. It is through this labeling and the consequent exclusion from normal interactions that the person takes on the trappings of a deviant; the child sees himself or herself as a criminal, may start associating with others who are viewed as criminals, and so forth.

A key notion is what labeling theorists, following Edwin Lemert (1951), call secondary deviance. In the customary labeling theory view, a person first commits primary deviation—some form of rule-breaking, such as experimentation with a drug, shoplifting, or acting depressed—and is penalized for it. The penalty can take a very simple form, such as informal ostracizing or a formal speeding ticket, or it may be informally or formally severe, such as a felony allegation or disowning the person from the family. Despite the penalty, the person may still be inclined to break the rules. This results in stronger penalties and, with these, greater rejection. Over time, a cycle is in place: (1) rule-breaking, (2) intolerance (including labeling) by others, (3) response by way of more extreme rule-breaking, and (4) conceptions of the self in accordance with the label. Secondary deviance is that stage, after the primary deviance, in which much of what the person or group does is a response to having been labeled. As the woman previously quoted put it, "From then on I was a depressive." She is thought of as a depressive, as if that is her identity or a very important part of it. Indeed, she went on to tell me that much of her time was then taken up with "being depressed." This included not only lack of sleep, "the blues," and other changes in affect, but also worrying about when the depression would hit again, assuring her husband that she could handle responsibility, dealing with potential employers who preferred not to hire persons considered mentally ill, and being invited by a patients' rights organization to become a member.

A variety of studies have produced similar findings. Robert Scott (1969) reports that blind people will frequently act docile, helpless, sad, spiritual, and aesthetic, which is what others expect of the blind. In a study of juvenile delinquents, researchers compared youths who had been apprehended and labeled as juvenile delinquents with a matched control group who performed similar acts with about the same frequency but were never picked up by police. The labeled group committed more delinquent acts in the future than did the nonlabeled group (Gold and Williams, 1972).

How people are labeled affects much more, however, than how they behave or feel, or with whom they associate. The type of labeling largely determines the kind of treatment they will receive. In a famous study that dramatically points this out—"On Being

Sane in Insane Places" (Rosenhan, 1973)—eight researchers, all sane by usual standards, became patients in mental hospitals. These pseudopatients pretended to hear voices at the time of their admission, but thereafter they acted as sanely as they could. They were treated by the hospital staff of nurses, psychiatrists, attendants, and others as if they were insane. They were avoided or were given the usual treatments for schizophrenia. Having been labeled schizophrenic, they were perceived by others as schizophrenic even though they did not exhibit the usual behaviors associated with schizophrenia. Indeed, they were discharged after lengthy stays, with the label "schizophrenia in remission." (Interestingly, the group within the hospitals who did not treat the pseudopatients as insane were the other patients, many of whom figured that the pseudopatients were journalists or researchers.)

Beyond the isolated hospital or other locality, there are larger, societywide variations in treatment according to label. Treatment is typically predicated upon the type of label employed. If a person is considered eccentric, he or she will probably be dealt with by family members or friends, but if considered mentally ill will be handled by psychiatrists or other mental health personnel. The importance of labeling in this regard can be most clearly seen, however, when a specific form of deviance is relabeled. When homosexuality is considered a moral crime, the persons are labeled and otherwise processed by the judicial system. When it is treated as an illness, the mental health establishment is involved. Similarly, when drug addicts are considered criminals, they are punished by the legal system; when they are thought of as sick, they are given methadone. Blame for the deviance also shifts. Deviants labeled as morally or criminally corrupt are blamed for their behaviors ("They should control themselves like the rest of us"), but deviants labeled as sick are not blameworthy (Conrad and Schneider, 1980: 27).

CRITIQUES

During the past few decades, more sociological research has derived from the labeling perspective than from any other model of deviance. Nevertheless, labeling theory has been criticized by every major school of contemporary sociology. Some say that labeling theory neglects the actual person labeled deviant, since labeling theorists do not explain primary deviance (Rogers and Buffalo, 1974); other critics argue just the opposite, that labeling theory stresses the individual too much (Davis, 1972). Some call labeling hypercritical of established social institutions (Lemert, 1972); others suggest that it perpetuates the status quo (Gouldner, 1968).

Let us consider three types of critiques, all of which are extensions of contemporary theoretical schools in sociology: neo-Marxist, empiricalist, and phenomenological.

Neo-Marxists

Following the more economic-oriented approach within Marxism, several sociologists have suggested that labeling theory ignores the importance of powerful members of society. Alvin Gouldner (1968) claims that labeling theorists refuse to recognize that deviance results from key institutions in society and that it sometimes serves to oppose those institutions. The first part of this claim is hard to refute in many cases. For instance, we know that as the national economy worsens (such as during recessions and depressions), the number of persons diagnosed as mentally ill increases (Brenner, 1977). The latter part of the claim is less clearly true. Certainly various sorts of robbery and white-collar crime are a form of battle with the dominant economic institutions, and revolutionaries are often considered deviant when they oppose the dominant social order. On the other hand, it is more difficult to think of obesity and physical disfigurement in these terms, although one might say that these sorts of deviance counter the cosmetic and clothing industries, hindering the emphasis within capitalism on fads and fashions as a way to enlarge markets for consumer goods. But how can one think in similar terms about those acts considered deviant such as masturbation and incest? This problem for the neo-Marxist position is more severe in the cases outside of "official deviances," where informal expectations are violated (examples include "brown nosers," "prudes," "party poopers," and "teacher's pets"). Here, persons seem to violate rules generally unrelated to large societal institutions, but rather directed at the perpetuation and smooth handling of interpersonal or small group relations. Such conduct, which may be very important although the broader society does not attend to it, has been called *relational deviance* (Denzin, 1970). One neo-Marxist has proposed that there should be distinctions made between those types of deviance that are linked to social class interests and those that are not (Gusfield, 1963).

Neo-Marxists typically have in mind deviance of the former type when they criticize labeling theory. "Writers of this field still do not try to relate the phenomenon of 'deviance' to larger social, historical, political, and economic interests. The emphasis is still on the 'deviant' and the 'problems' he presents to himself and others, not on the society within which he emerges and operates," writes Alexander Liazos (1972: 104). Neo-Marxists do not claim that labeling theory *cannot* deal with the role of the powerful in producing deviance, only that they *have* not. Surely it is true that most studies by labeling theorists have consisted of what Liazos calls "nuts, sluts, and perverts," but there is no reason why other groups cannot be studied from the labeling perspective. Nevertheless, the neo-Marxists want to distinguish between two types of deviants not usually separated by labeling theorists: the powerless and the powerful. The major cause or determinant of deviance by the powerless, in the neo-Marxist view, is the inequality in capitalist societies which prevents these persons from realizing their interests by other than deviant means (Taylor et al., 1973). On the other hand, the powerful commit deviance out of their greater opportunities or as part of their regular work. Neo-Marxists would prefer a concentration on the powerful, such as white-collar embezzlers who find themselves in the position of being able to steal (in contrast to ghetto burglars, who steal to eat or to buy convenience items), or the members of the Nixon White House, who saw their involvement in the Watergate burglary and related affairs as simply helping their country.

The neo-Marxist position entails some contradictions. The theorists define deviance as "conduct that is in violation of rules made largely by the power elite of a given society or group" (Thio, 1973: 1), and then declare that the proper subject matter for sociologists to study is those activities of the elite that harm others. On one level, it makes no sense to say that the elite are violating their own rules, since members of the elite often consider those "violations" acceptable.

Neo-Marxists criticize that labeling theorists treat persons like automatons. Gouldner (1968: 106) claims that in labeling theory the deviant is viewed as a product of society rather than as a rebel against it and therefore as a "passive nonentity who is responsible neither for his suffering nor its alleviation." One cannot, without contradiction, hold both that the deviant voluntarily chooses to commit an act and that deviance among the powerless is caused by the larger social structure.

Labeling theorists have claimed that their work brings into question the right of elite groups and "moral entrepreneurs" (see

Chapter 4) to define reality for everyone, and that labeling theory changes the conventional institutions of society (Becker, 1963). That this is accurate can be seen in examples such as the changes in involuntary commitment laws for psychiatric patients that have resulted in part from widespread discussion of labeling theory findings within social services establishments. In many places, it is now much more difficult than it was just two decades ago to commit someone to a mental institution if the person refuses such commitment. Neo-Marxists disagree that labeling has much to say about the really significant deviances, however, since political deviants have not been studied by labeling theorists.

Empiricalists

Several sociologists who do not ally themselves with one clear theoretical school (though they tend to imply structural functionalism in their writings) criticize labeling theory on various empirical grounds. They contend that there are weaknesses in labeling theory revealed by actual research.

One such claim is that labeling does not in fact result in more intense deviant activities or commitment, as the notion of secondary deviance would suggest. Some persons choose to be involved in deviant activities quite independently of whether or not they are labeled. Even within the studies conducted by labeling theorists themselves, one finds persons regularly involved in the use of marijuana (Becker, 1963) and in check forgery (Lemert, 1972) without at least official recognition such as arrest. Other obvious examples include secret drinkers, white-collar embezzlers who do not get caught, persons who regularly get high on household drugs without anyone else's knowledge, and persons who give up their criminal activities after prison terms. Or, like the depressive woman mentioned earlier, one can easily find people who have suffered only one episode of emotional illness who have nevertheless been labeled as mentally ill by hospital staffs and by their families (Gove, 1970).

An interesting debate on this issue occurred between Travis Hirschi and Edwin Lemert at the 1975 meeting of the American Sociological Association. Their discussion centered on the relevance of labeling theory of empirical studies of juvenile delinquency. Hirschi contended that labeling theory suffers from "dire empirical shortcomings." As evidence, he cited an investigation by the California Youth Authority of one-year recidivism rates among various parolee groups. Hirschi contended that because these rates do not differ significantly among parolees, persons assigned to regular probation units, and persons assigned to units involving intensive supervision, the major tenets of labeling theory have been disproved. (Parole and *probation* are different outcomes of processing by the criminal justice system, and therefore follow the application of the label *criminal*. At best, Hirschi was discussing the effects of the degree of supervision of persons labeled criminal, not the effects of labeling per se. To study the effects of labeling would require the comparison of persons labeled criminal with persons not so labeled.)

In his reply to Hirschi, Lemert cited data indicating that arrest record, age, race, demeanor, probation status, administrative unit of the officer, and presence or absence of interaction between police and juvenile affect both the tendency to arrest and the seriousness of the resulting charge. (In addition, Wilson [1968] found arrest rates of juveniles to be 50 percent higher for Western City than Eastern City, although crime rates did not differ markedly. Factors influencing these rates included concepts of what constitutes a record, the seriousness of the offense, racial attitudes, patrolling practices, and interaction with other officers.) Lemert summarized his position as follows: "In general I have found that studies of police and juvenile court processing of minors do not contradict the societal reaction view of delinquency; i.e., that choice making by agents of social control, influenced by values, interactions with others, social organization, availability of means and their costs, affect the designation of minors as delinquent and overall volume and rate."

More generally, Lemert's argument is that the usual empiricalist method of finding invariant relationships between variables (e.g., "if S, then Y") denies the relevance of choice in human action. The alternate conception of action found in labeling theory and symbolic interactionism sees humans responding to symbolic feedback concerning their actions. This, we believe, is a crucial difference between empiricalist conceptions of deviance and the labeling approach. The latter does not deny that certain acts—children breaking windows, individuals selling drugs, and individuals experiencing anxiety—exist. It does contend that what is made of these acts socially, and what implications they have for the individuals who commit them, depends on the symbols attached by actors, and that these symbols are applied through social interaction. This is as true for acts with far-reaching consequences as for those with less serious implications. In Texas, New Mexico, and Utah, if a man finds his wife with a lover and kills him, he is not guilty of any crime, yet if he kills his wife, either by design or accident, the act is considered murder (Kanowitz, 1969).

This response to empiricalists by labeling theorists insists upon a distinction between the labeling process and the behaviors of the deviant, and concentrates upon the former (Kitsuse, 1972; Spector and Kitsuse, 1977). With this in mind, one can think in a more sophisticated way about the matter than simply in terms of labeling causing deviance, the way a knife causes bleeding. Labeling may be viewed as something that occurs widely within society and is recognized as such. In the cases mentioned previously, some marijuana smokers, check forgers, law violators, psychiatric patients, and others may be fearful of the labeling that has been thrust upon them or that they suspect could later be administered, and thereby avoid the behaviors, or at least avoid getting caught.

There is more to the empiricalists' critique, however. Behind it is a notion that there is much more to deviance than the labeling process. On the one hand, certain acts are more likely to be labeled than others, at least under certain conditions. Jane Murphy (1976) has suggested, for instance, that those behaviors considered to be indicative of mental illness are roughly the same throughout the world. We also know that virtually all human groups prohibit incest and that some groups, such as Jews and homosexuals, are more frequently stigmatized than others. This sort of finding contradicts only the most radical labeling view that anything can and does get labeled deviant equally as often or as easily as anything else—but few, if any, labeling theorists hold this view.

On the other hand, the fact that certain persons and certain acts are more likely to be labeled deviant suggests that focusing primarily upon labeling is perhaps a lopsided view. Yet, when one turns to some of the empiricalist alternatives, they are not terribly promising. Quite a few depend upon "kinds of people" explanations and compare the incidence of physiological, psychological, and sociological variables between populations of officially designated deviants and others. Often this kind of research has something of a sociobiological flavor to it. A well-known example is the study by Glueck and Glueck (1956), which found mesomorphy (muscular body type) significantly more often among institutionalized delinquents than among nondelinquents. Does this relationship explain how mesomorphs become delinquent? Schur (1971) notes that association is not causation and that there are undoubtedly intervening factors in the relationship. It is possible that public officials consider mesomorphic boys more of a potential threat than their less muscular peers, and therefore incarcerate them more often. Another possibility is that mesomorphs have more friends than other boys. Because many delinquent acts are of the joyriding variety and are typically committed by groups, mesomorphs may be involved in these activities more often, simply as the result of being more popular with their peers. While demonstrations of statistical relationships between sets of variables are valid, they can provide only an incomplete understanding of deviance.

Other research points to the importance of genetic or personality factors in causing deviance. The difficulties are twofold in each case. First, we emit a great deal of behavior that is caused (or at least partly determined) by our genetic inheritance, but only a small part thereof is labeled deviant. We cannot explain what is considered deviant, nor can we explain the effects of such considerations, by way of genetics, unless we want to say that every interpretation, human interaction, and social structure is directly caused by genetics. Second, in many cases, a genetic predisposition is likely to produce within a population both deviant behavior and avoidance of such behavior. Suppose that my genetic makeup predisposes me to become easily intoxicated. When I experiment with alcohol as an adolescent, I become intoxicated more quickly than my friends. I may interpret this as a pleasant circumstance, enjoy feeling "loose," and turn to alcohol often. Or I may consider the intoxication experience as something embarrassing, physically nasty, or leading me to do things I do not want to do, and I may thus try to avoid alcohol. On the other hand, suppose that my genes make it difficult for me to become intoxicated. The same analysis holds. It may be a challenge for me to achieve intoxication, and I may work hard at it by using alcohol often; or, I may get sick from having to drink so much, or embarrassed that I cannot keep up with my peers, and thus avoid the stuff. In any of these cases, the labeling theorist wants to say that how others respond to my efforts will have something to do with my eventual actions with regard to drinking.

None of this is to say that empiricalists are wrong in their criticism that labeling theory cannot explain primary deviance or what is taken to be a deviant act. Labeling theory is not really a theory of deviance, because a full explanation of deviance must explain far more than does labeling theory. Unfortunately, though, this is not what the empiricalists have in mind when they dismiss labeling theory on the charge that it is only a set of sensitizing concepts (Schur, 1971; Blumer, 1954). Rather, the empiricalists say that labeling theory lacks testable propositions and that the findings of labeling theorists can be interpreted in many ways. One is hard pressed to locate any findings in the social sciences that can be tested in some pure, direct, and uncontroversial way. What the empiricalists are calling for is statistical evidence, which they see as more definitive. Instead, because they emphasize the diverse and partly hidden texture of social interaction, labeling theorists have most often employed qualitative research methods, particularly participant observation. As a result, they have been attacked for inability to generalize from their findings.

Phenomenologists

Those sociologists who follow the works of Alfred Schutz, in his interpretations of the philosopher Edmund Husserl, frequently identify themselves as *phenomenologists,* a term that has to do with a complex body of thought in philosophy. The sociologists' emphases are upon one aspect of phenomenological concerns, namely, the ways in which phenomena can be said to change by way of the person's interpretations of them. In the phenomenological view (Husserl, 1962, 1965), we best understand a thing in the world in terms of its own makeup and our ways of considering that thing. For instance, if I want to understand the moon, one way I can do so is by its chemical composition, another by the myths people have told about it, another by the way astronomers talk about it. In any case, there are two components to my knowledge of the moon: what the moon is in itself, and how I or others construct what it is. The standard scientific route to knowledge is a concern solely with what the object is, external to my way of looking, but, as the phenomenologists argue, varied types of views result in different conclusions. One way to understand the moon is within the theories of astronomy, another with chemistry, another with tribal myths, and so forth. The moon remains the same, and my explanations may be more or less true, depending upon the way of looking, but the knowledge does change according to my intentions. The social phenomenologists merely emphasize that to understand our knowledge of something involves understanding the object or phenomenon in question *and* our own intentions and ways of knowing (Glassner, 1980a).

When the phenomenologists in sociology have considered labeling theory, they have found it lacking in its attention to this latter concern—how persons make sense of their social world. They propose that labeling theorists should provide more detailed analyses of what labels mean to those labeled, to those doing the labeling, and to persons responding to others' labels (the audience). The ambition should be to discover how a social phenomenon comes to be seen in a certain way. In the phenomenologists' view, it is not enough, for instance, to show that when a city court judge labels an adolescent as a "juvenile delinquent," it has certain effects on the person so labeled. Instead, one needs to investigate how judges (and this particular judge) come to accept "juvenile delinquent" as something real in the world and to see particular persons as part of that reality; how the person labeled interprets the process and his or her own activities, or how the person contributes to or hinders the taken-for-granted nature of the label; and how other persons come to make up stories about the labeled person and build or sustain the social reality of "juvenile delinquency." In short, the goal is to discover how persons in their everyday affairs "construct their realities, how they account them, and what they account" (Philipson, 1972: 146).

The argument holds that labeling theorists are more like the empiricalists than they let on. For example, within labeling theory, the label is still considered as a cause, and the resulting deviant behavior (secondary deviance) as an effect. The task is to describe "how the array called society is assembled out of what members do, not out of the causes and effects of what they do" (McHugh, 1970: 155). This is an important issue that both empiricalists and labeling theorists have largely ignored.

Along the same line, labeling theorists have not gone far enough in developing categories other than those used by social control agents: "By locating deviance in 'traditional' areas, labeling sociologists take the perspective of officials. They further take the perspective of officials by defining deviance as what officials perceive as deviance" (Warren and Johnson, 1972: 81).

The suggestion is that sociologists need to look in places other than those provided by official categories in determining what constitutes deviance for social actors.

PROSPECTS FOR LABELING THEORY

As happens in other walks of life, when an idea in sociology proves intriguing and powerful, it can become a kind of fad that is used in place of a wide variety of other beneficial ideas. In the case of labeling theory, it appears that the initial insight—that labeling is an important aspect of deviance—has become so popular that our knowledge of deviance has suffered. On the one hand, this insight has not been examined very far beyond its original applications by sociologists such as Tannenbaum, Lemert, and Becker, even though Becker (1963) and Lemert (in Chapter 9) have encouraged such progress. At the same time, the notion of labeling has been called upon to explain far more than it possibly can.

Of the first problem, Jay Corzine and I have proposed that many of the criticisms considered above could be averted by broadening the notion of labeling to view three additional types of labeling: categorical, contextual, and potential (Glassner and Corzine, 1978). After discussing these, I will consider some appropriate restrictions on applications of the labeling perspective.

Categorical Labeling

Labeling theorists tend to restrict their research to relationships between small groups of persons, rather than looking also at the large-scale societal, global, or institutional concerns promoted by neo-Marxists and other sociologists. As a result, labeling theorists have tended not to question seriously three assumptions: (1) rules are enforced against only actual (or perceived) deviants, (2) successful labeling affects only those labeled, and (3) whether or not the label sticks depends primarily on the interaction that occurs between the designated recipient of the label and those involved in its attempted application. Thio (1973) recognizes the error in these assumptions and notes that "when a small minority of powerless people are successfully labeled as deviants . . . by the law-enforcer, the majority of powerless people are likely to be labeled by the general public as potentially deviant when compared to the powerful."

Although labeling theorists have recognized that some acts are "potentially deviant" (Becker, 1963), they have ignored that some groups of people are also "potentially deviant." An American result of this type of labeling has been the residential ghettoization of potential deviants: blacks, American Indians, hippies, and the aged. This labeling of categories of people as potentially deviant forms the stage on which attempts to label particular individuals are played out. Rotenberg (1974: 341) notes the importance of such categorical labels for the outcomes of attempts to label individuals: "There is a difference between a labeling process through which a wayward youth or a pauper is labeled a 'thief' and the case where a rich professional is so labeled. In the first case, the descriptive label 'thief' is categorically compatible with waywardness or poverty, in the sense that the actor is an outsider or failure to begin with. . . . In the second case, however, a labeling transformation process is needed to make the label stick."

That actions of social control agents directed toward groups of powerless people differ from those directed at others has perhaps been best demonstrated by studies of the "homeless men" who are the primary targets of public drunkenness statutes (Bittner, 1967; Spradley, 1970). The arrests of these men often have little to do with law violations, but may result from factors such as the need for jailhouse trustees or agricultural workers, presence in the wrong place at the wrong time, and refusal to passively submit to robbery and personal indignities at the hands of the police. Neither do they have any practical recourse to the legal system for the protection of their rights. In the words of Spradley (1970: 79), "drunks are defenseless, exploitable and expendable." The labeling as deviant of a respected member of society necessitates the transformation of identity stressed by labeling theorists (Lemert, 1972: 62–92) and others writing from an interactionist perspective (Garfinkel, 1956; Goffman, 1963). The labeling of a nonrespected member is more a reaffirmation of "what everyone has known about the individual all along." An analysis of the processes underlying categorical labeling and its relationship to the labeling of specific individuals is necessary for a full understanding of deviance and social control. Increased attention to categorical labeling may resolve the debate between labeling theorists and neo-Marxists concerning the role of deviance in maintaining the status quo. Categorical, rather than individual labeling, would logically prove more useful to powerful groups in preventing or obstructing major social and political change.

Contextual Labeling

Places, as well as people, are ascribed negative status, and individuals must consistently account for their physical presence in morally questionable settings. Contextual labeling is exemplified by a news item concerning a Chicago hotel whose computer programmers inadvertently caused cards thanking individuals for their patronage to be mailed to persons who had not stayed at the hotel. Before the error was corrected, numerous marital arguments and divorce proceedings occurred between the recipients of the cards and their spouses. With some notable exceptions (Polsky, 1969:

1–30), sociologists of deviance have neglected the negative status of places. Although sociologists define themselves as studying people rather than places, the moral status of physical locations becomes entwined in the social identities of individuals, and thereby becomes important to sociological analysis. "Redlining" by financial institutions and police patrol procedures create disadvantages for individuals on the basis of their residence. Most arrests for public drunkenness occur within the section of an urban area known as "Skid Row" (Spradley, 1970).

If Lofland (1969) is correct in asserting that physical location is becoming increasingly important as a shorthand for imputing relevant identities to individuals and groups in contemporary urban societies, the analysis of place as a factor in the construction of deviance will assume corresponding importance. Studies of contextual labeling in cases such as Spradley (1970) should prove useful in the understanding of both the labeling of groups (categorical labeling) and the labeling of individuals.

Potential Labeling

The focus of labeling theorists on deviant outcomes ignores that the perception of the possibility of being labeled influences people's choices. This perception leads to a common characteristic of deviance, where actors build attempts to conceal their activities. Thus, labeling affects social deviance not only because social controllers label actors and actors label themselves, as the labeling theorists note, but also because the phenomenon of labeling exists (potential labeling), and actors take it into consideration in making behavioral choices.

Potential labeling provides a theoretical link for the study of deviance among different social classes. While members of the upper classes are not typically redefined as deviant by themselves or others, even when the criminal law is breached (Sutherland, 1949; Geis, 1968), evidence indicates that they employ similar methods of masking their questionable activities as do members of the lower classes. Documented cases, which have received national attention, include price fixing in the electrical industry (Schur, 1969a) and the Watergate conspirators (Woodward and Bernstein, 1974). The linkage of "potential labeling" to "categorical labeling" may provide a basis for the inclusion of social structural factors in the labeling perspective.

Potential deviance also raises questions of labeling theory's assumption that the label is more important than antecedent conditions in development of a deviant identity and commitment to deviance (secondary deviance). In particular, labeling theorists and many phenomenologists (e.g., Matza, 1969) have stressed the importance of labeling by social control agents in the passage from primary to secondary deviance. Research findings by interactionists, as well as empiricalists, have not supported this assertion. Dank (1971) has documented the widespread acceptance of a deviant identity (the "coming out" process) by homosexuals in the absence of official labeling. The same general process has been studied among marijuana users (Becker, 1963: 41–78) and prostitutes (Bryan, 1965).

DELIMITING LABELING THEORY

Delimiting labeling theory helps to avoid some of the problems we raised earlier, but a kind of restriction is also in order. Labeling theory must be recognized for what it is: the application of some basic symbolic interactionist insights to the issues of deviant behaviors. Perhaps it would be helpful to rename this sociological enterprise "labeling studies." This may also help to end the misconception that because the labeling perspective has dealt primarily with the field of deviance, labeling is a process that occurs only in that area. Labels are symbols, and the construction and use of symbols are vital components of all human interaction. Therefore, the subject matter of "labeling studies" transcends the sociology of deviance (Becker, 1964).

Even with the sociology of deviance, some sense of limitation is needed. Labeling is frequently a *part* of the deviance process, rather than a decisive or fully explanatory factor. For instance, in my own studies of manic-depression and of drinking, labeling proved to be less significant in causing the behaviors or in exaggerating them than in stopping them. Labeling theorists have typically studied the negative effects of labeling, and the example of the woman who saw herself as mentally ill after labeling indicates that this aspect is present in my own findings. But at least as significant are the positive aspects. Several persons in the sample ceased to exhibit depressive or manic behavior once their family members called upon them to resume normal roles, as in the case of Elsa, a woman who had been labeled mentally ill. Incapacitated for several months, she had been prohibited from her usual activities as a homemaker and mother. Eventually, the family became unable or unwilling to do her work for her. As her sister put it: "Everybody is supposed to go after her and crawl after her and do whatever she wants, because she's 'sick.' I'm tired of it. I've had three years of always being there, taking care of her kids, and I see what she's doing to our mother. My mother is worn. She is sixty-one years old. . . . She works nights and watches those kids during the day. My mother wanted Elsa to go in the hospital, because she was sick, and even more because it's too hard watching three people instead of just the two kids. When my sister was home, my mother had to watch all three of them, and Elsa wouldn't lift a finger to help." The family told Elsa that they thought she was now "well enough to do her responsibilities," and soon thereafter she was pronounced "better" by the psychiatric staff at the hospital and was sent home (Glassner et al., 1979; Glassner, 1980b).

One might suspect that factors other than relabeling by her family brought about Elsa's change in behavior. In one case in our studies of drinking patterns, however, the effect of positive labeling is rather clear. In a study of Jewish drinking patterns (Glassner and Berg, 1980), we found several processes that contribute to the relatively low rates of alcoholism and alcohol abuse among Jews in comparison to other ethnic groups. One of these—the association of alcohol problems with non-Jews—involves a kind of potential labeling. Basically, the group as a unit defines alcohol abuse as something that happens to non-Jews, and this probably helps to protect Jews from excessive drinking.

Persons control their consumption by referring to social norms that prescribe how much of a given substance people like them usually consume. In the case of our sample, excessive or problematic consumption is considered a non-Jewish attribute. The saliency of this belief is evidenced by almost 70 percent of the relevant interviewees from our random sample telling us, although we did not even raise the issue, that alcohol problems are non-Jewish. "I mean that wasn't, isn't, a Jewish concept," one man explained. "Liquor and wine is part of Jewish, you know, holiday and tradition. More sociability, at parties." One woman recalled that she "was exposed to liquor plenty. Actually, my father worked for a beer company. It sounds like a stupid generalization, but non-Jewish people drink more heavily than Jewish people. That's a generalization I've been brought up with . . . and I still think it's true."

What our interviewees seemed to be telling us was that there is a double risk for Jews in being labeled alcoholics. There is the usual negative stigma of the alcoholism label, and in addition one is effectively considered no longer a member of one's own ethnic and religious group, since only non-Jews are said to be alcoholics. Ironically, this labeling within the Jewish group serves not only to help protect Jews from alcohol abuse, but at the same time makes it more difficult for the Jew who is having problems with alcohol to seek help for those problems. A recent newsletter quotes a psychologist's claim that "the Jewish alcohol abuser is . . . the most difficult to work with. They 'know' they don't exist. They believe they have the same reality as unicorns. This makes it very difficult for them to identify themselves as alcohol abusers" (Dropkin and Blume, n.d.).

Such cases illustrate the major point of this chapter: that labeling is consequential for the deviance process, and so must be included in most any explanation of deviance. Moreover, there is much more to both labeling and deviance than has been explored during the first decades of the existence of labeling theory.

Part II

Deviance, Power, and Conflict

Close to twenty years have now passed since Howard Becker's systematization of diverse trends of thought into the labeling theory of deviance. In the years since then, labeling theory has revitalized the study of deviance, generating a flood of research that has detailed the careers, experiences, and life-styles of persons defined as deviant. Without doubt, labeling theorists have added appreciably to our knowledge and understanding of the morally condemned.

Nevertheless, despite its unquestioned contributions, no other sociological perspective has been as characterized by criticism, defense, reformulation, apology, and repudiation as has labeling theory. As a consequence, the study of deviance has itself become the scene of continuous intellectual debate. Disagreement still rages over such fundamentals as what deviance really is, how one comes to be a deviant, and how we are to understand the relationship of deviance to conformity.

What accounts for this sometimes bitter controversy? As sociologists have long realized, the study of deviance is at the heart of the study of society. In uncovering disorder, we discover the sources upon which order rests; in uncovering immorality, we discover the boundaries within which morality is contained. The study of deviance is on the cutting edge of the sociological debate on the nature of social order.

All three chapters in Part II examine this intimate relationship between social order and deviance by examining the social context within which labeling processes occur. In this way, the study of deviance is integrated with such traditional macrosociological concerns as the study of society's normative structure, social class, and social formations, and the dynamics of organizational interests and behavior.

While labeling theorists have viewed deviance as reactions to rule-breaking behavior, little systematic attention has been paid to the issues of under what circumstances behavior will be understood as rule-breaking and under what circumstances rule-breaking behavior will provoke reaction.

Birenbaum and Lesieur (Chapter 4) explicitly address these issues in a manner that remains consistent with labeling theory by subordinating the normative concept of *rule* to the interactionist analysis of *expectations*. In this sense, they recognize that "what will be reacted to will depend on the nature of shared social expectations rather than on the behavior itself." Thus they overcome the split between normative theories of deviance (in which interaction is seen as determined by normative order) and labeling theory (in which normative order is merely treated as a resource brought into play during the labeling process).

Just as we understand social order the better for understanding deviance, it is also true that we can understand deviance the better for understanding order. To the student of deviance, social order is invariably problematic. Order does not operate automatically or independently of persons' intentions, motives, or actions. Rather, as Birenbaum and Lesieur show, the building blocks of social order—expectations, norms, and values—are differentially enforced in the course of persons' interactions with one another.

If one recognizes that social order is problematic, the kind of questions one asks about deviance are broadened to include the context within which expectations are or are not seen as breached. "The failure to meet expectations," Birenbaum and Lesieur note, "is not sufficient for identifying deviance." As an example, they show many instances in which we fail to apply (or are prevented from enforcing) norms. They cite permissiveness, the status of the deviant, the vagueness of the act as deviant, and the visibility of the deviant as four important factors that affect whether a norm will be enforced (or even be recognized as having been breached).

On other occasions, there may be conflict among groups over whether some form of behavior ought to be defined as deviant. Such conflict becomes a political issue as each group tries to impose its view on the others through political activities. The public

debate over marijuana, for example, is not limited to a disagreement over whether such use is "right" or "wrong," but includes the
far more fateful question of whether and which *penalties* should be
imposed for the use, possession, and sale of the substance.

In their chapter, Birenbaum and Lesieur present a view of
social order and deviance in which both are seen as "fluid": the
outcome of conflict, negotiation, and the differential availability
and use of power. They broaden the labeling approach to include
the contextual and situational features within which the application, imposition, or rejection of deviant labels plays a crucial
role.

This fluidity, ambiguity, and uncertainty, which sociologists
see as characterizing the concept of deviance, should not be taken
as drawbacks in its study. Rather, as Rock (1973: 23) argues, "the
outcome of such uncertainty may be a curiously fruitful one for the
sociologist of deviancy. He tends to resort to those areas where the
particular problematic states are experienced not so much by the
studied actors as by the sociologist himself. It is this sense of ambiguity which can prompt the sociologist into attaining understanding." Indeed, Rock (1967: 24) suggests that the study of deviance
requires the sociologist to surrender his commonsensical understanding of morality and, as Goffman (1969) describes it, "stumble
into awareness."

Still, if expectations, norms, and valves are the building blocks
of social order, power is the cement that holds this order together.
Labeling theorists have often been criticized for their alleged failure
to give "sufficient" attention to the role and significance of power.
Labeling theorists have responded that it was they who first raised
the issue of the role of power and political interests in deviance (cf.
Plummer, 1979). The very notion of societal reaction thus implies
an unequal distribution of power, which allows some persons to
label others as deviant. Moreover, in the concept of the "moral
entrepreneur" (Becker, 1963), labeling theory claims to have developed a model of the role of influential and powerful persons in the
creation and enforcement of rules.

It is this very notion of the moral entrepreneur that Ian Taylor
examines critically in Chapter 5. Taylor, one of the foremost critics
of the labeling approach to power, suggests that the concept of the
moral entrepreneur is too individualistic, allowing "considerable
power and influence . . . to committed individual moral entrepreneurs" and too subjective, assuming moral enterprise is the outcome of individuals' "prejudices, preferences, fears, desires, etc."

Such a conception of the role of power and political interests, Taylor argues, is too narrow.

Taylor suggests that labeling theory fails to situate deviance within the objective structural features of society. For Taylor, power is not a situational resource but the determinant of the very forms of deviance that are present in a society. What is required is to move a step beyond the concept of the individual moral entrepreneur to uncovering those conflicts among groups upon which moral enterprise is based. Taylor suggests that moral enterprises such as law-and-order campaigns are best understood as the ideological activity of powerful groups concerned with preserving or fostering their own interests while directing attention away from the true political and economic sources of public unrest.

So, according to Taylor, as "the structural problems of western society (and, especially in the U.S., its fiscal and energy problems) are becoming more severe . . . there is an increasing need to 'displace' the explanation of, and public focus on, these problems by ideological work on the threat from 'crimes,' from 'violence,' and from permissiveness."

Taylor is not arguing that there "really" are no crimes, but that the public's perception of crime is amplified and distorted such that "the attempt by right wing ideologists to explain the anxiety associated with the contemporary 'moment' of western capitalist society, in terms of homosexuals, feminists, or blacks . . . is, quite specifically, a mystification of the current situation in western societies." As a consequence of this "ideological work," many segments of the population cede greater authority to the government and the police to enable them to control these "threatening" elements.

True to form, the critiques by Taylor and other "new criminologists" have themselves come under criticism (Cohen, 1979; Rock, 1979). Nevertheless, whether or not one accepts Taylor's political orientation, there is no question that the "new criminologists" have directed the attention of many sociologists onto the interests and activities of those powerful enough to create and enforce definitions of deviance. The appearance of a book such as Schur's The Politics of Deviance (1980) indicates that labeling theorists are actively participating in researching this new interest.

Such a book as Schur's is, however, a departure from the typical concerns of labeling theorists. Thus, Kitsuse (1980) admits to a sense of "embarrassment" at the labeling theorists' failure to predict the development of politically organized deviant groups of which organized homosexuals are the most conspicuous example.

Even as they acknowledge the significance of the politics of deviance, labeling theorists still assign to power a different scope and a different social location than do critical theorists such as Taylor. For example, Schur (1980: 6) writes: "Although economic, legal, and direct political power may sometimes be involved (in deviance situations), what is most essentially at stake in such situations is the power or resource of moral standing or acceptability." By focusing on deviance *situations* rather than on social conditions, Schur retains the labeling theorists' interest in the moral dimension rather than the economic or political, which Taylor sees as basic.

The creation and enforcement of deviant definitions through moral enterprise by no means exhaust sociological interest in the relationship between power and deviance. Once sociologists began to interest themselves in the role of the powerful and to research their activities, they discovered the widespread extent and significance of deviance *among* the powerful. Indeed, given the scope of such deviance, it can well be argued that the crimes of the powerful are far more injurious to the public than are those of the more traditionally conceived deviants.

Nevertheless, as Charles Reasons (Chapter 6) points out, it was concerned citizens such as Ralph Nader, not sociologists, who first aroused public interest in the nature and dangers of organizational crime. Since the Watergate scandal, "crime at the top" has become a highly visible issue of great concern to the general public, and sociologists and criminologists have gradually come to take an interest in such phenomena.

In his discussion of organizational crime, Reasons deals with three categories of such crime: economic, human rights, and violent personal injury.

Most public interest is focused on economic crime because it is the most obviously harmful to the general public. Economic crime includes bribery, price fixing, fraud, and tax evasion. Such crime is surprisingly widespread given the generally expressed value of "corporate responsibility," and Reasons notes a study reporting that fully 11 percent of major American corporations "had been involved in at least one major delinquency." Given any corporation's understandable desire to keep its crimes secret (as would most deviants) and its greater resources and power for accomplishing this secrecy, the extent of actual corporate crime is quite likely greater than the official figures would reflect.

Human rights crimes may not hurt the individual's pocket as

economic crimes do, but they pose as much of a threat to the general public. The erosion of human rights as a consequence of governmental abuse of powers, illegality, and secrecy threaten the foundations of a democratic society.

Even more harmful to the public are violent personal injury crimes. Such crimes cause injuries and deaths to workers as a result of unsafe work practices or industrial diseases, kill and maim hundreds as a result of unsafe or harmful products, and, as in the case of pollution, pose a general threat to all of the public.

In the conclusion to Chapter 6, Reasons points out that while much empirical research on organizational crime still needs to be done, such research must be integrated with a theoretical perspective that places such crime within the broader sociopolitical context. Like Taylor and Jim Thomas (Chapter 10), Reasons argues for a critical Marxist perspective on crime and deviance.

4 SOCIAL VALUES AND EXPECTATIONS

ARNOLD BIRENBAUM

HENRY LESIEUR

Social interaction is, in part, made possible by shared *social expectations*, referring to collective beliefs about how others with specific titles or relationships will act in our presence. Expectations that are regarded as obligatory responses are defined as *norms*, often considered by members of society to be important for maintaining group life. Despite social expectations and norms, it has often been observed that there is no correspondence between what should be and what is (actual behavior). Moreover, we often fail to demand normative behavior or to punish some people for violating rules.

How is social order possible if there is a great deal of norm-violating behavior present in society? The purpose of this chapter is to identify the types of norms found in society, introduce the important concept of values, and explore the relationship between social expectations, norms, and deviant behavior. Some explanations are proffered for why norms are not always applied in appropriate situations.

The concepts of social expectations and values are central to any attempt to explain how society is possible. These concepts are also important in understanding the dynamics of conformity and nonconformity. That there are rules of conduct should be evident—who has not felt the shame associated with having others remind us of how we have been naughty? There are also rules concerning interaction, and how to act in certain situations, given the characteristics of ourselves and others (e.g., age, sex, position, or rank) and the context (e.g., work, home, or school). When individuals come into one another's presence, even for the first time, there is an excellent possibility that they will be able to get on with the business at hand without having to fully explain themselves. In short, the members of a society or community will have a similar set of expectations.

Expectations do not determine the outcome of interaction, but they do orient individuals to the likely behavior of others. Therefore, even action that is rule violating (e.g., lying or cheating) is social insofar as it recognizes that other human beings may impede or assist the actor. We often make our way through the world of humans and nature with what Schutz (1964) calls "common sense concepts," tacitly acknowledged beliefs about what to pay attention to and what to ignore.

Expectations serve only as models of behavior because human beings are capable of reacting in a variety of ways to what others do or say, and any individual's response may serve as a cue to another to alter expectations and responses. Therefore, commonsense concepts help us to interpret what is going on until these concepts are shown to be inappropriate. Then expectations are brought into line with the human and natural world. Sometimes, however, social expectations that are widely shared and preferred acquire a recondite quality, and regard conformity with these expectations as an important source of self-worth. These expectations may be called *values*.

Expectations that are collective are often emotionally shared, and any failure to comply may be regarded as a failure to live up to what is central to group life. Even when dealing with strangers, failures to maintain minimal levels of self-respect can produce expressions of revulsion, pity, terror, or anger. Consider how most people react to being approached by an unkempt panhandler. Respectable persons may walk out of their way to prevent such an encounter, shout an obscenity, avoid eye contact, or tell the vagrant to get a job. All of these responses are violations of the rules of civil behavior in public places, but all are permitted, or even encouraged, by bystanders. The rude behavior is an outcome of a situation that permits a reaction to a violation of a shared rule or norm concerning how people *should* act and appear in public places.

Social expectations can be conceived of both as predictive devices making for cooperative interaction and as the foundation of society. Social expectations, or rules, even when they are humanly constructed commonsense concepts, often acquire a life of their own. The French sociologist Emile Durkheim (1858–1917) called them "social facts." Durkheim (1895/1964b: 10) wrote that "a social fact is to be recognized by the power of external coercion which it exercises or is capable of exercising over individuals, and the presence of this power may be recognized in its turn either by the existence of some specific sanction or by the resistance offered against every individual effort that tends to violate it."

Recognition of the existence of social expectations does not indicate the universal acceptance of what is anticipated. Not every expected set of behaviors is approved or desired. The "collective conscience" (a term used by Durkheim) of a society may be found in strong reactions against those who break the rules. Sometimes efforts are made to anticipate rule-violating behavior, as when police set up a watch over a bank that may be robbed. And sometimes efforts are made to compensate victims of crime. State legislatures, for example, may anticipate that a certain number of muggings will occur, and will allocate monies to show support to the victims, without approving of, or accepting, the behavior of the muggers. Such official gestures indicate to the members of society that something is being done, even when the doing of them tacitly admits that detection and punishment by law enforcement officials are relatively ineffective.

Given the variety of social expectations that exist, how do some come to be considered important? It can be argued that rules represent society, and they serve to remind the members of society how much they depend on one another, and how much this dependence affords protection for the individual. Rule violations, therefore, stimulate and reinforce this sense of dependence when violators and victims (if present) are subject to some emotional reaction, perhaps anger in response to the former and sympathy in response to the latter. Maintaining social cohesion, Durkheim argued in *The Division of Labor in Society* (1893/1964a: 108), requires that punishment help restore belief in the rules, not among violators but among the upright.

> It is necessary, then, that it be affirmed forcibly at the very moment when it is contradicted, and the only meaning of affirming it is to express unanimous aversion which the crime continues to inspire, by an authentic act which can consist only in suffering inflicted upon the agent. Thus, while being the necessary product of the causes which engender it, this suffering is not a gratuitous

cruelty. It is the sign which witnesses that collective sentiments are always collective, that the communion of spirits in the same faith rests on a solid foundation, and accordingly, that it is repairing the evil which the crime inflicted upon society.

Rules, or norms (as sociologists designate them), are collective preferences or shared standards that depend on human activity in their support to remain significant. Unlike natural laws, norms do not operate independently of human participation. Norms come out of the everyday transactions in which people engage, and they guide their participation in group life. Consequently, norms are often linked to a sense of being part of something, such as a group, an organization, or a social class. All of these collectivities involve a definition of membership; that is, who is to belong to them, who is to be excluded, and, particularly, what activities and deportments are to be expected.

TYPES OF NORMS

There are norms that refer to the requirements for membership in groups or social occasions. These may be designated *rules of identity*, referring to the collective preferences concerning who has the right to be present at a given place or occasion. Social expectations, even when not overtly justified by collective preferences, tacitly exclude individuals who "everyone knows" will be uncomfortable or cause awkwardness or embarrassment to others (Goffman, 1963). The physically disabled person, for example, faces social as well as physical barriers when attempting to enjoy a party. Women who invaded male sanctuaries, such as a management position, a drinking place, and the Boston Marathon, were also treated with outright ostracism or hostility, or cast into a stereotyped role (Kanter, 1979).

An interesting example of violation of the norms of identity is found in the situation of mothers of mentally retarded children. When informed that their children will never develop normally, some mothers reacted as if membership in the family for a mentally retarded child was beyond possibility. In addition to considering placement in an institution, parents have expressed thoughts of revulsion at children who did not meet their expectations (Birenbaum, 1971).

There are norms in the form of informal expectations which relate to face-to-face interaction—*polite interaction rules*. These norms encompass wide-ranging preferences, from paying "civil inattention" to strangers in public transportation and how much room to leave others when passing on a busy street, to the appropriate amount of attention to display when someone is talking to you. Strong negative reactions have been elicited by researchers who have deliberately violated these informal expectations (Wolff, 1973; Levine, Vinson, and Wood, 1973). Rules related to politeness also refer to the remedies expected when initial expectations concerning face-to-face interaction are violated. Apologies and other acts in which blame is accepted and sorrow expressed for causing harm help to make face-to-face interaction continue when threatened by minor transgressions (Goffman, 1971).

Civil-legal rules go beyond face-to-face interaction and group membership. Laws are explicitly designed to regulate relationships between individuals, between individuals and collectivities, or between collectivities themselves. Laws are enacted by governments and sanctioned by the legitimate use of force; in modern societies, they are also written and categorized so that legal norms concerning regulation of businesses, for example, are separated from the laws concerning armed robbery. The right of governments to enforce the laws of the land gives them a special quality, justifying the use of force.

> It is not merely the question of the ultimate use of force—a criminal group can murder a member for violation of a rule—but law involves legitimacy of enactment, a mechanism for the adjudication of the guilt or innocence of one accused of a violation, and, above all, the ultimate use of force and coercion by an armed body that acts as the enforcer and is the embodiment of the power of the state (Birenbaum and Sagarin, 1976: 12).

A final type of norm that has been identified by sociologists is used to understand, interpret, or negotiate reality. These norms are identified as constituent rules (Garfinkel, 1967). The focus on this kind of norm is on the cognitive procedures that serve to organize experience and make it understandable or rational to people. No assumptions are made about the degree of commitment to rules held by users, or about how rules regulate and control actors. Rather, the problem for study, following this line of inquiry, is how conformity or deviance is produced through the manipulation of rules. What people use to make sense of reality can be based on rules built into language or gestural codes, and does not depend on any affective loyalty to the rules or what the rules represent (i.e., society). The rules are there because they work, and competent actors use them in an unthinking or un-self-conscious way.

With the introduction of the idea of constituent rules, Garfinkel and others have changed the way of looking at norms. Norms are not fixed or frozen in custom but must be forever recreated to fit the behavior and speech of actors. Social expectations are "accomplishments," rather than being external and constraining on individuals. Nonconformity, then, is not in the act itself but in its interpretation. It is a *recognition* of an accomplishment on the part of the person considered delinquent. The idea of how conformity and nonconformity through the use of rules is brought about is discussed in this complex passage (McHugh, 1970: 72): "Deviance is failure when conditions of failure are absent. A deviant act is a conventional act, whence it is deemed that the conditions of failure (accident, coercion, miracle) are not present, and thus the act under question was not inevitable."

NORMS AND DEVIANT BEHAVIOR

Reactions to rule violations and violators, whether affective or cognitive, are selective. There are many rules broken daily that are not viewed by the rule violator or others as particularly significant departures from social expectations. There are many people, for example, who are unmarried and cohabit, who jaywalk, or who smoke marijuana; they do not think badly of themselves and are not subject to sanction. The owners of a business who send a cash gift to the representative of a potential foreign buyer of their product do not see themselves, nor are they seen by all others, as wrongdoers. But *some* behaviors or personal characteristics do produce a reaction. What will be reacted to will depend on the nature of shared social expectations rather than on the behavior itself. Durkheim (1895/1964b: 69) reminds us of the normality of deviance even among those who seek to perfect themselves: "Imagine a society of saints, a perfect cloister of exemplary individuals. Crime, properly so called, will there be unknown; but faults which appear venial to the layman will create there the same scandal that the ordinary offense does in ordinary consciousness."

Deviance, then, involves some supposed or believed norm violation and a societal reaction that disvalues the person in question. An often cited definition of deviance, which encompasses these attributes, is provided by Edwin M. Schur (1971: 24): "Human behavior is deviant *to the extent that* it comes to be viewed as involving a *personally discreditable* departure from a group's normative expectations, *and it elicits* interpersonal or collective reactions that serve to 'isolate,' 'treat,' 'correct,' or 'punish' *individuals* engaged in such behavior." [Emphasis in the original.]

It is clear from anthropological evidence that all societies, like Durkheim's imaginary society of saints, produce deviance. The manifestations of deviance vary from society to society, and even the extremely violent person, by North American standards, may be considered harmless or indeed ordinary in another society. There is also little correlation between simple societies and a reduced rate of deviance. Wherever there are people living together, there will be "trouble," even when it takes a variety of forms (Edgerton, 1973: 25).

In some societies, violence is so institutionalized or preferred that it is encouraged, most likely as a means by which an aggressive and courageous populace is created. Erik Erickson (1950) has noted the use of slapping among the child-rearing practices of some of the Plains Indian nations. In societies that overtly encourage violence, the nonaggressive person with a nonviolent personality may appear out of place and be subject to scorn and ridicule (Edgerton, 1973). Chagnon (1968) has described the rituals of violence among the Yanomamo, a fierce people who make our daily dose of (nontelevised) violence appear timid in comparison.

Social expectations and values play a significant part, then, in the determination of deviance. The failure to meet expectations is not sufficient for identifying deviance. The person regarded as deviant is seen as disruptive of the constitutive rules of behavior, or the rules of identity, rather than of on-going social interaction. In this sense, deviance is viewed as a threat to one's own competency or the very rules used to reaffirm that competency. According to this concept, even persons who are not viewed as responsible for their disvalued appearance or behavior (e.g., a physically handicapped person) may be regarded as a threat to the rules themselves, because others (e.g., the nonhandicapped) are not certain as to which kinds of claims will be made, or what the implications are for the application of these rules.

The confusion and uncertainty produced by disability makes response to handicap interesting to the student of social expectations and deviance. Disability is rarely acquired in a conscious way, via an intentional misapplication of the recipes or formulas that constitute the culture of a society. Moreover, it can hardly be said that the disabled are attempting to directly violate the rules for personal gain, to fulfill some disrespectable desire, or even to change the rules of living. Acquiring a handicapped condition involves little intentional choice and can be considered as the crystallization of involuntary deviance into roles now performed by previously voluntary conformists. When a competent person becomes disabled, the very rules that define competency are called into question. Moreover, since the disabled person is still psychologically competent, he or she may start to question these rules since they proved to be unreliable.

Clearly, then, there is disagreement over rules and their definition. Social reality is defined by human beings in their efforts to bestow or maintain shared meanings. There may not be one set of shared meanings operative at any one time in society. The man who commits a crime of passion, such as murdering an unfaithful wife, may be viewed by some sectors of society as a hero (husbands) and merely a loathsome murderer by others (feminists).

There are group bases for multiple realities, and these constructed meanings may conflict. Sharp differences do exist as to what is believed and valued when different groups in society are considered. Thorsten Sellin (1979) proposed that culture conflict, particularly the conflict of norms between various ethnic groups, could be understood as a major explanation of crime. First, in a modern society, a variety of different styles of living are found alongside one another; these points of contact, in themselves, reduce the sense of moral absoluteness that conduct norms once held for members of an ethnic group. More important, there is a second basis for conflict: The person who seeks to "make it" in the wider society may have to violate strictly held ethnic, family, or community expectations. Culture conflict takes place when two groups having clashing codes live in contiguous areas, when there is migration, or when the law of one group is extended to cover the other.

The theory of culture conflict uses clashing conduct norms as an explanation to account for increasing rates of deviance. Culture conflict results from "processes of social differentiation, each with its own definitions of life situations, its own misunderstanding of the social values of other groups" (Sellin, 1979: 72). Therefore, there are clashing conduct norms for people born and raised in the same society, but who have acquired different knowledge, ability, and motivation. Culture conflict can be seen in the public debate over marijuana use and its legalization. Many millions of otherwise law-abiding North Americans have used this drug, and even bought and sold it. Still, other people have no desire for its legalization; yet many states have new laws that decriminalize the offense so that marijuana users will be fined rather than face lengthy jail sentences.

A strong belief in the importance of physical toughness for men is often adhered to by white working-class Americans, particularly migrants from rural southern towns. Even with a "moral" basis for fighting, men who express this belief run the risk of violating the law and being jailed. Hard-living people sometimes express the need to establish their independence through fighting: "But you know fighting ain't a good thing. It ain't a good thing, but goddammit, you got to stick up for yourself and you got to take care of yourself, and you can't let nobody push you around. Once you start letting somebody push you around, then other people are going to start pushing you around" (Howell, 1973: 296).

Social conflict theorists focus on power rather than norms, viewing conformity and deviance as the result of the domination over the forces of production (i.e., technology, the division of labor, capital) by a ruling class. In every society in which there are those who own and control, and those who must sell their labor in the marketplace to survive, there will be tension between these two groups. Ruling classes create laws and moral codes (e.g., the condemnation of gambling or desertion of the family) to protect their property and interests. Sometimes the laws appear to regulate those with power to command resources (e.g., statutes that mandate collective bargaining between management and labor). These laws create the illusion of equality and reduce the sense of being dominated on the part of those with little in the way of material resources.

Conflict theorists readily admit that many conventional criminal activities, such as burglary and larceny, are committed by the poor. Those persons without resources seek to get some since their deprivation makes money and consumer goods highly desirable. Even when the means are unequally distributed in society, the strong emphasis on success encourages criminality (Merton, 1957).

Social conflict theorists are also quick to point out that those who control the wealth of society often accumulate property in any way they can and eschew manifest social responsibilities, such as providing for the future. There are no legal restrictions on most corporations, for example, as to how they are to use their surplus capital. In the late 1970s, oil companies were not legally mandated to reinvest their close to 20 percent profits in exploration for fossil fuel deposits, or in the development of renewable energy sources that make use of various direct and indirect forms of solar power. In the United States, an oil company can invest in any enterprise that it pleases, including the purchase of department stores or banks.

The protection of private property appears to be a major value in a capitalist society, and criminal law in such a society helps the ruling class maintain its domination. One of the leading conflict criminologists, without taking into account the constitutional guarantee of judicial due process, flatly states that "control of crime becomes the coercive means of checking threats to the social and economic order, threats that result from a system of oppression and exploitation" (Quinney, 1979: 79). Even without such blanket assertions, it should be clear that criminal law is a political expression of the ruling class, setting limits to the forms of competition and conflict in society.

In societies in which traditional sources of identity are relics of the past (i.e., family, community, church), the acquisition of consumer goods is a way of being accorded status from others. Hence the persons who commit conventional crimes against property (e.g., theft, burglary, mugging) are as interested in possessing as much as those who uphold the law. While there are some career criminals, commitment to a life of crime is relatively limited, while the desire to have money and consumer items is strong. The deviant and the conformist both need to possess the signs of success in North American society. Other sources of self-worth based on the need for community, a feeling of strong interdependence, and direct connections with others may go unfulfilled (Slater, 1970).

SOCIAL EXPECTATIONS AND IDENTIFICATION OF DEVIANTS

Ideally, conformity is rewarded and deviance is punished. Legal statutes, ethical codes, or implicitly held expectations can be backed up by sanctions to rule violators. Some of these sanctions or punishments may be relatively minor and subtle, as when others express disapproval by raising an eyebrow, frowning, or even folding their arms across their chests. Other punishments may involve harsh words, physical assaults, or denial of access to desired or needed services. To punish a child, a parent may scream, "Why did you do that?", slap the child, or turn off the television set. Finally, there are legally enacted sentences for law violators that involve loss of life or liberty, or fines.

All of these examples are instances whereby social control is exercised; these are various mechanisms for maintaining conformity. Social control also involves condemning the act or the person, setting the act or the person apart from respectable society and its members. In many instances, the norm violator will help to condemn the delinquent act too, by showing some sense of sorrow or behaving contritely. He or she becomes, in Gusfield's (1967) terms, a repentant deviant. There may, however, be instances of harsh reactions to deviance that do not fit the transgression, encouraging the transgressor to believe that he or she is subject to unjust treatment. There are risks that a person who is severely punished becomes more deeply committed to deviance or loses respect for the agencies of social control (Matza, 1964). Alternatively, inaction or a weak or uncertain response may lead to more serious rule violations. Finally, the use of inappropriate forms of social control, such as pardons for indictable offenses, or allowing zealous police officers to plant evidence while apprehending suspected drug dealers, may be regarded by some members of society as itself a violation of the rules.

It has often been argued that the official identification of certain acts as criminal, and the imposition of severe penalties, is a benefit to society, reducing the frequency with which such acts are committed. Thus, imprisonment or capital punishment are seen as deterring crime. Alternatively, it has been argued that the social condemnation of the act (i.e., the seriousness with which it is viewed) accounts for the fact that people do not frequently commit that act. Further support for this latter explanation is the idea that informal social sanctions do act to discourage the performance of rule violations or at least promote the view that they are things that upright people do not do.

The law receives support from informal social sources. Erickson, Gibbs, and Jensen (1977) found that seriousness of the crime was inversely related to the frequency of self-reported acts, much in the same way that perceived certainty of punishment was related to frequency of law-violating behavior. Anderson, Chiricos, and Waldo (1977) found that the relative impact of several perceived informal sanctions proved slightly stronger than that of perceived certainty and severity of punishment when it came to self-reported marijuana use. Finally, Meier and Johnson (1977) reported that in a jurisdiction with severe penalties for the use of marijuana, friends' use was the most important factor associated with use or nonuse.

The social expectations found in many occupational and professional communities often constrain the identification of deviants within their ranks. A professional community may be limited by its own internal organization to evaluate and react to deviant behavior. The degree of supervision of physicians, for example, by other physicians is "itself limited by the norms of the group" (Merton, 1957: 343). Close supervision would be a violation in itself of the ethos or spirit of colleagueship in the social organization of this kind of work. The identification of deviants within a professional field may undermine the public's confidence in the competency of the profession. Therefore, too much activity in this area is often seen as demeaning to those who are effective performers of professional roles.

It should be evident from the discussion of legal penalties, informal sanctions, and the limits to professional self-regulation that social control mechanisms do not work consistently to punish deviance and reward conformity. First, it must be noted that there are waves of interest and concern about behaviors that generate the creation of new laws and elicit concern about their enforcement. The feminist movement has identified rape as an important social problem in North America (Rose, 1977). New medical forms of detection have increased the likelihood of identifying parents who physically abuse their children (Pfohl, 1977). The public concern with enforcement of antitrust laws has been cyclical, with law enforcement officials failing to "create a continuous identifiable body of criminal violators symbolizing and reinforcing reaction" (McCormick, 1977: 30), and the concern with the problem of monopolies has been reduced. Oligopolistic tendencies have been permitted to go uncorrected and are even regarded as necessary to economic prosperity. Control over markets has been demonstrated to be a source of higher prices to consumers and it reduces the necessity to modernize on the part of American industries (Galbraith and Salinger, 1978).

Second, the problem of who gets to be defined as deviant sometimes depends on perceived threats to political domination and social stability. Concerns about not wanting to appear weak, or a fear of subversion, can induce campaigns that cast persons, often with little evidence, into deviant roles. Political witch-hunts to smoke out members of the Communist party who were considered security threats have been discussed as a way societies express their corporate national interest, a collective ritual that renews social values (Bergesen, 1977). Recruitment for putative deviant roles is examined in Connor's (1972) detailed discussion and analysis of the Soviet purges of 1936–1938. On the basis of hearsay, thousands of the political and economic elite of the Soviet Union were arrested, tried, and sentenced for being responsible for the economic failures of that epoch. It appears that scapegoating can be conducted at almost any time and place, particularly when the apparatus of the state is available.

For the most part, discretion benefits the deviant. In the circumstances just discussed, however, deviants are created through arbitrary and capricious procedures. Use of agents provocateurs, entrapment, coercion, and torture to elicit confessions, as well as other less frequently used methods of deviancy, have been well documented (Blackstock, 1975; Halperin, et al., 1976; Karmen, 1974; Haskell and Yablonsky, 1978; Amnesty International, 1978–1981). The rationale behind the use of these methods is related to the supposed danger the deviant poses to society. Whether we are dealing with Black Panthers or Soviet dissidents, the threat is amplified, and violation of civil liberties by the state is justified. The results of such procedures are "extra" deviants who are grabbed into the net (Currie, 1968; Szasz, 1970; Solzhenitsyn, 1973; Conner, 1972).

Third, command over the means of communication enhances the capacity of groups in society to impose their version of reality and their definitions of deviance upon the social expectations of an entire society. "The chance that a group will get community support for its definition of unacceptable deviance depends on its relative power position. The greater the group's size, resources, efficiency, unity, articulateness, prestige, coordination with other groups, and access to the mass media and to decision-makers, the more likely it is to get its preferred norms legitimated" (Davis, 1975: 54).

In societies in which ruling elites directly control the nature of political activity and dissent, political statements or acts are treated as if they are the work of persons who cannot take care of themselves (Medvedev and Medvedev, 1971). A political act itself may be defined as criminal in the ordinary sense, the product of a mental incompetent, or a slander on the nation. Under loosely worded law, criticism can be considered an act of subversion.

Given these mechanisms for identifying deviance, how does it come to be that there is continuous rather than sporadic deviance? What factors account for this persistence of deviance? Certainly, norm violation must be allowed or even encouraged in society, and other factors must operate. In addition, not all deviance is punished. What features act to insulate some from punishment while others are negatively sanctioned?

WHY WE FAIL TO APPLY NORMS

Permissiveness

Deviance is not a hard and fast phenomenon. There are many situations in which a certain amount of deviance is allowed and

even encouraged. This is because, within limits, deviance is functional for the maintenance of the social structure. In allowing
some deviance, conformity with rules is thereby relaxed. Talcott
Parsons, Kingsley Davis, and Albert Cohen have noted that the
moral boundaries of a society are sufficiently flexible to permit
"safety valves" to operate and reduce socially structured strain.
The permissive atmosphere of parties where alcohol flows and the
existence of gambling in society despite laws against it are classic
examples of the safety valve in operation. Gambling, for example,
serves to stimulate alienated segments of the society. This keeps
alive hopes of social mobility for people who otherwise may have
turned to rebellion or despair. Permissiveness is not wild, however. Gambling is condemned by the Protestant Ethic, which
makes work and industriousness morally superior to such evils as
gambling and sloth. A compromise is reached with respect to gambling. Certain forms are allowed, others condemned. In addition,
gambling as mild entertainment is granted but gambling as an
alternative to work (and cheating and losing) is not. Other forms
of deviance serving this safety valve function include prostitution
and homosexuality. The prostitute, says Davis (1937), provides
impersonal sex to married clients, thereby keeping the marriage
intact. The impersonal nature of some homosexual behavior in
"tearooms" is noted by Humphreys (1970). Married Roman Catholics, whom Humphreys calls the "trade," frequent the tearooms
on a periodic basis. The tearoom, like the bordello, provides a
speedy and impersonal sexual alternative where a personal one
would threaten the marital relationship.

The moral boundaries of a community are never firmly established. They are fluid. Consequently, the boundaries of appropriate
behavior must be defined. The moral transgressor serves to clarify
the rules of appropriate behavior. Juveniles, for example, constantly
test the limits of appropriate behavior. Parents can limit this testing
by pointing to the bad boys in the neighborhood whose actions act
as boundary markers of socially acceptable performance. As Erikson (1966: 13) points out:

> Deviant behavior is not a simple kind of leakage which occurs
> when the machinery of society is in poor working order, but may
> be, in controlled quantities, an important condition for preserv-
> ing the stability of social life. Deviant forms of behavior, by
> marking the outer edges of group life, give the inner structure its
> special character and thus supply the framework within which
> the people of the group develop an orderly sense of their own
> cultural identity.

In this vein, the office clown and the localite who is "as nutty as a fruitcake," for example, fulfill positive functions for their confreres. They serve as boundary markers for acceptable behavior. In viewing reaction to them, others learn what they can and cannot do.

Further social support for deviance comes with contact with habituees. Insiders, either as a result of personal experience or learned attitudes, come to develop rather elaborate ideological supports for behavior others consider deviant. Victims (if there are any) are degraded or perceived to have earned their victim state. Pool, golf, and bowling hustlers look upon their victims as "suckers," "marks," and "fish." The fish is especially degraded—a fellow who is so stupid that he can be reeled in for replay after replay without catching on that he is being had. The principle "caveat emptor" is applied rather than the 1970s "caveat vendor." Where there is no victim, the action can be positively valued as a desired service, if that is the case. It can be looked at as a highly skilled occupation with status going to the most skilled. In other words, that which is condemned on the outside is praised on the inside. This is true for the fast-talking, fast-conning ability of the American confidence man (Maurer, 1974), the agility and nimble fingers of the "class cannon" (pickpocket) (Maurer, 1955), the eagle eye and steady hands of the pool hustler (Polsky, 1969), the money-moving ability of the gambling addict (Lesieur, 1977), and the knowledge of safes and explosives of the burglar (Letkemann, 1973).

Support from insiders, commonly received from habituees, is only a small element and part of larger, more inclusive patterns of discretion.

The ability and power to do nothing is exercised every day. In many situations, doing nothing is required. A rule of normal interaction is that "nothing unusual is happening" (Emerson, 1970). Hawkins and Tiedeman (1975: 114–117) note seven reasons this is true:

1. Cultural dictates exist as to who should and should not sanction and when. Individuals are supposed to be given a second chance in our society, and the general norm is "mind your own business."
2. Embarrassment reduces sanction initiation. Being wrong is worse than being right.
3. The accusor may have been involved in the deviance (victim-precipitated events are the clearest example of this).
4. The potential accusor has waited too long to respond. Con-

tinuation of nonresponse is likely in these situations. To do otherwise may produce accusations of cover-up prior to the report.

5. Desire to be benevolent to the offender is common. Juveniles are more likely to receive this treatment (Piliavin and Briar, 1964), as are people who are important to the group (Alvarez, 1968; Daniels, 1970).

6. A diffusion of responsibility occurs when there are many observers of an event.

7. The cost to the sanctioner may inhibit reaction. This factor is supported by studies in which victims did not report offenses to the police (Ennis, 1967).

Paying someone to overlook potentially embarrassing behavior is another source of insulation from punishment. Victimless crime in particular has been the producer of bribery and special considerations for the rule enforcers (Whyte, 1943; Gardiner, 1970). Corruption of authority has been organized into regularized payment systems when authorities have confronted organized forces (Knapp Commission, 1972). Not only does corruption exist in connection with violations of gambling, prostitution, pornography, and drugs, it has also been found in connection with violations of Sunday closing laws, construction regulations, health, restaurant, meat inspection on the federal level, and fire regulations on the municipal level (Knapp Commission, 1972; Chambliss, 1971; Schuck, 1972). Professional thieves have used "the fix" to ensure nonenforcement of the law (Sutherland, 1937), and ticket fixing is routine in many places (Gardiner, 1969).

While corruption is commonplace in some municipalities, codes of secrecy serve to buffer corrupt actions against any outward condemnation. Protection of the corrupted officials is so great in some situations that it takes a major scandal to do even minor things to effect change (Maas, 1973; Knapp Commission, 1972; Sheppard, 1978). In the long run, however, old patterns return (Gardiner, 1970), and the offenders are insulated from punishment again.

Status of Deviant

The upper social classes, the privileged, and whites have benefited most from discretionary procedures. The privileged and wealthy have been able to elicit support for deviant activities with much more ease than the lower classes. They are able to afford better lawyers, hire "experts" to testify at their trials, and engage in de-lays, where necessary, through the courtesy of top legal minds (Pa-tricia Hearst was a good example of this). Untoward behavior by professionals receives the courtesy of "professional review boards" that are notorious for secrecy and inaction (Carlin, 1966; McCleery, 1971). Quebec recently improved its system of review, for example, yet it is still almost impossible to find out what offense a disci-plined professional has been charged with. Decisions and names are published separately (Office des Professions du Québec, 1976). When we reach up the corporate ladders, the idea that "rank has its privileges" receives further confirmation. Corporations and their decision-makers have violated laws and committed decidedly devi-ant actions with impunity. Take the case of antitrust laws.

> No individual served a prison sentence for an antitrust violation during the first twenty years of enforcement. Even more telling, the first eleven imprisonments for antitrust convictions involved union and labor. . . . It was not until 1961 (with the Electrical Conspiracy case) that businessmen were actually imprisoned purely for price-fixing and monopolization (McCormick, 1977: 34). [Emphasis in the original.]

Comparisons of corporate with noncorporate criminals reveal that 1.8 percent of corporate offenders are imprisoned (typically for 30 days), whereas 46.06 percent of noncorporate offenders are im-prisoned (for an average of 43.9 months) (Gottfredson et al., 1978: 552–553).

For noncorporate offenders, social class is related to the type of offenses people commit. In turn, criminal sentences are related to offense.

> The average individual theft from the government in the 502 tax fraud convictions in 1969 was about $190,000. The average bur-glary in that year amounted to $321; the average auto theft, $992. Only 95 of the 502 people convicted of tax fraud were sentenced to prison, serving an average term of 9.5 months. . . . Of these people convicted in federal courts for burglary and auto theft, more than 60 percent were sentenced to prison, and the average time served was 28 months and 21 months respectively (Wright, 1973: 29).

Rank doesn't only have its privileges in formal processing. Higher status individuals are granted "idiosyncrasy credits" in the bank of conformity (Hollander, 1958). Because they are assumed to be more deserving, higher status individuals are granted rights to be deviant without social condemnation. This has been documented with middle- and upper-level employee drinking and condemnation of it (Roman, 1974). Also, the stigma of being a narcotic addict is lower for a physician or nurse than for the street addict (Winick, 1961; Poplar, 1969).

While rank has its privileges, rank also has its power. This power works in several directions. First of all, it enables the privileged to attain their privileges. This is because along with money comes power, which can be used to purchase and cajole others into giving privileges. Second, power buys secrecy through "no trespass" and other privacy laws. You have to get by the doorman or other gatekeepers (security guards, secretaries, etc.) before accusations of immorality can be made. Through these buffers, corporate decision-making achieves privacy. The end result is that acts that break rules are less likely to be discovered or studied, and rule-breakers are less likely to be punished.

Corporate power to reduce the impact of public condemnation has been studied by the Naderites at the Center for the Study of Responsive Law. Robert Fellmeth (1973) calls the relation between industrial giants and the agencies that regulate them the "regulatory-industrial complex." This term is accurate for many reasons. There is a high degree of informal contact between agency and industry. "Advisory committees" meet and "help" the agencies formulate policy. Public lobbying provides contact with federal and state legislators and executives. Widespread job interchanges exist (a revolving door), and Fellmeth calls these "deferred bribes." These features produce a corporate-government liaison which has the added feature of secrecy. This complex makes decisions that are for the most part favorable to industry. The result is a deferment and suspension of punishment for violations of rules. Whenever the above tactics fail, end runs to the executive branch of government can be made. A classic example of this type of end run occurred during the 1968 presidential campaign, when ITT, in its desire to have a favorable decision in connection with a merger with Hartford Insurance, made an offer of a $400,000 "commitment" to the San Diego Republican national convention. The "commitment" was discovered, and the convention was held in Miami as a result (Simpson, 1976). Ironically, ITT was still able to acquire Hartford Insurance after the bribe was publicized in Jack Anderson's column. Evidently, rank has its power.

Vagueness of Act as Deviant

Much behavior that should be called deviant achieves alternative definition. The line between deviant and normative is often vague, partly because of the fear of false accusation (i.e., did he "really" do it?). Suicide, for example, is subject to being defined as an accident (Douglas, 1967). In addition, potentially deviant persons will frequently desire to negotiate nondeviant status for themselves. These situations arise when the deviant status of the behavior is clear. Vagueness in the definition also exists.

Basically, deviance is a socially constructed phenomenon. Therefore, at any one time myriad forms of behavior will be in a state of definitional uncertainty or in the process of change. At one time, for example, coffee and tobacco were treated much like marijuana is today. People were punished for using them, and stocks were burned (Brecher, 1972). Obviously, the situation has changed. Abortion, euthanasia, witchcraft, and mental illness have been the subjects of heated controversy, and the accused have been able to use the controversies to their own advantage.

Research on employee theft has shown that the context is significant when defining an act as deviant. Horning (1970) found that pilferage of property of uncertain ownership was justified, whereas taking company or personal property was not. Perhaps the first to uncover the vagueness of definitions was Dalton (1959). He found that a large gray area exists in which the line between perquisites and outright theft is vague. This is because of pilferage rights, benefits, and privileges which may be attached to an office. The uncertainty of these rights is demonstrated in Gouldner's (1954) study of a gypsum plant that changed ownership. While the previous managers had an "indulgency pattern" whereby workers were allowed to take home wallboard for personal use, the new management denied these perquisites to the workers. In a sense, the definition of the *same* action changed from a nondeviant to a deviant one.

The meaning of deviance is also vague and subject to definitional disputes in interpersonal relations. While a rapist may hold that there are "good" women and "bad" ones, may think of his victim as thinking yes even though she says no, and may perceive her bralessness as a sexual invitation, the victim may perceive such thoughts as sexist and denying her rights of consent. Feminists have waged an attempt to change the male-dominated definitions, which, they believe, encourage rape.

Deviance is also vague because it quite often has positive consequences for the social system. Albert Cohen (1966) has summarized
seven ways in which deviance functions to the benefit of society.
First, deviance may be essential in combating red tape in bureaucracies. Frequently, the only solution is one that violates the rules.
In a sense, then, to save or aid the organization in certain circumstances will necessitate breaking the canons of that structure. Second, as noted, deviance can be a safety value that siphons off strain
and discontent in the social order. Third, the deviant person clarifies the rules for everyone else by testing the limits of propriety
within the community. Fourth, the deviant can serve to unite the
group. (In this instance, an internal enemy—the deviant—fulfills
similar functions as external enemies. In thinking about how to
combat the enemy, internal animosities are forgotten.) Fifth, the
group may be unified, but this time in behalf of the deviant. In an
effort to save an errant member (bring the person back into the fold,
as it were), internal discord may be set aside. Sixth, the deviant
serves a contrasting function. In contrasting oneself with the deviant, personal conformity is accented. The deviant serves as a reference point for community members. Last, deviance can operate as a
warning signal for defects in organizations. Excessive rule violation
may focus attention on weaknesses that wouldn't have been no-
ticed otherwise.

Visibility of Deviance

Structurally, in social and ecological fashion, deviants segregate,
and are segregated, into enclaves. These pockets serve to insulate
them from adverse reaction as well as to promote an "out of sight,
out of mind" atmosphere in the general population.

A critical mass of population density appears to be essential for
the formation of subcultural activity. A town of 20,000 may not be
able to support a gay bar, but one of 40,000 can more easily. The
likelihood of different types of gay bars will increase as urban size
increases. This increase enhances the sense of identity possible.
Without the critical mass, the feeling that you are part of some kind
of collective activity is diminished. Without a "leather bar" for
sadomasochistic homosexuality to be expressed in an overt manner, feeling part of this group is obviously reduced.

Ecological segregation was first studied intensively by members
of the Chicago school of sociology in the 1920s and 1930s. Maps of
Chicago were drawn, and the location of taxi dancehalls (Cressey,

1969), slums with their rooming house districts (Zorbaugh, 1929), juvenile delinquents (Shaw and McKay, 1972), gangs (Thrasher, 1963), and prostitutes (Reckless, 1969) were plotted. Heavy concentrations of deviance were found to be the rule rather than the exception. The areas in which deviance was located were called areas high in social disorganization. While sociologists today tend to think in terms of different types of social organization rather than assume that areas with high amounts of *overt* deviance are disorganized, these concentrations are still with us. In New York, pornography and prostitution are concentrated in the Times Square area, "Skid Row" is in the Bowery, heroin connections are in Harlem, overt homosexuality centers around Christopher Street in Greenwich Village, and professional thieves hang out in bars along 48th and 49th Streets between Sixth and Eighth Avenues. This wide spread is not common. Most cities have a Combat Zone (Boston) or Tenderloin (San Francisco), where the bulk of open deviance is concentrated. In any case, there tends to be a community in which the majority of deviance is located. In many cities, this is in the center of town or, alternatively, in the slums, where suburbanites and others come to be "serviced." The slums serve this function because of the neglect and resultant autonomy granted by the total social system (Clairmont, 1974). They are out of sight and out of mind. On top of this, servicing the wider community provides illegitimate opportunities where they are definitely appreciated. Structurally, a situation has been produced that practically guarantees the emergence of illegitimate services.

Segregation of lower class deviance has a dual effect. It produces a hidden, yet glamorous, quality to the behavior. This gives the deviants a sense of identity with others in like situations. Ironically, however, it also locates the behavior so it can be more easily controlled should those in power desire to do so.

The open and public nature of lower class deviance distinguishes it from hidden upper class deviance. Stinchcombe (1963) notes that the police are restricted by lack of ready access to private places. One could predict, therefore, that middle class call girls would be less likely to be arrested than lower class streetwalkers; drug-using physicians are more secure than street addicts; the executive drinker is safer than the Skid Row alcoholic; and the corporate water polluter is less vulnerable than the person who urinates in the subway station.

Segregation of deviance occurs in a different fashion in the professions. Because of the nature of independent professional practice, much deviance is beyond the ken of peers. When a matter such as incompetency becomes known among physicians, for example, a personal boycott occurs (Freidson, 1970); they stop referring patients to the physician, and he or she is snubbed. This encourages a movement beyond the observability of those who invoked the sanctions. Interestingly, a similar thing happens with drug addicts, alcoholics, and compulsive gamblers. When they are snubbed by their peers, they tend to move in one of two directions: becoming loners or becoming embedded in subcultures of addicts, alcoholics, or compulsive gamblers like themselves (Trice, 1966; Lesieur, 1977). Either movement has a self-reinforcing effect, further encouraging the career.

In an alternate fashion, some occupational groups will segregate deviance because the particular form of behavior functions for the benefit of the group. Violence among the police aids the officers. Violent cops tend to like a good fighter. When an "officer in distress" call comes over the radio, most police we have talked to agree that it is nice to have these guys around. As a result, complaints against these violent cops can have a potentially dangerous effect on an individual police officer's job. The stereotyped physical education teacher who becomes "dean of boys" and metes out physical punishment in junior high and high schools fulfills the same function in these settings. These teachers serve to keep the more recalcitrant students in line without upsetting the existing structure. At some schools, this teacher or administrator is used as a resource by other teachers when they need help. Consequently, he is not turned in so long as no evidence is left that could be used against him should a student complain (Kotarba, 1978).

To the end of advancement of the subsystem of the organization, higher ups, lawyers, and auditors working for the organization are shielded from knowledge of inappropriate behavior so they can say they didn't know about it. This is a common occurrence in corporations (Stone, 1975) as well as in public institutions (Kotarba, 1978). This shielding both protects higher ups and aids the organization to fulfill tasks in an unethical or illegal manner.

ENCOURAGING NONABSOLUTISTIC FORMS OF BELIEF

Deviance is encouraged in two major fashions: through collective support of others and through verbalized accounts for their own behavior, as voiced personally by the deviants. The support can be widespread—as noted in Gallup polls of community attitudes—or it can be achieved by contact with habituees. The verbalized accounts can be defensive responses to potential or actual condemnation, or they can be active, aggressive, political critiques of the system. With the active form, there is an attempt to go full circle in encouraging nonabsolutistic types of belief.

Normative Social Support from Others

When we consider behaviors that are not condemned by the great bulk of the population, there is normative social support for some deviant actions. In 1975, Gallup found that legalization of marijuana had the support of 25 percent of the public and 52 percent of college students.

In a survey by Boydell and Grindstaff (1972), the Canadian public was asked what types of punishment they would mete out to offenders. Public condemnation was greatest for assaultive offenses, followed by property crimes. With victimless offenses, however, there is widespread support for limited or no punishment, as Table 4.1 reveals.

While the attitudes presented in the table do not cause individuals to engage in victimless crimes, there is less of a condemnation and, hence, less of a deterrent effect. In essence, the absence of punishment serves as an object lesson for the individual who would engage in the activity. Such individuals will find out that others believe as they do (i.e., there is nothing wrong with the behavior). In some communities, this can come to have ideological support. Tolerance for deviance is greater among some ethnic groups than others. This is related to religion and culture of the ethnic subculture. Protestants are more likely to condemn drinking than Catholics. Blacks, Chinese, Italians, and Hispanics have favorable attitudes toward gambling.

SUMMARY

Societal expectations coexist with limitations, conditions, and distortions. This seeming paradox can be understood only in the context of a more thorough examination of the social fabric. To know that certain rules exist is not enough. There is frequent negotiation and disagreement over the nature of many of these rules. Whether abortion is homicide, whether marijuana is dangerous, and other issues are constantly being negotiated and debated heatedly. This fluid image of rules contrasts sharply with the Durkheimian notion

Table 4.1. **Percentage Distribution of Penalties Assigned for Crimes without Victims.**

Offenses	No Penalty	Fine	Probation	1 to 6 Months	6 Months or More	Execute	No Answer
Prostitute	28	26	16	23	4	—	3
Prostitute (client)	61	22	7	6	2	—	2
Homosexual	60	10	9	9	6	—	6
Gamble (with friend)	76	13	5	3	—	—	3
Gamble (professional)	54	31	7	5	1	2	2
Marijuana use	27	23	22	17	6	1	5
Hard drug use	15	13	26	26	16	—	4
Marijuana sell	4	9	6	23	52	1	5
Hard drug sell	1	4	3	11	75	2	4
Abortion (female)	56	11	14	9	6	—	4
Abortion (doctor)	41	21	10	7	17	—	4
Abortion (other)	4	6	2	19	64	—	6

SOURCE: Boydell and Grindstaff (1972: 176).

that rules are functional and serve to bind society against the violators. Disruptions of the collective conscience (widely agreed upon values) are becoming widely recognized as normal in modern society. In the name of morality and humanity, antiwar protesters violated laws in the late 1960s and early 1970s by burning and pouring blood on draft records. Similarly, anti-nuclear-power advocates have trespassed and destroyed property. These disruptions point to the predominant reality in society—that of power.

The powerful control the resources of rule creation and social control. Examples of this abound: a $20,000 birthday party is not illegal, but the person who would dare crash the party and steal liquor, presents, and the cake would be labeled a thief, a trespasser, and a disturber of the peace. On the other hand, if this thief is wealthy, he or she will be able to hire expert witnesses to try to prove temporary insanity. Why are the wealthy and powerful more able to insulate themselves from punishment? First of all, they make the rules. Second, deviance is more likely to be defined as falling within the jurisdiction of civil codes or professional review boards rather than requiring action by the criminal justice system. Third, they are granted "idiosyncracy credits." Fourth, their behavior is less open to public view.

Coming full circle, we see that support for violation of codes exists in different communities. This ranges from passive acceptance to the declaration that the subculture members are oppressed and not sinful or deviant. A comparison between blacks and other minorities and gays is made (Kameny, 1971; Hacker, 1971; Humphreys, 1972). Humphreys (1972: 9), in an analysis of the liberation movement, discusses the social oppression against homosexuals.

> Social oppression, at least as directed against those who reveal a preference for their own sex, takes three basic forms: *legal-physical*, in which certain behavior common to the stigmatized group is proscribed under threat of physical abuse or containment; *occupational-financial*, limiting the options for employment and financial gain for those stigmatized; and *ego-destructive*, by which the individual is made to feel morally inferior, self-hatred is encouraged, and a sense of valid identity is inhibited. [Emphasis in the original.]

Clearly, the object is to change the image of the homosexual from an immoral actor to an oppressed one. Other movements have taken on a similar form. Marijuana-smokers have organized NORML (Na tional Organization for the Reform of Marijuana Laws) and prostitutes have formed COYOTE (Call Off Your Old Tired Ethics), WED (Women Endorsing Decriminalization), and PONY (Prostitutes of New York). These movements declare that the deviants are not deviant but are oppressed. One solution to the oppression is legalization. Another solution—the one currently being taken—is compromise.

A movement toward liberalization of attitudes is taking place today. No longer can blacks, gays, the physically disabled, or others who have voiced a sense of oppression, be made the butt of dark humor. To do so is likely to bring on the stares and ostracism of listeners.

5 MORAL ENTERPRISE, MORAL PANIC, AND LAW-AND-ORDER CAMPAIGNS

IAN TAYLOR

The purpose of this chapter is to outline, and later to criticize, some of the writing by sociologists in the United States and England on the "campaigns" that occur in the process of bringing about changes in the scope of law. In other words, we are interested in the kinds of analyses undertaken by sociologists to explain the scope, target, intensity, and appeal of specifically political or religious or generally ideological campaigns that are conducted by various kinds of organizations and social groups in order to criminalize (to "outlaw") the behaviors of other social groups and individuals. We are looking at the process of the creation of deviance in public campaigns.

INTERACTIONISM AND THE THEORY OF MORAL ENTERPRISE

Students of crime and deviance who are cognizant of the past activities of people such as Anita Bryant in the United States and Canada (and Mary Whitehouse in England) will be well aware of the continuing truth of Howard Becker's now classic dictum in *Outsiders* (1963: 9) that:

> [Deviance] is created by society. I do not mean this in the sense in which it is ordinarily understood, in which the causes of deviance are located in the social situation of the deviant or in

the "social factors" which prompt his action. I mean, rather, that *social groups create deviance by making the rules whose infraction constitutes deviance* and by applying those rules to particular persons and labelling them as outsiders. From this point of view, deviance is not a quality of the act the person commits, but rather a consequence of the application by others of rules and sanctions to an "offender". The deviant is one to whom the label has been successfully applied; deviant behaviour is behaviour that people so label. [Emphasis in the original.]

It is not that homosexuality, for example, is essentially deviant, in the sense of being abnormal or unnatural (homosexuality has been approved of and celebrated in some cultures and in some historical periods). For homosexual preferences to be publicly proclaimed as deviant, some antihomosexual initiative is required on the part of what labeling theorists call "moral entrepreneurs." Committedly antihomosexual initiative encourages, and reproduces, a public definition of homosexuality as deviant.[1] It is precisely this kind of endeavor that was entered into by Anita Bryant and some other members of the radical Right in the last few years in the United States. Similar work has been undertaken by individuals and groups (mostly of the new "populist" Right) during the campaign against the Equal Rights Amendment in order to suggest that the woman who does not want to proceed with a pregnancy, or who wants to pursue a career other than homemaker, is in some sense deviating from some absolute and firmly established set of moral rules. In addition, over the last few decades, the Right has attempted to maintain the status of marijuana and certain soft chemical drugs as criminal—and therefore as more harmful than the more common consumption of nicotine, caffeine, and alcohol.[2]

Campaigns of this character—directed against the immorality of nuclear weapons, the unregulated use of nuclear energy, and other activities of the state and of the powerful in general—have also been conducted by members of the political Left over the years. However, they have met with less success and had less impact on the law and the sensitivities of the mass media than have the campaigns of the Right.

Such campaigns are by no means a recent feature of modern industrial society. Indeed, in both Europe and North America, throughout the nineteenth and twentieth centuries, there have been campaigns against what is now called "permissiveness" and also against "youth" (usually with a view toward demanding stricter punishment of delinquents) (Gillis, 1974). However, only with the development in the early 1960s of the "interactionist" approach to the study of deviance did these campaigns come to be examined as being a part of the cause of deviance, rather than being (as the campaigners themselves would suggest) simply a reaction to deviance. This reversal of the conventional view of "deviance creation" was most succinctly put by Edwin Lemert (1967: v), another prominent author in the interactionist literature on deviance. Lemert observed that there was, in his work, "a large turn away from older sociology which tended to rest heavily upon the idea that deviance leads to social control. I have come to believe that the reverse idea, i.e., social control leads to deviance, is equally tenable and the potentially richer premise for studying deviance in modern society."

Howard Becker illustrated his version of the interactionist theory of law creation in an examination of the passage of the Marijuana Tax Act by the United States Congress and Senate in 1937. Becker noted that this piece of legislation substantially prohibited the use of soft narcotics for all but medical purposes *at a time when there was very little evidence of marijuana or other soft drugs constituting a general social problem.* There had been very little popular or political anxiety over soft narcotic use in the early 1930s, and there was good evidence that its use was confined to very small numbers of people, restricted to certain ethnic subcultures. In other words, one would not have expected that there would be much support among powerful or influential groups in American society for the creation of a law that would be expensive to enforce, and that was occasioned by behavior that was relatively untroublesome to taxpayers.

Becker explains that the passage of the act, in these unpropitious circumstances, was the result of what he calls a *moral enterprise*, as well as the work of one highly committed and very well placed *moral entrepreneur*, Harry J. Anslinger, chief of the Federal Bureau of Narcotics in the 1930s. For Becker (1963: 148), a moral entrepreneur is an individual who is committed to bringing about a change in the dominant moral rules of society, via signifying new rules *in law*, and "He operates with an absolute ethic; what he sees is truly and totally evil with no qualification. Any means is justified to do away with it. The crusader is fervent and righteous, often self-righteous. . . . The crusader is not only interested in seeing to it that other people do what he thinks right. He believes that if they do what is right it will be good for them."

For Becker, the moral enterprise or moral crusade is not only an activity of outright reactionaries; it can also be pursued for what he calls "humanitarian" (progressive or liberal) ends. So:

> Prohibitionists [in the United States in the 1920s and 1930s] felt that they were not simply forcing their morals on others, but attempting to provide the conditions for a better way of life for people prevented by drink from realizing a truly good life. Abolitionists were not simply trying to prevent slave owners from doing the wrong things; they were trying to help slaves achieve a better life (Becker, 1963: 148).

Anslinger and the Federal Bureau of Narcotics in the 1930s operated on the basis of a set of ethical beliefs of this order, but the crucial feature of the publicity campaign that was launched against marijuana by the bureau in the 1930s was that it touched on the nerve centers of American morality and culture. The campaign of newspaper articles, advertisements, and films spoke not only of a drug that could reduce an individual's capacity for self-control (a key requirement of societies dominated by the Protestant Ethic) but also a drug that was taken, not to aid work or to reduce pain, but to achieve states of ecstasy. It was pleasure pursued without what Young (1970) called the "credit-card of work."

Becker (1963: 136) reflected that "because of our strong cultural emphases on pragmatism and utilitarianism, Americans usually feel uneasy and ambivalent about ecstatic experiences of any kind. But we do not condemn ecstatic experience when it is the by-product or reward of actions we consider proper in their own right, such as hard work or religious fervour. It is . . . when people pursue ecstasy for its own sake that we condemn their action as a search for 'illicit pleasure.' "

So the work undertaken by Anslinger and the bureau in the 1930s in order to identify marijuana as a danger to the American people (even though its use was very uncommon and restricted to certain subcultural groups) was successful because of the power of the anxiety that was created. It was in the interest of all Americans that marijuana should be identified in the most powerful way possible (in law) as deviant (and thereby abnormal) in order that the moral supports of the American way of life could be defended (in particular, the emphasis on individual responsibility and self-control, and the overwhelming cultural emphasis on work).

Becker's notion of moral enterprise is very general; it speaks of campaigns that are successful by virtue of their importance to a culture. It is also very individualistic; it allows considerable power and influence to the acts of committed individual moral entrepreneurs such as Harry Anslinger or Anita Bryant. It is a version of "moral crusades" that has been subject to some criticism from other sociologists of deviance in the United States working within the interactionist tradition.

MORAL ENTERPRISE BY ORGANIZATIONS

Donald T. Dickson, like Becker, was intrigued by the fact that the Marijuana Tax Act could have been enacted in a period when powerful interests in the population were largely unaffected and in no way threatened by soft drug use (Dickson, 1968). But Dickson's examination of Anslinger was not simply of an isolated, relatively powerful, but highly committed moral entrepreneur; it was also an examination of Anslinger in his capacity as a bureaucrat in charge of a large government agency. Large bureaucratic organizations like the Federal Bureau of Narcotics then had (and still have) a need to justify their existence to their paymasters, the federal government. One way in which an organization can do this is by attempting to persuade the public that "there is a job to be done" and that doing the job is within its capacity. Something more than an abstract and "absolute" moral ethic is involved in this process: What occurs is more like the mobilization of public opinion to support the bureaucratic organization (and, of course, to encourage a continued level of political and/or financial support for it from the government).

In the early 1930s, however, the Federal Bureau of Narcotics was in trouble. It had experienced a decline in the size of its operating budget, voted by Congress, of some 26 percent between 1932 and 1936, leaving the bureau with its lowest income for a decade. In part, this was a result of the Depression; but it was also due to the fact that drug use was what Dickson calls a "weakly held value" among the American public and on the mass media. It was the low budgetary endowment, and the consequent threat to the bureau's status and esteem (and, perhaps, its very existence), Dickson argues, that led the bureau to launch a mass of literature and radio broadcasts on the evils of marijuana. Significantly for Dickson's argument, the mass of the publicity came *after* the act, not before it; if Anslinger were indeed the archetypal moral entrepreneur of Becker's account, the passage of the act would have been a final victory in the moral crusade, rather than its beginning. But in a campaign in which the objective was to convince Congress, annually, of the persistent threat of drug use, the vigor of the bureau in combating it, and the necessity of continuing government financial support for the bureau, high levels of publicity were needed. Thus, by 1938, even though marijuana was an uncommon drug, one out of every four federal drug convictions involved marijuana use, and the bureau could claim to have successfully demonstrated the need for its own continued existence and support.

Dickson's interpretation of the bureau's activity around the Marijuana Tax Act directs attention away from individuals to organizational interests in explaining the origins of law creation, and alerts sociologists to the need to analyze the amount of power (especially in relation to governments) possessed by groups pressing for legal change. Evangelical efforts by individual moral entrepreneurs are unlikely to be successful in either criminalizing or decriminalizing behavior unless those efforts happen to coincide with the interests of an organization that has significant influence at the level of the Congress, the judiciary, and the state and federal legislatures.

SYMBOLIC CRUSADES

Other American sociological work on law creation has indicated that the power and influence of large (governmental) organizations is not essential in the process of bringing about changes in the definition of behavior as criminal and/or "deviant."

Joseph Gusfield's (1963: 17, 44) work on Prohibition in the United States is important in showing the enormous power of large social groups, united around a single issue, in breaking through the resistance of well-entrenched organizations including the police force,[3] and bringing about a reform of existing federal law. In 1919, the temperance movement in the United States, which was based on the Women's Christian Temperance Union founded in the nineteenth century, was successful in realizing its legislative aims (prohibition of the public sale and consumption of alcohol) precisely at a time when the social group from which its members were drawn—small-town middle America—felt most threatened by structural developments in the larger society. The temperance movement was, for Gusfield, a form of "status politics" whereby "members of a status group could strive to preserve, defend, or enhance the dominance and prestige of their style of life against threats from individuals or groups whose life-style differed from theirs." In organizing to bring about the passage of the 18th Amendment in 1919, the status group (the traditional middle class of small-town America) was attempting to affirm the dominance of the "rural, traditional, local, native, non-drinker" over the "urban, modern, cosmopolitan, foreign drinker." For Gusfield, therefore, the functions of law are to a considerable extent *symbolic* in proclaiming the values of particular, influential status groups (particularly in areas of morality and life-style); the sociologist should be interested in examining the ways in which these status groups operate, and the social conditions that make for their success or failure, in bringing about symbolic legal change.[4] In this sense, "laws" (and therefore also "crimes") are the social (and symbolic) accomplishments of particular interest groups, rather than being the abstractly "democratic" accomplishment spoken of by politicians, and rather than being an expression of a "general will," or the general needs of the social system (spoken of by functionalist sociology).[5]

Of course, it is also sometimes the case that a popular moral crusade will receive support from people whose motives (as Howard Becker [1963: 149] puts it) "are less pure than those of the crusader." Becker notes, without much further inquiry, that "some industrialists supported Prohibition because they felt it would provide them with a more manageable labour force." So, in some instances, essentially the moral crusade of a "status group" (symbolizing the *values* of the group) is appropriated, or taken up, for other *instrumental* purposes (profit-maximization, an orderly production line, etc.), especially those of influential social and economic interests like those of large industrial enterprise.

BEYOND MORAL ENTERPRISE

The investigation of law creation by Becker, Lemert, Dickson, Gusfield, and other American sociological writers in the 1960s was certainly very useful in shifting the focus of deviancy theory away from the deviant actor (and even the social contexts of the actor—family, subcultures, and environment) and in highlighting the importance of attempts by particular social groups (status groups, governmental organizations, industrial interests, etc.) in the moral enterprises that create law and therefore crime. This literature invited the sociologist to examine, and indeed to identify, the *interests* that underpin any particular campaign for legal change, and thus to recognize the attempts being made by these particular interests to represent themselves in law (as if they were universal, rather than particular, interests) as being undemocratic or even totalitarian.[6]

There are, however, at least two significant problems common to all the analyses of law creation we have examined. These revolve around (1) the implicit theory of the nature of political power and social structure in American (and, possibly, any modern industrial society) that is present in the work, and (2) the relative absence of a theory of the causes of moral enterprise.

Politics and Moral Enterprises

In attempting to identify the ways in which the law was often a symbol or a defense of particular social interests, interactionist sociologists were making two connected political points. On the one hand, they were attempting to show how the law could be biased or even repressive toward minority group interests, or toward what Becker (1963) called "subordinate populations." Homosexuals, alcoholics, prostitutes, users of soft drugs, and even people with unusual physical or basically harmless psychological tendencies could be subjected to harassment either by police or by social and psychiatric agencies. The fundamental message of the interactionist sociologist was that social control agencies should be less controlling and less oversensitive to people's expressions of diversity. By ceasing to label people who were "different" from the general public as "deviant," they would reduce the extent of any problems that deviant behavior might be causing others. This essentially liberal vision was later dubbed "radical non-intervention" by Edwin Schur. The implicit (and sometimes explicit) model society in this writing seemed often to be northern California in the late 1960s, a culture that was thought by Becker and Horowitz (1971) to clearly exhibit the qualities of civility and tolerance. The quest was for a society in which there would be a change of attitude (and thus a reduction in the amount of punitive or censorious social reaction) toward people whose behavioral preferences were different from those of the majority.

A prerequisite in the creation of such a degree of tolerance would be a reduction in the influence exercised over legal institutions and the content of law itself by bodies such as the Women's Christian Temperance Union and the Federal Bureau of Narcotics, as well as in the influence of individual entrepreneurs with an absolute moral ethic that they might want to impose on others "in their own interest." In order to reduce the extent of this social control, the special-interest groups pressing for control had first to be identified and exposed as having a particular (rather than general) interest in mind. A series of studies has been provoked by this interactionist tradition into the professional, class, elite, and religious interests that lie behind the pressure for child welfare legislation (Platt, 1969); the creation of a panic over hyperactivity among children (Schrag and Divoki, 1975); the campaigns against public display of pornography (Zurcher et al., 1971–1972); the demand for a legal continuing "repression" of drug use (Duster, 1970); and many other instances of what interactionists feel to be an unjustifiable demand for social control.[7]

So the politics of the literature on moral enterprise are really of a Romantic variety. In other words, problems of legal repression of minority groups are the result of misinformed, or in some cases malevolent, intentions on the part of interest groups that have more influence than they really "deserve," and the level of social control in a society is a product of the anxieties they have generated (often spuriously, as in the case of the Federal Bureau of Narcotics).

The main limitations in this liberal, the pluralist, concept of "social interest" have been identified by Isaac Balbus (1971). The operative conception is of an essentially subjective interest—a psychological state of mind of an individual (including his or her prejudices, preferences, fears, and desires). However, as Balbus (1971: 152) observes, "a person may be affected by something whether or not he realises it. . . . Evidence can be marshalled to demonstrate that an individual has an interest even if he is not aware of it or even that what an individual thinks is in his interest is in fact not in his interest."

In this case, for Balbus, we are conceiving of interest as an *objective interest* (independent of the psychological state of mind of the people involved). So to take just one example, while the white working class and lower middle class in Europe and North America might react to the entry of migrant black populations into their workplaces and their neighborhoods with prejudice and, very frequently, overt racism (the subjective interest), it would occur at the cost of a weakening of the common objective interests of the white and black populations in question. (Such objective interest demands unity on the part of working people caught in positions of exploitation by employers, landlords, supermarket chains, and other owners of capital.)

We would also argue, perhaps more contentiously, that the subjective belief of many working class people—that more severe sentences for "criminals" are necessary to restore a sense of order to working class communities—is incompatible with the objective interest of working class people. Prisons and juvenile institutions do not rehabilitate their inmates; they confirm the thief's and the vandal's rejection of the broader society, and thus they tend to reproduce a population, *within* the working class, of disorderly, antisocial minorities, who add to the already severe problems of decomposing working class communities. The objective interest of populations of such communities is in the creation of labor and housing markets, and therefore of living communities that are free from the contradictions and crises of a capitalist political economy.

Such a view of objective interest depends on a rather different view of the social structure of the United States (and other western societies) from that which is implicit in Becker, Lemert, Dickson, and Gusfield. In particular, it depends on the view that there is an ultimate conflict of interest between those who earn their livelihood through the sale of mental or manual labor and the owners of capital. These can be the traditional individual captains of industry, such as the Rockefellers and the Vanderbilts, or the massive corporate firms to which individuals are tied through shareholding. We shall return to this theory, but first we should observe that to hold to a theory that links social interest to social structure is to recognize that minds are changed not by persuasion (or even by majority democratic votes) but rather by force of circumstances (specifically, by changes in the social structure internal to a society). Holding to this position allows for the possibility that the concern expressed subjectively by an interest group (for example, alcohol abuse, as in the case of the prohibitionists) is objectively a form of false consciousness. Such concern may be a displacement of the real anxieties (in this case, the anxieties of a class whose position of influence in pioneer and agrarian America was rapidly declining in the face of the rise of the urban industrial middle class). Both of these realizations—the concrete rather than merely subjective relation between interests (or ideology) and social and economic conjunctures, and the possibility of social groups being mobilized against their own objective interest—are absolutely crucial to understanding the development of right wing movements in western society in the late 1970s.

The pluralist theory of politics and social structure, which was until recently accepted as truth in American political science and sociology (as well as in North American common sense), allows for no distinction between objectivity and subjectivity, as described by Balbus (1971). American society is seen as an open mix of ethnic, religious, and sociopolitical elements, structured to a limited extent by inequalities of influence and opportunity.[8] Insofar as a particular interest does achieve influence, and insofar as this influence encourages some elite domination to occur, this is said to be because of the absence of countervailing pressure—the kind that can be provided, and encouraged, by the work of social scientists, journalists, and democratically elected politicians. The theory is most clearly symbolized by Ralph Nader and his Raiders, who exposed the defects of Detroit cars, cat flea collars, and the political credentials of Congress. These areas were examined as if they were products of the inadequate attention paid by industrialists, individual large designers, and politicians to the "public interest," which is somehow an area free of contradictions of interest among the citizens (Nader, 1965; Green, 1972). In this sense, Nader is at one with the liberal interactionist sociologists who believe that a moral crusade should be mounted in the United States against undue moral, political, and economic influence exerted by other interests in the name of a real public interest.[9]

According to Nader, the extensive and eclectic nature of offenses committed against the public interest is evidence of the essentially very eclectic theory of political power and social structure that is pluralism: a picture of power and social structure that makes little sense of interest-group activity in the capitalist world in general in the 1970s and 1980s.

Causes of Moral Crusades

The crusades of individuals such as Harry Anslinger or of organizations such as the Women's Christian Temperance Union are the product of anxiety (indeed, an intolerant overanxiety) on the part of identifiable social interests. But only rarely are the social, economic, or political conditions that generate such anxiety, and thus the crusading movements, identified; only rarely do the interactionists try to speak about the conditions, which might aid a moral crusade in getting its objectives enshrined in state law.

One attempt to explain the origins of moral crusades was, however, undertaken by the British sociologist of deviance, Stan Cohen, in his *Folk Devils and Moral Panics* (1972). One of Cohen's aims was to explain the intensity of the social reaction in Britain to the activities of various working class youth groups that have emerged with some regularity since World War II. He was particularly interested in the motorcycle-riding youth groups that emerged at the seaside resorts of Brighton, Clacton, and Hastings on holiday weekends during 1964–1966. Cohen notes that only in the aftermath of mass media reports of "some trouble" involving "bike gangs" at the seaside, and the negative reaction of police and owners of seafront cafes and entertainment palaces, were the motorcycle-using youths actually polarized into exclusive groups representing the respectable working class "Mods" and the rough, lumpenproletarian "Rockers." He also shows how the process of social reaction against the youth groups achieved a momentum of its own, irrespective of the amount of property damage for which the youth groups could be thought responsible (it was not great) and irrespective of any troublesome behavior or incident. The panic generated in certain sections of the population, reproduced through the mass media, at the presence of groups of working class youths on motorcycles attempting to create some excitement on rainy and depressing holiday weekends did not need a firm daily basis in fact. Among the more telling examples of the mass media's coverage of the Mods and the Rockers were the stories carried by the *East Anglia Daily Times* on May 30, 1966,[10] and the *Dublin Evening News* on May 18, 1964.[11]

Examples of similar reportage of youth groups in North America are plentiful,[12] and the consequences are similar. Such reportage excites the process of "deviancy amplification,"[13] casting sections of youths in the role of outsiders and increasing their likelihood of becoming committed to such a role (when previously they had merely "drifted"). Cohen concludes that intense reactions—and the moral crusades that are often provoked by them (especially crusades for more repressive policies of juvenile justice)—must serve some larger societal function, rather than being merely an expression of a psychological interest (the dislike of youth). In particular, he argues, sociologists must examine the metaphorical contents of newspaper, police, and judicial comments on troublesome youths during periods of social reaction. For example, a striking feature of the British press' commentary on the motorcycle group members was an attempt to characterize the youths as being too affluent, the "spoilt product of the post-war Welfare State." This suggested to Cohen that the intensity of reaction was in some way related to the adult generation's attempt to make sense of massive social changes that had occurred in Britain since the war, especially the change that had occurred in the extent to which authority was accepted by youth. Traditional forms of authority (for example, the family, school, church, and army) had been rendered less relevant by improvements in the economic situation brought about by the postwar boom, as well as by the reforms, initiated by the Labour Government of 1945–1951, in the rigid class system of education. The antiauthoritarianism of youth—whether in the form of the explosion and appropriation of pop music, or in the form of youth subcultures (the Teddy Boys of 1953–1957, the Mods and the Rockers of 1964–1966, the Skinheads of 1967–1970, and the Punk Rockers of the late 1970s)—constitutes a massive threat to the views of social order the adult generation has come to take for granted. The visibility of youthful activity, the fascination of the mass media with violence, youth, and deviance, and the tendency of the media to look for convenient stereotypes in order to present its message[14] encourages the use of anxiety about youth as a metaphor for all kinds of broader anxieties that are in fact the product of changes in the social and economic structure. The society excites itself over recalcitrant youths in order to try to reaffirm its traditional moral values over a broad terrain. Cohen (1972: 9) thinks that the development of these anxieties (or "moral panics") over the consequences of rapid social change are predictable and universal to all societies:

> Societies appear to be subject, now and then, to periods of moral panic. A condition, episode, person or groups of persons emerges to become defined as a threat to societal values and interests; its nature is presented in a stylized and stereotypical fashion by the mass media; the moral barricades are manned by editors, bishops, politicians, and other right-thinking people; socially accredited experts pronounce their diagnoses and solutions; ways of coping are evolved or (more often) resorted to; the condition then disappears, submerges or deteriorates and becomes more visible. Sometimes the object of the panic is quite novel and at other times it is something which has been in existence long enough, but suddenly appears in the limelight. Sometimes the panic passes over and is forgotten, except in folklore and collective memory; at other times, it has more serious and long-lasting repercussions and might produce changes such as those in legal and social policy or even in the way society conceives itself.

The moral panic has a social function, therefore, in a classically Durkheimian sense.

> For the collective sentiments which are protected by the penal law of a people at a specified moment of its history to take

possession of the public conscience or for them to acquire a stronger hold where they have insufficient grip, they must acquire an intensity greater than that which they had hitherto had. The community as a whole must experience them more vividly, for it can acquire from no other source the greater force necessary to control these individuals who formerly were the most refractory (Durkheim, 1895/1964b: 67).

For both Durkheim and Cohen, the creation of these anxieties in a population is only in part, and indirectly, dependent on refractory behavior among individuals; it is a process that is dependent more directly on the necessity for *a community at a specified moment to take possession of the public conscience*. Sociologically, this analytical formulation is one that focuses the task of explanation on the identification of the conditions in social life that give rise to the demand (or felt need) for reintensification of social control (via taking possession of the collective conscience—the dominant morality, legal, and educational institutions, of a society).

As the collective conscience is reactivated in this way, society erects a "gallery of types . . . to show its members which roles should be avoided and which should be emulated . . . [and] groups [come to occupy] a constant position as folk devils: visible reminders of what we should not be" (Cohen, 1972: 10).

The gallery of types tends to overrepresent youths, precisely because youths have to be constantly subjected to the impact of the collective conscience before they are effectively socialized into their roles in the division of labor, and in the moral life of the community generally. Intensification of the societal reaction against the young occurs when the routine processes of socialization (for example, in schools or in the family) are thought to be ineffective (as in the case of the troublesome behavior of British working class youths in the late 1960s).

Cohen's argument is reminiscent of some of Hunter Thompson's (1966) remarks in his rather less orderly analysis of the moral panics in the early 1960s in America over the making of the Hell's Angels menace. Most Americans were concerned not so much with working class youths in general, however, as with the threatening image of the "motorcycle outlaws" in particular. According to Thompson, they were

as uniquely American as jazz. Nothing like them had ever existed. In some ways they appeared to be a kind of half breed anachronism, a human hangover from the era of the Wild West. Yet in other ways they were as new as television. There was absolutely no precedent, in the years after the Second World War, for large gangs of hoodlums on motorcycles, revelling in violence, worshipping mobility and thinking nothing of riding five hundred miles on a weekend . . . to whoop it up with other gangs of cyclists in some country hamlet entirely unprepared to handle even a dozen peaceful tourists. Many picturesque outback villages got their first taste of tourism not from families driving Fords or Chevrolets, but from clusters of boozing "city boys" on motorcycles (Thompson, 1966: 75).

Thompson's account of the reaction of the mass media and respectable citizenry to Hell's Angels uses many of the same images of social anxiety (over violence, affluence, sexuality, etc.) that are discussed in the British situation by Cohen. Thompson is well able to ridicule this social anxiety, and in his later works this is the subject of many more elaborate discussions.

The advantage of Cohen's "moral panic," over the theories of moral crusade developed in American deviance theory, is that it pays attention to the ongoing interrelationship of a changing social structure and dominant social morality. What Durkheim calls the "grip" of the dominant morality, or the collective conscience, is seen as being continually problematic. A constant reworking of the scope and application of moral rules is required (by newspaper editors, magistrates, priests, and other moral guardians of society) at all moments in the development of a social structure, in order that the existing rules do not lose their power of moral guidance and social control. So changes in social control are unlikely to arise entirely spuriously—as implied, for example, by Becker (1963) and Dickson (1968) in their analyses of the Marijuana Tax Act—simply because of the determination or the degree of influence of an interest group or government department. Such changes are likely to arise because of a real need to intensify the grip of the collective conscience at times when the relation between developments in the social structure (*especially* in the organization and development of the division of labor) and the collective conscience is particularly parlous.

Interesting, but relatively undiscussed,[15] in the case of the narcotics and alcohol legislation in the United States, is the relation between popular receptivity to the moral crusades conducted around these issues (or the power of the issues as a metaphor) and the anxieties of different elements in the American class structure. Such anxieties were created by the massive immigrations (especially from the third world) during 1860–1920 and the economic

cycle (in particular, the Great Depression, and its different consequences for agricultural sectors and the large financial capitals of
the East) from 1920 onward.

The creation of folk devils (like the drug user, the drinker, the
Mods and the Rockers, or other problematic groups) is a necessary
process. It symbolizes the threat to which the intensification of
social control is said to be a response. The process is spurious in
two senses: for example, in exaggerating and distorting the real
nature of drug or alcohol use, or of vandalism and hooliganism by
working class youth groups, and in displacing the real source of the
demand for the intensification of control. However, it is not spurious in the sense that it acts as the most effective carrier, or symbol,
of a process of intensification that is demanded by the particular
conjuncture of social structural development and the collective
conscience.

The work of American deviance theorists on the interest groups
involved in moral crusades needs to be extended further. Sociologists have to identify the relation between the emergence of an interest group (like the Women's Christian Temperance Union in the
early twentieth century), and the larger disjuncture in the relation of
social structure and "morality," rather than begin their analysis with
the investigation of an individual moral crusade, working backward
to a series of speculative accounts about the influence in the crusade
of cultural values, individuals, or organizations.

LAW-AND-ORDER CAMPAIGNS

Perhaps the most important work in the sociological investigation
of moral crusades is that of researchers at the Centre for Contemporary Cultural Studies at the University of Birmingham in England
(Hall et al., 1978). They focused on the alleged emergence of mugging in the United Kingdom during the winter of 1972–1973. In
particular, they examined the belief, expressed in one of the most
widely read newspapers in Britain, that "as crimes of violence esca-
late, a word common in the United States enters the British head-
lines: mugging. To our police, it's a frightening new strain of
crime" (Daily Mirror, August 17, 1972).

It is true that throughout 1972 and 1973 the British media was
preoccupied with the increasing violence that they alleged was occurring in society. (This violence was "seen" on school play-
grounds, in sports, and, crucially, in union picket lines during
strikes.) It is also true that some tragic violence did occur in those

years in the course of robberies in the street. The judiciary and the press thought that the situation was serious enough to warrant some very severe sentences for offenses categorized as muggings (for example, a sentence of twenty years on the sixteen-year-old half-caste, Paul Storey, by Mr. Justice Croom-Johnson at Birmingham Crown Court, in March 1973).

A closer examination of the development of the mugging epidemic by the Birmingham group revealed, however:

1. that the (statistical and other) evidence that was used to support the idea that there was a real increase in violent behavior in Britain was "weak and confused" (Hall et al., 1978: 17).

2. that street robberies, sometimes involving violence, are a well-known form of criminal activity in British cities, dating from the nineteenth century when they were known as "garrotting."

3. that the role of the press and the judiciary in sensitizing the public to the idea that the offenses being tried in court were a form of mugging (by implication a crime exported from America) was absolutely crucial.

Moreover, the investigation by the Birmingham group revealed that the Metropolitan Police in London had issued warnings via the mass media about the possibility of an outbreak of mugging, and had established an anti-mugging squad to patrol the trains on the London Underground System, in January and February 1972, some seven to eight months *before* the panic about mugging developed following a murder near Waterloo Station in August. In other words, "the organisational response on the ground long [predated] any official judicial or media expression of public anxiety. The situation was defined by the police as one requiring swift, vigorous, more-than-usual measures" (Hall et al., 1978: 40). The campaign over mugging was thus a campaign in which objectives and parameters were initiated by the police, but was responded to in the courts (with an ongoing "explanation" articulated through the mass media). Not only was it true that "social control" was leading to deviance, in the sense in which that phrase was intended by Lemert (1967); it was also the case that the rationale for social control and the "absolute reality" of the deviation in question were actually constructed *in advance* by social control agents working through the media. The media effectively symbolized the threatening nature of mugging by using references to the violence of Manhattan and Detroit. When courtroom hearings into arrests made by the anti-mugging squads and by uniformed police elsewhere began in late 1972 and early 1973, the press and its readers were able to congratulate the police on their foresight and on their firm and rapid response to a threatening behavior that was "obviously" on the increase.

The specific empirical question that interested the Birmingham Group was "the explanation [as to] how and why a version of . . . rather traditional street crime was perceived, at a certain point in the early 1970s, as a 'new strain of crime' " (Hall et al., 1978: 17). But of rather more consequence was the group's examination of the way in which the mugging panic was part of a larger law-and-order campaign. In this campaign, the police successfully provided "evidence" of the need for an increase in expenditure by the police, and also the need for an increase in their legal powers (especially in the areas of arrest and search),[16] and in which the existing institutions of the welfare state (especially in social work, education, and race relations) were put very much on the defensive. Crucially important in this campaign was the implicit question of race, in particular the policing of West Indian youths in the inner-city ghettos and the downtown streets of the major conurbations.[17] One consequence of the law-and-order campaign of the early to middle 1970s, in some ways anticipated by Hall et al., was the very prominent positions of race and immigration, and law and order in the issues raised by the Conservative Party in winning the general election in Britain in May 1979 (Taylor, 1980a, 1980b).

In dealing with these two questions, the Birmingham Group advances a clear distinction between three historical types of moral panic (Hall and Jefferson, 1975: 76–78).

The discrete moral panic of the kind described by Cohen in *Folk Devils and Moral Panics* (1972) is viewed as revolving around a dramatic event, and accompanied by public disquiet and action by agencies of social control (notably, the police and the magistracy). In Britain, according to the Birmingham Group, this discrete moral panic was characteristic of the early 1960s.

Crusades occur, according to the Birmingham Group, when individual moral panics are "mapped" or connected together, especially by moral entrepreneurs, in order to produce a speeded-up sequence. For example, in the late 1960s individual entrepreneurs attempted to connect the rise of a student counterculture, developments in soft-drug use, pornography, and sexual permissiveness generally as a single social development, arising out of weakness of established authority and also subversive of its future interests and people in general. In the late 1970s, controlling actions taken against students in both America and Europe tended to be justified in terms of public images of "students," which associated political rebelliousness with debauchery, weak personalities, and failure to internalize the appropriate respect for authority. Dramatic events, such as sit-ins on university premises, were used as confirmations of an already established image, rather than being considered (as in individual moral panics) the source of public (or entrepreneurial) activity.

For the 1970s, however, the Birmingham Group found it useful to speak of an "altered sequence" in which official reaction to events was already prepared, and articulated, in terms of the campaign for law and order. Throughout the decade, a massive sensitization of the public to a series of civil order problems occurred. In particular, the public was sensitized to the view that street crime, terrorism, violence, and homicides were the *source* of the breakdown that was then a part of everyday experience in British society. In other words, (1) there was a tendency for the control culture to always act in anticipation of a scare (such as the scare over mugging in 1972), and (2) a considerable amount of ideological work went into seeing mugging, for example, as a cause of the ruptures in civil society, rather than as a result. In popular talk about crime and violence (in the mass media), conventional criminological wisdom (which sees crime as resulting from problematic social arrangements) is reversed.

The mapping together of violence, permissiveness, rebelliousness, and disorder that was a part of the ideological work undertaken by individual moral entrepreneurs (for example, Vice President Spiro Agnew in the United States) in the 1960s became increasingly acceptable during the 1970s. This was partly due to the emergence of an influential and vociferous movement, the new, or radical, Right, which seemed to give respectability to views that were previously thought to be too extreme and too repressive by liberal, democratic societies with an ideological preference for pluralism and diversity. They were also becoming more acceptable, according to the Birmingham Group, because the structural problems of western society (and, especially in the United States, its fiscal and energy problems) were becoming much more severe (O'Connor, 1973; Gough, 1979). Moreover, there was an increasing need to displace public focus from structured problems onto the threat from crimes, from violence, and from permissiveness. For example, the right wing remains relatively silent on unemployment, which is now very high in all western societies and likely to increase, as a source of problems of order in civil society. Instead, it is very vocal on the existence of individuals who are said to be dangerous. In this way, the current social conditions in western society are made immune from radical criticism, and the source of problems is seen to reside in individual failings (which, of course, for an ideologist, is true as a matter of faith).

But the equation of the social problems of late industrial society with the existence of weak or evil individuals is not simply the result of the success of the subjective interests (the moral beliefs) of individual moral entrepreneurs. It corresponds to the objective interests of powerful groups in late capitalist society, who actually need to replace the structure of social control as a whole that existed in times of economic plenty (during the revolution of rising expectations) with a tighter, more repressive structure. As the fiscal and profitability crises of western states deepen, public expenditure on welfare (in its broadest sense) has to reduce. The major impact will be felt by the populations that have been most dependent on such subsidies—low-cost housing, health programs, and unemployment benefits. The increasing levels of unemployment in western society are likely to exacerbate the economic and personal insecurities of large sections of the working population. In addition, a process of marginalization of a large subordinate population is likely to occur in most western societies, whereby a substantial section of the population will be subjected to an increasing level of control by the police (prison, juvenile institutions, etc.) in particular, and by much more stringent systems of state welfare. This marginalization is likely to occur most intensively, however, among minority groups and among women and young people, who have in recent times made up what has been called the "reserve army of labour." The process is likely to be accelerated by the decline of world capitalism in the 1980s. As Schwendinger and Schwendinger (1976: 184) observe:

> The United States is . . . beset by long-term trends towards stagnation. The American economy no longer expands sufficiently to absorb most of its technologically displaced labour force—much less the new generations of workers. The rate of absorption has only surged for short periods during war-time or during a postwar boom. Generally the younger, the older and the most oppressed workers have been excluded from the labour market. Millions have become marginal. From an economic standpoint, these persons at any given time are either absolutely or relatively superfluous.

The decline in profitability and in expansion in the United States produces similar effects in other countries within an increasingly interconnected world economy. However, the consequences have to some extent varied according to the different political conditions in each country. In the old, declining economies of Britain and Italy, for example, the rates of unemployment that were common in North America were thought to be unacceptable politically, and were not allowed to develop until the early 1970s, largely because of the strength of the social-democratic parties and organized labor movements in those countries. As the crisis of world capital deepened in the late 1970s, however, there was a convergence in the problems of all the national economies. For the first time in its history, capitalism had to deal with the problems of declining profitability, high unemployment, and inflation all at the same time, throughout the world economy.

In such a global situation, the grip of ideologies of various descriptions put forth by the right wing will tend to intensify in capitalist societies, especially among the most economically and socially insecure sections of society (the lower middle class, in particular, which is dependent on the wealth created by productive labor, but which is also most committed to a belief in the independent producer). In stressing the threats posed to a society of independent producers from the collective movements of trade unionists, however, these ideologists tend to lose the support of working people, especially in a period of increasing unemployment and inflation for some sections of the working class. So the ideologies of the Right in the 1970s tended to place a considerable emphasis on issues that displaced the divisions of class, and the economic basis for marginalization (in capitalism) onto other terrains. The law-and-order campaigners in western societies in recent years have emphasized the moral inferiority of a wide variety of troublesome, rebellious, or generally undesirable populations. In the United States, for example, there has been considerable emphasis on the deviant and ungodly characteristics of homosexuals, of feminists (especially around the struggle for the Equal Rights Amendment), and of any individual or group that appears to threaten the sanctity of the nuclear family.[18] In addition, the anxieties fueled by the Right have been marshaled into the successful campaign for the reintroduction of capital punishment. In Britain, there has been a developing campaign, already described, around the issues of race and youth (a campaign that culminated, as unemployment rates started to increase rather dramatically, in the unification of several organizations of the extreme right wing into the fascist National Front). To this campaign has also recently been added a campaign, led by the judiciary and the police, for the reintroduction of capital punishment (Taylor, 1980a). And in Canada, elements of each of these movements have been present in disparate local campaigns around race (the Western Guard in Toronto and Vancouver); homosexuality (during Anita Bryant's visit to Toronto in 1978, subsequent to the murder of a young shoe cleaner by homosexuals in 1977); capital punishment (in a police campaign during the general election of 1979—Taylor, 1980b, 1980c); and unmanageable, recalcitrant youth (symbolized in the 10 P.M. curfew in Oakville, Ontario, in 1978).

A crucial feature of the various right wing ideologies that are achieving considerable influence in western societies is their ability to provide plausible explanations of the source of popular anxiety. The anxieties are a real feature of contemporary experience, but the explanations that are provided are ideological:

1. in the sense of being false (the material problems of later capitalist society are not even "in view" in the ideological work of the radical Right).

2. in the sense of working, as ideologies do, to provide an explanation of the anxieties in terms that appear to make sense to popular experience (changes in the ethnic composition of neighborhoods, reforms in the structure of authority at school and at work, changes in the levels of pay of the youthful labor force, etc.).

That the fears of the sections of the population that are attracted to the law-and-order campaigns, and to the radical Right, have a rational, explicable basis illustrates the point we made in criticizing the tendency of earlier deviancy theory to emphasize the spurious attribution of deviant characteristics by moral campaigners. Such a formulation underplays the relation between emergence of the ideological views of the radical Right and the problems of living being experienced by the population affected. It is in this sense that we argued that sociologists have to identify the relation between the emergence of an interest group and the larger disjuncture in the relation of social structure and morality. The explanation of economic and social anxiety felt by sections of the population as being a function of these changes is, of course, rational in part (changes to routine in a heavily socialized, conforming population are threatening). However, the attempt by right wing ideologists to explain the anxieties associated with the contemporary "moment" of western capitalist society, in terms of homosexuals, feminists, or blacks, or in terms of being in positions of political or social influence, or in terms of the activities of marginalized youths in the urban areas is, quite specifically, a mystification of the current situation in west- ern societies.

The law-and-order campaigns of the late 1970s (which were directed at minority ethnic groups, homosexuals, feminists, vio- lence, social workers, intellectuals, do-gooders, and many others) are in this sense elements in an ideological movement. This move- ment differed in overall character from the discrete moral panics of the 1960s in which the level and intensity of moral anxiety that was activated was circumscribed and specifically related to particu- lar events and, usually, the question of youth. It also differed from the moral enterprises spoken of by the American deviancy theo- rists, whereby individuals or organizations were seen as being in- volved in campaigns around single issues, in order to symbolize the status of an organization or social group, in an otherwise diverse and pluralistic society. In the literature on moral panics and on moral enterprises, the economic basis of the societies in question are left unexamined, and the inevitability of the liberal, pluralist coexistence of interests as the political form of western society is assumed. It is precisely that inevitability that the radical Right is attempting to disprove, and overturn, in its quest to replace the liberal and social democratic forms by a more traditional, authori- tarian form (it is involved in a reordering of the *fundamental forms* of authority, power, and law). It is precisely this movement that sociologists interested in the analysis of, and participation in, pro- cesses of legal and political change must now understand, and im- mediately confront.

NOTES

[1]We have in mind, of course, the considerable anthropological evidence on the cultural and historical variations in the social definition of homosexuality (Plum- mer, 1975). Plummer makes it quite clear that the explanation of homosexuality as a form of preferred sexual experience resides primarily in the different organization of socialization in different contexts (which may include social reaction, or labeling, but is not equivalent to it). The explanation of how homosexual preferences come to be liable for the definition of deviance involves a different order of question—in particular, the examination of the importance of the reproduction of the human species in order to ensure the inheritance of property.

[2]There is little doubt about the relative harmlessness of marijuana, especially when its effects are compared with those of legal drugs (alcohol, nicotine, caffeine, and pre- scription drugs) that are used routinely in most western societies. Cigarette-smoking

has been conclusively linked with a variety of fatal diseases, particularly of the heart and lung. Regular use of alcohol has been shown to relate very strongly to diseases of the liver and, through weight gain, the heart (Young, 1970). Zinburg and Weil's (1969) well-known experiments with soft drugs showed that any long-term physiological effects of soft-drug use were insignificant. Peterson (1977) suggested that "the most serious adverse consequences of any habit" have not surfaced in the case of marijuana, although there is good evidence to suggest that "the operation of a motor vehicle or complex psychomotor performance are clearly impaired by marijuana use in a manner somewhat similar to that of alcohol use."

The resistance of the political Right and center to call for the decriminalization of marijuana (coupled with a lack of pressure for criminalization of alcohol use) is therefore ideological. That is, the Right's position is one in which drugs that act to support a productive life (such as alcohol and prescription drugs) are legitimate and properly legal, while those that may encourage an unproductive attitude in the user are illegitimate and appropriately criminalized.

The continuing resistance of the political Right to the campaigns for the decriminalization of marijuana is in this sense *ideological*. It runs counter to the *factual* evidence of harmfulness, and is based on adherence to a political and social ideology that supports the use of incentives to production, including those that are chemically induced via the legitimate drugs, and requires (at present) the criminalization of drugs that may encourage an unproductive attitude in the user.

[3]The American police were concerned, in the period before 1919, that temperance laws would be unenforceable. In the 1920s, their experience in having to police the growth of the black market in alcohol more than confirmed their view. The period of Prohibition is a good illustration, indeed, of Becker's distinction between the *rule-creator* and the *rule-enforcer* (the police officer, traffic warden, some social workers, and others). Whereas moral entrepreneurs tend to confine their activities to the question of symbolizing their absolute moral ethic in changes in the law ("in the books"), in rule-creation, enforcers of rules are taken up with justifying their own productivity (for example, in making arrests), as well as with maintaining a workable relationship with the population(s) with which they must work. Neither of these two tasks makes for evangelism in law-enforcement, says Becker. As a result, the rule-enforcer tends to modify (and sometimes tends to ignore) the impact of "moralizing" legislation in carrying through the task of everyday law enforcement. "Modifications" in law enforcement during the period of Prohibition in the United States extended in some cases beyond mere connivance in avoidance of law enforcement to actual participation in the "rackets" (Allsop, 1961).

[4]One of the other critical consequences of "interest group" power in the definition of legality and illegality is the exclusion of a variety of socially harmful activities from legal definition and/or enforcement—as a result of the degree of power and influence exercised by the institutions and individuals engaged in these activities. Some of the best research in this area has been done on the way in which powerful agencies in North America and Europe avoid the impact of environmental legislation (Molotch, 1970; Gunningham, 1974) and also on the ways in which state legislation on the working conditions of the blue-collar working class is circumvented by employers (Carson, 1974). The work on moral enterprise by Becker, Dickson, and Gusfield is open to criticism for the extent to which it concentrates on crusades that were successful in bringing about legal change (even if only symbolically), without examining crusades—such as those conducted by environmentalists, trade union

organizers, civil libertarians, and radical groups—that have been less than fully successful in bringing about a *real change in the substantive enforcement of law* in western societies, precisely because of the fundamental structures of economic interest that dominate those societies.

[5]The functionalist view of law as being a reflection of the developing needs of the social system is evident not only in American sociological writing (like that of Merton, Parsons, and other authors working before the development of labeling theory); it is also apparent in the work of most lawyers and jurisprudential thinkers in the United States (as well as in Europe). Writing by lawyers on law tends to be couched in terms of an examination of the formal characteristics of legal rules rather than on their substantive application. That the legal rules do not generally discriminate between legal actors by reference to race, gender, or social position is taken as evidence of "equality." (Alas, the questions of power and influence in the enforcement and use of law are ignored, as are the distribution of professional lawyers in the social structure [differential access to law] and the possibility of people who are not qualified in law using the courts for their own purposes.)

[6]The idea of the sociologist being skeptical about the interests underpinning pressures for legal change is well illustrated by Cohen in his introductory essay to *Images of Deviance* (1971). Cohen insists on the sociologist responding to attempts to ascribe an "essentially" deviant character to behavior with the query, "Says who?" This insistence on *relativizing* any attempt to define behavior as deviant has led to the description of this version of criminology as "skeptical deviancy theory."

[7]Each of these campaigns (or moral crusades) is seen by the authors investigating them to have been accompanied by claims by their participants of what Becker would call a humanitarian variety: *They claimed to be operating in the general interest of all.* But in each case, the interactionist author shows that a special claim was being made by an organized social interest. In the case of the evolution of child welfare legislation in early twentieth-century America, Platt (1969) shows that the interests involved included those of American industrialists (through their families) concerned to provide a form of paternal protection (and thereby discipline) for the children in the new urban centers who might otherwise become unruly and dangerous elements in the adult population. The invention of hyperactivity in the 1960s is shown by Schrag and Divoky (1975) to have involved the creation of a new label for an old behavior, but a label that enabled psychiatrists to experiment with new forms of social control using drugs. The movements against pornography and soft-drug use are shown in turn to have symbolic significance for social groups whose politics and values are bound up at least ostensibly with conventionally "Protestant" and "repressed" heterosexual relationships within the nuclear family and with the consumption of legitimate, productive drugs. In each case, by implication, the argument is that there is no "proven" case that the increase of control over children, over pornography, and over drugs is in anyone's *real* interest: Social control has no observable function beyond that of symbolizing the particular values of a group.

[8]In Canada, the pluralism of sociology and politics is well-symbolized in the choice of the title *The Vertical Mosaic* by John Porter (1965) for his classical study of elite (rather than specifically class) formation.

[9]Nader differs from Becker, Lemert, and Gusfield, however, in being committed to increases in social control, and indeed to a very intensive monitoring of the productive and administrative activities of large corporations by law. In this sense, Nader's work is clear evidence of the one-sided focus of the interactionist sociologists on

activities that are only arguably harmful but nonetheless illegal, and their silence on activities that are more conclusively harmful while nonetheless quite unpoliced in modern American, and western, society.

[10]"Ton-up" is popular English slang for doing 100 miles per hour in a road vehicle (usually in a sports car or motorcycle).

[11]The "mutilated Mod" in this report turned out, on further reading, to be a young man in what the newspaper report called a "mod jacket" (the Mods wore open-necked shirts), aged 21–25 (the Mods were nearly all teenagers). The park in question was in Birmingham, some 150 miles from the various seaside resorts where the Mods and the Rockers incidents were occurring. Cohen observes that "newspapers farthest away from the source invariably carried the greatest distortions and inaccuracies" (Cohen, 1972: 42).

[12]Hunter Thompson's book on Hell's Angels carries many accounts of exaggerated and even spurious reportage of the motorcycle gang's activities in California in the 1960s, and is itself not immune from a generalized kind of impression-management.

[13]The concepts of interactionist sociology of deviance used here (deviancy amplification, commitment, drift) are drawn, respectively, from Leslie Wilkins, Howard Becker, and David Matza, but they are part of the common heritage of deviancy theory that is utilized elsewhere in this text.

[14]On the media's fascination with these themes, see the essay by Young (1974).

[15]The investigation of Canadian narcotics legislation in the early twentieth century by Cook (1969) would support this metaphorical interpretation, especially of debates held in the Canadian Parliament in 1922, in which the presence of an Asiatic immigrant group was linked to the distribution of opiate drugs in the country, and the "moral ruin of innocent young people" (Cook, 1969: 43). The classic American account is that of Lindesmith (1940).

[16]Descriptively, it makes some sense to speak of the police (in Britain and in North America) as being involved in a limited discrete moral enterprise in their own field of specialism. There is a considerable emphasis in police campaigns on the specifics of the criminal justice system, and on the way in which (the police allege) the scales of justice have been tilted too far in favor of the accused. But the police campaigns on law and order (and also on capital punishment) conducted in the British and Canadian general elections of May 1979 are also quite clearly articulated around the broad issue of politics and morality (the question of social order). And, the 1970s indeed witnessed the relatively unchecked entry of senior police officers into public political debates as if they were the equals (or superiors) of democratically elected representatives (rather than civil servants or public officials). In this respect, the police campaigns are the most politically successful insertions of right wing ideologies into the "liberal consensus" established during the postwar period.

[17]The *implicit* nature of the race/mugging connection in Britain was clearly important in the law-and-order ideology in the early 1970s. The new Right was opposed to the explicit use by the National Front of a poster in which "black muggers" were depicted, and the preponderance of blacks among those arrested for mugging made public. The implicitness of the race/crime connection was continued in discussions in the later 1970s of the use made by the police of a reactivated clause in a statute of 1824 (the Vagrancy Act), in which people thought to be behaving "suspiciously" on two separate occasions (even if only minutes apart) may be arrested. Liberal criticism of the use of the so-called sus charge is that it is an instrument used by the police for managing their *control* specifically over the black areas of the large cities (rather than being, authentically, an instrument of crime prevention). In 1978, a total

of 44 percent of the 2,331 arrested in London on sus charges were black. But police representatives and Conservative officials play down the racial implications of the sus charge. (In the same way, for Conservatives in the general election of May 1979, in their party's manifesto and in speeches, the connection between race and law and order was understood, and thus by the logic of ideology, commonsensical, and therefore more difficult to challenge.

[18]The centrality of the family in the political attack mounted on liberalism in the United States from the Right has been examined in a very helpful essay by Gordon and Hunter (1977). The defense of the family is seen as related to the defense of patriarchy (the power of the male head of the family to control others, including his wife and offspring), and thereby the work ethic to which working people have been socialized; and in this sense to be a reactionary force, working in defense of capital, inequality of the sexual division of labor, and double standards and repression in sexuality. But, as Gordon and Hunter also make clear, the family sometimes provides satisfactions, rewards, and comforts that are unobtainable, especially for subordinate populations, in the wider society. In the mass-media–dominated, impersonal society, these may include some individual identity and attention, and, especially in moments of social contradiction and crisis, some personal counseling and support. The family should not be idealized and romanticized (for it *is* an authoritarian institution); nor should it be abstractly condemned: Its functions and benefits can constitute a point of departure for personal support and also change (Gordon and Hunter, 1977: 17–19).

6 ORGANIZATIONAL CRIME

CHARLES E. REASONS

White-collar crime has received little attention by criminologists. Due to professional training, cultural conditioning, and problems of data access and analysis, until recently, few criminologists have attempted to study the crimes of the powerful. According to Newman (1958: 735):

> White-collar legislation represents the major formal controls imposed upon the occupational roles of the most powerful members of our society. Whether he likes it or not, the criminologist finds himself involved in an analysis of prestige, power, and differential privilege when he studies upperworld crime. He must be as conversant with data and theories from social stratification as he has been with studies of delinquency and crime within the setting of the urban slum. He must be able to cast his analysis not only in the framework of those who break laws, but in the context of those who make laws as well. . . . *No longer is the criminologist a middle-class observer studying lower-class behavior. He now looks upward at the most powerful and prestigeful strata, and his ingenuity in research and theory will be tested indeed!* [Emphasis added.]

One of the classic polemics concerning white-collar and corporate crime appeared in 1907, a work by E. A. Ross entitled *Sin and Society*. Ross, a sociologist who was imbued with the missionary zeal of his minister father and the progressive era muckraking of a Lincoln Steffens, identified the new emerging public enemy number one as the "criminaloid," or corporate criminal.[1] However, as is the nature of social thought generally and criminological thought specifically (Bloom and Reasons, 1978), the ideological climate changes, and crimes by the powerful gained little attention until the Depression, when Albert Morris's text, *Criminology*, compared criminals of the underworld with "the permissive criminals of the upperworld" (1935: 152). Subsequently, E. H. Sutherland (1949), an acknowledged pioneer in criminology and often noted leader in white-collar crime research, wrote *White Collar Crime*, a classic in the field.

White Collar Crime has remained a classic largely because few have followed in Sutherland's footsteps until recently. In his study of the seventy largest industrial and mercantile corporations in the United States, he revealed that they had been investigated by the government for violating various antitrust laws 980 times, and only 158 (16 percent) of these violations had been dealt with by the courts as criminal offenses, while the rest were dealt with through civil law and/or informal methods. Thus, he identified the bias in the operation of the law. However, he emphasized individual offenders rather than the organization per se, defining white-collar crime as "a crime committed by a person of respectability and high social status in the course of his occupation" (Sutherland, 1949: 9). This focus upon white-collar offenders and their modus operandi remains an important aspect of contemporary work.

During the cold war in the 1950s, little attention was given to crimes of the powerful, with the 1960s bringing a return to concern with the power and abuse of large corporations and government organizations. The leading figure in creating an atmosphere conducive to the study of white-collar crime during the last two decades has been Ralph Nader. An uncompromising lawyer who began by taking on General Motors, Nader and his associates (the Raiders) have researched, publicized, and politicized the crimes of corporations and regulatory agencies (McCorry, 1972). While some academics may not like his confrontational style and polemical analysis, Nader has undoubtedly helped foster the more academic research. Of course, he was not operating in a social vaccum. During the 1960s, citizens' organizations emerged to struggle against government crimes in Southeast Asia; the abuse of citizens at home by the FBI, the CIA, local police, and the Internal Revenue Service; corporate involvement in the "war effort"; and racial, sexual, and class oppression. In this context, Nader was able to rally massive support for his crusade against corporate criminals. Like E. A. Ross, Ralph Nader does not mince words when talking about such crimes and pointing out how these criminals are coddled compared to others.

The Chicago Seven kept twelve lawyers busy in the Justice Department. I've yet to hear one of Attorney General Mitchell's lawyers concerning himself with the Detroit Four. GM and Ford are criminals. This is serious enough to hand over to Vice President Agnew for action—but before he becomes interested we'll have to find polluters who wear beards and sandals[2] (McCorry, 1972: 306).

As is often the case, the intellectual community reflects the concerns of the larger society; therefore, criminologists have increasingly turned their attention to white-collar and corporate crime since the 1960s. Such book titles as *Crime at the Top: Deviance in Business and the Professions* (Johnson and Douglas, 1978), *Government Lawlessness in America* (Becker and Murray, 1971), *Illegal but Not Criminal: Business Crime in America* (Conklin, 1977), *White Collar Crime: Offenses in Business, Politics, and the Professions* (Geis and Meier, 1977), *Corporate and Governmental Deviance: Problems of Organizational Behavior in Contemporary Society* (Ermann and Lundman, 1978), *Corporate Crime in Canada* (Goff and Reasons, 1978), *Crimes of the Powerful* (Pearce, 1976), *White Collar Crime: Theory and Research* (Geis and Stotland, 1980), and *Illegal Corporate Behavior* (Clinard, 1979) give evidence to the growing concern with these offenses among academics. There have also been a number of national and international conferences on the topic, and local and national law-enforcement agencies in both Canada and the United States have established special units to investigate such offenses, while specialized prosecutional units have been formed to deal with these cases (Geis and Meier, 1977). The Sixth United Nations Congress on the Prevention of Crime and the Treatment of Offenders, held in Caracas, Venezuela, during August–September 1980, turned its attention for the first time to this subject, with one of its five major topics being *Crime and the Abuse of Power: Offenses and Offenders Beyond the Reach of the Law.*

As is evident from the preceding book titles, students of upperworld crime have different emphases, some focusing upon white-collar criminals and others upon organizational offenders.

FROM WHITE-COLLAR TO ORGANIZATIONAL STRUCTURE

Students of crime have traditionally viewed upperworld crime (or crime at the top) as white-collar crime—that is, crime committed by a person in a position of trust for his or her personal gain.[3] Therefore, emphasis has been placed upon individuals and their needs, goals, attitudes, and behavior. Theoretically and methodologically, research has largely been directed toward describing and explaining why persons in certain positions of trust violate the law (Geis and Meier, 1977). This individualistic and largely social-psychological approach has caused us to neglect the ever-increasing significance of organizations upon our daily lives. For example, it fails to adequately consider the physical harms that are a consequence of organizational offenses and does not deal with the special characteristics of illegal behavior in organizational settings. According to Schrager and Short (1978: 407–419): "Organizational crimes are illegal acts of omission or commission of an individual or a group of individuals in a legitimate formal organization in accordance with the operative goals of the organization, which have serious physical or economic impact on employees, consumers or the general public."

By making the distinction between white-collar and organizational crimes, we are recognizing the daily impact private and public organizations have upon our lives as workers, consumers, and members of the general public.[4] Therefore, the behavior of individuals is placed within the context of the organization. For example, while an employee who embezzles from the employer is guilty of a white-collar offense, the same employee may be involved in price fixing or misleading advertising as part of the policies, practices, and/or procedures of the organization. In the latter offenses, the white-collar offender is carrying out organizational goals. Such a distinction forces one to look at organizational changes and control as a means of redressing harms rather than solely individual sanction. For example, punishing a police officer for illegal entry or illegal mail opening may not alone remedy the practice if the organizational goals and practices of the police reinforce such behavior.

One student of organizations, Edward Gross (1980) argues that we must understand the emergence of corporate persons, show how biological persons were separated from corporate persons, and show how biological persons established the corporate environment with maximum freedom. He concludes:

> Crime is hence seen as an organizational contingency, with its own set of calculable costs, reflecting either a breakdown in the environment or a minimal set of "frictional" costs. We shall conclude by claiming that the network of corporate actors forms a *criminaloid conspiracy* (a conspiracy to control the environment), which has tendencies to result in crime. Thus, biological

persons do not, for the most part, seek to commit crimes (they prefer not to commit them), but come to see crime as occasionally inevitable in the search for larger goals. (Gross, 1980: 53). [Emphasis in the original.]

While there is evidence suggesting that legal sanctions may act as a deterrent to organizational crime (Hopkins, 1980), many students of crime have assumed that the public was not that concerned with such lawbreaking. However, organizational crimes are viewed as more serious by the public than criminologists have acknowledged. Schrager and Short (1980) found that crimes with the same type of impact were rated by respondents in a similar fashion whether they were common crimes or organizational crimes. Thus, when organizational crimes result in injury and death, they are viewed similarly to assault and homicide, while property destruction and theft do not receive as severe a condemnation. Traditionally, white-collar offenses have been viewed as economically harmful but not physically destructive. This has led observers of crime to suggest it is less important.

> I realize that muggers take much less from us than do corporate, syndicate and white collar criminals. I have little doubt that the average executive swindles more on his taxes and expense account than the average addict steals in a typical year. Moreover, I am well aware that concentrating on street crime provides yet another opportunity for picking on the poor, a campaign I have no wish to assist. It is a scandal that a bank embezzler gets six months while a hold-up man is hit with five years. Yet it is not entirely their disparate backgrounds that produce this discrimination.

> A face to face threat of bodily harm or possibly violent death is so terrifying to most people that the $20 or so stolen in a typical mugging must be multiplied many times if comparisons with other offenses are to be made. I have a hunch that a majority of city dwellers would accept a bargain under which if they would not be mugged this year they would be willing to allow white collar crime to take an extra ten percent of their incomes. Of course we are annoyed by corporate thievery that drives up prices, but the kind of dread included by thuggery has no dollar equivalent, or if it does, an extremely high one (Hacker, 1973: 9).

But while there is obvious physical danger and harm from some "street crimes," the belief that "suite crimes" are not violent is false.

Corporate crime kills and maims. It has been estimated, for example, that each year 200,000 to 500,000 workers are needlessly exposed to toxic agents such as radioactive materials and poisonous chemicals because of corporate failure to obey safety laws. And many of the 2.5 million temporary and 250,000 permanent worker disabilities from industrial accidents each year are the result of managerial acts that represent culpable failure to adhere to established standards (Geis, 1974: 246–247).

ORGANIZATIONAL CRIMES

As the theoretical distinction between white-collar and organizational crime is increasingly being made (Gross, 1978, 1980), varying types of organizational offenses have been noted. Schrager and Short (1978) identify three types of victims of organizational behavior based upon their relationship to the production of goods and services: (1) employees, (2) consumers, and (3) the general public. I have divided organizational offenses on the basis of type of crime into three categories: (1) economic crimes, (2) human rights crimes, and (3) violent personal injury crimes (Reasons, 1980). Combining both the aspects of the victim and the nature of the offense provides a conceptual typology for categorizing organizational crimes for further research (see Table 6.1).[5]

The following discussion will review the scope and nature of organizational crime in North America (the United States and Canada).

ECONOMIC CRIMES

What often comes to one's mind when corporate crime is mentioned are such things as misleading advertising, price fixing, bribery, and other types of economic offenses. In one of the few studies in this area in Canada, the six-month period from October 1974 to March 1975 was analyzed to determine the number of convictions and penalties under the Food and Drug Act, Hazardous Products Act, Weights and Measures Act, and Textile Labelling Act (Snider, 1978). Forty-one individuals or firms were convicted of fifty-nine charges, with an average fine of $442.50 per person or firm under the Food and Drug Act, with only one imprisoned. Under the Weights and Measures Act, eight firms or individuals were convicted on a total of eighteen charges, and $1,050 in fines were assessed, with no imprisonment. Finally, no prosecutions were

Table 6.1.   Organizational Crimes: A Typology.

Victim	Nature of Offense		
	ECONOMIC	HUMAN RIGHTS	VIOLENT
Employee	Failing to remit payroll deductions; pension fund abuse; violating minimum wage laws and other labor laws.	Restrictions on political activity, dress, and demeanor; union activity; public disclosure (e.g., Ellsberg and Pentagon Papers).	Deaths and injuries in workplace; industrial disease (e.g., from exposure to asbestos).
Consumer	Price fixing; monopolization; false advertising.	Misuse of credit information; restrictions on credit based on political, sexual, racial, and class bias.	Poor inspection, unsafe products (e.g., Ford Pinto, thalidomide).
Public	Bribery; misuse of public funds; cost overruns; oil spills.	Illegal surveillance; wiretaps; abuse of power by police, CIA, FBI, RCMP, and military (e.g., Watergate).	Police homicides; hazardous wastes; air and water pollutions; nuclear energy (e.g., Three Mile Island).

completed during this period under the Hazardous Products or Textile Labelling Acts.

The Combines Investigation Act, passed in 1889, is the key piece of legislation directed at corporations in Canada. Its purpose is largely to prohibit unfair marketing practices in the Canadian economy, including illegal monopolies, mergers, advertising, and other unfair practices. Between 1889 and 1972, there were 145 reports completed and 125 published by combines enforcers. Although there are provisions for up to two years incarceration, no one was put in jail during this period. Most of the prosecutions have been against smaller, less powerful corporations, with penalties being fines or orders of prohibition (Goff and Reasons, 1976, 1978).

In recent years, misleading advertising has largely occupied the enforcement staff, while price fixing, mergers, and monopolies have largely been neglected. However, these latter actions are potentially the most economically harmful. For example, it has been estimated that lost output due to monopolies and shared monopolies runs in the billions for the United States and Canada.

A U.S. study concludes that the overall cost of monopoly and shared monopoly in terms of lost production is somewhere between $48 billion and $60 billion annually. In Canada, lost output due to the same cause would be in the order of $4.5 to $6 billion dollars. The lost tax revenues alone from this wealth would go a long way towards ending poverty and pollution. The redistribution of income from monopoly profits that transfers income from consumers to shareholders is estimated at $2.3 billion annually in the U.S. and $2 to $3 billion in Canada. Monopolistic firms thus contribute to inequality, inflation and unemployment. Unemployment results since monopolies, as noted, significantly reduce output which in turn reduces the number of workers who would otherwise be producing (Gonick, 1975: 22).

Concentration and monopolization are often the consequences of mergers. Aggregate concentration (the percentage of economic activity accounted for by the largest firms in Canada) decreased from 1923 to 1975, while industrial concentration (the fraction of total activity in a given industry attributable to a fixed number of the largest corporations in that industry) increased in Canadian manufacturing industries from 1948 to 1972. Both aggregate and industrial concentration is higher in Canada than in the United States (Report of the Royal Commission, 1978). Prior to 1960, no mergers were successfully prosecuted by the Canadian government, while of the 3,572 mergers occurring between 1960 and 1972, nine were prosecuted and three convicted; the penalties assessed were two Orders of Prohibition and one fine of $40,000. Thus, since 1923, when mergers came under the auspices of the Combines Investigation Act, only 0.003 percent of the total number of mergers have been charged, resulting in 0.0005 percent of the mergers being convicted (Reasons and Goff, 1980). A recent price-fixing case resulted in a fine of $150,000 being levied against Levi Strauss for eight counts of price fixing. Although the largest fine assessed in such a case, the company made a net profit of $3.25 million in 1974 and $1.8 million in 1975, two of the years during which it fixed prices (Johnson and Douglas, 1978).

Research concerning economic crimes is more prevalent in the United States than in Canada. McCormick (1977) reviewed data on the Sherman Antitrust Act, and found that of 1,551 antitrust prosecutions instituted in the United States from 1890 to 1969, only 45 percent were criminal cases, although the laws are essentially criminal violations. Of the 536 cases resulting in some type of criminal conviction, only 26 (4.9 percent) led to actual serving of a prison sentence. The first eleven imprisonments involved union and labor defendants, while it was not until the Electrical Conspiracy case of 1961 that businessmen were imprisoned for price fixing and monopolization. It would appear that such competition laws in capitalist countries are not vigorously enforced (Reasons and Goff, 1980).

In the most recent and comprehensive analysis of corporate crime in the United States, Marshall B. Clinard (1979) and his associates empirically investigated 582 of the largest publicly owned corporations in the United States, gathering data on all enforcement actions against these corporations during 1975 and 1976. Clinard noted:

> Before one considers any findings from a study of corporate violations it is essential that one recognize the significance of the small frequencies of corporate cases and why they must be evaluated differently from statistics on ordinary crimes such as assault, larceny, or burglary. A single case of corporate law violation may involve millions and even billions of dollars of losses. . . . For example, in one case, the electrical price-fixing conspiracy of the 1960s, losses amounted to over $2 billion, a sum far greater than the total losses from the 3 million burglaries in any given year. At the same time, the average loss from a larceny theft is $165 and from a burglary $422, and the persons who commit these offenses may receive sentences of as much as five to ten years, or even longer. For the crimes committed by the large corporations the sole punishment often consists of warnings, consent orders, or comparatively small fines. (1979: xix)

Their findings were that more than 60 percent of these corporations had at least one enforcement action initiated against them during this period. More than three-fourths of all actions were in the manufacturing, environmental, and labor areas of violation, with large corporations being more criminal than smaller ones. More specifically, they had over 70 percent of the actions while making up less than one-half the corporations. The motor vehicle, drug, and oil-refining industries accounted for almost one-half of all violations, with 40 percent of them being serious or moderate in nature. Warnings and fines were the most prevalent sanctions, with 80 percent of the fines beng $5,000 or less. There were 56 executives convicted federally, with 62.5 percent receiving probations, 21.4 percent obtaining suspended sentences, and 28.6 percent going to jail. The sixteen officers were sent to jail for a total of 597 days, or 37.1 days per executive, with many having their sentences suspended after a few days of incarceration. Needless to say, such a record of combating crime would not do for "common crimes."

In Canada, there have been a number of recent revelations suggesting bribery and political kickbacks (Mathias, 1977; Urquhart, 1976; Conklin, 1978). In June 1979, five prominent businessmen were given two to five years in jail for their part in defrauding public agencies of more than $4.3 million between 1967 and 1976 through the rigging of bids on dredging contracts (Filiatreau, 1977). However, little systematic study has been conducted, with investigative journalists leading the way. More recent United States cases include that of former Vice President Agnew, who pleaded no contest to an income tax charge and numerous corporations admitting to various bribes overseas. Some of the larger bribes are as follows:

- Ashland Oil Inc. admits paying more than $300,000 to foreign officials, including $150,000 to President Albert Bernard Bongo of Gabon to retain mineral and refining rights.
- Burroughs Corp. admits that $1.5 million in corporate funds may have been used in improper payments to foreign officials.
- Exxon Corp. admits paying $740,000 to government officials and others in three countries. Admits its Italian subsidiary made $27 million in secret but legal contributions to seven Italian political parties.
- Gulf Oil Corp. admits paying $4 million to South Korea's ruling political party. Admits giving $460,000 to Bolivian officials—including a $110,000 helicopter to the late President Rene Barrientos Orutno—for oil rights.
- Lockheed Aircraft Corp. admits giving $202 million in commissions, payoffs, and bribes to foreign agents and government officials in the Netherlands, Italy, Japan, Turkey, and other countries. Admits that $22 million of this sum went for outright bribes.
- McDonnell Douglas Corp. admits paying $2.5 million in commissions and consultant fees between 1970 and 1975 to foreign government officials.
- Merck & Co., Inc. admits giving $3 million, largely in "commission-type payments," to employees of 36 foreign governments between 1968 and 1975.
- Northrop Corp. admits in part SEC charges that it paid $30 million in commissions and bribes to government officials

and agents in Holland, Iran, France, West Germany, Saudi Arabia, Brazil, Malaysia, and Taiwan.

- G. D. Searle & Co. admits paying $1.3 million to foreign governmental employees from 1973 to 1975 to "obtain sales of products or services."
- United Brands Co. admits paying $1,250,000 bribe to Honduran officials for a reduction in the banana export tax. Admits paying $750,000 to European officials. (Investigators say the payment was made to head off proposed Italian restrictions on banana imports.)

While corporate political contributions are legal in Canada, some argue that it is a practice in need of criminalizing (Urquhart, 1978; Reasons, 1980).[6] Also, the use of bribes by corporations has increasingly come under scrutiny, with the above-noted revelation that many United States multinational corporations are involved in bribing foreign customers and government officials.

In a review of corporate lawlessness, *Fortune* (Ross, 1980) found that of 1,043 major corporations , 117 (11 percent) had been involved in at least one major delinquency. Although the study excluded foreign bribes and kickbacks, the traditional crimes of bribery, criminal fraud, illegal political contributions, tax evasion, and criminal antitrust violations were frequent. The list of criminals included such familiar names as American Airlines, Bethlehem Steel, Carnation, DuPont, Firestone, Greyhound, Gulf & Western, 3M, Phillips Petroleum, Joseph E. Seagram, Jos. Schlitz Brewing, and Weyerhaeuser. Why are they criminal? Stress, time, the profit motive, and, ultimately, because of the lack of stigma and vigorous enforcement. As a celebrated corporate defense counsel states: "These business crimes are perceived by individual actors as victimless. We all grew up in an environment in which we learned that thou shalt not murder, rape, rob, probably not pay off a public official—but not that it was a crime to fix prices" (Ross, 1980: 58).

HUMAN RIGHTS CRIMES

In a democratic society, a fundamental right of the citizenry should be the right to know. Access to information upon which the government is making decisions and policies is essential to a government for the people. In Canada there is very little access to information that may be vital to citizens individually or collectively. In 1971 former federal Solicitor General Jean-Pierre Goyer circulated among five of his fellow Cabinet members a list of some twenty-five Canadians who were believed to be "subversives." It contained mainly civil servants and university professors thought to be organizing for the overthrow of the government. Subsequent blacklists were revealed, although they were denied by the Cabinet. Secret files on politicians, social activists, and others have been kept by the government. The Solicitor General's Department, R.C.M.P. Security Branch, and the Canadian Armed Forces keep files on political groups, business organizations, and individuals they regard as a threat to national security.[6] While such activities are largely legal, it is arguable that they should be prohibited by law in a democratic society.

The United States Congress passed the Freedom of Information Act in 1966 to increase public disclosure of government information. However, it was largely ineffective, because of bureaucratic discretion, delay, and cost, until amended in 1974. Subsequent to the 1974 amendments, thousands of requests have been made and numerous illegal acts by the government have been exposed, including CIA, FBI, and Department of Defense spying and disruption of domestic political groups (Prewitt and Verba, 1979). For example, a Freedom of Information Act lawsuit uncovered extensive spying and other illegal activities by the CIA against the late Dr. Martin Luther King, Jr.

The police in a democratic society should be subject to the rule of law and to control by the citizenry and their representatives. Within the last few years there have been increasing revelations concerning illegal and questionable activities of the Royal Canadian Mounted Police, including illegal wiretaps, kidnapping, using agents provocateurs, illegal mail opening, burglary, theft, destruction of property, and surveillance of suspected political activists in universities, unions, and native organizations, among others (Benedict, 1979; Mann and Lee, 1979). Throughout its history, the R.C.M.P. has conducted surveillance of political and social activists, particularly among labor unions (Brown and Brown, 1973). A Royal Commission (the McDonald Commission) was established to investigate these allegations, and its report, including recommendations, was released in the summer of 1980.[7] A United States Senate Select Committee on Intelligence Activities disclosed that the CIA illegally opened 215,000 letters in one of four mail intrusion projects and conducted domestic surveillance and prepared dossiers on

United States citizens. All of these activities were illegal. It discovered that the National Security Agency scanned all overseas telephone calls and cables between 1967 and 1973 in order to control 1,680 citizens involved in political dissent or suspected of being involved in narcotics or potential threats to the President. The FBI publicly acknowledges committing 238 burglaries against domestic political activists, opening mail illegally, and harassing people belonging to certain organizations. The Internal Revenue Service established dossiers on 8,585 political activists and 2,873 political organizations, while military intelligence spied on thousands of dissidents between 1967 and 1970, preparing dossiers on many citizens (Quinney, 1979; Report of the Senate, 1978; Commission on CIA Activities, 1978).

Probably one of the most well-known crimes of this century is Watergate. Perpetrated largely from the office of the President of the United States, it entailed such offenses as obstructing justice, illegal wiretaps, burglaries, misuse of public funds, income tax fraud, and illegal surveillance and harassment of political dissidents and opponents (Douglas, 1977; Wise, 1973; Eitzen, 1980). Due to these crimes, President Nixon resigned, Vice President Agnew was convicted, and several other political figures were convicted and sentenced to prison.

Criminologists are just beginning to inquire into the crimes committed by public officials. However, as one recent text observes:

> The list of crimes committed by public officials is a long one and includes the dismissal of persons from their jobs for revealing governmental corruption; discriminatory prosecution on the basis of political opinions; the manufacturing of evidence, including the use of perjured testimony; unlawful sentencing; the premeditated and unlawful repression of legal dissent; entrapment; illegal wiretapping; illegal treatment of prisoners; illegal denial of the right to vote; illegal awards of state and federal contracts; bribery to influence the political process; unlawful use of force by the police; and military war crimes (Sykes, 1978: 221).

The potential for abuse of civil rights and personal freedom is also evident in the increasing use of electronic eavesdropping. It appears that the Canadian Protection of Privacy Act introduced in 1974 is actually an erosion of the right of privacy (Title, 1978; Burns, 1975–1976). Unlike some other countries, evidence gained from illegal wiretaps may be admissible in court, and there is inadequate external review of the granting of legal wiretaps. Furthermore, the justification for legal wiretaps has largely been in terms of combating organized crime, although the evidence does not confirm its worth in this area. In the United States, a study by the General Accounting Office estimated that only 1.3 percent of some 17,528 FBI domestic intelligence investigations in 1974 resulted in prosecution and conviction (Report of the Senate, 1978).

Finally, some criminologists and social critics are arguing for the criminalization of behaviors that have obvious harm. Therefore, there are "victims without crimes" which need to be addressed (Swendinger and Swendinger, 1970, 1977). Individual and institutional discrimination on the basis of sex, age, race, ethnicity, sexual orientation, or class position is usually dealt with by civil, not criminal, laws. It is arguable that such practices and behavior strike at the very core of democratic egalitarian values and thus should receive the full attention of the criminal laws (MacKay, 1978; Reiman, 1979). For example, the history of racism in North America and its harmful effects on racial minorities are quite evident today (Blauner, 1972; Hughes and Kallen, 1974; Hill, 1978).

Apart from legal discrimination, there was both legally proscribed and/or condoned violence against racial minorities. This violence against minorities did not receive the attention of the criminal law, but the actions were surely criminal in moral terms (Graham and Gurr, 1969). Blacks were murdered at an alarming rate in North America by lynching, an illegal form of execution. Between 1882 and 1962, a total of 4,736 Americans were lynched, with 73 percent being black. Furthermore, approximately two-thirds of Native Americans were exterminated in the "winning" of the West (Reasons and Perdue, 1981). Federal, state, and local social control organizations contributed to this slaughter (Mouledoux, 1967; Pinkney, 1972). This brings us to the final category of crimes of violence.

VIOLENT PERSONAL INJURY CRIMES[8]

While there is obvious physical danger and harm from some "street crimes" such as murder and assault, the belief that organizational crimes are not violent is false. For example, the Ford Motor Company has lost several civil suits and was under indictment in Indiana for reckless homicide and criminal recklessness concerning the Pinto's fuel tanks. It was the first time an American corporation had been criminally prosecuted in a product-liability case. After eight weeks of testimony and twenty-five hours of jury deliberation, Ford was found not guilty on three counts of reckless homicide. While the maximum penalty was only $30,000, Ford officials feared that a finding of guilty would bring a flood of crime suits which would greatly cost the company. More specifically, it has been revealed in court that the representatives of this organization calculated that the costs of changing an unsafe gas tank were nearly three times the expected costs of suits arising due to deaths and injuries (Jacobson and Barnes, 1978; Globe and Mail, 1978). Table 6.2 is based upon a Ford internal memo of 1972, which calculated the *benefits* of not making changes to their Pinto gas tank compared to the costs of making such changes. It was obviously cheaper to continue to build an unsafe automobile. Thus, the policies and practices of the organization patently put profit over the saving of lives of consumers.[9] More recently, the National Highway Safety Administration has estimated that a defect in Ford's automatic transmission has caused 60 deaths, 1,100 injuries, and 3,700 accidents. Most of the deaths could have been avoided by a design improvement costing about 3¢ per car. While Ford knew of the problem for at least ten years, it rejected effective design improvements (Branan, 1980). The Center for Auto Safety claims there have been 128 deaths as a result of the defect, and Ford has 270 lawsuits pending against it, already losing a $4.4 million suit in April 1980. Internal documents revealed in that suit show that as early as 1971 Ford was warned of the defect by its principal engineer of the Chassis Safety Systems Department, but failed to act. It faces a massive recall of automobiles ("Massive Recall," 1980). Such a track record raises doubt about "Ford Has a Better Idea." Another example is the 1976 fire in Hamilton in the Wentworth Arms Hotel, which killed six people. Subsequent investigations found thirty safety violations, including the hotel procedure of turning off fire alarm bells at night to prevent false alarms ("30 Safety," 1978). Approximately twenty million serious injuries occur in the United States annually, permanently disabling 110,000 and killing 30,000 (Schrager and Short, 1978). An internationally known student of white-collar crimes states that "commercial fraud kills more people than are murdered by acts that come to be listed as criminal homicide in the Uniform Crime Reports" (Geis, 1975: 93). For example, aircraft manufacturers and drug companies, among others, have falsified test results in marketing unsafe products (McCaghy, 1976). Cosmetics, oral contraceptives, synthetic hormones, microwave ovens, children's sleepwear, pesticides, cleaning solutions and solvents, and X rays,

Table 6.2.   Profit over Life.

Benefits	Savings: 180 burn deaths, 180 serious burn injuries, 2,100 burned vehicles
	Unit cost: $200,000 per death, $67,000 per injury, $700 per vehicle
	Total benefit: 180 × (200,000) + 180 × (67,000) + 2,100 ($700) = 49.5 million
Costs	Sales: 11 million cars, 1.5 million light trucks
	Unit cost: $11 per car, $11 per truck
	Total cost: $11,000,000 × ($11) + 1,500,000 × ($11) = $137 million

SOURCE: The Sunday Times, February 12, 1978, p. 1.

among numerous other consumer goods, have been found to be unsafe and poorly regulated and/or marketed (Environmental Defense Fund, 1980). The number of deaths annually occurring from improper emergency care is twice that for homicide, while unneeded operations cost an estimated $5 billion a year and 16,000 lives (Reiman, 1979). Whether it be in manufactured products, services, or accommodations, violence against the consumer may be the result of an organization's policies and practices.

The general public has been subjected to a variety of physical harms, principally through pollution, hazardous substances, and maintenance of unsafe structures. For example, a dam collapsed at Buffalo Creek, West Virginia, killing scores of people and destroying the fabric of a community. While the "disaster" was a result of a company knowingly maintaining an illegal dam, a legal case is difficult to make given the problems of proving causation, foreseeability, and intent. There are innumerable substances that are illegally emitted into the air and potentially hazardous, if not lethal (Environmental Defense Fund, 1980). Methylmercury is a dangerous by-product of industrial pollution which results in cerebral and visual pathway damage (Pierce, 1972). For example, mercury poisoning from the Dryden Chemical plant in northwestern Ontario is evident in the native population (Singer and Rodgers, 1975). Arsenic poisoning of the general population of Yellowknife, Northwest Territories, is largely the consequence of two gold-mining operations (Tataryn, 1979). Many of these injuries involve illegal discharge of chemicals into the environment, such as the carbon tetrachloride spills and the contamination of the Louisville, Kentucky, sewer system (Filiatreau, 1977). The military sprayed more than ten million gallons of Agent Orange not only on the "enemy" in Vietnam, but also on its own soldiers. Containing dioxin, Agent

Orange is "one of the world's deadliest chemicals." In addition, the United States Army sprayed Winnipeg, Manitoba, Canada, some thirty-six times in 1953 as part of a chemical warfare experiment. Although the substance might have been dangerous to babies, elderly, the ill, or asthmatic persons, after twenty-seven years there is no real legal recourse. Ralph Nader states that "much more is lost in money and health through pollution than crimes of violence, yet only the latter is defined officially as violence" (Eitzen, 1980: 11–12). Current laws have minimal effect upon environmental pollution because it pays to violate the law.

The general public living in the vicinity of certain industries is assaulted daily. A National Cancer Institute study found the incidence of lung cancer above the national average in all thirty-six United States counties with smelters (Reiman, 1979). And, as the effects of Three Mile Island unfold, we will become aware of yet another potential crime against the public.

Possibly some of the largest crimes against the general public are crimes of war. The murder and ill-treatment of civilians and prisoners of war, the destruction of nonmilitary targets, and the illegal use of chemical warfare in Southeast Asia dwarf in magnitude the "garden variety" crimes of violence we are daily warned about (Quinney, 1979). Reiman (1979: 64) concludes that: "The most dangerous American crime ring since the days of Al Capone is the United States government. The Vietnam War, based on a history of deception predating even the lies we were told about the so-called Gulf of Tonkin incident, stands without peer in recent years in the annals of unnecessary carnage wrought by American hands."

Workers are daily assaulted on the job by unsafe working conditions and unhealthy chemicals (Reasons, Ross, and Paterson, 1981). The number of annual deaths from industrial disease is at least one hundred thousand in the United States, while the number in Canada is undoubtedly in the thousands (Tataryn, 1979). Many of these deaths are preventable through control of the environmental level of dangerous substances.

Most people think of violence as something bad and illegal that is perpetrated by a person or persons against another person or persons. Therefore, when mace is sprayed in our faces it is violence, while when we are forced to inhale asbestos dust at work, it is uncomfortable, but not violent. To violate is to disregard, fail to comply with, or act against the dictates or requirements of such things as an oath, treaty, law, terms, or conscience. While the inhalation of asbestos dust may not be unlawful, it *violates* the health of the worker.

Corporations have knowingly exposed their workers to lethal and injurious levels of hazardous materials. For example, the United States Occupational Safety and Health Administration (OSHA) imposed one of its heaviest fines against the nation's largest lead producer, N. L. Industries. They had knowingly allowed workers to be exposed to lead levels that exceeded permissible levels by more than a hundred times (Glasbeek and Rowland, 1979). Tataryn's 1979 book, *Dying for a Living: The Politics of Industrial Death*, documents the massive cover-up by the asbestos industry of its knowledge since the 1930s of the hazardous effects of asbestos. While this may be the subject of civil suits, criminal action is not available (although premeditated exposure to violent substances occurred).

Documents released in product liability suits against the asbestos industry in the United States show that a conscious, rational, well-organized cover-up of the ill-health effects of asbestos was engineered by representatives of Johns-Manville Corp., Raybestos-Manhattan Inc., and other asbestos companies. The Subcommittee on Crime of the Committee on the Judiciary, United States House of Representatives, notes in its report on Corporate Crime (1980: 24):

> South Carolina Circuit Court Judge James Price (who reviewed the material), is quoted as saying "it shows a pattern of denial and disease and attempts at suppression of information" so persuasive that he ordered a new trial for the family of a dead insulation worker whose earlier claim had been dismissed. Judge Price noted that correspondence further reflects a conscious effort by the industry in the 1930's to downplay, or arguably suppress the dissemination of information to employees and the public for fear of promotion of lawsuits. Judge Price also noted compensation disease claims filed by asbestos insulation workers against several companies—which quietly settled them—including eleven asbestosis cases settled out of court by Johns-Manville in 1933, all predating the time (1964) when these companies claim they first recognized the hazard to insulators.

Deaths and job injuries on the worksite are usually thought of as "accidents." However, it has been estimated that approximately 30 percent of job injuries in the United States are due to illegal working conditions, while another 24 percent are due to legal but unsafe conditions (Ashford, 1976). The maintenance of unsafe conditions is rational since the probability of detection is low and the penalties are relatively miniscule. For example, in the first three years of OSHA's existence, 95 percent of all covered employers were not inspected at all, and in 1973, 98 percent of the violations cited by inspectors were classified as nonserious, with an average penalty of $18.00 (Glasbeek and Rowland, 1979).

Apart from the moral argument to criminalize these acts which entail "victims without crimes," it is arguable that current criminal laws may be relevant. Glasbeek and Rowland (1979) make a case for the application of criminal negligence, duties of master to servant, assault, criminal breach of contract, traps likely to cause bodily harm, causing mischief, common nuisance, conspiracy, and murder from the Canadian Federal Criminal Code to violations of health and safety laws.[10]

SUMMARY

Most of the research in the area of organizational crimes has been atheoretical and purely descriptive. This is in part because much of it is done by journalists and/or social critics for policy reasons and consciousness raising. As noted earlier in this chapter, many criminologists continue to study from a white-collar crime perspective, emphasizing the kinds of people who commit such offenses and the kinds of environments that produce them (Reasons, 1975). Those who emphasize the characteristics of the organization as significant for understanding such offenses have drawn from the more traditional organizational theory.

The development of a critical, radical, and Marxist criminology within the last decade (Quinney, 1979) has brought attention to the sociology of law and the state as significant in understanding crime generally, and crimes by the powerful specifically (Reasons and Rich, 1978). Pearce (1976) places corporate crime in the United States within the context of a Marxist analysis. In *Class, State and Crime* (1977) and *Criminology* (1979), Quinney develops a Marxist analysis of organizational crimes. The first book identifies crimes of control (e.g., police crimes), crimes of government (e.g., Watergate), and crimes of domination (e.g., price fixing, sexism, racism—Quinney, 1977), although there is little analysis of these categories. In his criminology text, Quinney (1979) elaborates upon crimes of the state and crimes of the economy. In their analysis of competition legislation, Goff and Reasons (1978) and Reasons and Goff (1980) apply a conflict theory of laws and crime. As the sociology of law develops and a political economy of crime emerges, increasing analysis will be made of organizational crime from a critical per-

spective. A truly sociological study of crimes of the powerful necessitates an understanding of the broader sociopolitical context
within which it occurs.

NOTES

[1]During the late nineteenth and early twentieth century, there was an increasingly
vociferous campaign against the power and corruption of large corporations (Geis
and Meier, 1977).
[2]The irony of Nader asking Mitchell and Agnew to invoke the law is evident in their
subsequent criminality as part of the "Watergate 500."
[3]Edelhertz (1970) establishes four classes of white-collar crime including (1) *personal crimes* committed by persons operating on an individual, ad hoc basis, for
personal gain in a nonbusiness context such as income tax violation, bankruptcy,
and welfare and unemployment fraud, (2) *abuses of trust*, which are crimes in the
course of one's occupation which violate one's duty and loyalty, such as embezzlement, petty larceny, and false travel claims, (3) *business crimes*, which are crimes
incidental to, and in furtherance of, business operations, but not the central purpose
of operations, such as antitrust violations and fraud in advertising, and (4) *con
games*, where crime is the central activity of business, such as medical and health
frauds, land frauds, home improvement schemes, and personal improvement
schemes. This orientation or that based on occupational categories (Quinney, 1964;
Ross, 1970) still are lacking in addressing the peculiar aspects of organizations.
[4]By using the more inclusive term of organizational crime, one includes not only
violations of the law by legally incorporated corporations that are in business for
profit reasons, but also public organizations that may commit crimes, such as the
police.
[5]Although the focus of this paper is organizational crimes, this, of course, does not
mean white-collar crime is insignificant. Approximately $40 billion was lost due to
business crime in 1979 in the United States, according to the American Mutual
Insurance Alliance and the National Retail Merchants Association. In comparing
four traditional "common crimes" (auto theft, robbery, burglary, and larceny) with
four major types of white-collar crimes (embezzlement, forgery, tax evasion, and
fraud), white-collar crimes are three times as costly as the common crimes (Eitzen,
1980). In Canada, business crimes cost companies and consumers more than $4
billion in 1977 (Davis, 1978a). Insurance companies estimate that 30 percent of
company liquidations in North America are the result of fraud, although only an
estimated 5 percent of the criminals are apprehended and brought before the courts
(Davis, 1978b). For a good overview of largely traditional white-collar offenses, see
Conklin (1977) and McCaghy (1976). It should be noted that both research and
public attention regarding white-collar and organizational crime is much more advanced in the United States than in Canada. Furthermore, some of the "crimes"
mentioned here may not, strictly speaking, be criminal in a legal sense. However,
having a penal sanction (fine and/or sentence) attached to them qualifies them for
such a classification. Since the powerful have enormous ability to define what is
civil and criminal law, such an approach is necessary. Finally, it is arguable that
there are "victims without crimes" which need criminalization. Thus, the student of
crime must recognize that there are harms that should be criminalized and the

state's definition should not necessarily limit one's analysis (see Schwendinger and Schwendinger, 1970, 1977).

[6]There are approximately 15,000 or so files or types of records held by government institutions at the federal level distributed among eighty-seven government departments and institutions, with at least twenty-two types of records beyond the public realm. There are seventy-two federal statutes prohibiting release of certain records. While the Canadian Human Rights Act of 1977 provides access to government records, there are twenty-two exemptions, such as national defense or security, information given by confidential sources, and matters that might reveal information on individuals other than those making an inquiry. Also, the Minister of Justice has wide discretion in determining the "public benefit" in weighing whether to release or not release information. The most controversial and potentially damaging information will likely remain withheld because the burden of proof is upon the citizen to show what is specifically desired and why, while the opposite should be the case in a democracy.

[7]Like Presidential Commissions, Royal Commissions serve a number of useful political functions for those in power, not the least of which is appeasing the public by doing something about the issue (Rist, 1973).

[8]Schrager and Short (1978) deal exclusively with organizational violence perpetrated against employees, consumers, and the general public. The following section elaborates upon their discussion.

[9]The Firestone Tire and Rubber Co. recently paid a $500,000 fine for knowingly failing to recall defective tires ("$500,000 Settles Defective Tire Suit," 1980). It is too early to measure the violence due to such defects.

[10]While these are taken specifically from Canadian criminal law, varying United States statutes of a similar nature may be relevant.

Part III

Social Control and Social Change

In certain respects social control and social change are contradictory processes: Social change may occur when people deviate from community expectations in ways eventually defined as acceptable by a substantial proportion of members who initially opposed the questionable behavior. Present-day male hair length and the types of people now riding motorcycles exemplify changes that got their start twenty to thirty years ago as minor forms of difference. Similar transformations are now under way in the more seriously regarded areas of sexual behavior and marijuana use.

Social control refers to our attempts to avert originally unacceptable behavior or, once started, to correct or treat it. Through correcting or treating deviance, we hope to return errant members of the community to their former status of good, conforming citizens.

But society faces an awkward paradox: The more effective its social control measures, the fewer its social changes. The changes being considered here are, of course, only those stemming from initially objectionable practices of a minority of individuals. Change can also come from acceptable—indeed, respectable—spheres of life, such as art, science, industry, and entertainment.

Despite the possibility that all, or a major segment, of society might ultimately benefit from acts initially defined as deviant, we have accumulated an impressive list of what Walter Gove (Chapter 7) calls "strategies of intervention." These are ways of halting or trying to halt what those in control see as the unrelenting advance of aberrant patterns of behavior. One way they do this, Gove points out, is to study the underlying causes of the offensive activity and try to apply what they have learned. Alternatively, because objectionable acts are defined as such by the public, some agents of control may simply try to redefine them as unobjectionable, or at least as less objectionable. Various forms of deterrence have also been used, the most common of these being imprisonment and fining. Other intervention strategies include preventive measures, rewarding nondeviant behavior, and treating previously established patterns of deviance. The latter may amount to little more than amelioration of its undesirable aspects, as in the use of methadone to treat heroin and morphine withdrawal symptoms. Though it may seem like the community has acquiesced to the problem, some individuals, if left alone or discreetly advised, will eventually abandon their deviance of their own accord. In this situation, intervention is minimal. Since they vary in effectiveness, several strategies are commonly used, as officials strive to control various types of difference.

Lucius Seneca observed nearly two thousand years ago that "there is no genius without some touch of madness." Thus, mental illness, as madness is now euphemistically called, is one form of deviance to be controlled that is particularly important in a discussion of control and change. A wide variety of human material and cultural inventions start out as the wild ideas of a person or group identified at the time as somehow unbalanced. Gove reviews the treatment of the mentally ill in the United States from the early nineteenth century asylums onward. As is true of deviance in general, mental illness is only partially controllable, and by control we mean the application of one or more of the strategies of intervention. It follows that social change emanating from deviant sources is bound to take place occasionally, whether the source is mental illness or some other aberration.

Sagarin and Kelly (Chapter 8) describe how North American deviants try to have their cake and eat it by attempting to persuade society to accept or at least tolerate their "curious" ways. These authors identify three forms of the collective, formal promotion of deviance that can, and occasionally do, lead to social change. Certain deviant groups, for example, actively recruit as they attempt to expand their numbers. Or they proselytize, which is recruitment with a stress on change of personal values, attitudes, and beliefs. Nudists, marijuana users, and religious and political deviants commonly proselytize in their own special manner. Other groups, such as prostitutes and homosexuals, promote their deviance by propagandizing for the acceptance of their kind, their way of life, and the ideology they use to justify their differentness. Sagarin and Kelly note, too, how commercial interests may foster a type of deviance because of its profit potential. Today's production and distribution of pornography is a conspicuous instance of this form.

Over the years these efforts at formal promotion have produced limited changes in, for example, the public's attitude toward gays and marijuana users. How long this new climate of opinion will last remains to be seen, however. It could be short-lived.

The proposition that deviance spawns social change is, under certain conditions, reversible. Formal social changes can sometimes lead to deviance (e.g., prohibition) or, if the deviance already exists, to its official recognition and hence its public exposure (e.g., the Marijuana Tax Act of 1937). Sagarin and Kelly explain how legislation can suddenly transform legal behavior into illegal behavior, an enactment that may be the original inspiration of politicians or their response to the campaign of a muckraker. They also note that governments may try to stir up support for themselves by intentionally directing community attention to particular deviant or marginal ethnic groups, thereby publicizing their undesirable qualities and establishing a receptive mood for restrictive legal measures. Local crackdowns against homosexuals have been known to be motivated by such aims (Tripp, 1975).

Some forms of the collective, formal promotion of deviance fall outside the social control-social change theme being discussed here. One of these, say Sagarin and Kelly, is the work of the *agent provocateur*, whose incitements are officially sanctioned because those in power want to discredit those who threaten their regime. In some respects, provocation is akin to entrapment. In the latter, government agents engage in a type of deviance in an attempt to catch *flagrante delicto* people suspected of such behavior. However, enduring change in community values or behavior patterns is seldom intended in these forms and usually none occurs.

Returning to our theme of social control and social change, it appears that society's very attempts to control through strategies of intervention can, at times, set in motion the first three processes of collective, formal promotion (i.e., recruitment, propagandizing, and commercialization). It is as if the deviants, in response to an attack on their cherished way of life, organize a counterattack. This reaction helps explain why some attempts at control meet with limited success at best. Had the intolerant segments of the community left well enough alone, the deviants in question might have been content to carry on their activities without further promotion of them. With their existence threatened from without, however, they quickly develop ways of protecting themselves, which involve taking their case to the public, where they hope eventually to generate sympathy for their cause and possibly even find new adherents.

Obviously, only the tolerable forms of deviance mentioned in the introduction to this book have sufficient potential for public sympathy to make it worth the deviants' efforts to appeal to the larger community. Intolerable forms, particularly predatory crime, are hardly promotable in the sense of the present discussion. Public opinion is strongly opposed to such acts as murder, rape, or theft. People engaging in them are very likely to fail in any attempt to promote their deviant interests, should they even dare try to do so. Generally, however, the social control–social change framework is as applicable to intolerable deviance as it is to the tolerable variety.

Understanding the relationship between social control and social change is vital to our broader understanding of the nature and causes of deviance. No explanation of this kind of human behavior can ignore these two processes, even though they might appear on the surface to be mere societal reactions to activities of which the community disapproves.

7 THE FORMAL RESHAPING OF DEVIANCE

WALTER R. GOVE

While a colleague and I were jointly teaching a course in deviant behavior, my colleague made a distinction between the "conventional wisdom approach" typically taken by society and the "scientific approach" taken by sociologists. He suggested that society typically responded to social problems by taking direct, unsophisticated action that did not get at the core of the problem and thus did not alleviate it. For example, to deal with crime, the conventional wisdom approach would focus on such things as more police, more severe punishment, and better street lighting and would ignore the factors that motivate a person to commit a crime. In contrast, my colleague pointed out, sociologists would focus on the underlying problem that causes the troublesome behavior. For example, in explaining crime, the sociologist would look at such variables as the degree to which legitimate opportunities were available or unavailable to the different segments of society. The sociologist's analysis would thus lead to an understanding of the underlying cause of the problem and presumably insights into how to alleviate (or eliminate) it.

My colleague's argument was that conventional wisdom dealt only with the symptoms of an underlying problem and that such an approach, at best, could only temporarily alleviate the symptoms, for it left the underlying problem untouched. The sociological approach, he believed, if applied effectively, would eliminate the underlying problem, which in turn would lead to the elimination of the symptomatic behavior. It is my belief, however, that this model is probably no more useful, and is perhaps not even *as* useful, as the "conventional wisdom approach" when it comes to actually dealing with deviant behavior. Sociologists have indeed made some progress in understanding some of the underlying causes of some forms of deviant behavior. But a partial understanding of the causes of a particular problem does not mean that one knows how to deal with that problem once it exists. As Reiss (1970) has noted, most sociological research has little bearing on social policy. In part this is because questions that are theoretically important are frequently irrelevant to questions of policy.

Perhaps we need, as Reiss has suggested, a policy science. Some of the parameters that would shape such a science have been indicated by Gouldner (1957). He argues that a policy science will be concerned with locating independent variables, which not only have a major impact on the dependent variables in question but which are also amenable to control. Many independent variables that are of interest to the theoretical scientist will be of little interest to the applied scientist because (1) there is no technology for manipulating the independent variable, (2) the values of society prohibit its manipulation, and/or (3) the cost of manipulating the independent variable far outweighs the potential gain. Thus, policy scientists are concerned with locating variables that they have the technology to manipulate, that they will be allowed to manipulate, and that they can economically manipulate. Gouldner also suggests that applied social scientists will tend to use a systems analysis, for this approach points to the interdependence of variables, sensitizing the investigator to indirect as well as direct ways of manipulating a dependent variable and puts the investigator on guard against unforeseen and undesirable consequences.

In this chapter I will analyze different strategies for dealing with deviant behavior. I will be particularly concerned with the degree to which the strategies focus on independent variables that are significantly related to the dependent variable in question and for which there is (at least potentially) a technology of manipulation that is socially and economically feasible. I will then look at changes in how the mentally ill have been treated by society over the past twenty-five years as a case that highlights the processes involved in the formal shaping of deviance. I will conclude by relating the different strategies for intervention discussed in the first section to the actual changes that have occurred in the reshaping of the phenomenon we call mental illness.

STRATEGIES FOR INTERVENTION

Focus on the Underlying Causes

Deviant behaviors have multiple causes. Some of the causes are perhaps best viewed as *underlying causes,* such as inequities in the social structure, and others are best viewed as *immediate causes,* such as the opportunity to commit a crime. Historically, sociological research and theory have focused on underlying causes. However, a concern with the presumed underlying cause of a problematic behavior frequently has little relevance for the development of an effective strategy for dealing with that behavior.

As a simple example, let us look at the problem of environmental pollution. The symptoms of pollution are obvious: poor visibility, smarting eyes, stinking rivers and lakes, and poisonous residues—in short, a nasty and unhealthy environment. The underlying cause is not so obvious. Is it technology, capitalism, human greed, short-sightedness, or something else? How one answers this question will depend, at least in part, on one's conceptions of man, of technology, and of the just society. We can expect disagreement on such issues. Nevertheless, we can agree that pollution is a problem and we have technologies that will allow us to start controlling it. Furthermore, we know how to go about expanding these technologies. We have the ability to contain pollution. Prolonged debates on the underlying causes would probably increase dissension in our society and might even slow down our efforts to control pollution.

A problem that has received considerably more attention by social scientists is that of the riots by blacks in our society. Most people would agree that these riots constitute a social problem, for they create chaos, destroy property, cause injuries, and frequently result in deaths. But what is the underlying cause of the riots? According to the National Advisory Commission on Civil Disorders (1968), the underlying cause is white racism. But is it? We have had white racism for a very long time and during most of this time we have not had riots. We also know that seriously oppressed groups rarely rebel. Furthermore, the riots of the late sixties occurred after the major aspects of *de jure* segregation had been successfully attacked, and during a time when many blacks were experiencing an improvement in their position in the areas of income, education, type of occupation, and quality of housing (Palmore and Whittington, 1970). Thus, it appears to be incorrect to say that the oppression of blacks is the cause of the riots; rather, oppression is probably better seen as a predisposing factor.

If oppression cannot, by itself, account for the riots, then what can? There are a wide number of possible contributing factors. To some degree the riots can probably be attributed to the improvements blacks were experiencing, for in general it would appear that groups that in the past have experienced severe oppression but that have recently experienced a noticeable improvement in their condition tend to be revolutionary (Davies, 1962). The reason for this would appear to be the development of rising expectations and a shift in reference group. According to this argument, the oppressed originally evaluate themselves and their situation by making a comparison with others in their group. Subsequently, as the ideological and structural barriers that maintained their oppressed status break down, they start to compare themselves to those in the dominant group and they find that they are (relatively) deprived. The empirical evidence does indicate that the riots by blacks in our society are associated with a move to the North and are most apt to occur in cities where the attainment of blacks surpasses that of blacks living elsewhere and in cities where the disadvantaged position of blacks is relatively small[1] (Spilerman, 1970).

Given the fact that the riots by blacks have multiple causes and that white racism is probably best seen as a predisposing factor, what can be done about the riots? According to the National Advisory Commission on Civil Disorders (1968), the strategy should be to eliminate white racism. However, even if white racism were the underlying cause of the riots, such a strategy would not, at least in the short run, be effective. Even under the best of conditions (an absence of discrimination, combined with preferential treatment), it would require one generation, and probably two, to eliminate the effects of past racism. Put simply, the elimination of racism is not, by itself, a realistic strategy for the avoidance of riots in the next few decades. Furthermore, if the National Advisory Commission on Civil Disorders had been correct in their assessment of the cause of the riots during the late 1960s, the riots should have continued throughout the 1970s, as the basic changes in society that the Commission argued were necessary to prevent the riots were not implemented.

This example suggests that the strategy of focusing on the underlying causes of a social problem does not necessarily lead to an effective policy regarding that problem; for other examples, the reader is referred to Etzioni (1968). There are three especially important difficulties with this strategy. First, we frequently have, at best, a very rudimentary understanding of the underlying causes of a particular form of deviant behavior. Second, even when we are fairly certain what the underlying causes are (which is rare), we typically do not have a technology that enables the policy-maker to manipulate these causes effectively. Third, for many forms of deviant behavior, this strategy would require major changes in the social structure. In most cases it is unlikely that such changes can be implemented, for they require a massive and sustained effort while at the same time challenging the authority of important and powerful segments of society, which are in a position to eliminate, co-opt, or curtail the program.

The "war on poverty" is an example of an attempt to implement such a strategy. In essence it was aimed at eliminating the poverty culture and changing the social institutions that maintained that culture. But the "war on poverty" is correctly viewed as a failure. One of the reasons it failed is that it did not have a technology for eliminating the poverty culture. Much of its effort at change focused around attempts to get the very poor involved in self-help organizations—and these attempts were typically unsuccessful. (For an example of one of these programs, see Gove and Costner, 1969; for a more general review, see Curtis and Zurcher, 1971.) Such a focus, of course, tended not to get at the factors, such as unemployment, which produce poverty, and one might argue that these programs attempted to manipulate the "wrong" variables. When a particular program did get to the point of challenging the established authorities, the typical result was an effective effort by these authorities to eliminate or co-opt the program.

The cycle that the "war on poverty" went through is probably typical for programs based on this strategy. A fairly massive expenditure of money (much of it spent unwisely because nobody knows how to spend it wisely) and then a reaction (because someone's toes are being stepped on and/or because of the waste of money), which either channels the program into something "safe" or eliminates it. Unfortunately, such a cycle is apt to further increase the dissatisfaction of those the program was designed to help. Furthermore, those aspects of the program that were successful (in a massive program, some usually will be) are apt to be ignored, lost in the general reaction to the waste and frustration involved in the effort.[2]

I am not arguing that an interventionist should never focus attention on the underlying causes of a particular problem but only that a strategy based on the direct manipulation of the underlying causal variable(s) is apt to have a fairly limited range of effectiveness. I would note, however, that there is at least one area where such a strategy will frequently produce results. Some inequities in the social structure (such as those associated with race and sex) are amenable to legal challenge. The techniques for implementing such a challenge are fairly straightforward and, if a suit is successful, it may have far-reaching consequences. It is worth noting that probably one of the most effective (and controversial) aspects of the war on poverty was the legal assistance provided the poor. As the blacks in our society have discovered, a strategy based on legal challenges of social inequities will not solve all the problems of a group that is discriminated against, but it can, at least, remove certain important impediments.

Societal Reaction or Labeling Approach

Recently many social scientists have focused on the process by which certain types of behaviors come to be defined by society as deviant and have pointed to the consequences for the individual of being treated as a deviant. Implicit in much of this analysis is the view that (many) behaviors persist simply because society defines and responds to the behaviors as if they were deviant.

By not accepting society's definition of what deviant behavior is, the labeling theorists raise a number of interesting questions. One of the most intriguing questions deals with the relationship between what society defines as a problem and what may "objectively" be called a problem. For example, we may ask, is mental illness merely a social role into which certain persons are channeled, or are persons who are mentally ill really disturbed? In general, the labeling theorists have argued that mental illness is created by the societal reaction to persons who happen to be labeled mentally ill (e.g., Scheff, 1966). Similar arguments are made for other forms of deviant behavior. However, in the case of mental illness, it has been shown that most persons who are labeled mentally ill voluntarily seek care and are in fact seriously disturbed, and that the labeling explanation is largely (although not entirely) incorrect. Thus, although the labeling theorists raise important questions, they typically do not answer them very well, in part because they ignore the reality of deviance. Among other things, this means that a strategy for dealing with deviant behavior that is based on labeling theory would lead to a lack of societal intervention, and many serious and sometimes painful problems would not be treated.

A strategy for dealing with deviant behavior that is based on the societal reaction approach would be to redefine the situation so that behavior formerly viewed as a problem is no longer so viewed. On the surface, this might seem a reasonable, easy solution, particularly for deviant behaviors that do not directly harm others (for a discussion of such behaviors, see Schur, 1965). However, such a solution is not easily implemented, generally because it has serious implications for the society or group involved. Let us look, for example, at the Amish, who have rigorous rules that set them apart as a "particular" people. One problem the Amish regularly face is that of members who are attracted to various aspects of the modern industrial society. If these members take up some of the modern ways, the Amish treat them as deviants, excluding them from Amish society. This, of course, is generally painful to all concerned. A facile solution would be to have the Amish change their rules and thus retain their straying members. Unfortunately, a real relaxation in the rules that make them a "particular" people would destroy their culture. The point, of course, is that rules play a major role in defining and maintaining a culture, and a change in these rules means a change in the culture, frequently a serious change.

There are some situations in which the best solution is probably to change the rules. Most social scientists would no doubt agree that the elimination of prohibition is an excellent example of such a case. However, we should remember that prohibition did have its positive aspects. For example, the temperance movement was associated with a sharp decline in the number of persons hospitalized for alcoholic psychosis (Landis and Page, 1938). Perhaps the most important lesson to be learned from looking at the temperance movement is that the issue was probably not so much that of alcohol consumption but that of what components of society were to be dominant (e.g., Gusfield, 1963). To a large degree, the debate over marijuana is also essentially a debate about which values (and thus which group) in our society will be dominant (e.g., Goode, 1969). Such debates are essentially political debates, and although social scientists may quite appropriately point out some of the consequences of categorizing certain behaviors as deviant, the resolution of such debates will largely depend on the political strength of the parties involved and to some extent on the ability of the dominant party to impose its will on the weaker party. It is interesting to note that as the use of marijuana has been largely disassociated with a counterculture, the move to decriminalize its use has become increasingly successful. In short, redefining the rules of behavior in a society is a political process involving a contest between groups, and it is not a strategy that can be readily implemented by a social "engineer" through the manipulation of certain causal variables.

Deterrence Model

One of the most common strategies for dealing with deviant behavior is the use of punishment. Until recently, in spite of its widespread use, this approach, particularly as it is used at the societal level, has received relatively little attention from social scientists. However, the evidence from learning theory strongly suggests that if the performance of a particular act is quickly and consistently followed by punishment, the act will be performed much less frequently. Learning theory also suggests that severity of punishment will be inversely related to frequency of occurrence. Deterrence theory is derived directly from the principle of learning (or operant) theory, which treats a person's actions as almost solely a consequence of the rewards of a particular act exceeding the costs (or vice versa). I would emphasize that although in practice the purpose of punishment may be primarily punitive, the focus of deterrence theory is on preventing persons from performing particular acts because they perceive the negative consequences as outweighing the potential gains. It should be noted that the use of such things as bright street lights and mirrors in a store, which increase the (perceived) likelihood of being caught and thus being punished for an act, is consistent with a deterrence approach.

Recent evidence dealing with legal violations (Chambliss, 1966; Gibbs, 1975; Geerken and Gove, 1977) is generally consistent with the deterrence model, although it should be noted that most of the studies suffer from methodological problems (Chiricos and Gordon, 1970; Gibbs, 1975). In general, the strategy of increasing the (perceived) likelihood that one would be caught and punished for committing an illegal act would seem to be both socially acceptable and feasible. However, it should be noted that we know relatively little about how deterrence actually operates in a society as complex as ours (see the discussion in Geerken and Gove, 1975). We might note two obvious difficulties. First, learning theory suggests that it is important that sanctions be both quickly and consistently applied. However, for most types of criminal behavior, negative sanctions are only infrequently and unsystematically applied, and it is difficult to see how this can be greatly changed without drastic modifications in the social structure. Furthermore, there is frequently a substantial time lag between the deviant act and punishment. In part this time lag is due to the courts being overburdened and poorly administered. A truly effective deterrence system probably requires that the legal process be made much more efficient and effective so that the connection between the commission of a crime and being punished is much more easily perceived. Second, a fairly typical response when society becomes especially concerned about a particular type of violation is to impose an extremely stiff punishment. However, under the condition of severe punishment for a minor violation, such as speeding or marijuana use, a common response of the authorities is to be very lenient; i.e., to ignore the violation or to change the official violation to a more minor offense (see Ross and Campbell, 1968; Geerken and Gove, 1975). In such a case, of course, the effect of the stiff penalty is to decrease the likelihood of punishment and thus an "unreasonably" stiff penalty could conceivably even lead to an increase in violations.

Some persons probably feel that the elimination of a certain form of undesirable behavior through negative sanctions will only mean that the underlying problem will surface somewhere else. This may sometimes be the case, but it certainly is not always so. For example, a large proportion of shoplifting is done by middle class housewives. In general, the items they shoplift are not essential to themselves or to their families, but are luxuries they cannot justify spending money on but still want. Middle class housewives, when caught shoplifting, become extremely embarrassed, and it would appear that it is possible to largely eliminate their shoplifting through close surveillance and the consistent application of (mild) negative sanctions.[3]

Strategy of Prevention

This strategy is based on the type of procedure used in preventive medicine. Here, instead of focusing on what is presumed to be the underlying cause, the focus shifts to identifying the weak link (i.e., one that can be manipulated) in a complex causal process and then effectively manipulating that link so that the problem never develops. For example, in dealing with disease, the focus might be on eradication of an insect, purification of the water supply, or the development of a vaccine. An example of this strategy in the area of social behavior is the effort to eliminate the availability of handguns through gun control legislation. Here the assumption is that most murders are committed in a fit of anger and that many murders would not be committed if a gun were not readily available. In this case, there is relatively little concern with what causes anger and frustration but a great deal of concern with minimizing the ease with which frustration can be translated into murder. A major difference between gun control legislation and most preventive medicine is that almost everyone reacts favorably to preventive medicine, while gun control legislation challenges a cherished value of a substantial segment of our society.

A special version of the prevention strategy might be called prevention through education. Here the belief is that if we can change the knowledge of a person, he or she will act in a different and more desirable fashion. The weak link, in this case, is assumed to be the person's ignorance. This is a strategy that is used in birth control programs, in driver education, and in programs aimed at the prevention of drug abuse. If members of the public initially desire to commit the act in question, it would seem that this strategy would be ineffectual unless the educator can present new evidence that is very convincing to the audience about the negative consequences of the act. In many, if not most, cases, this would appear to be a very difficult task. In contrast, if the audience wants to prevent a particular outcome, such as conception, but lacks a technology which the educator can provide, such as birth control pills or the IUD, then this strategy would appear to hold great promise.

Incentives

Still another strategy for dealing with deviant behavior is to reward nondeviant behavior. This is so obvious that it would hardly deserve mention except for the fact that, because people frequently want to punish a violator, they may not turn to such a simple solution. Most of the proposals for controlling industrial pollution, for example, have focused on punitive measures. Perhaps as effective an approach (if not more effective, since industry would more readily accept it) would be the establishment of an incentive system for not polluting. Learning theory, of course, suggests that a combination of rewards and punishments is more effective than are either rewards or punishments by themselves.

Treatment

A very common strategy for dealing with certain problems of individuals is to treat the disorder once it becomes manifest. In general, treatment requires at least some cooperation on the part of the person being served, although there is considerable variation in how important this cooperation is. For some physical illnesses, we have technologies that will be effective as long as the patient will simply enter treatment. For many other physical and some emotional disorders, the continual cooperation of the patient is important, but as the patient usually desires to be cured, it should be possible to obtain such cooperation. (However, many doctors, by ignoring the social aspects of treatment, may in fact not obtain the patient's cooperation.) Thus, for many disorders, the key to treatment is the development of an effective technology. For some disorders, though, such as alcoholism and drug addiction, effective treatment requires that a person enter treatment voluntarily; this treatment is not an effective strategy for significantly reducing the rate of disorder at the societal level, unless it is also possible to influence motivations at this level.

Amelioration

Another way of dealing with some forms of deviant behavior might be called the strategy of amelioration. With this strategy, the aim is not to eliminate the problematic situation, but to minimize some of its painful aspects. An example of such a strategy would be the food stamp program. The goal of this program is not the elimination of poverty and the poverty culture, but the elimination of one of the painful aspects of being poor; namely, not having enough to eat. The national program for family assistance proposed by the Nixon administration may also be viewed as an amelioratory program. As initially presented, the program was designed to provide persons with sufficient funds to subsist on. However, many persons perceived this program as more than amelioratory, for they saw it as providing the poor with enough incentive and money to break out of the poverty culture (others felt it would have just the opposite effect). The differing interpretations of the family assistance program and its goals probably account for the eventual demise of the program. We should note that whether a program like family assistance is perceived as a success or failure will frequently depend on whether the goal was the amelioration of some of the painful aspects of a situation or the elimination of the situation itself.

Self-Curative Model

Some problems will solve themselves, given time and perhaps some limited assistance. The strategy that is called for in these situations is to assist processes already in operation and to prevent or minimize forces that would hinder these processes. Such a strategy might be called "protecting and facilitating."

This strategy would appear to be called for in dealing with certain adolescent behaviors such as juvenile delinquency. The adolescent role, to which juvenile delinquency is very closely tied, is a transitory one. In a few years the adolescent grows up, and if he or she has not been really caught up in a delinquent way of life (and relatively few have), the former adolescent acquires a job and a family and becomes a normal member of adult society. Perhaps the major question asked by policy-makers concerned with delinquency should not be what the underlying cause of delinquency is (broken homes, lack of opportunities, subcultural background) but how to keep adolescents from being so immersed in deviant behavior that they don't make the transition to normal adult roles.

At the present time, it appears that a protecting and facilitating strategy is one of the strategies called for in developing an effective policy for dealing with blacks in our society. More than a decade ago, Moynihan (1969) called for a policy of "benign neglect" toward blacks, which appears to be a version of this strategy. As noted earlier, blacks have been making very noticeable gains. Society can facilitate their advancement through such programs as compensatory education and preferential hiring, and it can protect their advancement by defusing or minimizing tense situations, such as those that promote riots and that are caused by riots. But regardless of what white society does, it is going to take a very long time before blacks occupy a position commensurate to that of whites in our society. Furthermore, actual advancement is going to depend to a large degree on the efforts made (or not made) by blacks. It may be that a policy aimed at immediate equality for blacks in all social and economic spheres (as contrasted to the legal sphere) would not only be unsuccessful but would actually, given realities of life, be a hindrance, for it would unrealistically raise expectations, heighten frustration, and generally be a divisive influence, which might impede black progress. It should be noted that a protecting and facilitating strategy calls for compromise, diplomacy, and a willingness to wait, and it is likely that many social scientists will find such a strategy theoretically and/or ideologically unattractive.

Social Intervention: An Overview

This section has enumerated various strategies for dealing with deviant behaviors and pointed out some of their strengths and weaknesses. The discussion of any particular strategy has of necessity been brief, and not all possible strategies have been dealt with. It is probably essential for an effective social policy to have specific goals and an awareness of what strategies can be realistically used to achieve them. Unfortunately, this requirement is frequently not met. All too often a problem is perceived and action is taken simply because there is a feeling that something should be done.

Just as problems have more than one cause, in attempting to deal with a particular problem one may want to use more than one strategy. Furthermore, the appropriate strategy for a particular problem may change over time. This may be due to a change in the nature of the problem. For example, if we look at the position of blacks in our society during the fifties and early sixties, probably the most effective strategy was to focus on the issue of legal inequality. However, now that legal impediments are noticeably less oppressive and blacks have been making progress on many fronts, a protecting and facilitating strategy that would assist processes already in operation would seem to be more appropriate. A shift in strategy may also be called for because of a shift in technology; for example, such a shift has occurred in the treatment of mental illness with the development of chemotherapy.

We will now consider at greater length the treatment of mental illness. This case is one of the few successful instances of social intervention on a large scale, and the revolution in treatment that has occurred in the past twenty-five years highlights many of the forms of intervention discussed above.

TREATMENT OF THE MENTALLY ILL

The development of state mental hospitals in the early part of the nineteenth century represented the first formal system of public care for the mentally ill in this country (Grob, 1966, 1973; Bockoven, 1972). They were founded during an era of social reform in response to the practice of incarcerating the insane in local almshouses, jails, or other facilities. In contrast to these settings, with their pattern of physical abuse, neglect, and ridicule, the early mental hospitals were viewed as institutions providing hope and humane care for the mentally ill. The first state mental hospitals, which practiced moral treatment, had high rates of recovery for persons who entered treatment early (Bockoven, 1972). The success of the first hospitals resulted in a reform movement, led by Dorothy Dix, to establish public mental hospitals throughout the country.

With the success of that reform movement, the hospitals soon became overcrowded with chronic mental patients who had formerly been cared for elsewhere; furthermore, the new hospitals were staffed by persons not trained in moral treatment, and soon the hospitals provided little more than custodial care. These institutions provided little in the way of treatment; the hospitals promoted institutionalism; and the number of chronically institutionalized mental patients increased each year from the middle 1800s until 1955 (the year that marks the start of the second revolution in the care of the mentally ill—and it is this revolution, and how it has reshaped the treatment of mental illness, with which we will be concerned).

There were a number of predisposing events leading up to the psychiatric revolution that started in 1955. During World War II, personnel entering the armed forces received a psychiatric screening, and a substantial number were found to be psychologically unfit. In the Army, a talented group of social scientists was organized and, using the best sampling survey and statistical techniques available, they studied the relationship of combat stress to the development of neurotic symptoms and morale problems. One of their major conclusions was that combat stress was a precipitator of emotional difficulties (e.g., Stouffer et al., 1949). Before World War II, Faris and Dunham (1938) had examined the ecological distribution of first admissions to mental hospitals in Chicago in the 1930s, and they found that diagnosis was related to the patients' areas of residence. Furthermore, the highest rates of hospitalization for mental illness occurred in residential areas with the highest rates of social disorganization. This careful study documented the importance of social variables in mental illness. The subsequent and more elaborate study in New Haven in the early fifties on social class and mental illness by Hollingshead and Redlick (1958) had an even more powerful effect, for it showed not only that social class was strongly related to the incidence of mental illness but also that persons in the lower classes had much poorer treatment.

In the 1950s there were three major studies that documented the high rate of untreated mental illness. One was the Midtown Manhattan study (Srole et al., 1962) done in downtown New York, another was the Sterling County study done in Sterling County, Nova Scotia (Leighton et al., 1963), and the third was a national survey of mental health conducted by Gurin et al. (1960). These studies used very different techniques, but they all concluded that there were a very substantial number of persons who needed psychiatric treatment but who were not receiving it. These studies built on the experience gained during and before World War II and were financed by the National Institute of Mental Health, which became operational in 1949. The evidence gained in these studies, combined with governmental involvement and a growing awareness of the magnitude of the problems associated with the mentally ill, resulted in a serious governmental effort to change mental health facilities and the way the mentally ill were treated. The background of the impetus for change and the goals are well elaborated in the Joint Commission on Mental Illness and Mental Health's *Action for Mental Health* (1961).

From a pragmatic point of view, the start of the actual revolution in psychiatric care started in 1955. Two things occurred at this time; the introduction of milieu therapy and the introduction of tranquilizers. Milieu therapy, which had been initiated earlier in Britain by Maxwell Jones (1953), had many parallels to moral treatment, being characterized by a social environment in which there was a high degree of freedom and an expectation that patients would act in a responsible fashion. Tranquilizers not only proved effective in controlling a patient's severe symptoms, but by constraining disrupting behavior they made it much easier to have an open door policy and to initiate an effective form of milieu therapy. The introduction of tranquilizers was rapidly followed by the introduction of antidepressants. From 1955 to the present there have been continuing advances in psychopharmacology, and the evidence for the effectiveness of the tranquilizers and antidepressants is now extremely strong (see the excellent review by Berger, 1978).

CHANGES IN RATES AND LOCATION OF TREATMENT

From 1955 to 1972, there was an increase each year in the number of patients admitted to public mental hospitals, at which point the admission rate leveled off and then began a slight decline. In spite of an increased admission rate, the resident population has declined every year since 1955. This reduction has been brought about by a very sharp decrease in the length of hospitalization. During this time there has been a sharp shift away from treatment in mental hospitals to treatment centers more closely tied to the community. Table 7.1 presents the number of inpatient and outpatient care episodes by type of psychiatric facility for the United States from 1955 to 1975. As these data show, the rate of inpatient hospitalizations has remained relatively constant, but there has been a marked change in the location of treatment, with more persons receiving inpatient treatment in general hospitals, community mental health centers, and, to a lesser extent, Veterans Administration (VA) hospitals. Furthermore, in all settings the length of treatment is now relatively brief. In 1975 the median length of inpatient care in public mental hospitals was twenty-six days, in private mental hospitals it was twenty days, in community mental health centers it was thirteen days, in VA hospitals (psychiatric admissions only) it was eighteen days, and in general hospitals (psychiatric admissions only) it was twelve days (Klerman and Schechter, 1979). The most striking characteristic of the data in Table 7.1 is the tremendous increase in the number of patients who received care in outpatient psychiatric clinics. Furthermore, many more persons were being treated by general physicians. According to Regier et al. (1978), in 1975 3.1 percent of the total United States population received treatment by mental health professionals, 0.5 percent received inpatient care in a nonpsychiatric setting, and 9.0 percent received treatment as outpatients by physicians. In total, 11.8 percent of the population received some form of psychiatric treatment from physicians during the year.

So many more persons now receive psychiatric treatment that it is difficult to imagine that the stigma of their treatment is acting as a master status (compare Becker, 1963) that persists in shaping their lives by socially placing them in the role of the (permanently) mentally ill. In addition, given the changes in the setting in which treatment occurs and the brevity of treatment, it is difficult to imagine that most mental patients are in the formal role of the mental patient for a long enough period of time to be socialized into the role of the chronically ill (compare Goffman, 1961).

CIVIL RIGHTS AND THE LAW

There has been a long history regarding the abuse of the civil rights of mental patients, with the case for such abuse being well argued by Goffman (1961), Szasz (1961), and Scheff (1966). Although I have argued that much of this abuse was more apparent than real (Gove, 1970, 1975), the evidence up through the sixties on the degree of abuse was inconclusive. However, due to court rulings, new laws, and changes in procedure, it is virtually impossible to make the case that the abuse of mental patients now is a serious general issue. (This is not to say that it may not be a serious issue with an occasional patient.) First of all, it should be noted that the issue of

Table 7.1. Number and Percent Distribution and Rate per 100,000 Population of Inpatient and Outpatient Care Episodes, in Selected Mental Health Facilities, by Type of Facility: United States, 1955, 1965, 1971, and 1975 (Provisional).[a]

Year	Total All Facilities	All Mental Services	Inpatient Services of:					Outpatient Psychiatric Services of:		
			State and County Mental Hospitals	Private Mental Hospitals	General Hospital Psychiatric Service (non-VA)	VA Psychiatric Inpatient Services	Federally Assisted Community Mental Health Center	All Outpatient Community Mental Services	Federally Assisted Community Mental Health Center	Other
						Rate per 100,000 Population				
1975	3033	847	283	78	268	101	117	2185	750	1435
1971	1977	843	365	62	266	87	64	1134	305	829
1965	1376	817	420	65	271	60		559		559
1955	1028	795	502	76	163	54		233		233

[a]In order to present trends on the same set of facilities over this interval, it has been necessary to exclude from this table the following: Private psychiatric office practice; psychiatric service modes of all types in hospitals or outpatient clinics of federal agencies other than the VA (e.g., Public Health Service, Indian Health Service, Department of Defense, Bureau of Prisons, etc.); inpatient service modes of multiservice facilities not shown in this table; all partial care episodes and outpatient episodes at VA hospitals.

SOURCE: Taube and Redick (1977: 6).

abuse deals almost entirely with committed patients. Virtually all committed patients are committed to public mental hospitals and, as noted above, these patients comprise only a small proportion of patients receiving psychiatric care. Furthermore, the majority of patients admitted to public mental hospitals are voluntary. In 1972, for the United States as a whole, 41.8 percent of the admissions involved civil commitments and the rate has declined substantially since then.

It is interesting to note that among persons who have graduated from grade school, there is no relationship between being committed to public mental hospitals and the amount of education they have (Meyer, 1974). This lack of relationship between education and civil commitment runs directly counter to the evidence of the fifties and early sixties, which suggested that persons with less education were more likely to be committed (e.g., see Hollingshead and Redlick, 1958; Rushing, 1978).

In 1971, in *Wyatt* v. *Stickney*, the Federal District Court in Alabama held that involuntarily committed patients "unquestionably have a constitutional right to receive such individual treatment as will give each of them a realistic opportunity to be cured or to improve his or her mental condition," and this has become the accepted standard for all hospitals. In 1975, in *O'Conner* v. *Donaldson*, the United States Supreme Court ruled that "a state cannot constitutionally confine a nondangerous individual who is capable of surviving safely in freedom by himself or with the help of willing and responsible family members or friends" (Crane et al., 1977: 827). As a consequence of this ruling, the Connecticut Valley Hospital (the defendant) instituted a systematic review of all involuntary patients at the hospital. Although the review found no other patients like O'Connor, it did find a substantial number of patients that could be cared for in other institutional settings, particularly nursing homes.

A systematic review of involuntary patients at specified periods is becoming standard practice in public mental hospitals, and a number of states had review boards long before this time (see Kerlins and Knudsen, 1976). Other states have set up systematic procedures to ensure that the rights of patients are protected. For example, in Michigan, all patients are notified of their rights as specified by a new mental health code, and each institution has a special person designated as a rights adviser who investigates complaints (Coye and Clifford, 1978). There is now a substantial body of evidence that right to treatment suits have been an effective agent of social change (Kaufman, 1979).

On April 30, 1979, in *Addington v. Texas*, the Supreme Court handed down a ruling that more clearly delineates the requirements for commitment. Persons can be committed only if they are at that time both mentally ill and dangerous to either themselves or others. Also, the evidence must be "clear and convincing." While the standard of proof is not as stringent as that required in criminal cases, in which the standard is "beyond a reasonable doubt," the ruling clearly indicates that it is almost as stringent. At that time, thirty-nine states already had laws requiring the standard used in criminal cases. It should also be noted that the Supreme Court has imposed stringent limits on how long defendants found incompetent to stand trial can be hospitalized (Steadman, 1979).

The court rulings are complemented by changes in the law. In 1965 the laws affecting the admissions to New York State mental hospitals were reformed and updated. These reforms, characterized at the time as "the most revolutionary in the country in the field of mental health in a century" (Wiley 1965: 2722), encouraged the use of voluntary admission procedures and required the conversion of all possible involuntary patients to a voluntary or informal status. The legislation abolished court certification of involuntary hospitalization and established a system of initial admissions based on medical judgment (two-physician certificates) for a two-week period. A number of legal safeguards were introduced. The law established a Mental Health Information Service, which guaranteed the patient was notified of his or her rights and the patient was automatically provided with legal assistance for a judicial hearing, which was to be held after two weeks in the cases where treatment was still deemed necessary and the patient had not changed to a voluntary or informal status. By 1969 only 7 percent of the patients requested a court hearing, and among those who requested a court hearing approximately 50 percent were released. Additional legal safeguards were introduced for involuntary patients hospitalized for more than sixty days (e.g., see Kumasaka et al., 1972; Morrissey, 1979).

In 1967 California passed the Lanterman-Petris-Short (LPS) Act, which limited all involuntary hospitalization to seventeen days and imposed very strict legal safeguards regarding both the requirements for commitment and the procedures to be used in commitment. Urmer (1978: 143) reports that "in the first two years post-LPS the average treatment duration of voluntary patients dropped from 75 days to 23 days." While the California law has received the most careful scrutiny, it has been used as a model for laws in other states (e.g., Sata and Goldenberg, 1977). Although there has been no recent systematic review of the present laws in the fifty states, it is common knowledge that new laws have been passed in most states that, on the average, are about as stringent as the statutes in California and New York and appear to follow the general tenor set by those laws.

PUBLIC ATTITUDES: MENTAL ILLNESS OR NERVOUS BREAKDOWN?

As Rabkin (1974) shows in her review of public attitudes toward mental illness, the literature is not clear on some issues. In large part this is probably due to methodological problems revolving around what is meant by the term "mental illness." In the past, I have speculated that one reason a substantial number of patients do not view themselves as mentally ill is that the stereotype of mental illness involves such a severe disorder and bizarre behavior that the majority of both mental patients and those they deal with recognize that the patient's condition does not conform to the popular conception of mental illness. Thus, I argued, although individuals may realize they need help, many mental patients will conclude that they are not really mentally ill (Gove, 1970, 1975). There is now strong evidence that this is the case. As the studies by Meile and Whitt (1980), Whitt et al. (1979), Askanasy (1974), Townsend (1976), and Rabkin (1979) indicate, lay persons have very stringent criteria for labeling someone mentally ill and they think of the mentally ill as both bizarre and seriously impaired. To them, most persons receiving psychiatric treatment, including a brief hospitalization, are suffering from a "nervous breakdown." Such persons are not perceived as mentally ill, even if they are in treatment, and the evidence indicates that they experience relatively little stigma. In short, the public stereotype of mental illness is so derogatory and bizarre that the vast majority of persons treated for mental illness do not conform to the stereotype and thus escape the label. This is especially true if "other" is a long-term acquaintance of the (ex-)mental patient and/or other sees the (ex-)patient after the more severe symptoms have been brought under control, which, as noted above, takes only a brief period of treatment.

While there is considerable evidence that the term *mental illness* conjures up a very negative image, most persons who receive treatment for mental illness experience relatively few problems from others following treatment, probably because they do not, and perhaps never did, correspond to what is perceived as a true case of mental illness. It has also been established that persons who have experience in dealing with the mentally ill are less rejecting than others and that, for family members, close ties tend to override the stigma of mental illness (Chin-shong, 1969; Kreisman and Joy, 1974). The evidence also indicates that employers don't discriminate against former mental patients (Olshansky et al., 1960; Huffine and Clausen, 1979). In fact, the study by Olmstead and Durham (1976) would suggest that being labeled an ex-mental patient is not stigmatizing.

CHRONIC MENTAL ILLNESS AND DEINSTITUTIONALIZATION PRACTICES

Although the vast majority of persons who receive treatment for mental illlness return to the community and, by and large, lead normal lives, this is not true of all patients. Many of the long-term patients released from mental hospitals, as a consequence of the deinstitutionalizing movement, were mentally impaired, had very limited social skills, and had no place to go. This is particularly true in California. Furthermore, for the minority of patients who have a severe form of mental illness, often with a biological base, continued maintenance therapy is necessary if the patient is to function at even a marginal level (see Davis, 1975, 1976). One of the major beliefs behind the deinstitutionalization movement was that treatment in the patient's community, where the patient would be close to friends and family, would facilitate rehabilitation. However, for the truly chronic patient, this has not turned out to be the case, and alternative forms of institutionalization have developed.

The first is a board-and-care (b & c) home. The b & c home is a privately owned, profit-making boarding house run specifically for the mentally ill. The staff is largely untrained and unsupervised. The sole source of support for the residents is state and federal funding (approximately $285 a month in California (Benson, 1979). There are a number of problems with the b & c home. As Lamb (1969: 132) states, some operators regard the b & c homes "almost solely as a business, squeezing excessive profits out of it at the expense of the residents." Other problems involve excessive drinking and theft, both of which are chronic problems (Lamb, 1969). As Lamb (1969), Benson (1979), and others note, the b & c home has come to take the place of the mental hospital for many chronic patients, but the care provided appears to be even less adequate than the care formerly provided by the mental hospital. Segal and Aviram (1978) and Lamb (1969) have observed that one of the steps needed is certification of facilities with respect to the quality of the social environment and the competency of the staff.

The second major facility in California for the chronically mentally ill is the long-term (L) institution—high-security, locked, long-term "convalescent homes" created specifically for the chronic and acutely disturbed mentally ill who cannot be maintained in a b & c situation (Benson, 1979). These facilities are also profit-making organizations plagued by a lack of trained personnel and are characterized by numerous serious problems (e.g., Bardach, 1972; Segal, 1974; American Justice Institute, 1974). One of the major problems is a lack of funds; as Benson (1979) states, funding for patients averages about $16 per day and, as a consequence, attempts to provide therapy are essentially nonexistent except for the use of medications.

In summary, as Morrissey (1979) notes in his study of New York, current practices tend to keep some persons out of mental hospitals who could benefit from help, and for the chronically mentally ill it is beginning to appear that the current deinstitutionalization practices sometimes result in a worse environment than was characteristic of the environment provided by the modern public mental hospital.

STRATEGIES OF INTERVENTION: THE CASE OF MENTAL ILLNESS

By and large, neither our society nor other societies have been very successful at being able to develop a strategy of intervention that both greatly reshapes the form of a significant type of deviant behavior and markedly reduces its negative impact. However, in the case of mental illness, such a reshaping is clearly what has happened. In 1955 half of the hospital beds in the United States were occupied by the mentally ill, and mental illness, especially in its more severe forms, was something truly to be dreaded. There was really no successful form of intervention; illness could last for a very prolonged time; and many persons who entered a mental hospital spent the rest of their lives there. Now the severe symptoms of mental illness can be rapidly and routinely brought under control. Many more people who have emotional difficulties receive treatment that effectively alleviates their suffering, whereas formerly they went untreated. There has also been a drastic change in the legal sphere regarding the role of mental patients. The old mental hospital described in many exposés is no longer a problem. Mental illness is still one of the most serious forms of deviant behavior; there is room for much improvement in treatment, and there are still chronically ill patients who are being treated very poorly by society. But the nature and magnitude of the problem has radically changed, and social intervention is now usually successful.

Let us now turn to look at the various strategies of intervention described in the first part of this chapter, to see what we can learn from the example of mental illness.

Focus on Underlying Causes

For all practical purposes, we still do not know what the underlying causes of mental illness are. The changes that have taken place have largely occurred based on only vague notions about the causes of mental illness. The discovery and use of tranquilizers and antidepressants occurred long before we had any idea why they are effective, and it is only recently that we have begun to understand how they work (Weissman and Klerman, 1978).

The fact that revolution in treatment occurred, although we did not know the underlying causes of mental illness, does not mean that such information is not useful. For example, we now know there is a biological component to schizophrenia and the affective disorders (e.g., Kety et al., 1975; Gershon et al., 1976; Reider and Gershon, 1978; Allen, 1976) and, drawing in part on this knowledge, we now know that for some individuals a lifelong use of medication will prevent a pattern of recurring episodes of mental illness and enable individuals to lead normal lives who could not have done so otherwise (Davis, 1975, 1976).

Labeling Theory of Mental Illness

With regard to mental illness, labeling theory holds essentially two propositions. The first is that there is nothing intrinsically the matter with persons labeled mentally ill, that persons are labeled mentally ill as an act of social control, and that persons who tend to be mentally ill are largely on the margins of society and have few resources. The second is that the societal reaction associated with the process of being labeled mentally ill is the major cause of stabilized forms of mental illness (Scheff, 1966; Gove, 1975). Labeling theory, which was explicitly developed as an alternative to the psychiatric perspective, had very little to do with initiating the psychiatric revolution discussed above. The psychiatric revolution grew directly out of the psychiatric perspective, and the labeling theory of mental illness was not clearly formulated until a decade after the revolution was started (see Scheff, 1966).

Labeling theory, nevertheless, has played a significant role as the psychiatric revolution has evolved. Books such as Goffman's *Asylums* (1961) greatly increased psychiatrists' awareness of the debilitating aspects of the traditional mental hospital. Perhaps more important, labeling theory provided much of the theoretical foundation for many of the court rulings and changes in the law. This was particularly true in California, in the case of the Lanterman-Petris-Short (LPS) Act, a fact that has been very well documented (e.g., Bardach, 1972; Benson, 1979). As noted above, the LPS Act has served as a model for other states. There have obviously been many beneficial aspects resulting from that Act, but at the same time it appears to have pushed the deinstitutionalization process too far too fast; one of its results has been the establishment in the communities of board and care homes and long-term facilities, which in many respects appear to provide worse treatment than was being provided by the modern mental hospital.

Deterrence Model

Although the deterrence perspective potentially applies to an area like crime, as a perspective it should theoretically have little to do with the psychiatric model of treatment. It should be recognized, however, that before 1955 patients were, in fact, often controlled through punishment or the threat of punishment. Although this practice created a very unpleasant environment, it did enable the staff to maintain control of the environment. Because punishment can deter behavior, we should be aware that, even in today's treatment centers, very disruptive patients almost undoubtedly are surreptitiously punished to control their behavior. Steadman (1979) found that, in the institution set up to deal with mentally incompetent offenders by psychiatrists who had a clear intention of avoiding a punitive atmosphere, such an atmosphere quickly developed due to the seriously disruptive and often violent behavior of the inmates.

Prevention

The psychiatric revolution contains excellent examples of attempts to deal with prevention. In the early sixties there was a massive community mental health movement, much of it aimed at preventing mental illness. One prong aimed at the prevention of mental illness by preventing its development; that is, by changing the factors in society that caused mental illness. But as no one knew how to do that, that effort quickly foundered in spite of a considerable expenditure of funds. The second prong was suicide centers, which were aimed at preventing suicide. As follow-up studies were conducted, it soon became clear that the suicide prevention centers were having no effect on the suicide rate (e.g., Light, 1973). Now such centers are typically called crisis centers, and due to the volume of activity it would appear that a number of people find them useful, but very little is known about what they actually accomplish.

A technique of prevention that has been a success is maintenance therapy, which involves persons who are biologically predisposed to either schizophrenia or the affective disorders and who take medication on a continuing basis to prevent an episode of mental illness. The evidence clearly shows that this preventive strategy works. It probably should be emphasized that the strategy involves the use of a technologically derived substance over which we have direct control. It perhaps also should be emphasized that with this strategy we have an effective technology of prevention but we have only a very rudimentary understanding of how that technology works.

Incentives

Incentives have been used effectively as part of token economies on back wards to get patients to perform in a relatively effective fashion. As far as I know, there is no good evidence that the incentive system on which token economies are based has ever been successfully transferred to open wards, which in turn lead the patients to "recover" and thus return to the community, where they can function effectively. I would note that with the deinstitutionalization movement, back wards are rapidly being phased out of existence and so the use of token economies in mental hospitals will probably become a thing of the past.

A situation in which incentives are important in the new era of psychiatry is in the treatment provided by board and care homes and in the long-term institutions. Both of these centers are run for profit, and the major incentive for the manager is to make a profit. The funds, provided by the state and federal governments, are clearly barely adequate for providing the essentials of life, and there is no built-in financial incentive for the manager to provide anything corresponding to adequate treatment. Until the incentive system is changed for the operation of these centers, we can anticipate that they will remain poor alternatives to the wards in a modern mental hospital.

Treatment

A major theme of this chapter is that the revolution in psychiatry was based on the discovery of an effective form of treatment—medication (i.e., tranquilizers and antidepressants). Tranquilizers have helped make milieu therapy possible. While the evidence tends to favor the sole use of medications over the sole use of psychotherapy, the research fairly consistently indicates that the combined use of medication and psychotherapy is more effective than either by itself. It might be noted that medications are more effective for severe disorders, where a patient is out of control and often out of contact with reality, while psychotherapy may be more beneficial where the problem appears to be of an intrapsychic nature and does not incapacitate the patient.

One of the more important things to keep in mind when looking at treatment as a strategy of intervention is that one waits for a "case" to develop and then one utilizes an effective technology for treatment. Thus (except for the treatment of persons who have already manifested signs of chronic illness), treatment is not aimed at prevention but at curing, or at least controlling, a condition once it has arisen.

Amelioration

As psychotherapeutic medications control symptoms but have no effect on the social situation, which frequently is the cause of the symptoms, the use of medication can be viewed as ameliorative (except in those cases where the cause of the disorder is clearly biological, where use of medications can be seen as clearly therapeutic). However, since persons in psychiatric treatment are also typically receiving some other form of treatment, such as psychotherapy, ameliorating symptoms through medication helps directly in the therapeutic process. Most psychiatric disorders eventually result in a spontaneous remission (after a few months). The control of the symptoms through medication, which shortens the time before remission and enables the person within a very brief period to function fairly effectively, thus plays a major role in preventing the development of the side effects of chronicity and institutionalism. It might be noted that with most physical diseases there is also a spontaneous remission if there is no treatment. Thus, there is a similarity in the treatment of many physical diseases and of mental illness, in that essentially the therapist, by controlling the symptoms, is largely speeding up a process that would eventually take care of itself.

Self-Curative Model

It has been estimated that in a given year 21.5 percent of the persons with a mental disorder do not receive treatment (Regier et al., 1978). Most of these persons apparently undergo a spontaneous remission and are excellent examples of the self-curative model in action. Furthermore, 54.1 percent of the persons who are mentally ill in a given year are treated by general physicians primarily through the use of medication. Most of these patients would also appear to be using the self-curative model to handle their problems, with the additional feature that they are using medication to temporarily ameliorate their emotional distress.

SUMMARY

Most forms of deviant behavior are not dealt with (shaped) effectively by society, although society may attempt a variety of forms of intervention. We have discussed eight forms of intervention and then applied them to the case of mental illness, which is unusual in that in the past twenty-five years fairly effective techniques of treatment have been developed and the nature and severity of the problem have changed substantially. We have thus related the various forms of intervention to the changes that have occurred in the treatment of mental illness in our society. From our discussion, it should be clear that many acts of intervention are ineffective, and that some of the acts that are effective are so for reasons not well understood. It should also be clear that, for most forms of deviant behavior, a variety of strategies are called for and the key strategy will typically involve the use of a variable that one can effectively manipulate. It should be reiterated that a focus on variables that can be manipulated will involve a very different approach from that used by those trying to understand the etiology of a particular form of deviant behavior, and there is apt to be some tension between a "pure" and an "applied" approach to different forms of deviant behavior.

NOTES

[1]Spilerman (1970) notes that the relationship between the relatively high attainment of blacks and riots largely disappears when the size of the black population is used as a control, and he argues that it is the size of the black population and not the characteristics of the blacks that is the cause of the riots. His data, however, only indicate that the size of the black population is related to the attainment of blacks and that both are related to riots. I would suggest that it is the relatively high attainment of blacks (and the concomitant high expectations) in cities with a large black population that may at least partially explain why such cities are prone to riots.

[2]For a strategy developed out of the war on poverty that would appear to hold considerable promise, see Zurcher and Key (1968).

[3]Store owners, however, are apparently reluctant to implement an effective policy for controlling shoplifting for fear of alienating their customers. For a detailed discussion of shoplifting, see Cameron (1964).

8 COLLECTIVE AND FORMAL PROMOTION OF DEVIANCE

EDWARD SAGARIN
ROBERT J. KELLY

In this chapter, we seek to distinguish the conditions under which deviance is a truly collective social enterprise engaging the entire society through its agents of control and their clients, patients, offenders, prisoners, and clinical cases.

Deviance is a broad contrapuntal term covering two distinct but tangibly linked populations: those who perform deviant acts and those who judge, evaluate, and control them. For the most part, the main theoretical streams in the study of deviance tend to focus on one or the other of these groups. It can be said in general that functionalist, anomie, interactionist, social and cultural support, and conflict theories are delimited to the deviants themselves. Whatever may be the deficiencies of labeling perspective (Gove, 1975; Montanino, 1977), it has made an effort to develop and elaborate on an orientation that focuses on the agents of control and management themselves. The global concept of "moral entrepreneurs," as formulated by Becker (1963), and the descriptive formulations of moral reform crusaders, as set forth by Gusfield (1963), were the first major steps in this direction. What was still needed, however, was a general theory of deviance embracing both the definers and the defined: those who get processed, treated, and incarcerated, and those who do the processing, treating, and incarcerating. Our attention is fixed on the rhetorics of deviance, the discourses of the rule enforcers and rule violators, and how their actions, ideology, and proselytizing promote deviant behavior in a social system.

By definition, deviance is thought of as behavior that is subject to negative social reaction, being disvalued by the society as an entity or by significant subgroups thereof. (For a definition of deviance, see Schur, 1971; for a discussion of definitions, see Sagarin, 1975: 1–66.)

Hence, it would be expected that deviant behavior would in one form or another be discouraged. Nevertheless, in a variety of ways, for many reasons, and by diverse elements, deviance is collectively, formally, and sometimes officially encouraged. The paradox here, of the collective encouragement of unwanted or undesired behavior, is not beyond explanation, and it is sometimes manifest because those encouraging the behavior are not the same groups as those who would label it as undesirable. Thus, there are examples of government agencies cooperating with private groups promoting deviance (sometimes insidiously) in order to strengthen or consolidate their own security, prestige, or material advantage. As an instance, crime waves have been shown to be, to a significant degree, the creation of law enforcement agencies and the news media (Fishman, 1978). It seems reasonable to assume that such collusion in the construction of fear enables the perpetrators to benefit economically, politically, or bureaucratically.

If the encouragers and discouragers of deviance were always separate entities in a society, the problem would be one of a simple conflict of forces. However, many complexities enter that transform the promotion of deviance into something that, from the viewpoint of sociological analysis, is anything but simple.

In a broad sense, the agents for the promotion of deviance fall into at least three categories:

1. the opponents of the deviant behavior (often social control agents having governmental or quasigovernmental authority).

2. the deviants themselves, seeking either to expand their influence and swell their ranks or to defend themselves from social ignominy (and in so doing become cast in the role of proselytizer and recruiter).

3. neutral groups that have a vested interest in neither the suppression nor the encouragement of deviance, but in the investigation of it, the publicizing of activities and persons (and in the

course of such work find themselves promoting what they have set out merely to describe or publicize). This group must also include physicians and other medical and health workers authorized to impute deviance—that is, those who confer "sick" labels and define and treat the disabled, handicapped, and infirm.

Within each of these three categories, there are different motivations, and the promotion of deviance takes on a variety of forms with vastly different consequences.

DEFINING *COLLECTIVE AND FORMAL*

To fit a definition of *collective and formal,* we would suggest that, to be collective, the promotion or encouragement of deviant activities, statuses, or belief systems occurs through some type of organized network or cultural consensus, in which there are cooperative and coordinated efforts. By formal, we would include action that is in accordance with social conventions, and is governmental or official, organizational (particularly through such structures as voluntary associations), or institutionalized and part of the legitimate activities and other (that is, normative) institutional practices in society. These latter would include mass media, scientific journals, and business organizations, among others.

Collective and formal thus includes *official,* but is not limited thereto, and may be *unofficial,* in the sense of not having been authorized by holders of governmental or private office.

If this appears to be all-encompassing, we would exclude such activities as recruitment into gang activities by juveniles, for although ceremonious and ritualized, it would not be formal in the sense here suggested. The reverse, a situation that would be formal but not collective, might be more unusual, but it could occur when one person, not authorized and not acting as agent or in consort with others, makes appeal for, and encourages, deviant activity or positions through the use of official channels. Although Watergate was a collective activity, some of the individually deviant acts were not, particularly in the obstruction of justice. However, the formal, as we employ the concept, would generally subsume collectivity, although not the reverse. Hence, for purposes of parsimony and to avoid redundancy, one can speak only of formal and imply collective, but both terms are used here because the collective nature of the promotion is a separate dimension.[1]

MODES AND SOURCES

Without claiming to be exhaustive in this preliminary discussion, and with acknowledged indebtedness to many who have investigated individual aspects of this question (although we know of no previous effort to deal with the entire subject), we would suggest that collective, formal promotion of deviance takes on the following forms, which will be discussed in greater detail in the body of this chapter.

1. Formerly normative behavior has been turned into deviance by legislative action or by social pressure by what have been termed the "moral entrepreneurs." Examples are found in prohibition, the contemporary campaign against smoking in public places, and, in the opinion of some, the antidrug laws.

2. Closely allied with the above, but where the source of the promotion of deviance is not legislative, are the muckrakers, often including very prestigious social scientists and better known journalists who arouse professional, judicial, popular, and regulatory agency indignation to transform a hitherto mildly disapproved of but widely tolerated behavior into one that more clearly fits into a definition of deviance. An example of such might be the campaign launched by Sutherland against corporate regulatory infractions, which he sought to have redefined as white-collar crime.

3. Official promotion of deviance, particularly in political activities that are oppositional in nature and that the government wishes to discredit, takes on the form of provocation, or what is more generally referred to as the actions of the agent provocateur.

4. Not unlike the agent provocateur in certain respects, there is the promotion or encouragement of illegal activity by the government or persons acting as agents of, or on behalf of, the government, for the purpose of promoting a crime that would not otherwise have occurred had the police not wanted to make an arrest. This concept has come to be known in American law as entrapment.

5. Powerful political forces sometimes seek to shift public hostility toward an entire group of people, racial or ethnic particularly but not exclusively. Deviance appears through the creation of scapegoats, in order to bring about social cohesion among others in the population and place the blame for the ills of the country not on national leaders, their policies, or the social system, but on some elements within the nation deemed undesirable.

6. In a very formal sense, some deviant groups, particularly when organized into voluntary associations, are dedicated to prose-

lytizing for their point of view, which may be of a religious, a political, or some other nature. Survival or success in the attainment of the goals may be largely dependent on the recruitment of new forces into the organization.

7. Other voluntary associations defensively propagandize for the social acceptance of their members, adherents, followers, and constituency. The propaganda may result in an open appeal for recruits, or the recruits may be brought into the ranks through an ideology that makes an alternate way of life increasingly appealing despite the hostility it invokes.

8. Deviance may be promoted by economic concerns, because it is part of the profit-making enterprise. In fact, many white-collar crimes, particularly price fixing and antitrust violations, are formally promoted deviance. Pornography is a striking example of commercially exploited deviance.[2]

MORAL ENTREPRENEURS AND MUCKRAKERS[3]

In *Outsiders*, Becker (1963) defines moral entrepreneurs as those individuals who create and enforce social rules of behavior. The moral entrepreneur operates with the conviction that society requires reformation and change in its moral and social structures, that it needs improvement. Typically, the reformers and crusaders are concerned with the achievement of certain objectives and do not usually attend to methods of implementation, leaving these technical matters in the hands of professionals and experts—in short, the enforcers.

Becker's perspective helps to clarify a central question in the study of collective and formal conceptions of deviance. It enables us to see how and why some acts and behaviors become defined as deviant; how definitions of deviance are sustained, modified, or rejected; and how those classified as deviant are treated and processed. Consequently, by examining the power and resources of those who create and impose deviant categories with those so labeled, we gain insight into how public perceptions of deviance evolve.

Perhaps the least obvious, but most important, example of moral entrepreneurial activity is that of the physician. Medical men and women have clear professional objectives: seeking out illness and helping the sick. In discovering and finding illness, they create social definitions and meanings where these may have been lacking before (Freidson, 1970). Since illness is undesirable and abnormal insofar as health is the norm, medical professionals engage in defining deviance and also enforce these definitions and meanings by treating those as sick who fit the definitions they promulgate. In the past two hundred years, doctors and medical researchers have declared many conditions and bodily states, formerly believed by lay society to be manifestations of immorality, emotional weakness, or mental deficiency, to be forms of illness. Thereby they relieve the afflicted of personal guilt and responsibility (Foucault, 1973, 1975). Thus, the "illness" of alcoholism, rather than the suffering individual, is condemned. And rather than punitive judgment and moral castigation, the sick and infirm become increasingly the objects of sympathy and pity who are held up to criticism and disapproval only if they fail to conform to the sociomedical regimens prescribed on their behalf or if they fail to cooperate enthusiastically with those formally authorized to help them regain their health or achieve an adequate adjustment.

Others in the field of health and medical care who may or may not be physicians, but who crusade vigorously to arouse public opinion, are more obvious examples of moral entrepreneurs. Within the medical-health profession and on the fringes of it are those who have sought to destigmatize certain diseases (such as leprosy) by exerting pressure to relabel it with another less fear-provoking term (Hansen's disease). Militant homosexual groups and sympathetic psychiatrists have successfully lobbied the American Psychiatric Association to remove homosexuality from its categories of disorders. This strategy of professionally destigmatizing homosexual activity seems to be predicated on the belief that in time public revulsion and hostility toward homosexuality will abate and, in turn, the social atmosphere will tolerate it to such an extent that homosexuals can rid themselves of putative internalized homophobia (Weinberg, 1972; Simpson, 1976). Here are illustrations of collective impression management (Goffman, 1959) wherein undesirable images are effaced by controlling what people see and hear (Gussow and Tracy, 1968).

Our emphasis so far has been primarily on the activities of health professionals who have in one way or another championed changes in social attitudes by demystifying and muting negative societal reactions to sickness and illness. However, most of the activities of health and medical moral entrepreneurs show a tendency to see illness (and hence deviance) where the public does not, or to see a major problem where the public sees a minor one. The campaign against smoking is a case in point, with formidable forces arrayed on both sides. Becker (1963: 18) points out that rules are created and maintained by segments of the public, implying that there is no universal consensus about them. "Instead," he writes, "they are the object of conflict and disagreement, part of the political process of society."

Indeed, so central are the concepts of conflict and power to the formal and collective promotion of deviance that the very perspective must, to a major degree, be built around them. With respect to prohibition—officially defined deviance—we come close to the position developed by Quinney (1970) that public policy is a manifestation of interest groups—and nothing more—in society.

Prohibition and its repeal are excellent examples of moral entrepreneurial activity touching upon deviance. Temperance forces managed through demonstrations, rallies, public meetings, court cases, political campaigns, and all other methods familiar to anyone who watched the civil rights and antiwar movements of the 1960s, to get Congress ultimately to declare alcohol manufacture, transportation, and sale illegal. There is more to the substance of a movement that goes against the cultural grain than moral persuasion and astute political manipulation. Gusfield (1967: 181) describes the issues succinctly: "The designation of culturally legitimate behaviour as deviant depends upon the superior power and organization of the designators. It becomes an issue of political conflict ranging group against group and culture against culture in the effort to determine whose morals are to be designated as deserving of public affirmation."

In the case of prohibition, the alcohol user and buyer was a publicly defined deviant who was neither sick nor guilt-ridden but in most instances an upholder of opposite norms. Efforts to stigmatize and shame alcohol users may have had some effects on the abstinence rates, but the legislative victory was largely dependent on votes and temperance pressure at the polls. Moreover, whatever the law, the public did not endorse the view, which was a central tenet of temperance philosophy, that alcohol was evil.

More important, the anti-alcohol crusades generated their own opposition and means of destruction. Since the nation as a whole could not bring itself to accept alcohol use as deviant, since it refused to perceive its behavior in this regard as sinful or shameful or even sick, the enactment and enforcement of the law stimulated the movement for its repeal. Cultural opposition translated into political opposition, and the movement was abandoned by many of its friends.

Similarly, the current campaign against smoking in the United States, which is based upon more credible scientific evidence and officially sponsored studies than the campaign against alcohol, has not made the desired impact because, as with the temperance movement, its appeals tend to be couched in moralistic language, although the medical aspect is by no means overlooked. Its rhetoric beseeches smokers to give up their "dirty habits," to think of the discomfort they cause others, to take note of the risks of fires. As with other moral crusades, the smoker is identified not as a sick or hopelessly addicted person (a strong case can be made for addiction) but as someone who chooses to smoke and to engage in a self-destructive habit. The scientific evidence suggests that nicotine addiction is as virulent and powerful as many other narcotic addictions, but the smoker is not perceived as an addict who needs help and understanding. There are no government-sponsored programs to help the addicted tobacco user, as there are for heroin addicts. Also, the antismoking campaign, again like the temperance movement, has produced a powerful opposition group. Precisely because smoking is legal and still generally tolerated almost everywhere, a pressure group has emerged to protect its vested economic interests in the tobacco industry. A coalition of tobacco growers, cigarette manufacturers, and labor unions have until now at least resisted attempts to abolish smoking altogether, to raise taxes on tobacco to punitive levels, or to restrict smoking (for the most part) except in the privacy of the user's home.

Stigmatizing the smoker as deviant by extraordinary measures will not succeed, it seems, for much the same reasons as prohibition failed. The partisans of abolition who demand radically repressive policies and employ moralistic redefinitions of smoking as deviant behavior seem doomed to defeat no matter how laudable their intentions, because of the social and cultural consensus needed to sustain a legal reformulation of formerly normative behavior as deviant, and because a phenomenon of this scope and size involves other complex issues, such as influential economic interests and biological and physiological factors, which taken together militate against the success of a moral crusade to eliminate smoking. The fate of the temperance movement was sealed because it was nothing more than an effort, lacking collective consent, at a formal redefinition of normative behavior as deviant. And it seems in general that the ingredient of public approval or assent is a necessary condition to facilitate the process of defining some forms of behavior as deviant or as normative (or normal).

PROVOCATION AND ENTRAPMENT

The use of the agent provocateur, particularly in political situations, is a worldwide phenomenon. The agent provocateur is more than a spy or a plant placed inside a political oppositionist movement by the power group in the society (or sometimes, probably more rarely, by a competitive oppositionist movement), whose purpose it is to garner information about the movement and pass it on to others. Such a person is properly termed an informer.[4] The aim of the informer is to obtain and pass on to enemies of a movement the greatest amount of details about its activities. He or she may have been a member of an organization or part of an informal group and then recruited by social control agents, or the task of infiltration might simply have been assigned. The informer is sometimes in the leadership of an oppositionist group, often makes contributions, attends meetings regularly, and seeks to act like any other loyal member, and perhaps with greater ardor than others (see Marx, 1974). While there is often disdain for informers, especially those recruited from within, as demonstrated by the pejorative tone of such a phrase as "stool pigeon," and while the government has been severely criticized for its use of such persons in legitimate, democratic movements that had as their aim pacifism, student action, and civil rights (see Karmen, 1974), there has also been considerable criticism of the government for failure to have its agents in the Ku Klux Klan, in violent-prone vigilante groups, in organized crime circles, and the like.

The agent provocateur goes beyond the level of the informer. An agent provocateur is a government agent, within the organization or movement, who encourages, suggests, and gives very active support and assistance to activities that, although seemingly militant and appealing, will serve to discredit a movement and are intended to lead its members and leaders into a cul de sac. Agents provocateurs seek to play an active part in an organization in order to lead it to defeat, bring its leadership into conflict with society, and bring its followers into disarray and dismay.

The agent provocateur is a promoter of deviance because he or she suggests violence and other activities that will promote outrage and that are inherently inimical to the group. This may include obscenities that will alienate part of the group's public following, and attacks of an intemperate nature on others within the organization for their reluctance to be supermilitant.

The agent provocateur, in the United States at least, is supposed to stop short of committing a serious crime or permitting it to be committed. However, elsewhere in the world and perhaps also in the United States, it is not unknown in the annals of political movements that an agent provocateur has committed murder or assisted in its commission. During the activist decade of the 1960s, agents provocateurs were known to have suggested that the American flag be burned in public, and they may have been responsible for the extreme bitterness that developed between various black militant leaders and groups.

Among the many instances of government-provoked and officially sponsored deviance, Marx (1974: 405, 406) notes:

> The FBI in Meridian, Mississippi, was reportedly involved in the payment of $36,500 to two members of the White Knights of the Ku Klux Klan to arrange for two other Klansmen to bomb a Jewish businessman's home. A trap was set in which one Klansman was killed and another arrested in the unsuccessful attempt.

> In demonstrations at the University of Alabama, a police agent reportedly urged violence, set fire to at least one campus building, and threw fire bombs and other objects at police. His actions were used to declare unlawful assemblies in which approximately 150 people were arrested.

> A police agent at Northeastern Illinois State College led an SDS (Students for a Democratic Society) sit-in and was expelled for two semesters for throwing the school's president off the stage.

In some ways related to the activities of agents provocateurs, one encounters what has come to be known in American law as entrapment.

The two differ in several important respects. In entrapment, the purpose is to make an arrest. The agent provocateur's goal is the discrediting and the maiming of a movement, and the arrest is not the end in itself, but a means toward the greater end of hurting (by decapitation, if there is arrest) an organization or a social movement. Further, the agent provocateur is always a part of the group that has been infiltrated, or that may even actually have been formed by the agent, whereas entrapment may take place during a chance encounter or among people who were otherwise strangers.

Although entrapment, like agent provocation, takes place in political protest movements (as suggesting a bombing or an assassination, urging that it be carried out, obtaining maps, destructive paraphernalia, and the like, and then making an arrest just on the eve of the event itself—if there is no mixup in the synchronization of police work, in which case the arrest might be made after the assassination!), entrapment is also found in such ordinary or relatively nonpolitical crimes as smuggling, sale of illegal drugs, and sexual solicitation. Cases of homosexual solicitation have been dismissed on the grounds of entrapment, although the defendant's interest in the activity was not denied, but it was argued by the United States Supreme Court that the police should not prey on the psychological weaknesses and problems of the citizenry.

What we have here, in short, are two types of official, usually governmental, promotion of deviance. It can be argued that in both types the deviance is episodic, on the one hand, and is designed to reduce deviance, in the long run, on the other. Hence, in this line of reasoning, any official promotion of deviance cannot be considered to have made a lasting contribution to the amplification of socially disapproved behavior. Stated differently, the government is here involved in increasing deviance—both its intensity and its quantity—as part of its system of social control, which is designed to reduce deviance and impose conformity. In each instance, social control is designed to be successful by isolating the deviant. The isolation can be through discreditation or mass isolation, or through arrest, which would involve individual isolation.

SCAPEGOATS: THE SEARCH FOR DEVIANTS

It would be difficult to find a more ideal-typical sample of the collective, formal, and official promotion of deviance than in the development of scapegoats.

The witchcraft and heresy hunting of the middle ages (Szasz, 1970) and of colonial America (Erikson, 1966) were frenzied efforts to arouse hostility against individuals and groups (who, in some instances, had slightly different traits, characteristics, and beliefs than others, though in many cases even this was not true, and the victims were chosen by chance, almost as if by lottery). This does not constitute the promotion of deviance in the sense that disapproved behavior is being sponsored, whether by government or by deviant people themselves or by others, but rather its manufacture, to use Szasz's word, or its complete fabrication. Thus, Szasz (1970: 3) writes: "The behaviour of persons whose conduct differs from that of their fellows—either by falling below the standards of the group or by surpassing them—constitutes a similar mystery and threat; the notions of demonic possession and madness supply a primitive theory for explaining such occurrences and appropriate methods for coping with them."

Kai Erikson (1966: 4), drawing upon Durkheim, notes that the deviant act "creates a sense of mutuality among the people of a community by supplying a focus for group feeling. Like a war, a flood, or some other emergency, deviance makes people more alert to the interests they share in common and draws attention to those values which constitute the 'collective conscience' of the community. Unless the rhythm of group life is punctuated by occasional moments of deviant behaviour, presumably, social organization would be impossible." While the sweeping statement in this last sentence, ending with the word "impossible," would seem to be overly strong, one can easily note that where governmental or other cultural leaders are seeking to bind together a community, with a sense of this collective conscience, it can utilize internal or external enemies. If, as sociologists have contended, outward hostility makes for internal cohesion, then the outward hostility can sometimes be created by focusing on deviants, real or imagined, in the society. These people become, in a social if not a literal sense, aliens, and for this purpose deviants are manufactured (witches), those already deviant are subject to the magnification of hostility (homosexuals), and the ire of the community is aroused against people not in the power group (blacks and Jews).

The creation of scapegoats is not necessarily conspiratorial and deliberate. People looking for causes for their misfortunes will find them, and at a time of misfortune there is a readiness to believe that the cause is to be found in the person of someone real and visible. There was an old folk saying in the United States during the period from the end of Reconstruction to the Second World War (when new enemies could be found and internal ones were no longer needed), that whenever the price of cotton went down, one could hear the cry of rape go up. Whether this would prove literally true when subject to historical analysis is not known, but in a broader sense the black and the Jew as scapegoat, particularly but not exclusively in nineteenth- and twentieth-century America and Germany, respectively, are examples of the promotion of deviance through the creation of a group of people on whom the deviant label, and the concomitant hostile and aggressive attitudes of powerful groups in society, could be placed. The era of McCarthyism, with its search for modern-day counterparts of witches in the form of traitors, Communists, homosexuals, and nonconformists in general, was an ill-begotten and only temporarily successful effort in the creation of deviance.

DEVIANTS AS PROMOTERS OF DEVIANCE

In some instances, it is in the nature of the deviant enterprise to promote its own activities, to gain converts, and to expand its sphere of influence. In fact, much of the public hostility may come from proselytizing, rather than from the rejection of belief systems and activities. If the deviant group were a self-contained collectivity, perhaps formally organized into a voluntary association, for the exchange of ideas on a view of the world not otherwise acceptable, few might care and many might dismiss the members as "harmless crackpots." Lofland (1966) has described a Doomsday Cult that was considered peculiar and rejected with the ridicule sufficient to give it deviant status. It was probably scorned rather than actively opposed precisely because there was little effort by its followers to convince (and coerce) the general public to join the very thin ranks. If people come together as atheists, Swedenborgians, and believers in (but not practitioners of) polygamy, there is little evidence that many will care about their activities.

Some noninstitutionalized religious groups are by their nature proselytizers, whether because they are led in such a direction by a mercenary leadership seeking to enrich the coffers by exploiting an ever larger clientele, or because the ideology of the members is infused with the belief that they are holders of "the truth," and that it is their mission to enlighten the masses still suffering in their ignorance. The Unification Church of the Reverend Sun Myung Moon (whose members are commonly referred to as "Moonies"), Jehovah's Witnesses, and many other cults have earned the disdain of the public more for their unflagging efforts to obtain converts than for their beliefs or activities.

This is not to deny other elements and activities that would bring scorn or hostility upon the group, but were it not for their propagandizing, these might be ignored. Americans generally look with disdain at marginal religious groups outside of the mainstream of society (although new ones can enter this mainstream, as Zen Buddhism seems to have done, with some degree of success among certain sectors of the population).

Thus, the energetic recruiting by deviant cults amplifies deviance in two almost self-contradictory manners: First, it increases the hostility of what might otherwise be an apathetic public; second, it brings a wider number of people within the organization or under its influence. In this sense, it serves to polarize, and the more successful it is in advancing its cause, the more successful it becomes in generating hostility toward itself.

In deviant political organizations, this two-edged activity is deliberately fostered, for the organization is inherently unsuccessful to the extent that it is ignored, at least publicly, by media, government, and others. While one can find numerous instances of small groups of political oppositionists who contented themselves with their usually clandestine weekly or monthly gatherings, and emigre groups in such havens for exiles as France or Switzerland, most politically conscious persons would consider their armchair philosophical musings and dreams of restoration as admissions of impotence. Activists adhering to politically oriented social movements know that their day of gaining power will not arrive by faith, patience, and discussion. That they require new adherents is a part of the self-evident credo of most political movements.

Whether a political opposition group is moving in the direction of gaining adherents, or of acting as a very small and tightly knit conspiracy, it is still seeking to spread its message, and hence to spread disapproved differentness. The position taken at a given moment is one of tactics, and for tactical reasons the deviant oppositionists may choose to publicize their activities rather than recruit followers. The publicizing may even be at the expense of losing followers, but this is viewed as a temporary, necessary, and unfortunate stage. It is probable that such groups as those responsible for various political kidnappings, bombings, and murders in Italy during the 1970s (including the murder of Aldo Moro) would be loathe to seek new members, and do not believe that they are winning new friends. On the other hand, they may believe that they are making the country ungovernable and preparing it for a takeover by themselves or forces like their own, and they would have some degree of historical precedent (each with innumerable differences) as they look at Cuba, British-mandated Palestine, and other areas of the world.

Nevertheless, it is in the nature of most dissident or oppositionist groups that they must seek recruits—in some instances, voters for their cause; in other instances, cadres that can be trained for leadership—and people who will provide financial assistance, as well as other types of followers. While ultimate success of their movement would result in a change in power relations so that the political deviants of yesterday become the acceptable power group of today, their successes can sharpen the lines of discord against them or can bring concessions to them, or some mixture of both. Such a combination is often seen in nationalist movements seeking political autonomy, where an effort is made to crush a movement by simultaneously repressing its foremost organized force and meeting some of its demands.

When deviants are propagandizing for their form of deviance, they are promoting the idea of social acceptance of their way, which would mean that their way would cease to be deviant. The official promotion of deviance thus is a self-contradictory or even a self-liquidating notion, for through its promotion it aspires to cease to be deviant.

This attempt to make normative or acceptable what was previously deviant is seen in many other social movements, in addition to the religious and the overtly political. Social movements can have more limited goals. Although the ramifications of these limited goals often reach into the inner core of major social institutions, this is not necessarily the case. It is probably true that broad environmentalist movements affect the political and economic structures of society, the relationships between corporate enterprises and government, the governmental control over the use and abuse of natural resources, but other movements can achieve their goals, or fail to achieve them, without strongly affecting the political-economic structures. This could be the case, for example, of campaigns to legalize and normalize marijuana-smoking, to legalize abortions, and to gain social and legal acceptability for homosexuality. This normalization, or more exactly the making of something normative that was formerly widely rejected and hence deviant, can be considered a process of destigmatization. A prime example of destigmatization that occurred in American society over the past few decades was in the decline of the worship of virginity and the "normalization" of nonmarital cohabitation. It is interesting that this took place without any formal campaign, with no organizations supporting such a movement and none constructed to oppose it.

There are organizations struggling for the social acceptance of some activities without urging that others take up the life, but only that those who so desire may be permitted to do so without negative legal or social sanctions. This would distinguish such persons from the political proselytizers or the religious cultists, who seek converts and without such conversion feel that their movements would be failures. One can urge the legalization and destigmatization of marijuana-smoking, or of the use of cocaine and heroin, for that matter, without wishing that the ranks of users and participants be swelled. And the same can be said of homosexuality and of other forms of sexuality that may not be accepted widely enough to please the practitioners.

The problem here is that, in defending the propriety of the activities for those who are voluntarily participating, and the social good that can be attained from destigmatization and decriminalization, one must present certain positive aspects, and downplay, ignore, or actively reject the negative aspects. If marijuana is portrayed as being harmless, nonaddictive, and free of other evil consequences, and if this portrayal is presented solely for the purpose of lifting the legal and social sanctions and developing more accepting attitudes, then this is almost certainly going to promote disapproved activity (that is, the marijuana-smoking) among the public. In fact, the present campaigns against cigarette-smoking, with the appeals to morality and to health care, are based on precisely the same train of thought but turned around; namely, that if the public is to be dissuaded from a type of behavior, this can be done by highlighting the negative consequences of its use. Thus, groups struggling for the legalization of marijuana and abortion may not be seeking to spread either of these activities, but the net effect of their campaigns can be to amplify both.

This contention, that decriminalization and destigmatization campaigns turn into the promotion rather than the defense of the activities, seems to be an issue in the gay rights movement. The answer to this, by the official organizations that are working toward the destigmatization of homosexuality, appears to be twofold. First, it is said to be most unlikely that persons with strong heterosexual orientations would be recruited to homosexuality by propaganda that "gay is good," or that lasting love is found about as frequently among homosexual groups as heterosexual, or that homosexuals are not more disturbed or pathological than are straight people. Second, if some persons, albeit a minority of those exposed to the propaganda, should choose the homosexual path, such persons would be making a free choice, say the groups supporting gay rights, and this is no more likely to result in difficulties or tragedy than if they embarked on heterosexuality (or at least need not be, if only the social sanctions were lifted).

This is not the place to discuss the merits of these arguments, but merely to point out that, by the nature of a voluntary association involved in the struggle for social acceptability of its way, there will be a strong tendency to make the picture of the life pretty, except for those ugly features that are imposed by the negative reactions of a hostile society. By contrast, a voluntary association of deviants concerned not with the normalization of deviance but the normalization of deviant people (the mending of their ways, so to speak) is likely to paint a vivid picture of the evils that await those who continue on the pathway to perdition. Thus, there are two types of voluntary associations of deviants—those who seek to change societal reactions and thus reduce deviance by gaining acceptance of their members, and those who wish to change their members or adherence and thus reduce deviance by having them comply with the normative order. The two types are exemplified by gay organizations, on the one hand, and by Alcoholics Anonymous, on the other. Only the former can be said to be involved in the formal amplification of deviance, although less deliberately than are politically deviant and religious proselytizing groups, and even then only to abolish the deviant character of their activity, and not the activity itself.

PROFIT IN DEVIANCE: CORPORATE AND PROFESSIONAL IMPROPRIETIES

Of course there is a profit in deviance. This may be profit in the form of nonmonetary gain, as goal attainment, pleasure, and the gratification of seeing results that may take on the deviant form of infliction of pain on others. But advantage is more generally thought of in its economic sense, and in that meaning, people benefit from the misfortunes of others. This may be an ironic validation of the old homily about silver linings in every cloud.

There is profit in anything: death, sickness, earthquakes, crime. As long as the thing exists, someone is going to make money out of it. One might be tempted to add that if people are going to make money out of something, they will cause it to exist. This is generally true, and abortions performed on women who are not pregnant, and the invention of other medical problems that require care and payment, are neat examples of just such a profit motive. But not everything works that way. There are people who exploit and capitalize on disasters such as earthquakes and tornadoes, but they cannot create them in the same way that one can make a fire. One might say with cynicism that they would if they could, but that would hardly be relevant except as a commentary on one's vision of society or of the human animal.

Corporate, white-collar, and professional deviance is sometimes, but not always, officially promoted, to the point where it is institutionalized. A bank does not want to have clerks or branch managers embezzle funds; in fact, if we can anthropomorphically speak of a bank wanting something (which the bank is incapable of doing, but the bankers, stockholders, management group, depositers, creditors, and government officials do have their wants), it would not want the branch manager to embezzle, and it would not want embezzlement by the president of the enterprise, either.

However, given the concept of deviance as behavior or status that is disvalued by various parts of the population but not necessarily by agreement among all, some corporate activities are of a nature that, whether legal or illegal, are discredited as improper by significant sections of the populace. Yet the actions continue, undisturbed and even escalating, buttressed by the collective support of the management group, of political influentials, and sometimes even by a labor group that has something to gain, albeit temporarily, and with much more to lose over longer periods.

SOCIAL AGENCIES AS PROMOTERS OF DEVIANCE

Social agencies handling people with difficulties and disabilities often must work toward destigmatization and acceptance of such persons in the community, and in that sense toward the removal of categories of clients from the negative sanctioning and effects of being seen as deviants. Goffman (1963) took note of the similarity of the problems of people who are stigmatized because of race or ethnicity, moral blemish or activities, and physical handicap. The latter have been termed "involuntry deviants," the term referring not to the fact that the deviance is unwanted, but that the status bringing about the deviance was the result of birth defect, sickness, accident, or other involuntary situation over which the individual has had no control (Montanino and Sagarin, 1977: 3–4).

It is one of the tasks of social agencies to assist families, or replace them, in offering care and assistance to the handicapped. The handicapped and their families are taught how to navigate through their social networks, sometimes to conceal their discreditable attribute, and sometimes to ignore it without concealment or to attempt to compensate for it or to "conquer" it.

Other methods of what Goffman (1963) calls the "management of spoiled identity" are probably learned more from peers met at the agencies than from social workers or people officially designated as teachers, such as joking about their problem and thus dismissing it as a serious impairment to social and personal functioning.

At the same time, an agency is itself a bureaucratic structure that has an interest in its own continuation, in being funded, in protecting the jobs of its employees (who may or may not be handicapped), and enlarging on its own field. As a major task, the agency frequently seeks to find employment for its clientele, but the finding of such employment is itself a job for agency people. If an agency would like to point to the large numbers of people it has assisted in becoming normal actors and who hence are no longer dependent wards, it cannot do so without emphasizing that there are tasks still to be performed, clientele not yet served (but through no fault of the agency, except that funding has been insufficient, and as a result the organization understaffed).

One might draw an analogy: What would happen to our prison wardens, correctional officials, and rehabilitative therapists, if the war on crime were so successful that people were universally deterred? No one seriously asks the question, or faces the potential problem of unemployment and displacement, because the possibility is remote beyond the level of speculation. But social agencies can have success so great that the clientele shrinks. A major example of this is the March of Dimes, which among other tasks stimulated research into the conquest of infantile paralysis, and when such research developed in a direction that made the continued fund-raising of the organization obsolete, the agency transformed itself by refocusing its interests on people suffering from other disabling diseases, including congenital defects (for the story of this transformation, see Sills, 1957).

A social agency does not create stigma, nor does it instill in people their retardation, their handicap, or their disability. But there is an elasticity to the number of people in need of supervision for a specifically disabling disorder. No matter what the handicap might be, there is no clear-cut line of delineation between the competent and normal, on the one hand, and the incompetent and dependent, on the other.

When there are social work jobs to be filled, more clients can be found. When there are large caseloads, fewer clients are defined as needing assistance (except for the purpose of decreasing caseloads or retaining or expanding staff). Again, there is the analogy to giving suspended sentences and placing people on probation. When there is room in the prisons, there is a Gresham's law at work: The beds will be filled (and beware of the hostile reaction to those who violate that law). The same can be said of hospital facilities: There will be more cases treated in hospitals not exclusively on the basis of medical needs, but on the basis of available beds and other facilities.

All of this, of course, affects mainly marginal cases, but it also affects official attitudes. In agencies, the amplification of deviance among the physically handicapped has been traced with meticulous care by Scott (1969), whose work is aptly entitled *The Making of Blind Men*. Blindness is seldom total; it is a term covering a condition of impaired sight, and under its rubric fall people with poor vision and a smaller number of people who lack vision entirely. For legal purposes, there is a clearly delineated distinction between the blind and all others, but for purposes of social functioning, independence, and competency in everyday life, no such line of demarcation can be drawn. It was Scott's contention that agencies take people, mainly with sight handicaps but not completely devoid of sight, and make them dependent persons, instead of turning them out into the world to live relatively normal lives. They learn to make brooms, instead of learning to be business executives and secretaries (where they could be extremely competent, but would meet considerable resistance by personnel managers). The agency has a vested interest in retaining and expanding its clientele, and in so doing it makes (socially) blind people out of biologically sight-handicapped.

There is a limit in the application of this thesis, but it is indisputable that, to some extent, and in certain types of disabilities, agencies perpetuate and promote deviant status despite themselves and their lofty intentions.

SUMMARY

The ways in which deviance is promoted in a society, ostensibly dedicated to its eradication, are varied and numerous. Here we have touched briefly on several of them.

Stebbins (1971: 115) has suggested that "after a certain stage of the deviant career the strategy of coping becomes one of remaining in one's deviant identity." What we have attempted to look at in this chapter are some of the sources of entering and of remaining in that identity, and while Stebbins focused specifically on one category of deviants, the nonprofessional criminal, we find the general thesis to be applicable to many other categories: the political and religious activist espousing deviant belief systems, the physically handicapped, the sexual deviant, and others.

There are many positive theoretical and empirical advantages in looking at the collective and formal features of deviance. An important result of investigating deviant behavior as a collective activity is that the focus of study is not limited to those who violate rules, occupy disvalued statuses, or are in other ways the objects of negative societal reaction. Such an orientation permits an inquiry into the interplay of forces, elements, and actors: the definers of deviance and the deviants themselves who together make up the deviant phenomena. As Becker (1963), Erikson (1966), and Freidson (1966) have noted, all of the major actors in deviant behavior are neither clearly nor fully appreciated—especially those who create the occasions for deviance, the rule creators and enforcers.

It has frequently been stated that no act or episode is intrinsically deviant. This is not to deny that some acts are intrinsically evil, but merely to assert that no empirical evidence has thus far been assembled to substantiate the view that deviance (that is, a trait, characteristic, or action that incites social hostility) inheres in a particular act or actor. Rather than exclusively attending to the psychology of an individual or group in seeking the origins of the trait itself, a more fruitful line of analysis ought to be sufficiently broad in scope to encompass, in addition to etiology, other elements and features salient to activities and behaviors that violate customary standards of acceptable and normal behavior.

What we are seeking here to show is that there are forces that encourage and discourage the violation of norms and rules. Acts of nonconformity, law-breaking, and rule infraction are denounced, condemned, or punished, depending upon the severity of the transgression, by a range of actors and agencies, all of whom are invested with the rights to speak and act on behalf of the community's legitimate order. "Professional degraders" represent the community of injured parties and are authorized to transform identities from normal to deviant. As Garfinkel (1956) observes, there is no society whose social structure does not provide, in its routine features, the conditions of identity degradation.

While the machinery of social control is erected to protect against the harmful effects of deviation, the formal apparatus of social control, as Erikson (1966) persuasively points out, is also designed to serve other important functions in preserving order. In censuring acts of behavior as deviant, the agencies of social control refine and concretize the meanings and applications of norms and also clarify the boundary contours of acceptable and nonacceptable behavior. Deviance is in this way cultivated by the very organizations devised to abolish it. In Erikson's (1966: 18) words: "Thus deviance cannot be dismissed simply as behaviour which *disrupts* stability in society, but may itself be, in controlled quantities, an important condition for *preserving* stability" (emphasis in the original).

In sum, the initial formal reactions of society to rule violators activate processes that are organized to control and eradicate deviance but that, paradoxically, promote, sustain, and encourage it.

Deviance might be formally promoted, normalized, or destigmatized by law, decree, administrative fiat, or other official means. Yet, these procedures in themselves do not seem to be sufficient guarantees of changed status and identity if these enactments lack collective social and cultural consensus. Conversely, mass opinion and general public agreement that some activity or group is deviant is not easily countered by formal sanctions to the contrary. The history of equal opportunity employment legislation, affirmative action policies, housing desegregation statutes, and prohibition—to cite just a few examples—shows that they have been resisted and circumvented frequently and consistently enough to suggest that though public opinion may be swayed and manipulated by mass media and legislation, a deeply ingrained matrix of values, beliefs, and attitudes cannot be "managed" easily and effectively in the short run.

In the long run, however, formal definitions of behavior as deviant, or redefinitions of deviance as normal, may help to create the necessary conditions for cultural and moral change in a desired direction. By formally and legally insisting that certain persons or behaviors be tolerated, by providing structures of opportunity, power, and persuasion previously denied those seeking acceptance, a society can be poised for change. In this connection, the civil rights and gay liberation movements share such a strategy in common: a demand for social access and participation mediated by litigations and other actions designed to reorient the moral and cultural consensus toward toleration of differentness.

Finally, it seems clear that the formal promotion of deviance by law or by governmental action is greatly facilitated by other organizational entities and persons strategically situated in positions and at points in the social and cultural core of the social system. Mass media, high-status persons, and other prestigious influentials make a discernible impact on public opinion and action, not by confronting it as much as by skillfully formulating and affirming it.

NOTES

[1]Collective might be absent but formal present in the promotion of certain disdained and disvalued ideas by scientists.

[2]Omitted from this discussion is a detailed consideration of the role of mass media and communications as mechanisms promoting deviance; how the work of the scientific community and prominent individual scientists often challenges popular beliefs and perceptions of health and sickness in society and are as a result encouraging deviant activities; and how language itself shapes our thinking about deviance by impressing upon us categories of thought and grammatical structures that mold our view of social reality.

[3]For a more detailed discussion of this topic, see Chapter 5.

[4]Those interested in the distinction between the informer and the informant should consult Sagarin and MacNamara (1970).

Part IV

Trends and Issues in Deviance Research

In the introduction to this volume, readers are subjected to some rather unpropitious language about the confused state of the study of deviance. There it is said that, as a result of two centuries of mixing morals with science, this field is now in ferment, as seen in the proliferation of theories, diverse methodologies, and ideological cross-currents. And the polemical character of some of the chapters in Parts I through III gives little comfort that these intellectual storms are likely to abate soon.

Over the years, however, something has been accomplished. Even while scholars continue to dispute various points of theory, method, and ideology, they have reached agreement on other points. Specifically, each theoretical advance has called attention, at times stridently, to knowledge gaps in established paradigms. Even the most staunch defenders of these challenged frameworks have eventually acknowledged many of the imputed weaknesses. The upshot of these critiques is that students of deviance have come to the realization that their paradigms, like those in other branches of sociology, have definite explanatory limitations. Each makes its distinct, albeit incomplete, contribution to our fuller understanding of aberrant behavior.

For example, few sociologists today would reject the proposition that officials selectively label deviants as such, while, informally, members of the larger community do much the same. Until the labeling theorists called attention to it, this process was largely ignored by mainstream criminologists and functionalists. A similar enlightenment occurred in connection with organizational crime. Though it took several decades for the idea to gain acceptance, modern deviance researchers acknowledge this practice as fact. In the article in which he introduced the term "white-collar crime," Sutherland (1940) observed that their identification with the middle class was beguiling criminologists into believing that property offenses were the exclusive domain of the lower classes.

A third instance of agreement centers on the radical criminology thesis: A significant number of a community's formal moral norms are not only enacted in accordance with the interests of powerful groups, but also enforced in sympathy with those interests. While labeling theorists were stressing the arbitrariness of norm application, radical criminologists were carrying this line of reasoning further by describing how self-interested groups exploit the legal machinery for their own ends. There are still arguments about just how successful the ascendant groups are in getting their laws passed and effectively enforced. But students of deviance concur that there is differential power, which is sometimes harnessed in a move to structure social life to the advantage of the powerful.

Given the agreements and disagreements among those who study deviance, what does the future hold? For one, it will bring further attempts to clarify unresolved theoretical and empirical issues. Chapter 9, by Lemert, exemplifies this trend. The future of deviance research will also contain new theoretical ventures. These will include the further application of the ethnomethodological (see Chapter 10) and the neo-Marxian (see Chapter 11) perspectives.

Lemert tackles a number of issues, some of which have come down to us from earlier evaluations and attempted revisions of the labeling framework. One vexing problem for all students of deviance, notwithstanding their theoretical proclivities, is the very definition of it. Following Karl Llewellyn's lead in the sociology of law, Lemert chooses to leave the central concept (of deviance) undefined. In harmony with the stance taken in the introduction to this book, he suggests that research on and theorizing about deviance proceed by identifying bodies of data concerned with the moral differentiation of groups of people.

The deviant act has also been the center of a certain amount of controversy. How important theoretically is this concept? Lemert demonstrates that particular acts are not necessarily prerequisite to becoming deviant. Moreover, whether an act is classified as deviant is greatly influenced by the culture in which it takes place.

A third major issue in the study of deviance is the role of social structures. One of its facets is how to bridge the theoretical gap between microsociological process and structure, which is a problem for all sociologists and one for which there is no easy solution. Another facet is the need to place types of deviance in historical and social context. Data on what Lemert calls "visible social structures," or medium-sized groups, can help eliminate this deficiency. The importance of social structures lies here, rather than in their questionable role as causes or producers of rates of deviance.

Answers to the question of what causes deviance are to be sought elsewhere. Based on Robert MacIver's theory of social causation, Lemert argues for a choice and feedback model in which objective and subjective elements in deviant individuals' personal, social, and physical environments are joined with their values and perceived costs to help them choose a line of action and evaluate its consequences. The reality of deviance, says Lemert, is not exclusively a social reality.

Wieder and Wright, in Chapter 10, address an issue in the study of deviance of special concern to ethnomethodologists. It has to do with the nature of the rules of behavior whose infraction constitutes the deviance sociologists and other social scientists examine. Functionalists and labeling theorists have tended to assume that such rules are operating—that there is general community agreement about their meaning and about how typical members should apply them in their daily lives. Ethnomethodologists note that many scholars see society's moral rules as scientifically unproblematic, as prescriptions or proscriptions for behavior sufficiently clear-cut to justify turning their attention to other matters.

Ethnomethodologists view the meaning and application of rules, moral and otherwise, as situationally determined. These processes rest on the ways community members define what is happening in particular settings with reference to their reasons for being there. Ethnomethodology seeks to discover the general methods people use in these circumstances. For this branch of sociology, however, deviance is only one of many rule-governed areas of behavior open to ethnomethodological analysis.

Wieder and Wright observe that rules and norms in the traditional conception of conformity and deviance are treated much like the rules of a game. Such rules are known beforehand in sufficient detail to enable the players to complete the contest. They are self-contained, unequivocal, and immutable; no further information is needed to apply them. But everyday life is seldom so simple.

Wieder and Wright review the research that shows how knowledge of a rule is, alone, inadequate as an explanation of situated behavior. The commonsensical reasoning people use in applying the rule must also be analyzed.

Thomas would steer the study of deviance on a different course from that of either Lemert or Wieder and Wright. In Chapter 11 he contends that the conventional paradigms used to study moral difference are candidates for the intellectual scrap heap—and no amount of methodological or theoretical tinkering will make them workable again, for they direct attention, almost exclusively, to deviants and their aberrant behavior, while ignoring the abuses of political and economic power, legislative interest groups, corporate bribers, industrial polluters, and the like. In other words, the study of deviance as it has evolved to the present both supports and perpetrates the established order.

What is needed, Thomas insists, is not additional new theoretical directions, but a single, bold, new paradigmatic "destination." The paradigm Thomas has in mind is Marxian, but one excluding the radical ideas of Thomas Hobbes; the conflict theory of such sociologists as Dahrendorf, Vold, Sutherland, and Simmel; and the controlology of Jason Ditton. Rather, our new theoretical destination should emphasize the relationship between political and economic forces, on the one hand, and exploitative and discriminatory social arrangements, on the other. British and American scholars have been developing their own positions along these lines for some time.

The Marxian perspective envisaged by Thomas has a strong humanistic streak running through it. Its task is to identify those aspects of routine human existence that are unnecessarily constraining, especially those unnecessarily restrictive of personal freedom, and to suggest ways of eliminating the practices contributing to these conditions. People need to be given the opportunity to realize their individual potential. To the extent that they are harnessed to a program of emancipatory social change, the conventional paradigms in deviance research may be useful.

In certain respects, Thomas's proposal jibes with what biologist Gunther Stent (1978) and others are saying these days about the progress of science. They claim no grounds exist for supposing that new scientific developments can continue into the future at the same high rate as in the recent past. We shall soon be at a point where all the fundamental discoveries will have been made.

Should this assessment hold for the social sciences as well, the following reorientation may occur with them.

> The major task of the social scientist will consist of the codification of scientific findings and then translation into terms that the ordinary person can understand, equipping the average person with sufficient competence at least to ask the right questions. . . . The charge that the early sociologists assigned to themselves was, in an age of science, to find a way to maintain sufficient social unity to get the collective work of the world accomplished. It would seem to be time for sociologists to rededicate themselves to this task, but enriched by all they have learned in the meantime. Possibly the renewed interest in the sociology of everyday life is a move in the right direction: dedication to a task of communication, raising the level of understanding of the ordinary people to a point where they comprehend the fundamentals of science and society and are able . . . to participate directly in the management of their futures (Martindale, 1981: 628).

Perhaps this is the common bond that will eventually unite those who study deviance. At the very least, there is little in Martindale's remarks with which they could disagree, even though they may sometimes have strikingly different blueprints for the future of their scientific specialty.

9 ISSUES IN THE STUDY OF DEVIANCE

EDWIN M. LEMERT

In the past decade and a half, a substantial amount of commentary and criticism has been directed at the societal reaction and labeling theories of deviance. The quality of the criticism has been uneven at best and some of it has been uninformed by careful consideration of what those credited with developing the prevailing theories of deviance have in fact said. In many instances, complex ideas about deviance have been restated so simplistically that their criticism becomes a spurious exercise in logic or is followed by citing data whose relevance is questionable. In the context of the controversial and sometimes polemic discussions, labeling theory often appears to be a creation of its critics, bent on destruction of that which never was (see Hirschi, 1973; Gove, 1975).

Criticisms of the "new" conceptions of deviance can be understood best in terms of their basic assumptions, their postulates, or the grounds of knowledge from which they derive. Some of the criticisms predictably have come from those identified with positivism, best represented in the field of traditional criminology, whose advocates have sought to discover the causes of crime in the attributes of individuals or in measurable aspects of their environments. Other critical voices have been raised among writers associated with functionalism, likewise among a newer coterie of radical sociologists. Finally, a kind of revisionist criticism can be found among friendly critics who accept in a general way the labeling conception of deviance but recognize the need for its more explicit formulation.

The number of specific criticisms of the theories in question is quite large, and so diverse that to sort them out or reply to them all would be an overwhelming, if not a self-defeating, task. For this reason, my discussion will be focused around several issues whose resolution is crucial to the clarification and development of a heuristic model for the study of deviance. This will attempt to reduce some of the confusion that now pervades the field—confusion that stems in large part from differences in definitions of its subject matter, and in models or paradigms that underlie related research, if not opposing conceptions of the nature of social science itself.

ISSUE OF DEFINITION

Gibbs (1966) more or less inaugurated criticism of the new conceptions of deviance in a carefully phrased analysis that exposed a serious flaw in the fourfold schema Becker (1963) used to define the subject matter of his labeling theory. The scheme included two kinds of rule breaking, one of which was designated as "secret deviant" despite Becker's pivotal idea that deviance is behavior that groups perceive and label as such. On its face this poses a contradiction, for it admits the existence of secret deviance apart from, or independent of, that constituted by those who apply the rules. Thus deviance is defined as perceived behavior but the term also is applied to behavior not perceived. Further ambiguity lies in Becker's illustrations of secret deviance: sadomasochistic fetishism and homosexuality do not seem well chosen for the purpose because in our society *most* sexual behavior is concealed or hidden from others. Logically this compels recognition that there is secret conformity, and so the term *secret* further loses its discriminating value. A similar kind of confusion is inherent in Becker's category of "falsely accused" deviance, which is perceived as deviant behavior but subsumed as conformity because no rule breaking occurs.

NORM-BASED DEFINITION OF DEVIANCE

Gibbs's critique of Becker, also given attention by Pollner (1974), reveals that there is less of a break and discontinuity between labeling theory and the traditional positivist conception of deviance than ordinarily is believed. The difficulty this creates lies in the continued reliance upon a rule- or norm-based definition of deviance while proposing to study it as a process (Lemert, 1975). This raises the important question of whether to study rules as members of a community utilize them in pursuing their everyday purposes or to study rules as they are deduced or inferred by the methods of positivist social science. Put somewhat differently, the question is whether to inquire into how acting members of a community conceive rules or to study their actions with a conception of rules devised by sociologists and imposed on their actions. Presumably, the answer will depend on which is the better basis for explaining that which in a large sense I here call *moral differentiation*.

Gibbs (1966: 9–14) favored the positivist view of deviance mainly on the grounds that labeling theory is ambiguous and fails to deal sufficiently with the causes and incidence of deviant acts. He stated his conclusion as a " . . . preference to identify deviant acts by reference to norms and treat reactions as a contingent property." The opposing view is well put by Kitsuse (1972: 14): "If we follow Gibbs' proposal that deviant acts be identified by reference to norms independent of the reactions to those acts, sociologists may find that (community) members ignore, dismiss and even applaud acts that sociologists classify as unambiguously clear violations of norms.

SOME REALISM ABOUT NORMS AND THE DEFINITION OF DEVIANCE

The issue that exists among sociologists over the importance of rules in defining deviance is strongly reminiscent of the controversy carried on in years past in jurisprudence by the legal realists, who attacked the long-held assumptions that the decisions of judges were determined by legal rules having an independent existence that they "discovered" by logic and analysis. Today the contention of the legal realists that rules are problematical influences in the administration of the law and that the law is largely what judges, legislators, lawyers, and others do is taken for granted. Sociologists who prefer to study rules as separate subject matter risk erring in the direction of the older discredited jurisprudence. Evidence for this lies in the tendency of sociologists to reify norms, in effect treating them as entities that cause people to conduct themselves in certain ways (Lemert, 1972). This conjures up an image of people who carry on their daily routines by consulting rule books, codes, or laws, and directing their behavior accordingly.

All of this ignores the patent fact that human beings make rules, change them as they deem fit, use them in many ways, and even get along without them, depending on how they *evaluate* them in relation to their ends. If this postulate is accepted, above all that human beings are evaluating creatures, then an important intervening process is introduced into the study of deviance that distinguishes it from the methods of positivism. This refers to human choice and the influence of values.

The variable and contingent influence of rules is best clarified by considering the nature of values that enter into the process of evaluation and the choices people make when confronted with alternative means of reaching their ends. While such alternatives were comparatively few in small, isolated, low-energy societies of the past, they have increased greatly in modern industrial societies, whose cultures and social organization have become vastly differentiated. Much of this is due to innovations in science and technology that have contributed to widespread secularization of values.

These changes have altered greatly the relationship between rules and values, which in simpler societies more frequently had fixed relationships to one another. Many values once regarded as sacred have become secularized, or the processes of differentiation have made them so remote and artificial that many persons are willing to consider them merely as alternate means to their ends, or as negotiable and expendable costs of attaining goals. These changes have been very uneven and distributed in different ways so that what is deemed an inviolate truth, a God-given right, or sacred morality by one person or group may be held low in importance by others, dismissed from consideration or regarded as outmoded prejudice. This has important consequences for the kind of acts people are willing to engage in and what they will tolerate by others. Trying to predict the invocation of rules based on the aggregation of values becomes a complex exercise in social dynamics rather than one of structured responses.

There is still another cogent reason for doubting that rules alone can be the basis for defining deviance in modern society, namely their great proliferation—a veritable avalanche in the form of regulations, standards, official guidelines, ordinances, statutes, and judicial decisions. Much of this overwhelming accretion has grown out of regulatory or administrative laws, amongst which, for example, can be found rules for meat inspection by the United States Department of Agriculture crammed into a book so thick no inspector can ever hope to master them (Schuck, 1972). Likewise, penal codes grow apace, as do those for health, education, and welfare. It was for this reason that as early as the 1930s the legal realists insisted that the problem of modern-day judges is not how to reach a conclusion from a rule but rather what rule to select from a plethora of legal precedents. This is dramatically illustrated in a modern Ohio case, which involved the violation of a restrictive covenant having to do with the sale of dance training courses by those who have purchased them (*Arthur Murray Dance Studios* v. *Ohio*):

> This is not one of those questions on which the legal researcher cannot find enough to quench his thirst. To the contrary there is so much authority that it drowns him. It is a sea—vast and vacillating. One can fish out of it any kind of strange support for anything if he lives so long. This deep and unsettled sea pertaining to an employee's convenant not to compete with his employer after termination of employment is really seven seas.

And there follows eighty-three periodical citations, twenty-one annotations, fifteen encyclopedia sources, twenty treatises, seven digests, and two restatements, plus a separate selection from all of these for the state of Ohio.

This comes close to saying that judges can arrive at any finding they wish—a conclusion also applicable to a California deputy district attorney, who pointed to a copy of the state penal code and said, "That's a wonderful book, you can do almost anything you want to with it." But this ignores the fact that there are individuals and groups in the justice system with whom prosecutors and judges interact and share the power to decide who and how suspects are charged with the commission of crimes. Any portrayal of individuals acting alone to interpret or apply criminal law is misleading because usually the final action is the result of a series of choices in which the values of different individuals and groups are aggregated through interaction.

What has been said emphasizes the multiplicity of rules at hand in modern society and also the diverse and provisional nature of their use. But this does not justify an extreme conclusion that rules do not exist or that they play no part in the process with which deviance is defined, or perhaps better, socially designated. Seen as influences, they may be either important or unimportant elements in the outcome of the process. They become subordinate factors in a more generic model of explanation, present in some instances, absent in others, utilized for one purpose at one time and for a different purpose at another, sometimes being invoked by human beings as ends in themselves—even as absolutes in the sense in which the positivists see them.

LEAVING DEVIANCE UNDEFINED

The difficulty of defining deviance by reference to rules and norms plus the need to begin with a more generic conception of deviance suggests that it is much better to leave it undefined rather than to try to agree on its meaning by stipulation. While this defies scholarly convention, it has a precedent in the work of Karl Llewellyn (1973), who chose to avoid any definition of law in his numerous writings. Instead he elected to write about *legal matters*, leaving it to others to supply the connotative limits of his term. There are some very good reasons for doing this, among them that: (1) definitions are nearly always vulnerable to exceptions, (2) they can lead to contradictions and paradoxes, and (3) they invite reification and tautologies. However, Llewellyn's chief reason for bypassing definition, and that emphasized here, lay in his broad conception of law as part of social control and in his conviction that definitions "are likely to exclude things we may want to study" (Llewellyn, 1973: 178).

Analogously, the study of deviance can best proceed by identifying bodies of data through primitive, ontological recognition rather than by formal definition. In this larger sense, "deviance matters" deal with the process of differentiation, how people become differentiated, and what moral significance is attached to their differences. The center of concern is moral ideas, their rise and fall, and their invocation and application either as informal social designations or as administrative categories by agencies of social control. While moral evaluations and judgments may do no more than express "moral indignation," in all cases they are part and parcel of informal and formal social control that make up the overall societal reaction to deviance. Whenever persons and their actions mutually differentiate through processes of stigmatization, rejection, isolation, segregation, punishment, treatment, or rehabilitation, they are data for the study of deviance. The concepts chosen for the related research and the mode of analysis necessarily will be oriented to particular bodies of data under investigation.

THE DEVIANT ACT AS AN ISSUE

A great deal of controversy over the current conceptions of deviance has centered around the significance of the deviant act. Societal reaction and labeling theorists in some instances have been charged with slighting its importance and leaving the impression that persons are arbitrarily selected by agents of social control and fixed with a deviant label. A closely related objection to labeling theory is that it pays no attention to the problem of the etiology of deviant acts. Some writers contend that by ignoring deviant acts and dwelling on the variation in their social definitions, the deviance theories revive an outmoded cultural relativism that makes no recognition of possible universal or transcultural forms of deviance.

While Gibbs (1966) indicated a preference for concentrating on the study of norm-defined deviant acts because of the lack of clarity in labeling theory, Merton and Nisbet (1971) adhere to a functionalist view that the sociologist conceives deviant actions differently than the "social system does" and that he is concerned with deviant behavior, not persons. In particular, the Merton-Nisbet–style sociologist wants to discover how differing rates and forms of deviant behavior are produced by characteristics of social structure. Accordingly, explaining these and the social reactions to them are two separate questions, and merging the two abandons the basic question of why particular acts vary from one population to another, why certain persons engage in the acts, and why an act is deviant in one society but not in another. Consistent with these statements, Merton and Nisbet use the terms *deviant behavior, rule breaking,* and *acts* interchangeably.

Merton and Nisbet's insistence that social structure produces rates of deviance is made without any real refutation of the thesis of Kitsuse and Cicourel (1963) that persons or social organizations generate statistics about deviance by defining, recording, and tabulating cases for political and administrative purposes, rather than purely technical. This restates in a somewhat different context the issue already discussed, namely whether sociologists or the active participants in the on-going activities of society decide if deviance exists and to what degree. It is significant to add here that in many instances those sociologists who have undertaken the more objective type of analysis of rates of deviance have relied on data taken from the records of public agencies. The unreliability of such data for measuring the kind of highly abstracted "acts" that Merton, Nisbet, and others give an independent existence has received a good deal of comment. The post-functionalist theories of deviance do not necessarily reject the importance of investigating such rates but rather insist that they are measures of past social interactions rather than of abstracted acts in a technical sense.

It is true that labeling and societal reaction theorists have not shown much interest in trying to discover rates of deviance. However, the criticism that they disregard the importance of the deviant act does not stand up well in the light of their commitment to descriptive methods that stress appreciation of its specific, diverse, and contextual nature. This assumes that human acts cannot be understood fully apart from their meaning or evaluation, which in turn are understandable only in terms of present and past social interactions. Societal reaction theory includes observations of deviance—namely, values and valuation—which ordinarily positivists refuse to acknowledge or insist are not scientifically knowable.

The wisdom of making such observations is demonstrated in those areas of deviance where it can be understood only by focusing on their "value added" or reactional aspects. Physically handicapped persons do not become deviant because of particular acts that break rules—a conclusion especially conspicuous in cases of persons who have cosmetic defects, such as scars, birthmarks, misshapen features, or uncoordinated bodily movements. Much the same is true of stuttering, which so far has defied research efforts to show that any particular kinds of speech lead to its onset. Again, to date efforts at defining problem drinking or alcoholism by measures of the quantity and frequency of alcohol consumption have been unavailing. Finally, although there is some fervid disagreement about the matter, it seems doubtful that any classifiable acts or symptoms can be identified consistently as mental disease.

The best evidence that specific acts are not prerequisites of deviance and that the status of deviant can be purely ascribed is brought out by materials on witchcraft and sorcery, phenomena whose existence good positivists must surely deny. Gluckman (1965: 175) noted this:

> Not all disturbances of social relations arise from breaches of rules of right conduct. A marked characteristic of tribal society is that natural misfortunes are ascribed to evil wishes of witches or sorcerers, to the anger of spirits affronted by neglect of themselves . . . and to rightful curses by appropriate persons.

Selby (1974: 92) asserts that witchcraft among the Zapotec is a test case of the idea that inherent qualities of behavior are not required in order for persons to be labeled deviant. The people in question typically are curers who under certain conditions are subject to ostracism as witches. Selby writes that " . . . the villagers say that 'sometimes they are witches,' but there is no one in the village who performs witchcraft either by sticking pins in dolls or muttering incantations."

DEVIANT ACTS AND THE NEW CRIMINOLOGY

Some of the strongest objections to labeling and societal reaction theories for their assumed neglect of deviant acts have come from those in the field of delinquency research and criminology, often appearing in debates over the "new criminology," which grew out of deviancy theory in the British Isles. Those aligned with a more traditional positivist methodology in the field generally hold that crime is a violation of law and that actions of police or courts are substantially accurate certifications of homogeneous acts that transgress consensual norms. A qualified position taken by some writers recognizes ambiguities in the definitions of crimes but claims that there are certain acts, such as robbery, that "everyone knows" are crimes, and that are universally recognized as such. From this it is reasoned that societal reaction theory, because it takes the definition of crimes to be problematical, revives and propagates a form of naïve cultural relativism.

Contrary to these claims, it can be pointed out that there are quite a few legally defined transgressions that do not require the commission of specific actions; for example, the so-called status offenses of juveniles—incorrigibility, running away, truancy, and "being in moral danger." But, more significantly, there are also adult crimes without specific behavioral correlates, the most obvious one being conspiracy, in which no overt act need be committed in order to be accused or found guilty. American antitrust laws do not forbid acts as such but rather "combinations" in restraint of trade, so that something as conventional as carrying a briefcase to lunch at a restaurant may be taken to be criminal if a judge or a jury determines that it signified intent to set prices illegally on a manufactured product.

When scrutiny is turned from American society to those societies that have experienced socialist revolutions, it is abundantly clear that specificity of acts is not an absolute requirement for the designation of crimes. While these nations, like others, have penal codes, they usually have contained some very generalized provision for the punishment of counterrevolutionary crimes. These, called crimes by analogy, are illustrated by the following excerpt from a Chinese communist code: "Those with a counterrevolutionary purpose who commit crimes not covered in this act may be given punishments which are comparable to the crimes committed" (Li, 1970: 86).

In Russia, during the Stalinist era, the possession of foreign postage stamps was sufficient for arrest and punishment as a counterrevolutionary (Gilksman, 1954). In Czechoslovakia, after the Communists took power, an accident damaging another vehicle became a crime if the vehicle belonged to the State but not if it belonged to a private citizen. And although the Czechs had no law against bestiality, in one case a man in their country was convicted for sexual intercourse with a cow because it was an undignified use of state property (Ulc, 1972).

It is possible to argue, as Fuller (1968) does, that such occurrences do not reflect law, or that they are "bad" law or pathology of law and that no "true" crimes were committed. Nevertheless, the fact remains that large numbers of people at one time or another in such societies have been charged, tried, convicted, and imprisoned as criminals on such grounds. Only in a highly ideal "ought" sense can political influences be excluded from the study of criminal law. Where courts and law enforcement are directly subordinated to political authority and official ideology, it is much easier than it is in our society to see how crime may be ascribed through such influences in the absence of specificity of charges.

The insistence that there always must be discernible acts before there can be crime comes close to absurdity when it is recalled that failure to act can be forbidden by law as well as describable acts. Instances of this kind are offenses of nonsupport of dependents, failure to answer a summons, negligence in operating machinery, failure to register for military duty, failure to report taxable income, and even failure to file census reports. Some writers try to evade this illogicality (i.e., making both acts and nonacts crimes) by referring to "acts of omission," but obviously this is no more than a fiction.

CULTURAL RELATIVISM AND DEVIANT ACTS

The belief that certain forms of conduct are more or less inherently criminal, or that they are universally recognized as such in different cultures, is an old one. Recently this idea has reappeared in criticisms Walker (1974) makes of the new criminology. He grants that there are some conditions under which the passage of new laws and their enforcement creates deviance, such as England's imposition of a tax on tea drunk by Americans and missionary laws forbidding nudity and adultery among South Sea natives. However, he goes on to say that "this Eden ideology is quite inapplicable to crimes such as murder, rape, robbery and burglary, which have been serious crimes in every civilized culture—and most uncivilized ones—for many generations" (Walker, 1974: 58).

What this says, literally, is little more than that certain crimes have been crimes, leaving it unclear whether the writer means conceptions of crimes or the actions and behavior they presume to represent. If he merely means the conceptions, then there is some support for his claim, but if he means the actions and behavior they subsume, a heavy weight of opinion runs to the contrary. This is well summarized in Znaniecki's discussion (1952: 332) of attempts to discover the substance of universalistic crimes:

> Can these classifications of transgressions be scientifically tested and validated by comparative analysis . . . ? Quite a few cultural scientists believe that they can, especially those criminologists who accept the system of criminal law maintained by their own society and assume its generalizations were originally based on a comparative study of the actions therein classified as crimes. . . . Nevertheless attempts—like that of Garafalo—to discover essential similarities between actions classified as crimes in all societies at all periods have failed.
>
> The reason for this is clear. All prohibitive rules define and classify actions as experienced and evaluated by those who promulgate the rules from the point of view of standards and norms they consider binding. Hence the agents who perform such prohibited actions *ex definitione* do not conform with these standards and norms, such a classification by itself contains no information as to what the actions really are from the standpoint of the agents themselves.

There is, to be sure, agreement among anthropologists that universal moral standards or ethics exist; all societies recognize and disapprove of such things as homicide, theft, lying, adultery, sexual promiscuity, and incest. But while evidence of such universalistic ethics can be found, as Linton (1952) made clear, the likenesses are primarily conceptual in nature, and, in his words, " . . . variation rages rampant as to details of proscribed instrumentalities and sanctions." Thus, taking the life of another human being is universally condemned, but at different times and in different cultures, infanticide, uxoricide, and parricide have been socially tolerated solutions to human problems, as well as killing in self-defense, in duels, and in instances where adulterers are caught *en flagrante*.

may be claimed that these are merely "exceptions to the s" but detailed examination makes it doubtful that actions or interactions claimed to be the same type of crime in different cultures ever have the common elements necessary to provoke similar societal reactions. Theft in the Cook Islands usually has involved taking coconuts from the trees of others and, under certain circumstances, usually drunkenness, helping oneself to food in an underground oven, neither of which is ever likely to be experienced by Americans. Moreover, kinship lines among Cook Islanders were so ramified that the ownership of coconuts, in reality ownership of only a right to the product of the trees, often could be challenged by legitimate claims to the "stolen" property. Theft in such instances was made even more ambiguous by the importance Polynesians attach to the values of sharing and hospitality. This emphasizes what is generally true; namely, that more than one value ordinarily comes into play in the human judgments that produce deviance.

While it is possible to say that universal values exist, nevertheless, the relation of such values to specific acts, the persons involved, and the surrounding situations making for deviance are highly variable between, and also within, cultures. An important corollary of this is that while different societies may have a number of similar values, the order in which these values can be satisfied varies greatly. Likewise, the orders of value satisfaction vary with time. Thus, although homicide presently in our society is considered to be among the most serious of crimes, there have been localities in the past where the theft of a horse was more likely to beget hanging than killing another human being. Finally, it has to be said that in most, if not all, societies, the constraints of value orders, whatever they may be, usually are applicable only to the recognized members of the society, the "in-group." So while homicide may be forbidden within the group, killing of a member of a different tribe, or even of an opposing clan in the same society, may be permissible or even applauded.

Trying to ascertain the order in which values are likely to be satisfied in particular situations is very much at the center of the study of deviance. Thus far, the emphasis in this chapter has been on the dynamic interactional process by which such value orders are reached. Parenthetically, it must be acknowledged that value orders may have been established by past interactions and incorporated into relatively stable patterns of action, guarded by rules and ideology, and transmitted as part of a culture. Deviance from such patterns is readily perceived and deviants dealt with routinely by established means of social control. The description of such patterns in small, slowly changing societies has long occupied anthropologists, who usually refer to them as structured, or as part of the social structure. Few will deny the reality of such structured patterns, but the degree to which they exist, and their linkage into larger configurations taken to be social systems, is an unsettled issue. This is particularly true in highly differentiated industrial societies. In order to emphasize the problematical nature of such linkages between patterned actions, structure will be used here in its generic sense, confining the use of the term to its plural form.

SOCIAL STRUCTURES AND DEVIANCE

Functionalists understandably have been affronted by labeling theory because it pays scant attention to questions of how social structures generate deviant acts and why their incidence or rates vary among populations and societies. Unfortunately, such questions do not carry inquiry into the relationship between social structures and the societal reaction in its processual or interactional aspects. But much the same criticism is applicable to labeling theory, which throws little light on the possible connections between interaction, process, and structures. The shortcoming in reality is a more general shortcoming of sociology, and the difficulty in large part is inherent in the notion of process itself. Despite the lengthy history of its use in sociology, the concept, as Bain (1933) noted years ago, has never been satisfactory. This resulted from the study of process or processes formally, as separate phenomena minus cultural content. While the shift to a symbolic interactionist conception of process brought meanings into analysis, the associated concepts of "self," "me," and "other" are insufficient for the study of social structure (Lemert, 1974).

The theoretical gap between process and social structure has been an unmistakable weakness of a number of the studies carried out by deviance sociologists. This comes out in their narrow preoccupation with the interaction between deviants and agents of social control, in a failure to locate them with reference to particular social structures, and reporting their results in the ethnographic present. This has prompted the criticism that labeling theory is both astructural and ahistorical (N. Davis, 1975). Many of the studies in question do not give the provenience of their data and the time period for which their conclusions are applicable. In some instances, provenience has been deliberately concealed and it must be learned informally or guessed at.

Without detracting from the merit of Goffman's (1961) contributions to deviance study, it must be said that his conclusions about total institutions and deviance, which came from research at St. Elizabeth's Hospital, failed to consider the possible effects of its special organizational features. Yet this is the hospital where the notorious "Whitehouse cases" (persons arrested and detained by the United States Secret Service for threats to the President) were sent, and where Ezra Pound was held virtually as a political prisoner for many years; and it also lies in the area of the Third United States District Court of Appeals when came the Durham rule, modifying the grounds of insanity pleas in criminal cases. It has had close administrative ties with the National Institute of Mental Health. Taken together, these facts suggest that a larger organizational analysis of "asylums" might have been worth pursuing, if for no other reason than to discover the limits within which generalizations about total institutions are valid.

THE RADICAL CRITIQUE

Among the more strident protests that prevailing deviance theory disregards, the larger organizational implications of deviance are those aired by radical sociologists. They carry forward the burden of C. Wright Mills's (1943) ideas, which condemned the social pathologists of his day for their fragmentary, nontheoretical treatments of social problems and for their failure to reckon with structural phenomena of stratification and concentration of power. Latter-day radical sociologists claim that deviance sociologists misdirect their research efforts by focusing on the interaction between deviants and agents of social control who are no more than middle or lower management people having little influence in making laws and policies that define and are used to control deviants. The radical sociologists assert that acceptance of a state definition of crime (by law) restricts inquiry to visible forms of deviance and overlooks what is, in their estimation, more serious deviance (Liazos, 1972; Taylor, Walton, and Young, 1973).

Sociologists on the sinistral side insist that the ideological commitments of those in power and antagonisms due to class differences are the causes of deviance. These they define as the violations of politically defined human rights: to food, shelter, dignity, and self-determination. Specifically, such violations are caused by racism, sexism, and inequality. Sociologists, the radicals urge, should be studying such things as political corruption, deception, and genocide. The objective of their work should be the revolutionary transformation of society.

According to the radical ideology, deviants ordinarily studied by sociologists are victims of an oppressive social system. Paradoxically, however, this same passive portrayal of deviants has been cited by some critics as one of the major faults of labeling theory (Gouldner, 1968). The counter-theme is that deviants are, or are becoming, active, self-determining rebels against oppressive social structures. Their transformation theoretically comes from cultivation of a collective consciousness of their exploited status and by the deliberate politicizing of their deviance; e.g., using the commission of crimes or other visible deviance as a means to attack the established political order (Hills, 1980).

Collective action to change the status of deviants on closer scrutiny proves to have been most apparent in the United States among homosexuals, the physically handicapped, prison inmates, and prostitutes. In each case, social action has been less radical than libertarian in its goals and less unified than pluralistic, and any connections they may have with the black civil rights and women's liberation movements are tenuous at best.

Politicization and liberation are terms easily used, but, unfortunately, little effort has been made to clarify their meanings or to discover their organizational ramifications. Media presentations of deviants as politicized or liberated need considerable discounting, and the assertions of social scientists who describe deviant behavior as "alternative life-styles" need empirical demonstration. That political movements may degenerate and become cloaks for crime and other deviance is an ever-present possibility (Dillon and Lahane, 1973). It is also true that libertarian representations in media and in social science writings may ignore the possibility that seen in its full context, much deviance is merely banal or pathetic rather than political (Taylor and Taylor, 1968).

A more generic basis for discussing this issue can be found in the insightful comments of Matza (1969) on pathos. He notes the tendency in "naturalistic" presentations to romanticize deviance in contrast to the older absolutist tendency to designate it as pathology. Recognizing that there is diversity in deviance carries the responsibility to give equal recognition to its nonromantic, sordid, and destructive aspects as well as to those aspects that, in Matza's words, are socially tenable. Some theoretical means is needed to relate the variable quality and tenability of deviance to its patterned context or social structure.

Weighed in the balance, the radical critical conception of deviance appears more as an ideology of activism than as scholarly analysis, and more rhetoric than substantial conceptualization suited to sustained empirical inquiry and research. The imputed existence of ideologically homogeneous elites or classes with disguised or conspiratorial purposes and endowed with widespread power to exploit deviants is difficult to prove or disprove. A similar reservation applies to statements that sexism, racism, and inequality cause deviance, which tend to be no more than simple assertions without explicit formulations to show how this happens.

STRUCTURES OF THE MIDDLE RANGE

The most that can be said for radical sociology at this point is that it does a modest service in recalling the need for the historical study of deviance and reemphasizing the necessity to place it in a larger sociocultural and political context. However, it remains to be determined at what level of social structure inquiries into deviance can be pursued and still be manageable as research enterprises. Some of the features of modern society suggest the answer. One is the salience of large-scale associations that are organized around a limited set of purposes and that make no effort to satisfy a full range of human values. This specialization is no less true of agencies dealing with deviants than it is of business and industrial corporations.

While the predominance of large public associations can be assumed, the nature and extent of their interorganizational ties and their connections with small groups and individuals is problematical (i.e., they must be discovered by empirical research). Moreover, because of the specialized way in which they are organized, the particular issues that arise in their interaction and the values at stake are crucial in trying to foretell whether they will become involved in the social control of deviance. So, for example, a taxpayers' association may try to influence public policies that affect police and correctional organizations in order to try to keep down the costs of government, but are unlikely to spend funds and staff time on issues irrelevant to the interests of property owners, such as repealing laws against sex offenses.

For this and related reasons, the study of deviance can best start with conceptual orientations to bodies of data dealing with visible social structures rather than assume the existence of an over-arching social system or pervasive ideological influence binding groups and individuals together in a common morality. The path of analysis begun in this fashion may ramify into various levels of governmental or economic structures, such as can be demonstrated by studies of public policy and the social control of narcotic drugs (McCoy, 1972; Newsday Staff, 1973). However, it is easier to propose such research than to carry it out; problems of access to data, inference, and proof tend to grow with the magnitude of the social structures postulated as significant.

SOCIAL STRUCTURE AND DEVIANCE: INTERIM CONCLUSIONS

Although I have taken a stand against structural or functional theories of deviance as they are conventionally understood, nonetheless, social structures in the sense of the position of groups and individuals at the point of their interaction are of great significance in any attempt to predict the pattern of action in which deviance emerges. Values of people who are filled with moral indignation over the acts of others may have little importance if they are not organized and brought to bear in situations in which they can influence the societal reaction. Conversely, persons and groups, even though they count as no more than a minority, may be so situated that their specialized values, rather than those of others, shape new moral ideas or preserve the old.

The aspects of social structures that are relevant for the study of deviance include codes specifying the place and manner of determining laws and policies, arrangements designed to stop the flow of some kinds of information and facilitate others, rules for control over meetings, and methods of communication that create or impede effective group action. Such features are part of the power structure of every community and society (Cottrell, 1972).

The ideological importance given to law in American society, its apotheosis of "sacred rights" and assumed inviolability of its procedures, means that courts, judges, and lawyers are strongly positioned to forge criminal sanctions for deviance and control their administration. One effect of this is to obscure the problematical nature of law, in which informal interaction, the "law" in action, or negotiation takes precedence over vaunted formal procedures. Another effect is to conceal the extent to which law comes to rest on indeterminate concepts, such as "reasonable," "due process," and "good faith," all of which get their substance from human evaluation. More accurate appraisal of legal structures that recognizes such "realities" can be made from comparisons across societies and cultures.

The special limited meaning given to the concept of social structure is heuristic. The main conclusion to be left at this point is that social structure does not cause deviance nor does it in my view produce rates of deviance. This, however, is not merely a denial of the large assumptions of a theory of functionalism so much as it is an assertion about the nature of causation itself. This raises a final issue in deviance studies, more fundamental than any so far examined.

ISSUE OF CAUSATION: REVISIONIST VIEWS

Kitsuse (1972) insightfully pointed out a confusion in Becker's (1963) theory of deviance in that it starts with rule breaking as an a priori fact, which is then converted into deviance by the application of the rules a group has created. Thus, rules preexist but they are also created and applied through symbolic interaction. It is left unclear whether deviance has an independent existence, which is then officially certified, or whether it is an emergent phenomenon in which acts as well as their meanings change and become deviant as a result of symbolic communication. A similar kind of confusion or "subtle shift in emphasis" was detected by Kitsuse (1972) in my early (Lemert, 1951) statement of the societal reaction theory of deviance. To wit: I postulated the independent or empirically verifiable existence of modalities or norms of behavior and deviations from them, to which there are societal reactions ranging from social approval through social disapproval. This stood in contrast to my other statements that deviance should be studied as a process of moral differentiation and individuation.

The ambiguity in societal reaction theory detected by Kitsuse speaks of the difficulties those striving for innovative ideas have in disengaging themselves from the issues, questions, and methodologies of their eras. Becker unwisely got caught up by the attractive symmetry of the fourfold table, while I was beguiled by the behavioral studies of conformity being carried out by psychologists and legal realists of the time.

In behalf of Becker and myself, although we acknowledged the prior or separate existence of "something out there"—rule breaking or variation from norms—nevertheless, we made process the starting point for analysis: labeling for Becker; social control for myself. Unfortunately, the ambiguities in both theories allowed or encouraged critics, friendly and unfriendly, to cast them into the format of normal science. Process was ignored or paid lip service, while some single aspect or referent of social control, such as arrest, dishonorable discharge from the armed forces, or referral of shoplifters to police by store detectives, was selected as an independent variable to be related by conventional quantitative methods to the occurrence or magnitude of deviance. Needless to say, not much unequivocal validation has emerged. At the same time, responsible critics admit that few studies have been designed specifically to test societal reaction theory, and some conclude that no theory worthy of the term has been developed. Thus, Tittle (1975: 176) states, "Labelists must get down to serious theoretical business. Evasiveness, lauding of ambiguity and hiding behind a facade of sensitizing concepts will no longer suffice."

THEORY OR NONTHEORY

The validity of this last charge may be settled partially by looking at the way labelists characterize their writings. Tannenbaum (1938) calls his formulation of delinquency and crime a point of view; Becker (1963) speaks of his ideas as a perspective that tells how something becomes other than what it was, and says that the value of labeling theory will be gauged by "increased understanding of things formerly obscure." Scheff (1975) calls his labeling theory of mental illness a sensitizing theory originated to discount the medical model and to "clear the air"; he concedes that this is not literally true but that it can be used to evaluate evidence in a provisional way and is the best way to interpret existing studies in his area. Although I can't recall having stated the purpose of societal reaction theory, I have always believed that the ultimate purpose of social science is prediction or some rough estimate of what is going to happen next. Spector and Kitsuse (1977), the chief revisionists of societal reaction and labeling theories, believe that their purpose should be to *describe and explain* the definitional process (of deviance and social problems) and the collective activities that get organized around these assertions or claims.

Obviously, ambiguity still lurks here, beclouding any effort to determine just what form these characterizations of the respective scholarly works amount to: humanism, social philosophy, speculative theory, or science? All of which recall an older, and wise, observation by MacIver (1942: 375) that "the perplexities of social causation have fostered a tendency to resort to modes of explanation that avoid or seem to avoid the causal challenge."

NEED FOR AN ANALYTICAL MODEL

Schur (1975: 287), another revisionist of labeling theory, comes closest to agreeing that the societal reaction perspective or its sensitizing concepts need to be developed or "become parts of genuine theories that serve the ends of science." He also insightfully notes what I take to be the main stumbling block to such a task; namely, the unquestioned insistence of its critics that the societal reaction orientation "should prove its worth as a theory of deviance causation in the traditional sense." Unfortunately, Schur does not pursue this line of thought and simply argues for a change in subject matter from microanalysis of the origins of deviant identity to the study of rule creation and rule change at "various levels," thus adopting what Mankoff (1971) terms macrolabeling analysis.

The revisionist position taken by Spector and Kitsuse (1977) like Schur's seeks to shift the study of deviance (and social problems) to macrosociological concerns arrived at from a different direction than a functionalist route. As already noted, this means that deviance theory should describe and explain the process by which morally objectionable conditions or behavior are asserted to exist. However, these writers leave it unclear whether in carrying out such a task sociologists perform in the capacity of scientists.

While Mankoff (1971), Schur (1975), Spector and Kitsuse (1977), and Rains (1975) have demarcated new areas for deviance study and indicated what should be explained, they have not in my estimation provided a theoretical model for doing so. While Davis (1975) lists formal requirements for developing a model to study social control, including causal structure, at the same time she disavows the existence of deviance. Despite this, deviance is defined in a rather formal way as a kind of conflict. Furthermore, causation becomes statements about relationships between variables—how they co-vary. Thus, while labeling theorists bypass the causal question, a formal statement of conflict theory returns to a traditional mechanical model of causation.

An important reason why labelists may have failed to originate a working model for the study of deviance is that the symbolic interactionist concept of process derived from Mead, to which I

assume that Schur, Spector and Kitsuse, and others give their allegiance, is by its nature insufficient for macrosociological analysis. I
have given my reasons for believing this elsewhere (Lemert, 1974)
but here I will simply say that Mead dwelled primarily on interin-
dividual interaction and socialization; he never developed a conception of groups or of society other than as generalized extensions
of self-consciousness or as that of the "larger self."

It is also likely that labeling theorists distort the idea of interaction; by adopting the perspective of the individual or of the so-
called underdog, social control is described unilaterally, and social
interaction takes on an asymmetrical quality that precludes appreciation of its mutuality. Full interactional analysis must show how
individual and aggregate responses of deviants through resistance,
deflection, mitigation, and negotiation become influences that re-
shape the societal reaction. While some writers (Rogers and Buffalo, 1974) have attacked the view of the deviant as a victim and
have shown how deviants "fight back," Cohen (1965) and Mills
(1959) stated explicitly the need to analyze the relationship of deviants and their milieu in interactional terms. In Cohen's (1965: 11)
words: "The interaction process may be analyzed from the standpoint of its consequences for stability or change in the normative
structure itself.... Deviance may prompt re-examination of the
boundaries of the normatively permissible, resulting in ... reformulation of the rule or implicit changes in its meaning, so that
deviant becomes defined as nondeviant or nondeviant as deviant."

Spector and Kitsuse (1977) say that labeling theorists and value
conflict theorists have been sensitive to this last issue, the charge of
subjectivism made by their critics. By this they mean that labelists
have recognized the importance of objective conditions or of objective behavior as well as the definitional processes involved in the
production of deviance and social problems. However, they refer to
this as the "balanced approach" and reject it on the grounds that "it
reduces the social construction of reality, an accomplishment of
members of society, to a mere mechanical reaction to exterior
forces" (Spector and Kitsuse, 1977: 589). Instead, they say that individuals and groups define, respond, and act toward putative conditions (i.e., those commonly thought or reckoned to exist).

Whether by this means these writers escape the dilemma of
subjectivism in deviance study is questionable. This becomes
clearer in another of their statements (Spector and Kitsuse, 1977:
78): " ... it is not such an extreme position to urge that sociologists
of social problems set aside the issue of the objective basis of al-

leged conditions, even to the extent of remaining indifferent to their existence." Here is a "subtle shift" by the authors from concern with people to concern with sociologists. Most certainly the people or agents of social control do not set aside questions of the existence of objective conditions in making judgments about deviance, nor do they ignore questions of the creditability and consequences of their judgments about objective conditions.

If it is accepted that theoretical models must reflect the reality they represent, then a model must be devised for the study of deviance that reveals how people take objective conditions into account in making judgments about deviance by others and by themselves. This pertains not only to external social facts but also to physical and biological facts. Their inclusion is imperative if the study of deviance is to move beyond static, cross-sectional researches to that of the emergence and dynamics inherent in its conception as a process of differentiation.

A CHOICE AND FEEDBACK MODEL

There is good reason to believe that Cooley's (1902) conception of social interaction is superior to Mead's for the kind of macrosociological work toward which Schur, Mankoff, Davis, and others say deviance study is or should be moving. This is because Cooley's formulations deal with groups and institutions, their differentiation, expansion, contraction, and disappearance, all as part of a tentative process in which influences move back and forth between groups and individuals, as well as between mutually influencing groups. Furthermore, Cooley clearly distinguishes between generalizations about certain kinds of recurrent social phenomena that result in more or less constant rates: marriages, divorces, suicides, the proportion of income spent on food, and generalizations applicable to situations in which social and physical influences get organized into some new and emergent form. The latter take place through human agencies in which evaluation occurs in a context of group interaction. Specifically, Cooley recognizes the importance of *social intelligence* in deliberating, calculating, weighing, and sorting out values leading to choices for individual and collective action. Toulmin (1970: 2) clarifies further the nature of this evaluational process in which things called factors or variables in mechanical models of causation are modified and reduced to influences, thus making possible the use of a different kind of model of causation:

Everything has causes; some of the things we do have reasons too. When our actions are done for reasons, these reasons enter into the causal explanation of our actions. But they do so indirectly by way of the "rational arts"—moral reflection, practical deliberation and intellectual calculation . . . and they do so without losing their rational character of "having force for us rather than forcing us", of "carrying weight with us" rather than overpowering us, of being "compelling" rather than compulsive.

It is evaluation in this sense, which provides the core of a model for studying deviance, that considers how influences are organized, that shows the interplay between objective and subjective factors, and that leaves room for human choice without leaving scientific ground.

COTTRELL AND THE FEEDBACK CONCEPT

However valuable it is, it is necessary to go beyond Cooley's early notions of evaluation and social intelligence to show in more detail what consequences human choices have on the process by which deviance emerges. A good deal is owed to Cottrell (1972) for his novel use of the concept of feedback to explicate more precisely what Cooley meant by the tentative social process. Feedback, a term coming from engineering and mathematical model-making, refers to the use of a small amount of energy to convey back to a machine the on-going direction, speed, and other physical aspects of its operation, which can through a servomechanism energize self-corrective adjustments. However, Cottrell uses the term in a descriptive way, meaning to convey back to individuals or groups the consequences of prior choices, which is to say whether their choices produced results according to their expectations or not. In general, when they do, an emergent or preexisting pattern of action is reinforced or the tentative social process is extended. When they do not, subsequent choices become problematical, especially over the long run. Cottrell emphasizes that human choices are not invariate in a mechanical sense, to which may be added that they are not analogues of stimulus response behavior of experimental animals, as often portrayed by behavioristic psychology.

The possibilities or consequences of a human choice are several, at least:

1. It may perpetuate a pattern of action—a set of rules, or the persistence of deviance.

2. It may alter the pattern of action—rules are changed.

3. It may weaken, undermine, or erode the pattern.

4. It may so change the pattern and situation that choice is no longer possible.

5. It may destroy the person or persons making the choice.

VALUES AND COSTS

Cottrell's (1972) model distinguishes between the act of evaluation and the pattern of action that expresses the order in which values get satisfied. Value is defined as that which within physical and biological limits influences choice; hence, values are observed or inferred from the choices people make. Presumably, values exist in a hierarchy, but the opportunity for individuals to satisfy them in some ideal or free-choice order seldom occurs because persons must seek their ends in a world of limited means and usually through the instrumentality of organized groups. Consequently, a give-and-take occurs in group interaction in which individuals sacrifice some values in order to satisfy others. Those sacrificed values become costs of particular choices or costs of achieving preferred ends.

It is here, in the consideration of costs, that "objective factors," such as time, energy, monetary expenditures, and stress, enter into individual evaluations and collective interaction. The most important observation to make is that while objective conditions do not directly "cause" human choices or action, they can, nevertheless, change the costs of satisfying an existing order of values and so alter choices and a pattern of action. For example, greater driving time needed by police to deliver drunks to a detoxification center may cut down the number of arrests for intoxication even though the police still hold to an order of protective and charitable values that previously led to their making larger numbers of arrests. The need for increased court appearances by police, choked court calendars, lack of jail space, and accelerated demands on the county budget all can alter choices and change patterns of action by law enforcement people without any changes in the value systems of the individuals and groups involved.

A final point, no less important than the previous one, is that while changed or increased costs may be perceived or learned through symbolic interaction, they also may be perceived through direct experience with the material world and the human body, and sometimes they can't be perceived in any other way. It is doubtful whether the deeper meaning of a craving for alcohol or for heroin can be communicated symbolically, although others who have experienced them may certify their existence. In an opposite vein, it can scarcely be said that the resistance encountered in nurses and in some physicians to acceptance of alcoholism as a disease is learned symbolically; rather, it comes from appreciation of the untenability of the alcoholic's reactions in a medical treatment setting.

If it is accepted that there is perception of deviance through direct feedback from the physical environment and from the biological organism, then objective and subjective facts may be brought together in an analytical model that is still within the bounds of social science. The reality of deviance no longer will need to be exclusively conceived as social reality. Likewise, a solution to the problem raised by the "oversocialized conception of man" (Wrong, 1961) in sociology may be dealt with other than by simply ignoring it.

10 NORMS, CONFORMITY, AND DEVIANCE

D. LAWRENCE WIEDER
CHARLES W. WRIGHT

The problem of deviance as it is formulated within any system of thought is contingent, if not dependent, upon aspects of the general system of thought in which it is couched. For example, a Lombrosian positivist (as well as a modern genetic determinist—say, a "sociobiologist") is able to view crime as largely explicable biologically, because the positivistic general system of "sociology" finds values given in nature, reifies criminal law, and, therefore, takes the existence, structure, and content of the law for granted. A full understanding of the "problem of deviance" (i.e., its position within a thought system, the puzzles that it raises, and the solutions offered to those puzzles) benefits from an analysis of the general system of thought as it bears most directly upon the study of deviance. In large part, this paper is concerned with explicating the image of social life that has guided sociological thinking about deviance for a number of years. As such, it is a commentary on general sociological theory as it bears upon the development of the study of deviance.

Modern sociologies of deviance are not inclined to make the positivistic error of taking the law or other patterned aspects of social life for granted. Nevertheless, the conceptualization of deviance found within these systems is most always associated with the notion of a normative pattern (a norm, rule, or law). Modern functionalism is unequivocal on this point. For example, Parsons (1951: 250) comments that " . . . deviance is a motivated tendency for an actor to behave in contravention of one or more institutionalized patterns. Merton (1971: 827) also makes his position clear. At the end of a critical comment directed toward labeling theory, he remarks: " . . . no rule, no rule violating behavior." Upon this foundation, functionalism has raised a series of questions concerning the matter of the violation of social patterns. How are social patterns established for the actor? What leads the actor to withdraw commitment from such patterns once they have been established? How do subcultures emerge that exist in opposition to the pattern? What is the role of major institutions in this process? How are tendencies to the violation of these patterns counteracted? What functional significance do such patterns possess (i.e., what is their functional relationship to the system of social life in which they are embedded)? These questions are logically founded on the functionalist conception of deviance. They would not be reasonable questions to ask in light of some other conceptions of deviance.

In contrast, labeling theory holds that behavior is not intrinsically deviant and is made so only in the process of being reacted to as deviant. Further, it is held that this reaction occurs in the context of someone's interests. In the situation of reaction, rules are formulated and/or elaborated upon and applied to the behavior of the purported deviant. Labeling theory conceives of the relation of rules to deviance[1] in a manner that is different from the point of view of functionalism, but rules still are clearly implicated as a major element, if not the major element, of study within the perspective. As Becker (1963: 9) notes, in a comment that shifts the focus of the study of deviance from the act to the rules it may be seen as violating, " . . . social groups create deviance by making the rules whose infraction constitutes deviance and by applying those rules to particular people and labeling them outsiders." Although there are fundamental differences between the approaches of labeling theory and functionalism (see Wright and Randall, 1978), the two share the inclusion of this "pattern element." From both these perspectives, the rules are there to be violated and/or applied. And, from the labeling perspective, if rules are not already there, they can be created. For labeling theorists, the crucial questions concerning rules include the conditions necessary for the emergence of a rule, whose interests are represented in the formulation of a rule, the role of rules in social life, to whom the rule will be applied, and the effect of the application of rules on an actor. These questions, and not those posed by the functionalists, are logically founded on the labeling theorists' conception of deviance. As a matter of practice, followers of labeling theory and functionalism have not made rules and norms phenomena for investigation in their own right. That is, they do not ask: What sorts of things are rules (or norms) in the first place? Rather, the features of rules (or norms) are stipulated by definition. Rules (or norms), with the features given them by definition, are then assumed to be in operation in social interaction and, in turn, are employed in the analysis of deviance.

Foundational questions concerning the basic features of the phenomena are thus ignored in stipulating those features by constructing definitions. Furthermore, these questions are ruled "out of order" as unreasonable, for they seek clarification of the seemingly obvious matters that any sociologist already "knows" before he or she becomes a sociologist. What could be more obvious than the properties of ordinary rules as any citizen might know them? Yet, as we shall see, asking foundational questions not only brings to the surface conceptual features and issues that are not at all obvious, but such a line of questioning permits the formulation of cogent empirical questions of the sort that bear upon theoretical disputes as well.

Our method for raising foundational questions relies upon ethnomethodological reasoning and lines of theoretical and empirical inquiry that stem from that reasoning. Among the tasks that they have undertaken, ethnomethodologists have sought to clarify the idea of rule-governed actions. Two similar lines of inquiry have concerned the logical-theoretical properties of the normative paradigm (Wilson, 1970) and the game-model of social interaction (Garfinkel, 1963). Here we will employ and elaborate the game-model and its specification of rules.

By proceeding in this fashion, we will typify and clarify the model that tacitly undergirds the functional approach to deviance, as associated with such scholars as Talcott Parsons, Robert Merton, Albert Cohen, Richard Cloward, and Lloyd Ohlin, as well as others. Insofar as the architects and practitioners of labeling theory have sipped from this fountain (and we think they have in important respects), this analysis will bear upon their work as well. Our focus is upon the general model, for it is this model that is the generally unclarified and partially tacit foundation for the conceptualization of the theoretical problem of deviance. By clarifying the model in this fashion, we are in a position to ask what sorts of phenomenon rules are in the first place in a way that is relevant to functionalist and labeling theorist conceptions. This clarification will enable us to exhibit some of the powerful claims and propositions that can be based on the model and to examine the ways it is empirically cogent and empirically "testable" in the sense of being well or poorly fitted to empirical states of affairs.

We will then be in a position to raise issue with the image of rule, conformity, and deviance, which is projected by the underlying model. We shall find that propositions that are warranted on the basis of ethnographic observation of the processes of following a rule and of witnessing someone else's conformity or deviance from a rule are inconsistent with the model and, in turn, with the traditional conception. Ethnomethodological conceptions of rules, conformity, and deviance are, however, consistent with these direct observations and, in part, are based upon them. The final sections of this chapter, then, exhibit an ethnomethodological imagery for the analysis of rules, norms, conformity, and deviance.

WHAT IS ETHNOMETHODOLOGY?

Since much of our exposition depends upon, and concerns, ethnomethodological analysis, a brief explanation of this mode of analysis is in order. First to be explained is that awkward term *ethnomethodology*. What does it mean and what connection does it have to actual ethnomethodological work (Garfinkel, 1974)? *Ethno* means "folk" or "the people." *Ethnomethods* thus are "folk methods." Ethnomethodology does not refer to a method of doing social science (although it does have some distinctive methods and reflects a particular philosophy of social science) but to a phenomenon—an object to be studied. At the analytic level, ethnomethodology refers to a frame of analysis that inspects social life with respect to the methods that societal members employ in living their lives. Initially, the concern for members' methods focused on the production and utilization of commonsensical knowledge—roughly equivalent to cognitive and normative culture. But the notion quickly became expanded to include the production of orderly activities. The idea of method, of course, calls our attention to the stepwise accomplishment of some state of affairs. A metaphor that is helpful here is the building of a model airplane. The instructions and the person's temporally extended way of carrying out those instructions constitute the person's method. There is an absolute correlation between method and achieved product (the fully constructed model airplane). To examine the method is to examine the resulting object's mode of being organized—we may say its "constitution."

The current ethnomethodological heuristic treats the seemingly stable or given features of a social setting (e.g., its gender composition, its castelike structure, or its sense as objective—its sense as "there" for anyone) as the collective achievement of the setting's participants. "The transformation of 'social facts' into processual accomplishments is a paradigmatic principle of ethnomethodological inquiry" (Pollner, 1978: 269). Any socially recognized social state of affairs is to be examined as the accomplishment of the parties to those affairs.

The social recognition of social states of affairs is accomplished through everyday methods. In effect, these are the culturally given and culturally transmitted methods of reasonable thinking. They consist in any reasonable person's methods of determining truth and relevance. They include the definite ways of answering questions such as: Is this statement true? Is this statement possibly true? Is that statement probably true? Is this equivalent to that? Does this cause that? Is this description complete? What kind of bias or distortion is involved here? What is this?

Just as these are questions that may be asked by scientists, they are also questions that—in the context of everyday life—are asked by judges, juries, police officers, social workers, business executives, carpenters, and supermarket shoppers. The methods employed in answering these questions as they appear in everyday life produce those phenomena that sociologists focus upon as objects of study. That is, these methods produce what sociologists treat as data. Further, it is upon these data that the sociologist bases his or her theories of the social world. But, until the recent past, sociologists have done very little to examine the processes associated with the production of these objects of study. In this sense, the data are simply "taken for granted." Douglas (1967: vii) comments concerning the development of his own work on suicide: "After having amassed and carefully analyzed a great deal of material on suicide rates, I encountered some of the early criticisms of official suicide statistics. It came as something of a shock to me to realize that I had not given any careful consideration to my fundamental source of information about the phenomena being studied."

Focusing upon the nature of the production of the data, we are led to raise questions about the production of a "crime rate" or the production of a particular crime; what is the reasoning by which citizens are led to treat an event as a crime? For example, how (or through what lines of reasoning) might a woman understand some particular sexual act as an act of rape? And, should she decide to report it to the authorities, how will they treat her report of the occurrence? Through what set of procedures will the police treat the report as "well founded"? Or, on the other hand, with what procedure will the police "unfound" the report? Answers to these questions require that the observer make constant reference to the everyday reasoning of the members of the group engaging in the actual production of events as events of a particular kind. Sociologists, in accepting this data, have tended to assume that this level of reasoning is "normative" (i.e., it is shared by the members of the relevant group as a more or less clear set of rules supported by a system of sanctions). Members' employment of rules with these proposed properties establishes the nature of any particular event in a way that does not require interpretational work. In short, it has been argued that an event exists as preinterpreted within the context of a stable normative order, an order that transcends, but is visible within, a particular situation. However, the very fact that the citizen may understand an act as a rape and believe that she is making reference to a transcendent normative order that defines it as such, while the authorities may not so understand the event and may believe, as the citizen does, that their understanding is grounded in the very same transcendent normative order, suggests the relevance and import of interpretive work in any determination that a rape has or has not occurred.

The phenomena of "socially recognized suicides" and "socially recognized suicide rates" provide a similar example of the production of events that has been extensively treated by ethnomethodologists. In formulating the question, the ethnomethodologist sets aside (brackets) any concern of his or her own with whether or not a suicide actually happened. That question is the ethnomethodologist's *phenomenon*. By treating such issues as pure "topics of study" (Zimmerman and Pollner, 1970: 81–92), the ethnomethodologist is in the position to treat the procedures and results of all sorts of inquiry (done by laypersons or professionals) under the notion that "every feature of sense, of fact, of method . . . is [a] managed accomplishment. . . . [All the scientific or rational features of such] practices and results . . . are acquired and assured only through particular, located organizations of artful practices" (Garfinkel, 1967: 32). The question is then: What are the particular, located, artful practices—the methods and knowledge—whereby an event becomes recognized and established as a suicide? That is, how is the *determination accomplished* that the event is an actual case of suicide or any other type of act? It was this sort of concern that led Garfinkel (1967: 11–18) to investigate the methodology of the "psychological autopsies" that were undertaken by the Los Angeles Suicide Prevention Center for the Los Angeles Medical Examiner-Coroner's office.

Among the tasks that coroners or medical examiners are assigned is the determination of a death as a suicide. What knowledge must we have of the reasoning of the medical examiner in order to understand the process by which this determination is made, and therefore (for us) the process by which the suicide is "produced"? In the first place, we are obliged to follow the examiner into the concrete situation, which involves the possibility of suicide. It is in the situation that we can observe and perhaps decipher the process of reasoning that leads to the determination.

Garfinkel found that although the staff had been taught elaborate rules of correct procedure, and although they were trained in scientific procedure and scientific decision-making, all such rules and decision-making methods "in the actual situation were [known] to consist of recipes, proverbs, slogans, and partially formulated plans of action" (Garfinkel, 1967: 13). It was the actual situation in its details, and not the rules of correct procedure, to which the staff was primarily responsive. Rules were reworked and fitted to the situation—not vice versa. In reasoning with the contingencies of the situation, the staff employed their interpretive skills in assessing the significance and potential meaning of all the details: the dishes piled in the sink, the cigarette butts on the floor, a half-empty bottle of pills, the fact that this corpse is that of the eminently successful Smedley Phipps. The staff knows, too, that Smedley's adoring girlfriend (whom he was planning to marry) has arrived on the scene, that the examiner must deal with Smedley's wife, who is awaiting his call, and that there have been inquiries made by Smedley's priest and Smedley's insurance company. Also relevant as aspects of this situation, as the examiner and his staff experience it, are the views of their superiors (what they had said they thought of the last decision made in a case "like this") and the views of the community of medical examiners at large (for example,g what would other medical examiners make of the various particulars in the case—the pills, the bottle, and the corpse—and what would they make of such features of the process of investigation as the time spent on this case?). Garfinkel notes considerations such as these as some of the elements of the general process of determining that a suicide did or did not occur.

There are no rules (or norms) that have the capacity to determine what medical examiners will understand as significant (worthy of attention) or how the significant aspects will be understood. Indeed, not only is there no set of rules external to the examiner that cause his action, but there is no complete and determinate set of rules to which the examiner could simply refer to answer the questions he runs up against—how to respond to the various aspects of the situation, how to choose what is relevant to the situation and what is not, and so forth.

ETHNOMETHODOLOGY AND THE STUDY OF DEVIANCE

Deviance, like other matters that are known to, and dealt with by, members of societies, is, for ethnomethodologists, a phenomenon for members' recognition (Garfinkel and Sacks, 1970). Whatever it is, it can become an object for ethnomethodological analysis, because laypersons and professionals recognize and treat it. Since ethnomethodological studies seek to discover the general methods (and their invariant properties) of these processes of recognition and treatment, they do not develop a theory of deviance in the conventional sense—a theory that would concern the causes of deviance. Nonetheless, deviance and its specific manifestations (e.g., crime or mental illness), as recognized by citizens, police, psychiatrists, prosecutors, defense attorneys, judges, and juries, do furnish very handy examples for ethnomethodological inquiry. This is so, in part, because in the arena of deviance recognition and treatment, the details of commonsensical reasoning are made public matters. It is, for example, the specific task of prosecuting and defense attorneys to make certain lines of reasoning lucid and visible. There is, then, a set of ethnomethodological studies of deviance, even though there is no specific "ethnomethodological conception" or "ethnomethodological theory" of deviance. Instead, the studies concern the commonsensical recognition of deviance at various levels—as illustrated in the work of Pollner (1978), McHugh (1970), and Sudnow (1975).

Pollner clarifies Becker's labeling conception of deviance by contrasting it with ethnomethodology, because the two views have the surface appearance of similarity. Pollner notes a fundamental strain in Becker's work. On the one hand, Becker seems to say that deviance is an act that is labeled as such by a reactive audience. This aspect of Becker's approach is in general harmony with the perspective of ethnomethodology and could be developed along ethnomethodological lines. However, this conception is qualified by the inclusion of "mundane" assumptions or "common sense" within Becker's analytic apparatus. Becker's view contains the assumption of inherently deviant acts in the form of inherently rule-violating acts. This view " . . . presuppose[s] an act whose properties are defined by some method or criteria other than the observed response of the community" (Pollner, 1978: 273). Insofar as a theory of deviance includes such a proposition, it includes in its investigatory (analytic) apparatus central elements of the commonsensical view that deviance exists independently of "us" that it pretends to investigate. The result is not only to confound the relationship between the observer's analytic apparatus and the object of study, but to take important aspects of the object of investigation for granted. Rather than pursue this course, Pollner recommends a stronger and more consistent labeling theory, one that eliminates some of the logical anomalies that have troubled the theory from its outset.[2] This stronger rendition of labeling theory " . . . recommends that deviance consists entirely and exclusively of the activities through which it is realized as such" (Pollner, 1978: 279). This view eliminates any other basis of the determination of deviance other than the commonsensical determination that a particular act is or was an act of deviance. The focus of study, then, is solely and unequivocally upon the processes of common sense as it arrives at such determinations, hence (and at the same moment) constituting the object to which it refers.

McHugh (1970) formulates the invariant properties of commonsensical conceptions of deviance. First, the act must be apprehended by the participants as an act which possesses "conventionality." By this he means that the act is regarded as one that need not have occurred. The recognition of the act as such involves a commonsensical consideration of the "conditions of failure" with respect to the attempt at rule following. For an act to be "conventional," it must occur in a context within which the conditions of failure are perceived to be absent. Thus, an action conceived as involving an effort to follow a rule, but in an impossible (failure-determined) situation, is not recognized within societies as "conventional." Therefore, it is not recognized as deviance.

Second, members assess the "theoreticity" of the reasoning that stands behind the "questionable" act. The issue concerns the actor's knowledge or type of awareness. The question is: Did the actor know what he or she was doing? Since certain actors (e.g., children and psychotics) are not regarded as fully aware of what they are doing, their failures in following rules are not regarded as punishable or deviant. McHugh argues, then, that certain commonsensical determinations are invariantly part of the recognition of an act as deviant; namely, the determination that the act is both "conventional" and "theoretic." Sudnow examines common sense as it constructs and employs deviant concepts. His research concerns the determination of the categories of criminality as they are employed by persons in the criminal justice system in the conduct of their everyday affairs. "Here, the categories of criminal law are not regarded as useful or not, as objects to be either adopted, adapted, or ignored; rather they are seen as constituting the basic conceptual equipment with which such people as judges, lawyers, policemen and probation workers organize their everyday activity" (Sudnow, 1975: 289). Focusing on public defenders, Sudnow finds that court personnel employ categories that specify the typical or normal features of certain types of action. For example, they employ categories that specify the "typical burglary," or the "typical child molestation," as well as the "typical burglar" and the "typical child molester." These typifications possess numerous features other than those specified by, or derivable from, criminal statute. Hence, one cannot refer simply to statute to determine the categories that are in actual play in the dispensation of cases that come to the attention of the court.

The "normal" or "typical" act of burglary is understood as an act occurring in a certain locale of the community, committed by persons familiar with the terrain, in solitary, uncoordinated activity, who pursue certain objects, and whose appearance, demeanor, and talk is of such-and-such a kind. It is furthermore the case that the construct, "typical burglary," takes into account burglaries as they are understood in this community and at this time. Hence, the typical burglary occurring in this community, X, may be understood by public defenders as distinct from typical burglaries in community Y. At the same time, typical burglaries of past years may be distinct from "today's typical burglaries." It is these features that the public defender takes into account when making the decision, "Is this or is this not a 'burglary' case I have before me?" Having acquired the relevant information in these terms, the public defender can decide whether "this instance" fits the category of a "typical burglary," a "typical child molestation," and so on.

Having determined that the case is a "typical" one of whatever kind, the defender, in conjunction with the prosecuting attorney, "deals" with the case in a routinized way. For example, a "typical burglary" is reducible to a petty theft, a "typical child molestation" to "loitering by a schoolhouse." The reduction within the "deal" is accomplished primarily by way of an unstated recipe that the public defender and the prosecuting attorney work out. The recipe is a method by which the aims of the two parties are accomplished. First, the charge must be sufficiently reduced so that the "typical burglar" will accept the deal, thereby avoiding trial—an interest most parties to the court have in common. Second, the public defender and the prosecuting attorney intend that the "typical burglar" (etc.) "gets his due" (i.e., they both wish to see that "justice," as embedded in their commonsensical and everyday reasoning, is done).

ETHNOMETHODOLOGY, SOCIOLOGY, AND COMMON SENSE

Why engage in studies of this sort of phenomena? In particular, why study the methods of commonsensical reasoning that professional social scientists and laypersons employ in making the most commonplace determinations? Those social scientists who embark on ethnomethodological study and investigation are convinced that there is no alternative. If one is to aim for a rigorous discipline concerned with social life, then one must investigate commonsensical thinking, for social science theorizing and empirical practice are founded on it.

Let us briefly examine the substance of this conviction. If we look around at the scenes of our everyday lives, we can see and experience the massive standardization of some features of those scenes. In innumerable ways, the social organization of ordinary places or ordinary scenes shows standardization, regularity, and repetivity. Furthermore, the conventional concepts of sociology— norm, role, status, and so on—are easy enough to apply to such scenes. If we chose, we could quantitatively investigate what happens in such scenes. Thus we have affairs that are experientially standardized—they show regularities, they are conceptualizable in terms of, or related to, their immediate causal structure, and they can be systematically counted and classified.

While we do experience the scenes of our everyday lives as structured, our experience of structure and our capacity to recognize the affairs as structured, countable, and classifiable relies on tacitly held knowledge and tacit modes of reason. This knowledge and these modes of reasoning are essential to our everyday experience and our social scientific findings. Our experience and findings rest upon tacit modes of reasoning and tacitly held knowledge that is nowhere specified. The tacitly known interpenetrates the systematic knowledge of the social sciences, but it is not a formal, acknowledged part of it. It is a mode of knowing and reasoning that social scientists and their subjects know together. While this taken-for-granted corpus of commonsensical knowledge and its methodology becomes explicit from time to time, it is explicit only in fragments. There are points in some sociological studies at which the investigator can see it directly. Whenever the participant observer asks him/herself how to recognize those affairs that are to be described in the field notes, he or she gets a glance at it. Investigators get a similar glance over the course of content analysis or in constructing histories from written documents. The contemporary style of questionnaire, with its fixed choices, tends to remove the modern survey researcher from these situations, but the investigator can see his or her own essentially necessary tacit reasoning come into play when judgments concerning face validity need to be made.

The theoretical and empirical objects of the social sciences rest on the tacit foundations of the corpus of common knowledge and its methods. This may be most easily seen in the cluster of ideas surrounding the concept of norm. Common sense is brought into play and, in effect, becomes part of the norm itself whenever we ask questions such as the following: What is the rule? What is compliance with the rule? How must we act in a case like this? Are these two rules in conflict?

If rules and other conventions were somehow transparent and self-contained, then the corpus of commonsensical knowledge and its methods would simply be part of common culture as we traditionally conceive it. It would pose no special foundational problems. Indeed, in the social sciences, norms are frequently treated in just this way (i.e., they are reasoned about *as if* they were transparent and self-contained). Norms are then treated as if they were rules of a game.

RULES IN GAMES

The features of rules and norms within the traditional conception of conformity and deviance are brought to the surface by describing them within the framework of the game model. This method of analyzing normative concepts also shows us what empirical matters we should examine in assessing the adequacy of the traditional conceptions. Further, this method of analysis throws the difference between ethnomethodological and traditional conceptions of normative phenomena into stark relief. The game model is a sort of purification of the conventional idea of culture and culturally determined regularities. It is implied in traditional sociological ideas, especially those connected with Durkheim and Parsons. When social scientists attempt to reason rigorously with certain kinds of sociological data, they imply that the model is appropriate.

Put positively, if the model were appropriate—if it matched actual social life or were not incongruent with that life—very powerful deductions, predictions, and mathematical manipulation would be possible. If social life could be adequately described in terms of the idealized portrait of the game-model, there would be little point in studying commonsensical reasoning. Everything that might be known about common sense would already be fully specified by a detailed description of rules. As we shall see, however, despite the great promise of the game-model, it is not adequate as a description of actual social life. Further, its tacit use in sociological theorizing obscures the true phenomena of norms, compliance to norms, and deviance from norms. Showing the specific ways in which the game-model is inadequate and how necessary it is to directly investigate commonsensical reasoning with norms first requires a close inspection of the game-model itself.

Because of its complexity, we first define a game and then offer a game-model interpretation of the concept of normative order. This, then, will serve as a point of departure for an empirical and an ethnomethodological examination of rules, conformity, and deviance.

BASIC GAME MODEL AND THE NORMATIVE-CULTURE IDEA

The primary ingredients of games were specified by Garfinkel (1963) as a constituent of his early research on normative orders. We employ his conceptions here and adapt and extend them. We emphasize those features of games that represent a rigorous analytic model that articulates the sociological vision.

From the game-model vantage point, interest in the person is defined exclusively as interest in the player of the game. A player is one who seeks to comply with a common set of rules. These common rules are, in Garfinkel's formulation, basic rules of the game. Basic rules have three features, the "constitutive expectancies," which render the rules reciprocally binding:

1. Whatsoever the rule specifies, compliance with it is obligatory. Such rules may not be suspended on the grounds of personal desire, immediate gratifications, plans, individual interests, or undesirable consequences.

2. The player regards these same requirements as binding on fellow players just as they are binding on him.

3. The player regards these expectancies as fully reciprocal. Not only are they binding on him and the other, but both know this as well. Each expects to insist on compliance and expects that compliance will be insisted upon with regard to their own conduct.

In the game, any rule with these features is a basic rule. Basic rules typically define territories of play, legally possible plays, and sequences of play.

Many ensembles of basic rules are possible that define different games. Changes in a single rule of the game are potentially more profound in their consequences for the players' situation than they would seem to appear in the content of the changed rule. This is so for two reasons. First, the rules fit together in such a way that alterations in one rule have ramifying consequences across the whole set of rules. For example, reducing the territory of play in chess may eliminate the legal possibilities of certain types of moves. Second, compliance with each set of basic rules generates a game-furnished structure.[3] These game-furnished structures refer to all those patterns or regularities not mentioned in the rules that, nonetheless, are produced by compliance with the rules and that are relevant to the players' choices or strategies. They include such affairs as the amount and type of information the player has about the other player's situation (e.g., the players of chess have complete information about the current state of the game, while the players of the poker game five card stud have limited information about the other players' situations). They also include certain patterned regularities of action (e.g., the rules in chess, which specify the starting state of the board and the possible legal moves for each piece, which generate certain moves as the only legal initial moves). Those game-furnished structures that are altered by a change in a single rule are often not predictable by mere inspection of the rule in question, but depend on that rule in conjunction with other rules.

The basic rules of the game define all the possible legal occurrences in that game. Further, they define and partition the domain of possible play in terms of a set of "categorical possibilities" (Garfinkel, 1963: 194). The categorical possibilities describe the meaning of all events that occur within the game-possible events and game-possible actions (i.e., they describe all the states of affairs that can be discriminated as game-relevant different states of affairs). Thus we have one set—all the legal possibilities—which is further partitioned in terms of all the game-relevant different states of affairs. The basic rules require that a player devise the play to fall within all the legal possibilities, whereas a choice is permitted, according to his or her strategy, among successive assemblies of game-relevant different states of affairs.

The concepts of *categorical possibilities* and *game-possible events and actions* are further specified by noting that although the game is played by rearranging the positions of a physically observable object or objects with respect to a system of temporal-spatial coordinates, interest in such juxtapositions is directed toward what they indicate or signify and not toward the physical display as such. A certain arrangement of colors and figures upon five pasteboard cards signifies a full house in poker. The full house is the event in poker, the event described as a categorical possibility, not the spatio-temporal arrangement of pasteboard. Although a number of different full houses are depicted in the categorical possibilities, each type of full house may be visible in a variety of spatio-temporal displays. For example, the same full house may be displayed in cards from different card decks that are of various sizes and colors, and that employ different emblems for the different suits (spades, clubs, etc.).

Garfinkel (1963: 195) refers to these spatio-temporal arrangements as behaviors, and he refers to the signified occurrences as game-possible actions. "Basic rules then [frame] the possible events of play that observed behaviors can signify." An adequate or competent grasp of the basic rules provides the player with the criteria for recognizing game-possible actions. These criteria furnish the player with the grounds or "coding rules" for classifying a behavioral display as: (1) one or another game-possible action, (2) outside the field of play (i.e., game-irrelevant), or (3) a rule-violating game-relevant event. It should be emphasized that if a behavioral occurrence does not alter the game-relevant state of affairs—affairs describable in game-possible action terms—then, from the standpoint of the game, it did not happen. The activity of eating a sandwich during a poker game would ordinarily be such a sequence of behavior, even if the sandwich was eaten from a hand that held cards.

Rules are violated through behaviors that actually *alter* the arrangement of categorical possibilities.

Different sets of basic rules define different arrays of behavior as game-relevant, and they may assign the same behavioral display to differing game-possible actions. The basic rules thus function as what Schutz (1962) termed a scheme of interpretation and a scheme of expression through which one recognizes the other players' behavior as game actions and through which a player channels his or her own behavior so that it will be recognizable to other players as game actions.

The point was summarized by Garfinkel (1963: 195) in saying, "The basic rules provide a behavior's *sense* as action. They are the terms in which a player decides . . . 'What happened?' " Use of the basic rules as a scheme of interpretation and expression defines, for each player, the common intersubjective meanings of game events. It makes the significance of any given physical array *objective* (accessible to any one of us who knows the basic rules) as the selfsame state of affairs. This means that "what happened" is equally visible to anyone who knows the rules, whether they are players or judges. No special perspective *that matters* for the game is provided by the perspective of the player.

The objective quality of the intersubjective significance of a spatio-temporal display depends upon two characteristic features of rules of the game. The rules are independent of events in the game in the sense that they are not altered by plays of the game. And the details of their application are independent of the context or particulars in each case (i.e., the rules of application can be mechanically applied and do not require interpretive reasoning to fit them to the context and particulars). These two features guarantee a once-and-for-all quality to recognized game events. The judgment that it was *this* rather than *that* which occurred remains untouched by subsequent events in the game. The workings of these two features also importantly guarantee the equivalence among all events or actions that are classified as instances of the same categorical possibility.

The game contains the ground for its own description as long as the players are motivated to comply with the basic rules. A nonplayer who knows these rules is in a position to describe the events of the game as they appear to the players. Not only can such an outsider describe "what happened," objectively speaking, but he or she can also describe "what could have happened." Since the basic rules generate an ensemble of categorical possibilities in the form of all the possible occurrences in this game-world and all the possible co-occurrences in this game-world, certain structural arrangements are attributable to the features of any particular set of basic rules.

This set of structural arrangements, the game-furnished structures, and the sequences of legal possibilities are predictable and inferable from the set of basic rules. The basic rules, then, function as a sort of theory of the game in much the same way that a grammar functions as a theory of its language. Further, the basic rules set the terms for a theory of the players' strategy. A theory of rational play, for example, would be stated in terms of rules for choosing among different game-relevant states of affairs.

GAME-MODEL INTERPRETATION OF RULES IN EVERYDAY LIFE

Despite the fact that many features of games—for example, their temporally encapsulated character—recommend that games not be treated as simulations of everyday life (Garfinkel, 1967), the various relationships between rules, conduct, appearances and their objects, players, and situations of play as they occur in games can be treated as a provisional model of rules and everyday conduct. Parsons (1965), among others, has employed just such an idea. The elements of games specified above serve as a logically rigorous analytic model, which permits clear and cogent inferences. The sociological theorist may decide to interpret institutionalized patterns of normative culture as basic rules of the game. This decision furnishes normative culture with a clear and definite sense, and it gives normative culture the same theoretical status that grammars have in the hands of linguists. It makes logically defensible a set of inferences and operative assumptions that are central to traditional sociological theorizing. Indeed, it gives that enterprise the grounds for portraying:

1. "what can happen" as a distinct and limited set of possibilities
2. "what did happen" as a selection from among those possibilities
3. the terms for predicting "what will happen"
4. that the prediction "what will happen" will fall within the legal possibilities
5. predictions concerning certain game-furnished structural regularities

6. that all these descriptions are objective (i.e., that their terms consistently refer to logically equivalent states of affairs, that the terms are not dependent on context for their interpretation or reasoned use, and that the terms mean the same thing to all observers and participants)

Upon the game-theoretic construal of normative culture, the society is a single game. Each concrete situation is a "subroutine" or "subsection" of an over-arching game. The metaphor of basic rules is tempered in its application here. There is no precise equivalence for the episodic character of an instance of the game or for a move in the game. The episodic character of complete games and events in games is associated with there being time outside the game in which decisions relevant to the game (e.g., determining what the rules are) are made. In contrast, lived-through everyday life is incessantly on-going and continuous. It is, in the terms of our metaphor, as if the game never ceases, and it encompasses all concrete situations. There are no "time-outs," as it were (at least, there are no "time-outs" to a broader context). There may be "time-outs" from everyday life, such as going to plays, engaging in games, doing scientific theory, and the like, but these other realities have everyday life as their context and not the other way around (Schutz, 1962). The actual features of everyday life within the society are observable only "from within." There is no "outside," in the sense that there is for games. Our last assertion points to a distinctive feature of institutionalized patterns of normative culture (i.e., that they are not listed "outside" the situations in which they are somehow employed). If we imagine looking for a book of rules lying alongside our real-life situations that corresponds to a rule book for a game, we find new places to look.

Durkheim (1964a) formulated the definitive sociological solution to this problem—the problem of the empirical status of a transcendent moral order. Durkheim, in *The Division of Labor*, defines normative orders as those that, if violated, bring out corrective responses in societal members. It is the order as actually enforced. In this formulation, Durkheim provides the social sciences with an apparently rigorous device for detecting the real normative order and distinguishing it from competing idealized or ideological versions.

Durkheim ties the observation of actual normative orders to concrete, lived-through situations. While normative orders are observable first-hand only in concrete situations, they are understood as *transcending* those situations and as linking any given situation to other situations so that the situations go together as parts of the same society. Norms that are observed in their enforcement in concrete situations are conceived of as expressions of one transcending normative order.

The interpretation of norms as they are enforced as expressions of a transcending normative order, the very conception of such a transcending order, and the relationship between situation and society as part and whole tied together by a transcending normative order all depend on something like a game-model interpretation of normative culture. That is, the conception of a transcending normative order incorporates the property of basic rules that the rules are prior to and independent of the situations in which they are employed. This feature requires, in turn, that the rules have the features of stability of sense, unequivocality, and mechanical application. If these interdependent and overlapping features are not demonstrable features of norms as enforced, then the theoretical power of the Durkheimian vision and its current incarnations are seriously undermined.

Institutionalized patterns of normative culture understood as basic rules equip the analyst with a scheme of interpretation with which he or she can rigorously portray "what can happen" as a distinct and limited set of possibilities and "what did happen" as a selection from among those possibilities. On the basis of the terms of such a rigorous portrait, the analyst may make a related set of logical inferences about the patterns of conduct that occur in the society under study. The analyst is in the position to predict:

1. A general pattern of conduct that flows from compliance with the rules.

2. A secondary set of predictions about conduct not falling within the general patterns so that it will be unrecognizable as an event in the society or will be responded to as an act of deviance.

3. An ensemble of patterns of conduct, "game-furnished structures," which is not depicted in the rules but which, nonetheless, follows from compliance with them.

The interpretation of normative culture as basic rules attributes the basic rule properties of stability, unequivocality, and mechanical applicability to normative culture and, in turn, warrants treating as objective the descriptions and predictions that result from the interpretation's use. The results are objective in the sense that their descriptive terms consistently refer to logically equivalent states of affairs; the terms are not dependent on context for their interpretation or reasoned use; and the terms have the same meaning for all observers and members.

ETHNOMETHODOLOGICAL STUDIES OF RULES

Are rules in actual social life mechanically applicable and, hence, stable and unequivocal? The judgment can only be made by observing rules in use in actual situations of their use. The fact that a set of players or societal members could formulate what looks like the same rule outside the situation of its actual use might tell us that they are oriented to the "same" rule but not that the rule was mechanically applicable. There is an element of paradox in saying this, however, since lack of mechanical application renders the expression, "the same rule," uncertain.

Rules, which examine—as they are used in—actual on-going concrete situations, have been examined in a host of ethnomethodological studies.[4] These studies have uncovered features of rules in use that are incompatible with mechanical application, stability, and unequivocality. Instead, ethnomethodologists have found that tacit knowledge is employed in the interpretation of rules; common sense extends rules to meet the circumstance of their use; situations of rule use are commonsensical situations of choice, rather than logically depictable situations; single rules have etcetera features, and sets of rules have etcetera provisions; rules are so context-dependent that they escape objective or literal description; and, in other ways, rules are dependent on the artful, temporally extended, innovative practices of competent members.

These studies are focused upon rules in use, including the observation of rules as they are used as guides of conduct, as standards for judging the conduct of others, as topics to be discovered, and as warrants for the objectivity of some practice or result. The subjects of these studies have included students taking IQ tests (Mackay, 1974; Roth, 1974), sociologists doing coding (Garfinkel, 1967; Leiter, 1969), teachers making decisions about students' performances (Leiter, 1974, 1976), parolees' complying with the convict code and the rules of parole (Wieder, 1974), sociologists observing rules as topics (Wieder and Zimmerman, 1976), social welfare workers' scheduling clients (Wieder and Zimmerman, 1970), detectives' use of investigative procedures (Sanders, 1977), police officers' application of the law (Sanders and Daudistel, 1976), police officers' enforcing the law and keeping the peace (Bittner,

1967), and probation officers' determining what a probationer has done (Cicourel, 1968).

In all these cases, the statement of a rule by itself was found to be inadequate for explicitly defining its prospective sense in the actual situations of its use. The rule user had to employ common-sensical reasoning to connect the rule to the situation. This was invariably done by awaiting the actual occasions of the rule's use so that unforeseen particulars could be taken into account. No matter how much effort is devoted to the rational anticipation of all possibilities, the actual situations of naturally occurring social life hold surprises for those who live in them. No matter how explicit a rule is, it is not mechanically applied.

What mechanical applicability means and how it is not a necessary feature of rules as they are actually employed are exemplified in these studies from the three standpoints that concern us here. Lack of mechanical applicability and the associated equivocality of rules are visible from the several standpoints of (1) the person attempting to comply with the rule, (2) the person judging compliance with the rule, and (3) the analyst. Let us recall that in a mechanically applicable rule, the action that mechanically fits the rule's criteria is "automatically" in accord with the rule's intent. Further, from the standpoint of the member, the judge, and the analyst, those spatio-temporally observable behaviors may be "coded" by reference to the rule—and the acting person's intent is thereby correctly uncovered as the same intent from all three standpoints.

Rules and coventions are still phenomena for ethnomethodologists, but what they consist of is taken to be a matter to be discovered—a pure topic of research and not a resource. By converting norms, compliance, and deviance into pure topics of research, ethnomethodologists do not attribute to norms those properties formulated by Durkheim that are clarified in the game-model. They do not attribute to norms the properties of stability of sense, unequivocality, mechanical applicability, and trans-situationality (situation transcendence). The operative word here is "attribute." Because conventional sociologists attribute these properties to observed normative phenomena, they place themselves in the position to draw inferences of the sort we have described. Those inferences are just the sort that conventional sociologists and laypersons find interesting, for they offer at least a partial answer to practical and moral questions (e.g., who is likely to commit a crime, why they will do so, and what might be done to prevent it). These inferences are based on "reasonable" assumptions, which are made by professional sociologists and laypersons alike (Zimmerman and Pollner, 1970).

But if the analyst joins the societal member in making the very same assumptions, phenomena such as norms and the "how" of the assumptions upon which they rest—how they are made, how they are reasoned with, how they are made reasonable—cannot be made topics of empirical investigation. In the interests of bringing normative phenomena and their foundations into clear view, ethnomethodologists stand back from the assumptions that enter into the folk definition and normative phenomena and attempt to observe the phenomena first-hand.

Zimmerman and Wieder (1970: 288) have proposed three steps to facilitate the first-hand observation of normatively governed conduct: "The first step is to suspend the assumption that social conduct is rule governed, or based in or mounted from shared meanings or systems of symbols shared in common."

To "suspend" an assumption does not mean to negate or deny it. Instead, to "suspend" means "do not rely upon" and "do not make use of" it. Especially, do not make use of the assumption that social conduct is rule-governed to draw further inferences about what it is that one is seeing or to connect one thing that one has observed to another thing that one has observed in a routine, automatic, taken-for-granted manner (i.e., as a matter of assumption). In suspending the assumptions, one still *notices* the inference that its use would yield and one would *note* the observations that its use would connect. But now one *notes* these inferences and connections as phenomena—things to be observed—and notes the phenomena of folk reasoning that are actually part of the phenomena, "normatively governed conduct." How this is the case is the focus of the next step of our procedure (Zimmerman and Wieder, 1970: 288): "The second step is to observe that the regular, coherent, connected patterns of social life are *described* and *explained* in just such terms, or close relatives of them, by laymen and professional sociologists alike."

This step directs our attention to the talk, the conversations, and the stories in which societal members describe their own society in normative terms. In the folk reasoning of societal members, which is made visible in talk, normative ideas and the assumptions that sustain those ideas are invoked to characterize the surrounding scene and to connect one affair to another. Ethnomethodologists investigate this use of normative ideas and assumptions as their phenomena. They do not appropriate and refine these ideas in order to press them into theoretical service, as is done, for example, in the game-model rendition of normative phenomena. In noticing that norms are phenomena for members—that they are explicitly recognized and talked about (Garfinkel, 1967)—ethnomethodologists also note the part this recognition and talk plays in the very scenes in which it is done. Zimmerman and Wieder (1970: 228) put the matter procedurally: "The third step is [to examine the ways in which] the appearances of described and explained patterns of orderly social activities are *appearances* produced . . . by and through such procedures as analyzing, describing, or explaining an event as an instance of compliance (or noncompliance) with a rule."

With this step, the ethnomethodologist explores the ways in which members of society account for (describe and explain) the social order they experience around them, *and* the ethnomethodologist explores the achievements of that accounting work. Here the investigator is sensitive to the ways in which the order as described and the order as experienced are reflexively related (i.e., that they are constituents of each other). Through their talking about the surrounding scene, participants show one another how activities and events are parts of a social order. Activities and events are known as parts of a social order by a community of participants through the recognizing and noting work that is carried out over the course of social interaction. The three steps of the analytic procedure lead to more specific questions about the content of these social interactions (Zimmerman and Wieder, 1970: 290):

> How are members going about the task of investigating the scenes of their actions so that they see and report patterning and structure, often by reference to normative and motivational constructions? How are events being analyzed so that they appear as being connected? By what procedures are descriptions being done so that they portray order? How is the factual character of such accounts established? How is the sense or appearance of a world in common and common understanding concerning its shared features accomplished?

To give these questions substance, we now turn to a study in which they were asked. Among sociologists, there is a long tradition[5] of explaining the orderly behavior of inmates of prisons and reformatories by referring to a set of rules, the "convict code." The convict code includes prohibitions (e.g., "don't snitch"—that is, do not be an informer) and positive injunctions (e.g., "be loyal to your fellow inmates"). The rules of the convict code explain orderly patterns of inmate behavior in their relationships with one another and with the staff in the same way that the rules of a game explain the orderly patterns of behavior within the game.

In studying a halfway house for narcotic addicts who have been parolled from prison, Wieder (1974) encountered the same sorts of phenomena that had been recognized within this tradition. Like the social scientists who had preceded him, Wieder heard, *as a sociologist*, the convict code being expressed in interviews and in overheard remarks. *As an ethnomethodologist*, Wieder noted, and took as a point of departure for close investigation, a feature of the rules that the sociologists had surely seen but that was submerged in the game-model assumptions of their analytic apparatus—that the rules formulated by sociologists observing prison life were founded on the talk of the inmates and other participants. What the other investigators observed had been made available to Wieder through interactions in the setting he had brought under study. Those interactions simultaneously "reported on" the setting while being a feature of the very process they "reported on." The setting as *described* by participants is a part of that selfsame setting as *experienced* by participants. Things as described and things as experienced are reflexively related (Garfinkel, 1967).

What happens in these interactions that leads the participant observer to formulate rules? In the halfway house, Wieder came to see that in conversations that occurred between participants (the residents and the staff, the residents and the researcher, the staff and the researcher), the participants instructed one another on how to "see" the behavior of the residents. They did this by pointing out the relevance of the convict code to any particular resident's circumstances and by noting the ways in which some particular behavior was motivated by it.

Reflecting upon his own experiences, Wieder discovered that residents persuasively taught him and the staff some of the uses of the convict code. Residents often explained or commented upon what they were doing, sometimes "spontaneously," sometimes in response to a query. In these commentaries, residents used what Wieder and the staff understood to be portions of the code and its language. By "telling the code," residents presented their conduct as goal-directed and required and sanctioned by others. Residents also thereby pointed to the particular action in question as an "instance" of a pattern (a part of that pattern), and they noted the rule that required that action and made it sensible. Residents taught the staff and the researcher how to see the sense of resident conduct by providing them the means to see the environment of the halfway house from the standpoint of the residents.

Rules, as phenomena in a setting, are encountered as members' formulations, spoken folk-concepts. In using these rules, by "telling" them, members identify particular behaviors as instances of a type and relate those behaviors to the rules that warrant or "cause" them. Members as participants in social scenes thereby preanalyze those scenes for the sociologists who may happen to come upon them. Rules as spoken folk-concepts function as schemes of interpretation in a way that may be compared to rules of the game as schemes of interpretation. Here, however, the rule as a scheme of interpretation is initially encountered in its interpretive function. The analyst encounters the rule in its use (in its being spoken), wherein members are involved in explaining actions in much the same way that social scientists do. In citing rules, members show the motivated sense of what they or their fellows are doing; they show the reasonableness of what they are doing; and often they note the required or necessary, and thus justifiable, sense of what they are doing. Using rules (speaking of rules) formulates the very setting in which those rules are spoken of as schemes of interpretation.

Rules encountered in this fashion, however, are not locatable or visible in the neatly ordered and preassembled fashion of a rule book. Wieder found that the rules of the code were available to him in only occasionally identified bits and pieces. Hearing resident talk as "telling the code" required interpretive work. Wieder (1974: 184–186) described some of this interpretive work as follows.

> Equipped with what I understood to be a preliminary and partial version of the residents' definition of their situation (which was contained in the title, "The Code", and several maxims), I saw that other pronouncements of residents were untitled extensions of this same line of talk. I used whatever "pieces" of the code I had collected at that point as a scheme for interpreting further talk as extensions of what I had heard "up to now". Garfinkel (1967: 78), following Mannheim, calls this kind of procedure "the documentary method of interpretation", describing it in the following terms: "The method consists of treating an actual appearance as 'the document of', as 'pointing to', as 'standing on behalf of' a presupposed underlying pattern. Not only is the underlying pattern derived from its individual documentary evidences, but the individual documentary evidences, in their turn, are interpreted on the basis of 'what is known' about the underlying pattern. Each is used to elaborate the other."

An example of the use of this method is provided by the interpretation of a remark I overheard during my first week at the halfway house. I passed a resident who was wandering through the halls after the committee meetings on Wednesday night. He said to staff and all others within hearing, "Where can I find that meeting where I can get an overnight pass?" On the basis of what I had already learned, I understood him to be saying, "I'm not going to that meeting because I'm interested in participating in the program of the halfway house. I'm going to that meeting just because I would like to collect the reward of an overnight pass and for no other reason. I'm not a kiss-ass. Everyone who is in hearing distance should understand that I'm not kissing up to staff. My behavior really is in conformity with the code, though without hearing this (reference to an overnight pass), you might think otherwise." I thereby collected another "piece" of talk which, when put together with utterances I had heard up to that point (which permitted me to see the "sense" of this remark) and used with utterances I had yet to collect, was employed by me to formulate the general maxim, "Show your loyalty to the residents." . . .

In this fashion, I employed my collection of "pieces" as a self-elaborating schema. Each newly encountered "piece" of talk was simultaneously rendered sensible by interpreting it in terms of the developing relevancies of the code and was, at the same time, more evidence of the existence of that code. Furthermore, the interpreted "piece" then functioned as part of the elaborated schema itself and was used in the interpretation of still further "pieces" of talk [and in the interpretation of newly encountered "pieces" of action].

Thus, seeing and describing the behaviors of residents as coherently and more or less stably motivated required the work of actively interpreting the pieces of talk and action that one heard and saw. By actively interpreting, an observer actively *constitutes* the well-organized character of the setting. A layer of sense is thus contributed to the social scene as it is experienced by the observer. This layer of sense is a constituent of the experientially real scene that is the immediate situation and the possible object of his or her descriptions to others.

Where rules and rule-like objects occur, they function as schemes of interpretation. In these very ordinary and common situations, particular organizations of the lived environment as experienced by witnesses (observer-listeners) are the product of actively interpreting that which is seen and heard in terms of these rules and rule-like schemes of interpretation. These rules and rule-like devices are themselves the products of active interpretation of observed and heard "bits and pieces." These two lines of interpretation, however, are interdependent and mutually sustaining and elaborating moments of the same continuous interpretive process. In this view, rules do not *exist as independent* affairs, as they do in the game-model. Instead, they *subsist as dependent* constituents of on-going (temporally extended) perceptual-interpretive-descriptive acts. They have no finally, specifiable once-and-for-all sense. They are open and subsist in open sets of rules. Always tied to concrete courses of experience and description, they are continuously being given new "life" and new substance in every next grasp or description of a concrete rule-related act—an act of one's own or an act of another person. Rules organize the very occasions in which they occur as constituents.

Employing rules as descriptions and schemes of interpretation is every member's work. An examination of Wieder's (1974) conversations with the staff shows some of the ways that the staff engaged in this interpretive work; that is, the staff described and explained events in the setting by using the code as the residents' definition of the situation. The staff did this in conversations with Wieder, with one another, and even with the residents. When they did this explanatory work, they too identified events as "instances" of a pattern. They too tied together different kinds of actions as being essentially the same through an ascribed pattern of underlying motivation that made out differing actions as essentially the same. In one case, a staff member identified the burning of a mattress, being reluctant to participate in the group, and ridiculing a cooperative resident as all having the same meaning. They had the same meaning because they all displayed the residents' hostility to the staff and their loyalty to other residents and were, thus, actions prescribed by maxims of the convict code. In giving explanations by way of the code, the staff drew together events in the setting and thereby perceived the setting as organized.

In their conversations with each other, staff and residents engaged in a variety of forms of folk-sociological analysis. They identified observable, regular, repetitive patterns of behavior, they did analyses of members' definitions of their situations, and they explained the regular patterns of behavior by referring their production to a rule (a statement of a rule) that required persons to act in the observed fashion. "Analyzing" human behavior in this way is work that members routinely do in getting through interactions in which socially important matters are achieved (responsibilities are being assigned, choices are being defined and made, strategies are being chosen, advice about how to treat others is being given, or demands for action are being asserted). In contexts such as these, rules as spoken are members' methods for doing things.

The ways in which *speaking* a rule formulates a setting (achieves an organization of it) *and* is an accomplishing state-of-affairs-altering act is vividly illustrated by "telling" the rule about snitching (informing) at the halfway house (Wieder, 1974: 168–170).

> When talking with residents, staff and I often had a relatively friendly line of conversation terminated by a resident's saying, "You know I won't snitch". Hearing such an utterance functioned to re-crystalize the immediate interaction as the present center of one's experiential world. "You know I won't snitch", multiformulated the immediate environment, its surrounding social structures, and the connections between this interaction and the surrounding social structures. It (a) told what had just happened—e.g., "You just asked me to snitch". It (b) formulated what the resident was doing in saying that phrase—e.g., "I am saying that this is my answer to your question. My answer is not to answer". It (c) formulated the resident's motives for saying what he was saying and doing what he was doing—e.g., "I'm not answering in order to avoid snitching". Since snitching was morally inappropriate for residents, the utterance, therefore, formulated the sensible and proper grounds of the refusal to answer the question. It (d) formulated (in the fashion of pointing to) the immediate relationship between the listener (staff or myself) and teller (resident) by re-locating the conversation in the context of the persisting role relationships between the parties—e.g., "For you to ask me that, would be asking me to snitch". Thus saying, "You know I won't snitch", operated as a renunciation, or a reminder of the role relationships involved and the appropriate relations between members of those categories. It placed the ongoing occasion in the context of what both parties knew about their overriding trans-situational relationships. It (e) was one more formulation of the features of the persisting role relationship between hearer and teller—e.g., "You are an agent [for state researcher] and I am a resident-parolee. Some things you might ask me involve informing on my fellow residents. Residents do not inform on their fellows. We call that snitching". Besides reminding the participants of a trans-situational role relationship, the features of that trans-situational role relationship were originally and continuously formulated through such utterances as, "You know I won't snitch".

Beyond the multi-formulative character of this single utterance, it was also a consequential move in the very "game" that it formulated. As a move in that field of action which it formulated, it pointed to the contingencies in that field as they were altered by this move. Furthermore, the utterance as a move obtained its sense and impact from those altered contingencies. Much of the persuasiveness of "telling the code" consisted in its character as a move in the field of action which it also defined. By saying, "You know I won't snitch", (a) the resident negatively sanctioned the prior conduct of the staff member or myself. Saying that the question called for snitching was morally evaluating it and rebuffing me or the staff. The utterances (b) called for and almost always obtained a cessation of that line of the conversation. It was, therefore, consequential in terminating that line of talk. In terminating what line of talk, it (c) left me or staff ignorant of what we would have learned by [asking] the question had it been answered. And it (d) signaled the consequences of rejecting the resident's utterance or the course of action it suggested. By saying, "You know I won't snitch", the resident pointed to what he would do if the staff persisted. He "said" he would not comply, irrespective of the staff's wishes. He thereby warned that the conversation would turn nasty if staff or I did not retreat from the question. He also pointed to the staff's obligation (or my obligation) to be competent in the affairs of residents. To refuse to acknowledge the sense and appropriateness of the resident's response was to risk being seen as incompetent in the eyes of all other residents and staff. Finally, by noting that what was being requested was *snitching*, a resident pointed to the consequences for himself if he were to go ahead and answer the question. The potential consequences for him could include beatings and even death. Since staff was obliged to protect residents, this fate was also consequential for them. The potential consequences of refusing to accept the credibility of the resident's response made that response persuasive.

In the view portrayed here, rules (and, in turn, conformity and deviance) are not abstract affairs that transcend situations that are conceived in the idealized game-model of rules in rule books. Instead, they subsist in such practices as giving explanations by rule. As Wieder and Zimmerman (1976: 120) put it:

> [These procedures] are methods which are employed within concrete here and now occasions which make those occasions organized as aspects of the setting for members. They are a means whereby discrete here and now events are seen and named as parts of a pattern which temporally and spatially extends beyond

the here and now. They are means whereby the necessary or inevitable character of the flow of events is seen and effectively asserted. Through their accounting practices . . . societal members make their conduct and the conduct of others recognizable as events-in-a-social-order. Just what those events are socially explicitly recognized as, or merely acknowledged as, depends upon the production and acceptance of such accounting work. The sense that the social world and all its constituent objects has for those residing in it thus depends on this important accounting work. Furthermore, this same accounting work is an act in the very field of action that it makes accountable or formulates. Accounts (e.g., an explanation by rule) simultaneously organize a world while operating in or on that very same organized world.

NOTES

[1]See Pollner (1974).
[2]This difficulty is most clearly discerned by reference to the category of "secret deviance." Clearly, such a concept is not easily associated with a theory that defines deviance as that which is reacted to as such, since, if the activity is "secret," it cannot provoke "reaction."
[3]The game-furnished structures approximately correspond to Garfinkel's game-furnished conditions (1963: 191–193).
[4]Bittner, 1965, 1967; Cicourel, 1968, 1973, 1974; Eglin, 1974; Garfinkel, 1967; Garfinkel and Sacks, 1970; Leiter, 1969, 1974, 1976, 1980; Mehan, 1974; Mehan and Wood, 1975; Roth, 1974; Sacks, 1963; Sudnow, 1975; Wieder, 1970, 1974; Wieder and Zimmerman, 1976; Wilson, 1970; Zimmerman, 1970, 1978; Zimmerman and Pollner, 1970; Zimmerman and Wieder, 1970.
[5]Haynor and Asch, 1939, 1940; Clemmer, 1940; Weinberg, 1942; Haynor, 1943; Schragg, 1944, 1954; Caldwell, 1956; Ohlin, 1956; Sykes, 1956; Galtung, 1958; Cressey and Krasowski, 1959; Grusky, 1959; Cloward, 1960; Sykes and Messinger, 1960; Johnson, 1961; McLeery, 1961a, 1961b; Wheeler, 1961; Garbedian, 1963, 1964; Tittle and Tittle, 1964; Ward and Kassebaum, 1965; Wilmer, 1965; Berk, 1966; Street, Vintner, and Perrow, 1966; Studt, Messinger, and Wilson, 1968.

11 NEW DIRECTIONS IN DEVIANCE RESEARCH

JIM THOMAS

Reefer Madness, a government-inspired antimarijuana fright film of the mid-1930s, dramatized the sleazy life of marijuana-smokers as one of crazed depravity in which all those in contact with the "killer weed" were viewed as categorically pathological, destined necessarily to suffer tragically. In *Reefer Madness*, deviance required retribution so that the social order would be preserved. *Reefer Madness* addressed marijuana-smoking in much the same way—although far more dramatically—than most contemporary social scientists address deviance: as *stigmatized behavior* that has been *predefined* either explicitly or implicitly as requiring *control, containment,* or *monitoring*. By the very act of identifying a set of behaviors as appropriate for deviance research, researchers—no matter how permissive or well-intentioned their own personal ideology—perpetuate a view of the social world that includes value premises reflecting the nature of that world and the proper (or nondeviant) behaviors within it. Probably more than any other subarea of social inquiry, deviance research seems supported by an undisclosed normative structure and by hidden power relations that remain, for the researcher, unproblematic (for example, Gouldner, 1968, 1971; Liazos, 1972, 1974; N. Davis, 1975; Spitzer, 1975, 1977; Smart, 1977; S. Cohen, 1979; Platt, 1977). Implicitly immoral behavior (e.g., sexual promiscuity, prostitution, homosexuality, obtaining an abortion, purchasing or purveying pornography, becoming involved in a love tryst), pathological behavior (e.g., crime, delinquency, substance abuse), groups characterized by social stigmatization (e.g., the handicapped, divorcees, illegitimate children, "hitmen and muggers"), and, more recently, so-called bourgeois deviance (e.g., white-collar crime, compulsive gambling, student activism, membership in religious sects, smoking cigarettes) are consistently preferred as objects of analysis over abuses of political or economic power, political surveillance agents, legislative interest groups, or corporate bribers and industrial polluters.

The point to be made is that deviant behavior is contingent upon *social definitions* that emerge as products of specific social, political, and economic circumstances and reflects shifts in social norms, values, and goals, as well as in social and researcher ideology (e.g., Schur, 1980). Lofland (1969) has convincingly argued that the concept of deviance embodies a form of social conflict in that it is not simply that the *behaviors* are in question; it also involves people competing over the right to name the world. As a concept, deviance also reflects specific power relations because it entails the capacity of some group, usually the dominant social group, to impose its tacit definitions of the world and of the proper order of things upon both its own and upon other social groups. As Rock (1973: 59) has suggested: "In a sense, conceptions of deviancy are not more than the organizing beliefs which guide the activities of people who sustain rule-breaking behavior. They cannot be understood independently of a society's power structure and social groupings."

Deviancy researchers, nonetheless, have tended to plunge into their analysis by *assuming the normative stance* implied by, and reflected in, the meanings of such behaviors. This has resulted in an ideologically-based acceptance of the adequacy and legitimacy of the chosen topic rather than a challenging or questioning of the underlying ideology that itself supports the meaning of the concepts and definitions of deviancy research. This serves to support and perpetuate the existing social and political order, and, as Thomas et al. (1980) have shown in a related argument, serves as a subtle control mechanism by maintaining the legitimacy of those power relations that direct our attention to disapproved behaviors.

The central thesis of this chapter is simply this: Despite apparent theoretical and methodological shifts, contemporary deviancy research has changed little in the past several decades. The various thematic and theoretical transformations, beginning with the Chicago and functionalist schools in deviancy research and continuing through labeling and conflict theories of the 1970s, shared fundamental paradigmatic features. As a consequence, differences between perspectives may be more apparent than real, and the result is that deviancy research that proceeds from conventional paradigms is rapidly becoming exhausted as fruitful for social inquiry. Unproblematic concepts, stereotypical definitions and conceptions of "deviant," and conservative ideological implications have subverted even the labeling perspective—considered by some to be a liberal, even radical, antidote to the politically conservative approaches of the 1950s and 1960s. The solution to this problem of theoretical and ideological impoverishment does not lie in the generation of new theories, expansion of empirical limits, or greater emphasis on "bottom dog" rather than "top dog" research (e.g., Becker, 1967). The position taken in this essay is that deviancy research, as reflected in the dominant social science paradigms, is a *dead-end endeavor*, in that 1) loosely articulated "theories" of disapproved behavior proliferate almost as fast as new "facts," without substantively adding to our social understanding, and 2) the questions asked and the answers provided, while initially provocative and seductive, leave us, as does a short-term lover, perhaps momentarily exhilarated, but essentially and consistently unfulfilled, and, over the long term, empty.

What is needed is not new twists on increasingly differentiated topics, but rather a substantively new perspective—a new paradigm, one capable of addressing human behavior in a way that neither blames nor stigmatizes the observed behaviors. What is needed is not simply new directions to the same old destinations, but new destinations that go beyond the conventional conceptions of deviance and deviants.

PARADIGMS

Classification of deviancy research by theories, topics, or "schools" has tended to exaggerate the differences between competing perspectives within similar paradigms and thus ignore fundamental commonalities that tie many theoretical perspectives together. One way to avoid this problem is by classifying research according to the paradigm on which it is based.

The concept of paradigm in the social sciences is often vague, and critics of sociology in particular have argued about which (or even whether) dominant paradigms exist in the social sciences. The concept is useful, nonetheless. Discussions of paradigms have in-

cluded those by Ritzer (1975), Truman (1965), Bryant (1975), Fallding (1972), and Dawe (1970, 1971). Although the term has been
defined in various ways (see, for example, Useem, 1976; Kuhn,
1970; Eckberg and Hill, 1979), Ritzer's (1975: 157) remains quite
useful. He views a paradigm as ". . . a fundamental image of the
subject matter within a science. It serves to define what should be
studied, what questions should be asked, and how they should be
asked, and what rules should be followed in interpreting the
answer obtained. The paradigm is the broadest unit of consensus
within a science and serves to differentiate one scientific community (or sub-community) from another. It subsumes, defines, and
inter-relates exemplars, theories, methods and instruments that exist within it."

As Alford (1975) has argued, this concept allows us to avoid the
interfaces of logical adherence and deductive consistency which
the terms *theory* or *model* convey, yet provides a sense of the epistemological structure that guides inquiry by allowing for an identification of the background assumptions and ontological presuppositions underlying research. While an analysis of theoretical approaches allows for an analysis of specific explanatory positions
within paradigms, an analysis of the paradigm itself allows for a
classification instrument that subsumes competing theories, yet retains the basic epistemological features common to competing theories. An analysis of paradigms provides insights into the problems
of subject-object, fact-value, and theory-praxis,[1] each of which takes
on a specific character depending upon the paradigm employed.

Modifying Ritzer's classification system, three distinct paradigmatic categories can be identified in deviancy research. First, the
social facts paradigm focuses on objects of research as existing
independently from the perceiving subject (that is, it separates the
knowing subject from the object to be known). This perspective
reflects a form of objectivism, which at its simplest means that our
concepts correspond more or less exactly with the objects to which
they refer. The goal of research is one of viewing the topic as an
independently existing object that can be understood primarily
through describing, classifying, or correlating the manifest features
of the object. In the social sciences, this approach poses as the
primary problematic concepts those such as norms, values, or roles,
and in sociological theory, it is typically represented by, for example, such perspectives as positivism, systems theory, or conflict
positions. The fact that such approaches as conflict and positivist
views—often thought to be incompatible—can be categorized on

the basis of fundamental common features indicates the utility of classification by paradigms.

Second, the *social constructionist paradigm* focuses on the manner in which the reconstruction of the social world is a product of the activity of the human subject, and includes such acts as interpretation, negotiation, and meaning acquisition as features that constitute how we enact a social environment. This paradigm is represented by qualitative interactionist approaches (e.g., labeling and existential positions) and Weberian-oriented analysis. Finally, the *dialectical Marxian paradigm* offers both new directions and destinations for social research.

Social Facts Paradigm

The social factist approach typically views the program of deviancy research as one of compiling facts or identifying correlations between the causes of disapproved behaviors (the independent variable) and the specific behaviors caused (the dependent variable). Viewing people as acted upon, social facts practitioners focus upon so-called objective truth, or on how objects in the social world influence and constrain people to behave as they do. Examples include sociological positivism (e.g., broken homes "cause" delinquency), Durkheimian approaches (e.g., anomie theories), and conflict theory. Four interrelated features characterize the social factist position. First, knowledge is reducible to an independent objective element, which ". . . presents us with society conceived of as a thing-like facticity standing over against its individual members with coercive controls and molding them in its socializing processes" (Berger and Pullberg, 1964: 196). Hearn (1973–1974: 143) reminds us that for practitioners of this view, ". . . the reflective powers of cognition become drastically minimized as thought becomes defined in terms of a unified scientific order wherein factual knowledge is derivable from and subsumed under natural scientific principles." This latter feature permeates especially the works of positivist deviancy researchers who attempt to locate factors that cause deviancy (e.g., Hawkes, 1975; Turner and Rosen, 1967; Hakim, Ovadia, and Weinblatt, 1978; Foster, Dinitz, and Reckless, 1972; Hirschi and Selvin, 1966; Hagan and Leon, 1977).

Second, social factists deny the phenomenal relationship between the knowing subject and the object to be known. By objectifying knowledge and focusing upon this objectified imagery as explicit or implicit "variables" that correspond to "reality," the subject-object gap becomes intensified and the subjective element (i.e., how knowing subjects themselves participate in constructing the object to be known) is eliminated as relevant for analysis. That is deviance is not conceptualized as a product of, and as shaped by, human activity, and it is not understood, even in part, by grasping the meanings imputed to behaviors by knowledge-constituting subjects (whether these latter be the deviants, those doing the defining, or even the researchers themselves). Rather, deviance becomes viewed as preexisting phenomena that are "already there," and the practical side of the concept—that is, how it is created in consciousness—is ignored.

Third, the social factist approach is ahistorical in that it rejects as problematic the historicity underlying deviancy. By concealing the historical configurations that shape and predefine behavioral options, as well as which definitions count as "deviant," social factists present a one-sided and distorted—and thereby inadequate—image of the social nature of behavior. In fact, behavior is removed from the realm of social activity—removed as historical praxis (that is, human practical activity)—and social factist approaches thus eliminate one of the crucial components of the sociology of deviance—the social aspect—and reinsert instead a reified, mystified, and distorted vision of norms, power, and behaviors as existing independently from human subjectivity. For those social factists who do attempt to describe changes in definitions of deviance over time, and thus view their own work as historical, chronological correlations become confused with historical analysis, and discussion of temporal sequences is erroneously taken to be "history."

Finally, social factists view "scientific knowledge" as a neutral, disinterested affair, one unconnected to political, ethical, or other value issues. The presuppositions that guide selection of topics, shape interpretations, and suggest uses for outcomes of research are not included as problematic. This paradigm maintains a radical separation between facts and values and adheres to the belief in the possibility and the necessity of "value-free" inquiry. As a consequence, definitions of deviance are seldom examined for the value biases they may contain as part of the research, and the result is the acceptance of "official" or dominant definitions of disapproved behaviors. In contrast to the program of critical or Marxian perspectives, which attempt to "scientifically" demonstrate the constraining features either of norm-violating behavior or of definitions of such behavior, by identifying the class-based genesis of the social arrangements that support the deviant-defining ideology with the intent of providing theoretically-grounded strategies for possible social emancipation from such constraints, the social factists not only find such a program undesirable, but see it as "scientifically" impossible.

Because the social facts paradigm excludes so much from its analytic program, it offers at best only limited insights, which may possess potential for being integrated (as data) into other paradigms. However, as a basis for analysis into the sociology of deviance, or as a guide to practical—especially emancipatory—activity, it appears quite unworthy as a future direction in deviancy research.

In sum, the distinguishing feature of the social facts approach is the radical severance of, and total emphasis upon, the object of knowledge. Rather than recognize the object of disapproved behaviors as mediated by subjective factors (such as human interpretations or meaning imposition), the social facts position attempts to remove from both the methodology and from theory all traces of subjectivity. By contrast, the social constructionist view discussed next inverts this relationship by deemphasizing the object of knowledge and emphasizing instead the knowing subject as the primary focal point of research.

Social Constructionist Paradigm

The social constructionist paradigm emphasizes people as acting upon their world, and the research goal is that of describing the processes through which the subject (people) constructs the social world. In this view, deviance is seen as a social process, and researchers typically examine how persons actively participate in making the conditions for, adapting to the label of, or actually doing, deviance. As Table 11.1 indicates, this paradigm differs in a number of fundamental ways from the others. Social constructionists, for example, set as the primary research task the displaying of how persons account for their everyday, taken-for-granted world, or how people make sense of the common stock of social meanings required in order to structure their lives and interpret and react to their experiences. The general methods are those that provide data from which to build qualitative descriptions of the explicit conditions under which individuals give or accept accounts of the "world as fact," and how, when norms are violated, the violator attempts to justify or manage the subsequent situations. The task for inquiry centers upon disclosing and displaying meaning networks, and emphasizes the understanding of the meanings of a social situation within the specific context in which such meanings occur.

In sociology, social constructionist work has been developed particularly by Weberian (*Verstehen*) analysis, but in deviance research it is typified primarily by interactionist sociology. Particularly influential have been ethnomethodologists (e.g., Cicourel, 1968; Garfinkel, 1967; Coulter, 1973), existential sociologists (e.g., Douglas, 1972; Lofland, 1969), dramaturgical analysts (Manning, 1972, 1975, 1977; Goffman, 1959, 1963, 1967, 1969, 1971), and, especially, labeling theorists (Lemert, 1951; Becker, 1963, 1974; Gusfield, 1955, 1967; Scheff, 1974). Although their ideas and approaches may vary dramatically, social constructionists share a common premise: Behaviors are social acts (rather than social facts) and can be understood by grasping the manner in which meanings are created, exchanged, and maintained through the manipulation of social symbols. Persons bring into each social experience a "stock of knowledge," which, if shared (or "common"), provides the framework through which symbolically-mediated meanings are exchanged. The goal of inquiry thus becomes a rigorous and systematic description of how persons, in their everyday life, create and exchange these meanings and thus acquire and employ shared knowledge through which, and upon which, social interaction is conducted and social institutions function, and through which most of us experience our everyday situations.

This paradigm has been called subjectivistic in that it studies knowledge from the standpoint of the subject of knowledge. Unlike social factists, who emphasize the primacy of the object, the knowledge-constituting subject becomes the focal point of analysis. But this requires the deemphasis, if not the actual elimination, of the object in that the object becomes viewed as a reflection or outcome of subjective activity rather than a mutually delimiting component of an interactive process through which both are affected and thereby transformed. Thus, the subject-object distinction is maintained as it is for social factists, although the emphasis is on subject rather than object. By focusing on the mental states or meanings of the subject and the corresponding behaviors prompted by these mental states, social constructionist views of deviance exchange the objectivism of positivism for a neo-Kantian subjectivism in which categories of knowledge, concepts, and other attendant apparatuses of knowing become understood as existing within the cognitive activity of the subject. This leads to reification of categories and of intellectual activity in that there is no examination of

Table 11.1. Summary of Dominant Paradigms in Deviancy Research.

Paradigm	Key Features	Typical Perspectives	Goals of Research	Program of Research	Typical Methods and Data Manipulation Techniques
Social facts	Subject-object distinction Fact-value distinction Primacy of facts Persons acted upon A historical Separation of theory and practice Objectivistic	Positivism Functionalism Biosociology Anomie theory Conflict theory	Obtain objective data Identify causal antecedents (positivism) Correlate observed variables Establish function of observed relationships (functionalism) Identify competing interests that generate conflict and social change (conflict theory)	Obtain "objective" knowledge Application of rules of science in disinterested (i.e., value-neutral) manner Verification and reliability testing of knowledge	Hypothesis construction and statistical analysis Abstract generalizations; use of secondary sources; typology construction (e.g., functionalism) Survey techniques Case studies "Official" records and statistics
Social constructionist	Subject-object distinction Primacy of subject of knowledge Persons act upon Maintain fact-value distinction (although not as radically as social factists)	Labeling theory Dramaturgical analysis Existential sociology Ethnomethodology	Examine social conditions in which deviance and control procedures are created by human subjects Examine how behaviors emerge as negotiated features of the social world, how persons in organizations, power positions, reform movements, or deviant groups enact their environments in a conscious, intentional manner	General program of enlightened understanding Latent program of critique of society and existing social conditions Understanding of social processes underlying production of deviant behavior and control apparatus Search for social meanings of deviance	Ethnographies Participant observation Impressionistic and systematic observation Interviewing
Marxian perspectives	Focus on class relations Deviance reflects social arrangements of capitalism Facts and values inseparable Attempts to overcome subject-object distinction Theory of deviancy must guide practice to overcome unnecessary forms of social domination Dialectical and historical analysis	Marxian theory Critical criminology "Radical" political economy "Radical" critiques of cultural and ideology (critical theory)	Examine interconnections between elements of social life and economic order Identify production of consciousness as a component of social experience contingent upon one's position in production relations of society Examine deviant behavior and control as mediated by such factors as class conflict, social interactions that serve to maintain existing social arrangements, dominant ideological views of "right and wrong," or social order	Knowledge about deviance seen as means of understanding larger social questions, such as how classes maintain domination in society Knowledge is a possible weapon in struggle to change society Radical social change	Dialectical method Documentary research Historical analysis Class analysis Statistical techniques not excluded, but used as part of broader technique of analysis Interaction techniques not excluded, but used as part of broader technique of analysis

296

how subjects create knowledge in relation to the prior social conditions in which social concepts, rules of interpretation, and even research and language itself are embedded.

In addition to the subject-object separation, the social constructionist paradigm maintains the fact-value and theory-praxis distinction. This occurs not because of the belief in the necessity for such a distinction, as for social factists, but because of the lack of paradigmatic development capable of unifying theoretically derived imperatives for constructing values and action. This approach also ignores the historical configurations that shape both the content of commonsensical understandings (or "typifications" of the world) and the social structure itself, which in part shapes and delimits how we apprehend and negotiate our symbolic and material world. Beneath these systems of social rules, shared assumptions, common modes of expression, and attitudinal and belief systems lie historically shaped elements that predefine, limit, guide, and channel the manner in which we consciously experience the world and interpret and respond to that experience.

Social constructionist approaches have provided the sociology of deviance with invaluable sensitizing concepts, and have profoundly altered the way in which we study deviance. Nonetheless, the current state of this paradigm is such that there appear to be no new developments remaining, and even most practitioners of labeling theory have moved on to different areas of research or have reduced their own expectations for the perspective. Although both social facts and social constructionist paradigms have left a considerable legacy, and although they continue to have limited, though necessary, utility, they appear to lead to a dead end because they simply do not provide adequate understandings either of the topic of deviancy or of the relationship of deviancy research itself to its topic.

Radical Perspectives and Marxian Paradigms: New Directions for the 1980s

The third paradigm derives primarily from the writings of Karl Marx. This Marxian paradigm[2] is a fruitful, but certainly controversial, approach—as recent debates suggest (e.g., Inciardi, 1980; Platt and Takagi, 1979). It seems to offer a powerful new direction by which to avoid the traditional obstacles to understanding suggested in the preceding discussion.

It is not always clear what constitutes a Marxian approach and what does not. Most researchers assume that any so-called radical perspective is a Marxian perspective, while others argue that only those researchers with "politically correct" analyses illustrating the need to overthrow the "ruling class" can be called authentic Marxists. One value of classifying deviance research by paradigms is that it help us to distinguish the differences between approaches that are simply radical or conflict-oriented, which often derive from a social facts paradigm, and Marxian approaches. Before discussing the Marxian paradigm, it might be useful first to distinguish between apparently similar approaches that seem to be gaining popularity as possible new directions in the coming decade, in order to clearly illustrate why they are in fact variants of dead-end paradigms.

Radical Approaches

One current direction reflecting attempts to address such often-ignored issues in deviance as power relations, sources and meanings of deviance, and the content of disapproved behavior targetted for social control, may loosely be termed *radical analysis*. Although not actually "new" (it has, after all, been influenced by several centuries of intellectual traditions), this perspective has become increasingly adapted to deviancy research. The term *radical* here denotes a political orientation that the social order is askew, rather than a shared theoretical or methodological commitment, and the position consists of several variations, not all of which are compatible with the others. Some of these perspectives have been with us since the mid-seventeenth century, others for only a few decades, and still others are in an embryonic stage. But they are each loosely connected by several shared features. First, and perhaps most important, they have all been generally clumped together (erroneously) as *conflict theories*[3] because they assume that the primary characteristics that shape social interaction and social structure reflect competing values and norms, and struggles over power and material and symbolic resources. This competition contributes to contradictory features of social life and institutions, which tend to generate social, political, and economic conflicts, which in turn shape social life and interaction. More simply, a radical perspective begins from the premise that the social order is based on *dissensus*, not (as for functionalists, for example) *consensus*. Radical views are usually traced back to the seventeenth-century philosopher Thomas Hobbes (1967, 1971), who argued that because individuals desire their own good, the natural state of humanity is one of conflict, with each person attempting to maximize personal benefits at the expense of others. This makes social antagonism and struggle a natural feature of the social order. Hobbes (1967: 277–278) wrote: "Further, since men by natural passion are divers ways offensive one to another, every many thinking well of himself, and hating to see the same in others, they must needs provoke one another by words, and other signs of contempt and hatred, which are incident to all comparison, till at last they must determine the pre-eminence by strength of force and body."

Given the natural cupidity of the human species, it is only natural that battles for possession of resources (whether material or symbolic) occur normally, and, for Hobbes (1967: 279), it follows "that the stronger must enjoy it alone, and that it be decided by battle who is the stronger." For this reason, people live in a continual state of hostility. Yet, Hobbes was a rationalist, not a pessimist, cynic, or nihilist. He argued that reason is a critically important tool that allows us to overcome the morass of conflict and allows us to create that great Leviathan called the state, which represents the public citizen. The state mediates between primitive human desires and the rational need for freedom and well-being.

Second, radical analysts are guided by the Hobbesian view that definitions of norms and values are a source of conflict over who has the right to name the world. This perspective is further guided by the Hobbesian assumption that the state functions to mediate (that is, to intervene with the intention of resolving) the conflicts over these definitions of acceptable and unacceptable behaviors. This means that for radical theorists, not only the behaviors of individuals are important to study, but also the nature of the power relations that define some behaviors as permissible and not others. Further, some researchers suggest that the state is not so much a rational mediator between conflicting interests, but itself is a tool, a mechanism in shaping deviant labels that maintain the power and privilege of dominant groups against those persons less powerful. This view of the state is also central to Marxian theory. In this view, deviance may reflect state-aided attempts to oppress targeted behaviors rather than indicate behavioral disorders.

Third, radical theorists rarely focus solely on individual behavior, but instead concentrate on how social features reflect conflicting values, norms, or laws. That is, radical perspectives tend to be macroanalysis. Finally, the radical perspective contains a sometimes implicit, but more often explicit, political position, usually one that defends particular forms of political activity, opposes the oppressive or arbitrary nature of repressive definitions of behavior, or attempts to present a radical approach to resolving social problems that generate or facilitate disapproved behaviors, such as poverty or racism.

Although these four features are shared by all radical researchers, they are developed in substantially different directions. Distinguishing between two general variations, we can identify prominent differences, thereby allowing us to evaluate the potential of each for guiding us to not only new directions, but to new destinations in deviance research. This will also help us understand why a Marxian paradigm is set apart from these other approaches.

Conflict Perspectives

Perhaps in part because the Red Scare of the 1950s led to so-called political witch hunts and persecution of many persons even suspected of possessing overly liberal political values (e.g., Caute, 1978), Marxian thought was not developed or applied to any significant degree until the mid-1960s. Instead, a relatively safe theoretical position known as *conflict theory* emerged.[4] In order to distinguish between Marxian positions on one hand and positions that derive from non-Marxian premises but often employ similar concepts on the other, it is convenient to apply the term *conflict theory* to those positions that subscribed to, but do not substantially go beyond, the Hobbesian position outlined above. Chambliss and Seidman (1971) have summarized the position in four propositions:

1. Society at every moment is subject to change; social change is continuous.
2. Every society experiences at every moment social conflicts.
3. Every element in a society contributes to change.
4. Every society rests upon constraint of some members by others.

Unlike the Chicago and related schools, which held that deviance was the outcome of structural disjunctions that either "caused" or facilitated deviance, conflict theories hold that deviance (defined loosely as those behaviors proscribed by power-wielding groups) is a natural state of social affairs, since deviance, whatever the individual's motivation, is at root a reflection of unequal power distribution. Put more simply, deviance is a conflict between at least two parties, one the superordinate, who makes and enforces the rules, and the other the subordinate, whose behaviors violate those rules (Horowitz and Liebowitz, 1968).

Like labeling perspectives, conflict theory is sensitive to the manner in which the deviant label comes to be applied to certain behaviors. Unlike labeling theory, neither the imputation nor the acceptance of the label is the primary focal point for analysis. The research focus is instead the power relations between labeler and labeled, the interests served by particular labels, or the selective allocation of power and resources against specific behaviors and subordinate groups. That is, the task for research is primarily political.

> The political questions inherent in a conflict model of deviance focus on the use of social control in society. What behavior is forbidden? How is this behavior controlled? At issue is a conflict between individual freedom and social restraint, with social disorder (anarchy) and authoritarian social control (Leviathan) as the polar expressions. The resolution of this conflict entails a political decision about how much social disorder will be tolerated at the expense of how much social control. This choice cannot be confronted as long as deviance is relegated to the arena of administrative policy-making (Horowitz and Liebowitz, 1968: 283).

The value of conflict theory has been twofold. First, it has sensitized researchers who are uncomfortable with much of the rhetoric and poor scholarship of some Marxians to many of the issues shared by the two positions. Conflict theory remains a bridge between liberal and radical politics that many conflict theorists attempt to straddle. Second, especially during the 1950s and early 1960s, it served as a buffer between conservative social theories and the need for a critical examination of social institutions during an era of both political and intellectual repression by state and private control agencies. Conflict theory has been viewed by critics, particularly Marxians, as not going "far enough" in challenging existing social relations or in not digging deep enough into the underlying political economy or ideology that supports existing social institutions. These criticisms may be valid, but they tend to detract from and thus minimize the role that this perspective played during one of the most intellectually repressive eras in United States history. Conflict theory filled a critical void when other theories were either silent or still in embryo.

Unlike symbolic interactionist perspectives, which focus on how the *subject* of knowledge creates a world built up from meanings and competent interpretations of those meanings, or the Marxian paradigm, which sees the social world as a dialectical outcome of objective and subjective factors, conflict theory tends to focus on the *object* of knowledge. That is, the research concern is one of seeing how social factors (conflict, interests, power, and status as objective variables) act upon individuals or groups in ways that create deviance. This serves to present a one-sided view of social reality in that it overemphasizes how persons are acted upon by external conditions, and deemphasizes how persons as thinking, feeling, willing creatures create and maintain their own *context for action.*

Conflict theorists, despite their critical examination of power relations, do accept the existing social arrangements of contemporary society insofar as they perceive the fundamental premises of a capitalist society as adequate for resolving existing problems and conflicts. Reorganization of the social structure itself and implementation of a new social order are not part of the conflict theory program. Nor is deviance viewed as historically contingent upon values that are embedded in normative and ideological systems that have evolved in response to specific sociopolitical or cultural transformations. Finally, conflict theorists do not examine the sources of the types of acts and the types of control available to deviants or controllers at a particular historical moment. Other than describe power inequities and sources of conflict, this perspective does not offer adequate potential for addressing fundamental issues. This is the primary feature separating conflict from Marxian theorists. But before comparing the two positions, we should next examine a position related to conflict theory, that of controlology.

Controlology

Controlology, a term coined by Jason Ditton (1979), is a recent direction that attempts to display the dynamics of social control agents and their techniques in constraining disapproved behaviors. This perspective is a variant of conflict theory in that it shares the assumptions, direction, and paradigmatic (i.e., social factist) and political orientation of conflict theory. Its uniqueness lies in the emphasis placed on the agents of control as they respond to disapproved behaviors, rather than on the genesis of the behaviors themselves (as, by contrast, did the Chicago school and anomie theorists), or upon the processes of learning deviant behaviors (e.g., as do the symbolic interactionists, especially labeling theorists), or upon the relationship between political economy, class, and structural and ideological features of control and behavior (e.g., Marxian positions). This has also been called the *social control perspective* by N. Davis (1975), who provides one of the most coherent statements of this position. Key concepts include power, authority, political systems, conflict, sanctions, and other variables that may provide indices of unequal power relations (e.g., Davis, 1975). Although conflict theories in general and control theories in particular are often associated with Marxian assumptions and premises (e.g., Nettlar, 1978; Davis, 1975; Empey, 1978), such a judgment, as we shall see, is unfounded, as Table 11.1 indicates. Control theory often uses the terminology of Marxian analysis (e.g., *class, state, bourgeoisie, ruling classes*) and shares *prima facie* political similarities (e.g., rejection of "bourgeois politics," sympathy with radical and militant social movements, support of social change) with Marxian analysis. It also suggests similar conclusions, such as the belief that the "capitalist state" may generate deviancy, that laws function primarily to suppress individuals and repress behavior (e.g., Roby, 1969; Chambliss, 1975; Nonet, 1976), that control agents may *cause* deviance (e.g., Hawkins and Tiedeman, 1975; Marx, 1980a, 1980b), or, in its most extreme form, that there are no *crime waves*, only *control waves* (Ditton, 1979).

The central program of controlology is to reveal the structures of control as they reinforce, create, shape, or otherwise underlie suppression of disapproved behavior. The essential problem with controlology, as with conflict theory, from which it derives, is that despite the ambitious program of social criticism and the accompanying reform suggested, and despite also its sensitizing value to topics and problems not addressed by other perspectives, there is substantially no new theoretical development of this perspective over those they claim to replace. At best, they remain supplemental, for they do not offer an adequate account of the political, economic, social, or ideological conditions that shape behavior and control the social arrangements from which all behavior derives. Unlike symbolic interactionist approaches, neither conflict nor control theories examine adequately how individuals themselves create a social world, including the meanings of behavior, social structures, or even the very language within which we carry on discourse about deviance (e.g., Burton and Carlen, 1979).

This is not, of course, to suggest that *any* theory can ever be so complete as to offer a definitive, universal, permanent body of *truth*. It may be possible, however, to provide a theory of society capable of generating a theory of subjective and objective behavior. This is the project of Marxian approaches, which to varying degrees of success reflect attempts to develop a theory of society that is also capable of contributing to the understanding of so-called deviant behavior without necessarily having a specific "theory of deviance."

Marxian Paradigm

This paradigm—itself a radical approach—has existed since the mid-nineteenth century. It may be seen as a new direction in deviance research because only in recent years has the potential of Marxian inquiry been systematically redirected and developed in North America. Now that the stigma of the former polemical excesses of some Marxian writers of the past two decades has begun to subside, Marxian inquiry has become a new field of both theoretical and empirical application to social research in general, including deviancy research.

Marxian theories are perhaps the most misunderstood of all research perspectives. This is in part because of an ideological suspicion of left-leaning ideas, which has been compounded by a tendency among some Marxians toward polemics and rhetoric rather than analysis and cogent argument. It has also been due partly to the confusion over the meaning of "Marxian analysis," which is not helped by large numbers of writers who identify themselves as Marxists, often without any understanding of Marxian methodology, and by the use of Marxian concepts or political-economic variables (such as class, ideology, monopoly, and economic base) in ways not consistent with a Marxian position. Any position that does not, at a minimum, at least attempt to proceed from an analysis based on the relationship between political-economic forces (such as productive relations, class conflict, the "logic" of capitalism, and the corresponding social arrangements of exploitation and discrimination) should not be considered Marxian. Nor should an argument be considered Marxian simply because it appears hostile toward capitalism, takes a strident stand against the status quo, advocates militance on social issues, or uses "buzz words" usually associated with Marxian thought.

Among Marxian deviancy researchers there have been two influential positions. The first has been loosely termed the new criminology, and despite the name, it is not limited to criminology, but pertains to social deviance in general. This position is associated particularly with British scholars (e.g., Smart, 1977; Taylor, 1971; Taylor and Taylor, 1973; Young, 1973, 1974; Taylor, Walton, and Young, 1973, 1975; Cohen and Taylor, 1972). It is useful to compare this position with more recent North American research in order to illustrate not only the nature of the Marxian paradigm, but to show the variations between practitioners.

The New Criminology.[5] The British school reflected an attempt to go beyond the positivism that adherents of this new position saw as a dominating influence on deviance research in both North America and Britain. It was an attempt to critique the existing state of deviancy theory, and to *demystify* (or expose) the power relations that were perceived to underlie research concepts, propositions, and methodology, and to examine the results and purposes of research as a means of maintaining existing power relations. Unlike conflict theory, the new criminology began as an attack on utilitarian and positivistic criminology and was intended to replace such perspectives with one that expanded the conceptual framework of social control research beyond legalistic, official, or conventionally normative prescriptions of behavior (Taylor, Walton, and Young, 1973). The initial works of the new criminologists did not attempt to develop an alternative theoretical framework appropriate for new conceptual, stronger theoretical, or revised, analytic formulations. Instead, the writings reflected, for the most part, attempts to reveal (or demystify) the ideological biases, the control implications, and the partial nature of existing studies, and to form alternative politically grounded research statements such that deviancy research would become a form of social and political activism (e.g., Gibson, 1970; Taylor, 1971; Damer, 1974), or to clarify the state of criminology and deviancy research (e.g., Platt, 1975; Taylor, Walton, and Young, 1973).

Although claiming to ground their approach in a Marxian historical materialism, their conceptualization and formulation of a theoretical framework appropriate for this task remained limited to conventional analyses within a politically informed, but methodologically conventional, stance (Curry, 1974). Their argument that a dialectical position would have to break down the arbitrary academic divisions of deviancy research and ground inquiry in a framework capable of apprehending the structural and class differences existing within and between capitalist society was certainly worthwhile. Unfortunately, their theoretical development fell short of their goal, and empirical research consisted primarily of reconceptualizing alternative deviancy topics in the vocabulary of Marxian theory rather than proceeding from a rigorously applied conceptual apparatus built up from a dialectical and historical epistemological base. The new criminology focuses especially upon current social problems as topics, such as the media's role in generating deviance (Young, 1974; Hall, 1974), social control in socialist societies (Loney, 1973), the weather underground in the United States (Walton, 1973), the "deviant as hero" views of workplace pilferage (Mars, 1974), and prison life (Cohen and Taylor, 1972). These studies are invariably interesting, serve to alert other practitioners to political and ideological issues, and are exceptionally valuable for raising questions that have not previously been systematically addressed. Nonetheless, the analytic development has not promoted a sustained assault on conventional deviancy (or social) theory, or helped in guiding this new research direction toward more powerful theoretical reformulations. The studies have tended to focus, as did the studies of social reaction theorists, on those topics that were dramatic (crime, social problems) and that tended also to be those most conducive to supporting their general thesis that, in capitalist societies, the rich and the powerful are more able to name the world and thus define unacceptable behaviors than are the rest of us. A second weakness of these studies has been the failure to examine the fundamental assumptions of their approach within the context of the epistemological model from which they were taken, which led to a conceptual gap between a new Marxian direction and the ad hoc employment of Marxian insights. This left its adherents, as Cohen (1979) brilliantly illustrates, with an often untenable political (and moral) position in which deviance was seen to be the result primarily of a capitalist society that produces crime and deviancy. This led to a utopian view of society in which the ideal would be to eliminate all forms of control. As Cohen (1979: 42) argues, this is questionable, since the very nature of society implies some sort of "social glue" in the form of rules, tacit understandings, interactional norms, and other mechanisms required to avoid total chaos and ensure at least minimal social interaction. Finally, the lack of a practical component in the theory, basic to any Marxian position, was missing. A practical component refers to a set of principles or guidelines that allow for the examination of how concrete, practical social activity is, at root, the basis of creation and interpretation of meaning, social structure, and interaction in society, and in turn, of how precepts for social action can be derived directly from our theory (rather than from a separate set of political beliefs). Deviant labels and deviants were viewed, implicitly, as caused by capitalism, and capitalism was viewed as an external variable, so to speak, as something existing apart from social members. This precluded the possibility of a theoretical understanding of the relationship between individuals and social involvement in the creation of meaning. It was undialectical because it could not, at the theoretical level, see that deviance, rather than being an effect of capitalism, might instead reflect forms of mediation, or might in fact be tangential to capitalist social structure (e.g., such behaviors as cigarette smoking or unusual clothing fads). When new criminologists did discuss such issues, it was from their political position, not from their theoretical position. Commenting on the failure of the new criminology, Cohen (1979: 19) reflected, "It was as if we had drafted the blueprint for a new bomb, even constructed bits of it, left it lying around—and then run rapidly in other directions."

North American Marxians. The social crises of the 1960s and the emergent social movements and corresponding theoretical developments, particularly in the United States, inspired the development of various forms of Marxian and critical thought in North America. The early works of C. Wright Mills, Alvin Gouldner, William Chambliss, Jerome Skolnick, Irving Horowitz, and Ralf Dahrendorf, although only marginally Marxian, nonetheless stimulated younger scholars, who were most profoundly affected both intellectually and politically by the events of the 1960s, particularly antiwar and civil rights struggles. Sustained by their older mentors—products of the politically restrained 1940s and 1950s—and by the proliferation of leftist-oriented journals, study groups, associations, conferences, and other forms of mutual support networks, considerable social theory was redirected—despite the often conflicting, contradictory, and even outrageous propositions—toward a distinct Marxian paradigm.

As in Britain, research tended to be political. But in North America, Marxian deviancy research has continued to be a stimulating and developing intellectual force. From the mid-1970s, Marxian deviancy research has mushroomed, and it has followed two general directions. The first direction embodied emphasis of topics such as crime and delinquency. Stimulated particularly by the works of Quinney (1970, 1974, 1975, 1977), Schwendinger and Schwendinger (1974, 1975, 1976), and Platt (1977), this position attempted to demystify contemporary approaches to deviancy research by examining the premises, political implications, or results and purposes of competing perspectives. Prompted by the social and political crises of the Vietnam era, many researchers proceeded from an intuitive—rather than a well-developed—Marxian position, and attempted to connect on an ad hoc basis their Marxian concepts and politics into other, often incompatible, frameworks. Quinney, for example, in his early works, attempted to integrate phenomenology with Marxian premises and argued that definitions of crime were a means for the bourgeoisie to maintain its advantageous position in class struggle. What distinguished Quinney's work from the British school was, at root, his intent to redirect Marxian inquiry toward questions of human subjectivity, especially the problems of meaning and interaction. Platt (1975, 1977) suggested a similar argument for examining delinquency and juvenile justice. Others, such as McNall and Johnson (1975), Grabiner (1975), and Young (1971), used their critiques of interactionist approaches to illustrate the then newly emergent potential of Marxian theory.

These approaches, despite their flaws, challenged the dominant definitions of deviance and the inequitable application of the definitions to particular social groups, and, most important, attempted to link the meanings and applications of disapproved behaviors to an unjust social system that generated conditions that caused, shaped, or encouraged the commission of disapproved acts. In short, this perspective attempted to integrate structural and interactional issues, and although these researchers often reflected the same weaknesses as the British school, the American Marxians appeared more willing to struggle with fundamental epistemological and methodological questions in order to bring adequate theoretical and conceptual formulations to research.

A second Marxian direction developed and refined the theoretical and empirical problems facing Marxian research. Challenged both by hostile critics and, especially, by other Marxians, who recognized and aggressively addressed the inadequacies and unresolved theoretical problems, these researchers attempted to clarify and develop Marxian thought. Some (e.g., Thio, 1973; Harring, 1977) attempted to display the class nature of political rules or policies by tracing the sources or applications of power to the class-bound ideology of capitalism. Others (e.g., Liazos, 1974; Platt, 1977; Scull, 1977) argued that delinquency research in general, and the juvenile justice system in particular, reflected attempts by a ruling elite to shore up an eroding social edifice that was decaying because of the logic of the social order upon which it was based. These works typify recent Marxian studies examining deviance within the context of racism, sexism, alienation, power, poverty, or imperialism, which all have roots in the fundamental productive forces of society. Typical of explicit formulations of the Marxian paradigm is the work of Spitzer (1975, 1977, 1981), whose attempt to develop a dialectical theory of deviance has focused on officially defined sanctions (either tacitly, through policy or institutional reinforcement of preferred norms and behaviors, or formally, through legally proscribing behavior). Spitzer contended that deviance production reflects the processes through which a society's population is structurally reproduced and shaped, channeled, and manipulated by social categories defined as deviant. Spitzer (1975: 642) has suggested a research strategy from which to proceed: "Problem populations [i.e., deviants] tend to share a number of social characteristics, but most important among them is the fact that their behavior, personal qualities and/or position threaten the *social relations of production* in capitalist societies." Spitzer then identified five areas that may, when threatened, prompt control attempts:

1. Capitalist modes of appropriating products of human labor.
2. Social conditions of production.
3. Patterns of distribution and consumption.
4. Processes of socialization for productive and nonproductive roles.
5. Ideology underlying capitalist society.

This argument is not totally convincing in that there seem to be a variety of behaviors that may derive from precapitalist historical moments (such as religious or ideological anachronisms that are retained in norms, cultural taboos, prescriptions and proscriptions, and in law), or that do not, even in a broad and imaginative interpretation, seem to necessarily contravene the logic or method of capitalist production. Nonetheless, as a preliminary theoretical examination and as a heuristic statement, Spitzer has indicated a power direction from which we are offered the possibility of resolving the apparent flaws, a direction more fully developed in his more recent work (Spitzer, 1981).

One theoretical nub of the Marxian position is that social control arrangements are ultimately a response to structurally generated and historically contingent behaviors that result in problems for class society. For Marxians, an analysis of the historical nature of the social arrangements required for capitalist economy will allow identification of those forms of control of problem populations likely to be used to protect and sustain that economic order. Some Marxians, building on the works of Offe (1972, 1973, 1975), O'Connor (1975),

Wright (1979), Therborn (1980), and other capitalist state theorists, view the production of deviance and criminality as a reflection of state attempts to mediate problems in capitalist society. Some radical theorists who locate the source of deviance production within the structure of the capitalist state include Balbus (1977) and Heydebrand (1977), who each link the production of law and public policy to the power of contemporary state organization and the processes that form the criminal justice system. Others have attempted to display the relationship between such factors as race and class and ideology in the social organization of prisons or street gangs (e.g., Thomas, 1981a, 1981b), or between class, state, and white-collar crime (e.g., Young, 1978, 1980). Still others have examined the political consequences of deviance. In an analysis of Marxian theories of crime, for example, Wenger and Bonomo (1978) examine the thesis that problem populations represent "progressive" social praxis. They cogently illustrate the impoverishment of these perspectives, and suggest that such analysis and interpretations tend to be the result of ad hoc and mechanical application of Marxian theory and concepts rather than carefully considered and conceptualized theoretical analysis. The significance of such work as Wenger and Bonomo's is that it reflects powerful critiques of Marxian research by other Marxians, using as criteria more fully developed formulations of theory and concepts, and making it clear that ad hoc concepts, questionable scholarship, and political rhetoric are not acceptable elements of the Marxian paradigm.

Critics of Marxian deviancy research have tended to ridicule the paradigm for its simplistic arguments (e.g., capitalism causes deviance) and highly contentious discourse (e.g., "eliminate capitalism and we eliminate deviance," "bourgeois theorists are lackeys of the ruling class"). Critics also have opposed it as tautological in that everything tends to be explained in terms of capitalism. As a consequence, there occur spurious correlations between deviance (the dependent variable) and capitalism (the independent variable) because of a presumed, rather than demonstrated, empirical connection. But if the discussion above has been successful, it should be clear that the paradigm currently is just in its infancy, and that many of these criticisms are directed not so much at the Marxian paradigm as at radical perspectives that are quite inconsistent with Marxian research. In recent years, Marxians have recognized that it is no longer sufficient to simply demystify other theories of deviancy. It is necessary to assume responsibility for formulating propositions appropriate to the task of constructing a powerful direction for studying both society and deviance. It is also not sufficient to issue a politically impassioned cry from the heart against social injustice, or to simply blame injustice upon a particular economic or political system, and then assume that "because our cause is just, our thoughts are true."

What, then, does a Marxian paradigm offer us that other approaches do not? First, it offers an understanding of the basic social fabric from which both meanings and contents of problem populations are woven. It suggests, as did both functionalism and the Chicago school, that deviance may be a rational response to irrational situations. Unlike the Chicago school, however, it requires that we must examine the sources of the conflicts that generate both the definitions and the form and content of control responses of those holding the power to name the world and those attempting to live in that world as nonconformists. It requires, in short, an understanding of nothing less than how social arrangements are created and maintained. But unlike the symbolic interactionists who share this project, a Marxian approach goes further in arguing that social symbols and the rules by which they are manipulated to create social order do not come out of a vacuum, but are historically specific in that they are shaped by how persons are socially organized to reproduce themselves both materially and symbolically. This also separates the Marxian from the conflict approach. Conflict researchers do not focus so much on the fundamental roots of conflict, but rather on the acts of conflict themselves, regardless of the source. Second, current Marxian dialectical approaches recognize the role of the state in maintaining definitions of disapproved behaviors and especially in creating the machinery for suppressing such behaviors. For this reason, Marxian research has tended to focus on legal and policing systems, and this is one reason why so much Marxian deviancy research examines crime, delinquency, and official forms of social control. As Horowitz and Liebowitz (1968) have reminded us, the decision to treat disapproved behaviors as a social problem (or, conversely, not to treat them at all) is a political decision, which must also become part of the research problem. Third, the role of ideology as a means of generating throughout society a peaceful—rather than a coercive—means of sustaining values and beliefs that function to sustain preferred behaviors is a critically important topic for Marxian deviance research, especially as a means for examining the very premises of our own research approach. Ideology supports both the traditional research questions and methods, and, as a consequence, research may not only shape the values and norms by which we disapprove of some behaviors, but can also create a practical bond between research (e.g., which questions are or are not asked, and how we formulate our answers) and the society such research serves (e.g., Shaw, 1975; Thomas et al., 1980). Marxian inquiry thus becomes not only an analysis of disapproved behavior and problem populations but also a study of the sources and the contents of consciousness that support the definitions of such behavior as "disapproved."

Marxian deviancy research is, then, not primarily concerned with attitudes, values, or self-esteem as factors that produce deviance, although, certainly, such research need not be excluded from a dialectical paradigm. Nor is dialectical deviancy research primarily concerned with such concepts as "secondary deviance," or other interactionist conceptions. A dialectical approach is concerned with concepts that are perceived to transcend these former directions. A Marxian position offers conceptual tools that include the concepts of social practice, mode of production, the distinction between an "economic base" and a "superstructure" of appropriate social arrangements, social class, relations of production, social reproduction, the labor theory of value, class conflict, and ideological hegemony as elements of the basic conceptual framework from which deviancy research proceeds. This leads not only to the understanding of a specific disapproved act, but relates disapproved behaviors to the larger social and cultural context in which these behaviors occur.

Contrary to the assertions of many critics, Marxian theory is not an all-encompassing, definitive body of truth, and it cannot (nor do its adherents claim ability to) answer every question one might pose about deviance. The approach is not an idealistic attempt to establish a utopia in which disapproved behaviors will not exist. The Marxian approach may, however, offer a more comprehensive tool for examining the relationship between social structure and individual behavior by taking as its starting point the analysis of the production of the social order and social arrangements that provide the context for both behavior and for control. It allows understanding of specific disapproved behaviors that may occur within *specific social settings* at specific historical moments (whether such moments be those of a general epoch, such as nineteenth-century industrial society, or a shorter period, such as substance abuse in the 1970s).

In sum, it is crucial to remember, as C. Wright Mills (1971) reminded us nearly a quarter of a century ago, that there are three types of Marxians: the vulgar Marxists, typified by political and intellectual rigidity, who substitute narrow-minded and blind application of unproblematic rhetoric, slogans, and terminology for rigorous analysis; the sophisticated Marxists, who tend to see Marx's writings as a sacred text and argue *ex cathedra* over their true meaning and how these meanings should be translated into sensible statements given contemporary social changes; and the plain Marxists, who attempt to develop the methodological, conceptual, theoretical, and political value of a Marxian position. The plain Marxists attempt to recognize and resolve the conceptual and theoretical difficulties of a Marxian framework while developing it also as an empirical research tool. Ironically, contemporary directions in Marxian research are exciting for the same reason that they are open to criticism: They remain undeveloped, yet tantalizingly promising. We must remember Gouldner's (1971) observation that the socially concerned youths of the 1960s, who are the young professors of the 1980s, are still too young to have matured intellectually. A single decade is hardly sufficient to develop a complex theory or to have produced an unflawed theoretical or methodological research approach. Theory is not created overnight, but results from a process (or, in Marxian terms, a dialectic) of development. This process is formed by, and is the outcome of, social, intellectual, political, and ideological conflicts and confrontations, which in turn generate modification and refinement of premises and assumptions as well as of direction and outcome. The Marxian paradigm, in short, offers, more than any other single perspective, the directions and the destinations needed for both social and deviancy research in the coming years.

SUMMARY

There is more at stake in selection of a research paradigm or perspective than simply topics or epistemological issues. Each of the three paradigms we have identified correspond to what have been termed *cognitive interests* (Habermas, 1972). Cognition refers to the processes by which we appropriate the symbolic and material world through our social activity and through our consciousness. Interests are those practical purposes or intentions that we wish to fulfill through our activity. Knowledge provides a cognitive map that guides our interpretation and practical activity (Childe, 1956; Manning, 1972). Cognitive maps provide a perspective, a way of viewing, and thereby suggest ways of acting. Such maps reflect the location and perspective of the observer (Manning, 1972). Cognitive interests, therefore, are the particular orientations that shape how we perceive an object, shape how an object is construed in our thinking, and, above all, shape the intents and purposes we project for an object. Social factist paradigms are guided by technical (or instrumental) interests, social constructionist paradigms by hermeneutical interests, and a Marxian paradigm by emancipatory interests.

Technical interests are the orientation toward technical rules in which empirical knowledge becomes an instrument for guiding policy and decision-making. This orientation has for its program the extension of technical power and mastery and control over the natural and social world, and the method for this program is seen as the extension of empirical limits and examination of how the objective world acts upon persons inhabiting it. From this orientation, deviance research usually (but not always, as conflict theory shows) tends to acquire knowledge that can be used to control delinquency. Even conflict theory, which does not take a control perspective, nonetheless approaches its topic from this same technical (although not political) basis at the fundamental epistemological level.

Hermeneutic interests are grounded in historical and descriptive sciences, and are represented, for example, by symbolic interactionism and Weber's *Verstehen* sociology. The practical interest here is one of imputing meaning to objects or social phenomena, and has for its program the task of eliminating misunderstanding of meanings. This is done by focusing on the processes and techniques by which people acquire and exchange meaning through the use of social symbols. The empirical-analytic sciences of the social facts paradigm, because of their narrow orientation and limited research program, tend to distort scientific communication in that they exclude from examination the meanings and assumptions of their own concept and theories, assuming that empirical variables derived from specific theories correspond with self-existent "things" (e.g., Habermas, 1972: 307). The social constructionist paradigm instead attempts to examine the normative systems in order to understand meanings rather than to "read off" observations from the observed phenomena.

The third cognitive orientation is that of emancipation and corresponds to the program of Marxian, especially Critical, theories. The task for this orientation is to identify features of social existence that produce unnecessary social constraints, and to describe how human freedom is constricted, thus indicating directions for social change. Adherents to this orientation would not exclude such narrower programs as causal analysis, for example, but would insist that such a program is but one of a series of tasks in a larger program of emancipatory theoretical and practical social activity. Nor would this orientation exclude hermeneutic programmatic goals, but would simply add that they do not go far enough. For Marxian and Critical theorists, conventional theories of deviancy, such as those we have described above, are derived from the categories of labor, language, and power, and therefore reflect more or less exactly the existing social order. In this view, our theories themselves may tell us as much about the social world as any given sociology topic. The Marxian project of emancipation, as Horkheimer (1972: 210) has suggested, ". . . is motivated today by the effort really to transcend the tension and to abolish the opposition between the individual's purposefulness, spontaneity, and rationality, and those work-process relationships on which society is built. Critical thought has a concept of man as in conflict with himself until this opposition is removed."

The opposition Horkheimer describes is one between social system and forms of production and interaction versus the needs of persons to develop their full human potential. The removal of this opposition will contribute to the emancipation of persons by allowing them to realize their potential as human beings, or at least by allowing them to *attempt* to realize this potential.

This is especially critical for deviancy research. The social factist positions, limited as they are by the questions they pose (and by those questions that remain unasked), by their unproblematic view of control, by the assumption that commonsensical or officially defined conceptions of disapproved behavior are legitimate categories of deviance, and limited especially by the insistence upon the severance of subject from object and facts from values, promote a view of behavior and control that links control to research—either directly, as in many federally funded research projects, or indirectly, as in ideologically bound perspectives (e.g., Thomas, 1980). Social constructionists, taking intersubjective understanding as their project, also retain the fact-value and subject-object distinction, and likewise cannot generate any action-guiding "ought" statements or scientifically based norms for guiding social activity. By perpetuating the pejorative connotations of disapproved behavior, deviancy research becomes a subtle, yet powerful, apology for the existing social order by remaining within an ideologically bound research framework, and by employing the appropriate conceptual and theoretical apparatus for that framework that directly links social science research with mechanisms that maintain the status quo. Used in this sense, ideologies become world views, and as M. Shaw (1972) reminds us, despite their partial and possibly critical insights, these views may prevent us from understanding the social relations we are examining because these world views may be conceptually and theoretically limited to conventional definitions and assumptions. As a consequence, conceptions of deviance and the appropriate research methods for studying disapproved behavior may become socially patterned and methodologically constrained. It is precisely because of this inability of most deviancy research to acknowledge and examine such patternings and constraints that new directions and destinations are needed. By examining existing perspectives and suggesting how these are inadequate, it has been possible to compare current directions in deviancy research with Marxian directions that promise a new path and new cognitive maps for the future. For at stake in our discussion of new directions has not simply been the issue of new topics, new methods, or even novel concepts for research. There is at stake nothing less than social control, political power, and a more humane social world. Conventional perspectives and paradigms maintain existing social arrangements by *what they do not do*, and for this reason we have judged them inadequate. To continue the original metaphor, they remain dead-end avenues to undesirable destinations. If this chapter has been successful, then there should be little doubt that although other paradigms indeed have valuable uses, whatever our personal politics, the dialectical paradigm, with its emancipatory orientation, offers the most exciting new direction for the future.

NOTES

[1]The *fact-value problem* is based on the difficulty of deriving statements of value from statements of fact. For example, we can agree that some roses are red, and we can identify without too much disagreement other features of roses (they have petals and thorns, and they grow on vines). These are "facts." There is, however, nothing in these facts that allows us to say that roses are beautiful. That is, we cannot generate values (e.g., beauty, freedom) from the objective data of our theories. The *subject-object problem* involves the question of how a thinking subject can know objects in the world. For some thinkers, objects have invariant properties, and the task of knowledge production is to identify, classify, and correlate these properties. Other thinkers argue that the mind itself is most important because it perceives and interprets these properties (i.e., we bring to external objects in the world our own mental apparatus, which generates concepts that may or may not correspond to the

real properties of the object). The former position typifies social factists; the latter, social constructionists. The *theory-practice problem* refers to cognitive interests, which guide particular ways of looking at the world. The problem of most theories is that they ignore the practical or applied uses for which theories and knowledge are developed, and are often, for this reason, seen as "neutral."

Marxian theories attempt to overcome these problems in several ways. The subject-object problem is addressed by displaying how the social world is constructed through a dialectical process of activity between both the thinking subject and the objects in the world as a historical outcome of transformations of language, social structure, culture, and production. The fact-value problem is addressed by recognizing that values themselves are social constructs, and thus can be examined scientifically. Further, some values (e.g., freedom) derive from an implicit view of human nature in which the existence of factors that suppress the development of human potential are viewed as unnatural, so to speak. From a "scientific" examination of the nature of human social activity, we can put forth such "ought" statements as "racism and sexism are wrong" as scientific statements rather than simply as value judgments or opinions. Such value statements are considered scientific because they refer to explicit objects that can be analyzed through research (e.g., social control, repression). Finally, the theory-practice task for Marxians is one of integrating social knowledge within a political program or set of action statements that will allow knowledge to be used for socially emancipatory activity.

[2]There is considerable debate among Marxians whether in fact there can even be a special "Marxian theory" of deviance. Because Marxian theory is a general theory of society (although by no means, as some critics suggest, an all-encompassing one), it is possible to examine deviance from a Marxian perspective, and that is the position taken in this chapter. There is no attempt to identify or describe the features of such a position, which is attempted elsewhere (Thomas, forthcoming). Because of the variants among writers influenced by Marx's writings, the term *Marxian* is preferred to *Marxist*, since the former connotes an affinity toward the paradigm rather than adherence to specific political or ideological beliefs, dogma, premises, and theories.

[3]These perspectives are often called conflict theory, but the term *theory* is used too loosely to be meaningful. Although a specific researcher may claim to provide a theory of society or of deviancy, there is in fact no set of interconnected postulates of a law-like nature containing deductively derived hypotheses that are empirically falsifiable. Further, the perspective is too diverse and internally inconsistent to warrant such a label, although some recent research of the criminal justice process (e.g., Lizotte, 1978; Jacobs and Britt, 1979) has suggested useful directions for theory-building.

[4]Although conflict theory was developed prior to the 1960s, particularly by the social theorist Ralf Dahrendorf (1958a, 1958b, 1963) and the criminologist George Vold (1958), it has also been associated with the Chicago school (usually called "culture conflict" theory) and E. H. Sutherland (1939). The roots of conflict theory, however, are radically different from those of the Chicago school's "web of life" metaphors and biotic models of society. Derived particularly from the early works of Simmel, who saw conflict as a means of resolving social dualisms and attaining unity "even if it be through the annihilation of one of the conflicting parties" (1955: 13), and Lewis Coser (1958), who attempted to integrate functional (or consensus) theory with conflict premises, the conflict theorists share, at root, little with the cultural conflict perspective. For one concise summary of these and other features of a conflict perspective, see Rex (1973).

⁵This position is also referred to as critical criminology. Critical criminology refers to the critique of social factors underlying deviant behavior, and especially to critiques of theories of deviance. It does not, as is often erroneously assumed, refer to critical theory. Critical theory is a philosophical position that derives from Georg Lukács and the Frankfurt school of the 1930s and 1940s, and was influenced more recently by the works of Jürgen Habermas and Albrecht Wellmer; it is reflected in journals such as *Telos*.

BIBLIOGRAPHY

ALFORD, R. R.
  1975   "Paradigms of Relations between State and Society." In L. N. Lindberg, R. Alford, C. Crouch, and C. Offe (Eds.), *Stress and Contradiction in Modern Capitalism.* Lexington, Mass.: Lexington Books, pp. 145–159.
ALLEN, M.
  1976   "Twin Studies of Affective Illness." *Archives of General Psychiatry 33: 1476–1489.*
ALLSOP, K.
  1961   *The Bootleggers.* London: Hutchinson.
ALVAREZ, R.
  1968   "Informal Reactions to Deviance in Simulated Work Organizations: A Laboratory Experiment." *American Sociological Review* 33 (December): 895–912.
AMERICAN JUSTICE INSTITUTE
  1974   *After Care Evaluation Report for Santa Clara County: First Year Report.* Sacramento.
AMNESTY INTERNATIONAL
  1978–81   *Amnesty Action.* New York: Amnesty International, U.S.A.
ANDERSON, L. S., T. G. CHIRICOS, and G. P. WALDO
  1977   "Formal and Informal Sanctions: A Comparison of Deterrent Effects." *Social Problems* 25 (October): 103–114.
ANDERSON, N.
  1923   *The Hobo.* Chicago: University of Chicago Press.
ARNOLD, D. O.
  1970   *The Sociology of Subcultures.* Berkeley: Glendessary Press.

ARTHUR MURRAY DANCE STUDIOS v OHIO 105 NE 2d. 685 Ohio.

ASHFORD, N. A.
1976, 1977   Crisis in the Workplace: Occupational Disease and Injury.
Cambridge, Mass.: M.I.T. Press.

ASKANASY, A.
1974   Attitudes Toward Mental Patients: A Study Across Cultures. The
Hague, Holland: Mouton.

BAIN, R.
1933   The Concept of Social Process, Twenty Sixth Annual Meetings of
the American Sociological Society. Washington, D.C., pp. 10–18.

BALBUS, I. D.
1971   "The Concept of Interest in Pluralist and Marxian Analysis."
Politics and Society 1 (February).
1977   The Dialectics of Legal Repression: Black Rebels before the
American Criminal Courts. New Brunswick, N.J.: Transaction
Books.

BARDACH, E.
1972   The Skill Factor in Politics: Repealing the Mental Commitment
Laws in California. Berkeley: University of California Press.

BECKER, H.
1963   Outsiders: Studies in the Sociology of Deviance. New York: Free
Press.
1964   "Introduction." The Other Side Perspectives on Deviance. New
York: Free Press, pp. 1–6.
1967   "Whose Side Are We On?" Social Problems 14 (Winter): 239–
247.
1974   "Labelling Theory Reconsidered." In P. Rock and M. McIntosh
(Eds.), Deviance and Social Control. London: Tavistock, pp. 41–
66.
1981   Review of The Labelling of Deviance by W. Gove. Society, forthcoming.

BECKER, H. S., and I. L. HOROWITZ
1971   "The Culture of Civility." In H. S. Becker (Ed.), Culture and
Civility in San Francisco. Chicago: Aldine.

BECKER, T. L., and V. C. MURRAY
1971   Government Lawlessness in America. New York: Oxford University Press.

BENEDICT, M.
1979   "Past Imperfect, Future Tense." The Canadian (February 3): 4–6.

BENSON, P.
1979   "Labeling Theory and Community Care of the Mentally Ill in
California: The Relationship of Social Theory and Ideology to
Public Policy." Presented at the annual meeting of the Southern
Sociological Society. Atlanta (April).

BERGER, P.
1978   "Medical Treatment of Mental Illness: Psychopharmacological

Therapeutics Revolutionize Psychiatric Care and Present Scientific and Ethical Challenges to Society." *Science* 200: 974–981.

BERGER, P., and S. PULLBERG
  1964   "Reification and the Sociological Critique of Consciousness." *History and Theory* IV(1): 194–211.

BERGESEN, A. J.
  1977   "Political Witch Hunts: The Sacred and Subversive in Cross-national Perspective." *American Sociological Review* 42 (April): 220–232.

BERK, B.
  1966   "Organizational Goals and Inmate Organization." *American Journal of Sociology* LXXI: 522–534.

BIRENBAUM, A.
  1971   "The Recognition and Acceptance of Stigma." *Sociological Symposium* 7 (Fall): 15–22.

BIRENBAUM, A., and SAGARIN, E.
  1976   *Norms and Human Behavior.* New York: Praeger.

BITTNER, E.
  1965   "The Concept of Organization." *Social Research* 32: 239–258.
  1967   "The Police on Skid Row." *American Sociological Review* 32: 699–715.

BLACKSTOCK, N.
  1975   *Cointelpro: The FBI's Secret War on Political Freedom.* New York: Vintage.

BLAUNER, R.
  1972   *Racial Oppression in America.* New York: Harper & Row.

BLOCK, M. K., F. C. NOLD, and J. G. SIDAK
  1978   *The Deterrent Effect of Antitrust Enforcement: A Theoretical and Empirical Analysis.* Stanford University, Palo Alto, Calif.: Hoover Institution.

BLOOM, D. M., and C. E. REASONS
  1978   "Ideology and Crime: A Study in the Sociology of Knowledge." *International Journal of Criminology and Penology* 6(July): 19–30.

BLUMER, H.
  1954   "What Is Wrong with Social Theory." *American Sociological Review* 19: 3–10.
  1969   *Symbolic Interactionism: Perspective and Method.* Englewood Cliffs, N.J.: Prentice-Hall.

BOCKOVEN, J. S.
  1972   *Moral Treatment in American Society* (2nd Edition). New York: Springer-Verlag.

BOYDELL, C. L., and C. GRINDSTAFF
  1972   "Public Opinion and the Criminal Law: An Empirical Test of Public Attitudes Toward Legal Sanctions." In C. L. Boydell, C. F. Grindstaff, and P. C. Whitehead (Eds.), *Deviant Behavior and*

Societal Reaction. Toronto: Holt, Rinehart and Winston, pp. 165–180.

BRANAN, K.
1980   "Killer Reverse Roams Highways, Victim Warns." The Calgary Herald (August 7): E1.

BRECHER, E. M., and THE EDITORS OF CONSUMER REPORTS
1972   Licit and Illicit Drugs. Boston: Little, Brown and Co.

BRENNER, M. H.
1977   "Personal Stability and Economic Insecurity." Social Policy 8: 2–4.

BROWN, L., and C. BROWN
1973   An Unauthorized History of the R.C.M.P. Toronto: James Lorrimer.

BRYAN, J. H.
1965   "Apprenticeships in Prostitution." Social Problems 12: 287–297.
1966   "Occupational Ideologies and Individual Attitudes of Call Girls." Social Problems 13 (Spring): 441–450.

BRYANT, C. G. A.
1975   "Kuhn, Paradigms and Sociology." British Journal of Sociology 3 (September): 354–359.

BURNS, P.
1975–76   "Electronic Eavesdropping and the Federal Response: Cloning a Hybrid." University of British Columbia Law Review 10: 36–63.

BURTON, F., and P. CARLEN
1979   Official Discourse: On Discourse Analysis, Government Publications, Ideology and the State. Boston: Routledge and Kegan Paul.

CALDWELL, M. G.
1956   "Group Dynamics in the Prison Community." Journal of Criminal Law, Criminology and Police Science 46: 648–657.

CAMERON, M.
1964   The Booster and the Snitch. New York: Free Press.

CARLIN, J.
1966   Lawyer's Ethics: A Survey of the New York City Bar. New York: Russell Sage Foundation.

CARSON, W. G.
1974   "Symbolic and Instrumental Dimensions of Early Factory Legislation: A Case Study in the Social Origins of Criminal Law." In R. Hood (Ed.), Crime, Criminology and Public Policy. London: Heinemann.

CAUTE, D.
1978   The Great Fear: The Anti-Communist Purge under Truman and Eisenhower. New York: Simon and Schuster.

CAVAN, S.
1966   Liquor License: A Ethnography of Bar Behavior. Chicago: Aldine.

CHAGNON, N.
1978   *Yanomamo: The Fierce People.* New York: Holt, Rinehart and Winston.

CHAMBLISS, W. J.
1966   "The Deterrent Influence of Punishment." *Crime and Delinquency* (January): 70–75.
1971   "Vice, Corruption, Bureaucracy and Power." *Wisconsin Law Review* (4): 1150–1173.
1975   "The Political Economy of Crime: A Comparative Study of Nigeria and the U.S.A." In I. Taylor, P. Walton, and J. Young (Eds.), *The New Criminology: For a Social Theory of Deviance.* Boston: Routledge and Kegan Paul, pp. 167–179.

CHAMBLISS, W. J., and R. J. SEIDMAN
1971   *Law, Order and Power.* Reading, Mass.: Addison-Wesley.

CHILDE, V. G.
1956   *Society and Knowledge.* New York: Harper and Bros.

CHIN-SHONG, E.
1969   "Rejection of the Mentally Ill: The Effects of Personal Ties versus Perception of Danger." Presented at the annual meeting of the American Sociological Association. San Francisco (September).

CHIRICOS, T., and W. GORDON
1970   "Punishment and Crime: An Examination of Some Empirical Evidence." *Social Problems* 18 (Fall): 200–219.

CICOUREL, A. V.
1968   *The Social Organization of Juvenile Justice.* New York: Wiley.
1973   *Cognitive Sociology.* London: Penguin.
1974   *Theory and Method in a Study of Argentine Fertility.* New York: Wiley.

CLAIRMONT, D.
1974   "The Development of a Deviance Service Center." In J. Haas and B. Shaffir (Eds.), *Decency and Deviance.* Toronto: McClelland and Stewart, pp. 30–42.

CLEMMER, D.
1940   *The Prison Community.* Boston: Christopher Publishing House.

CLINARD, M. B.
1979   *Illegal Corporate Behavior.* Washington, D.C.: U.S. Government Printing Office.

CLOWARD, R. A.
1960   "Social Control in the Prison." In R. Cloward et al., *Theoretical Studies in Social Organization of the Prison.* New York: Social Science Research Council, pp. 20–48.

CLOWARD, R. A., and L. E. OHLIN
1961   *Delinquency and Opportunity: A Theory of Delinquent Gangs.* New York: Free Press.

COHEN, A.
1955   *Delinquent Boys: The Culture of the Gang.* New York: Free Press.
1965   "The Sociology of the Deviant Act: Anomie Theory and Beyond." *American Sociological Review* 30: 5–15.
1966   *Deviance and Social Control.* Englewood Cliffs, N.J.: Prentice-Hall.
COHEN, S. (Ed.)
1971   *Images of Deviance.* London: Penguin.
COHEN, S.
1972   *Folk Devils and Moral Panics.* London: MacGibbon and Kee.
1979   "Guilt, Justice and Tolerance: Some Old Concepts for a New Criminology." In D. Downes and P. Rock (Eds.), *Deviant Interpretations.* New York: Barnes and Noble, pp. 17–51.
COHEN, S., and L. TAYLOR
1972   *Psychological Survival: The Experience of Long-Term Imprisonment.* New York: Pantheon.
COMMISSION ON CIA ACTIVITIES WITHIN THE UNITED STATES
1978   "The CIA's Mail Intercepts." In M. D. Ermann and R. J. Lundman (Eds.), *Corporate and Governmental Deviance: Problems of Organizational Behavior in Contemporary Society.* New York: Oxford University Press, pp. 174–185.
CONKLIN, J. E.
1977   *Illegal But Not Criminal: Business in America.* Englewood Cliffs, N.J.: Prentice-Hall.
CONNOR, W. D.
1972   "The Manufacture of Deviance: The Case of the Soviet Purge, 1936–1938." *American Sociological Review* 37 (August): 403–413.
CONRAD, P., and J. SCHNEIDER
1980   *Deviance and Medicalization.* St. Louis: Mosby.
COOK, S. J.
1969   "Canadian Narcotics Legislation, 1908–1923; A Conflict Model Interpretation." *Canadian Review of Sociology and Anthropology* 6(1) (February): 36–46.
COOLEY, C. H.
1902   *Human Nature and the Social Order.* New York: Scribner's.
COSER, L. A.
1956   *The Functions of Social Conflict.* New York: Free Press.
COTTRELL, W. F.
1972   *Technology, Man and Progress.* Columbus: Charles E. Merrill, Chapter I.
COULTER, J.
1973   *Approaches to Insanity.* London: Martin Robertson and Co.
COYE, J., and D. CLIFFORD
1978   "A One-year Report on Rights Violations under Michigan's New

Protection System." *Hospital and Community Psychiatry* 22: 528–533.

CRANE, L., H. ZONANA, and S. WISER
1977   "Implications of the Donaldson Decision: A Model for Periodic Review of Committed Patients." *Hospital and Community Psychiatry* 28: 827–833.

CRESPO, M.
1973   *Becoming Deviant: The Career of the School Skipper*. Master's thesis, McGill University.

1974   "The Career of the School Skipper." In J. Haas and B. Shaffir (Eds.), *Decency and Deviance*. Toronto: McClelland and Stewart, pp. 129–145.

CRESSEY, D. R., and W. KRASOWSKI
1959   "Inmate Organization and Anomie in American Prisons and Soviet Labor Camps." *American Journal of Sociology* 65: 59–67.

CRESSEY, P. G.
1969   *The Taxi-Dance Hall*. Montclair, N.J.: Paterson-Smith. Reprint of 1932 edition originally published by the University of Chicago.

CURRIE, E. P.
1968   "Crimes Without Criminals: Witchcraft and its Control in Renaissance Europe." *Law and Society Review* 3 (August): 7–32. Reprinted in F. J. Davis and R. Stivers (Eds.), *The Collective Definition of Deviance*. New York: Free Press, 1975, pp. 296–316.

CURRY, E.
1974   "Review: The New Criminology." *Issues in Criminology* 9 (Spring): 133–142.

CURTIS, R., and L. ZURCHER
1971   "Voluntary Associations and the Social Integration of the Poor." *Social Problems* 18 (Winter): 339–537.

DAHRENDORF, R.
1958a   "Toward a Theory of Social Conflict." *Journal of Conflict Resolution* II: 170–183.

1958b   "Out of Utopia: Toward a Re-orientation of Sociological Analysis." *American Journal of Sociology* 64 (September): 115–127.

1963   *Class and Class Conflict in Industrial Society*. Palo Alto, Calif.: Stanford University Press.

DALTON, M.
1959   *Men Who Manage*. New York: Wiley.

DAMER, S.
1974   "Wine Alley: The Sociology of a Dreadful Enclosure." *Sociological Review* 22 (May): 221–248.

DANIELS, A. K.
1970   "Development of the Scapegoat in Sensitivity Training Sessions." In T. Shibutani (Ed.), *Human Nature and Collective Behavior*. Englewood Cliffs, N.J.: Prentice-Hall.

<header>326   BIBLIOGRAPHY</header>

DANK, B. M.
1971   "Coming Out in the Gay World." *Psychiatry* 34: 180–197.
DAVIES, J.
1962   "Toward a Theory of Revolution." *American Sociological Review* 27 (February): 5–19.
DAVIS, F.
1967   "Why All of Us May Be Hippies Someday." *Trans-action* 5 (December): 10–18.
DAVIS, F. J.
1975   "Beliefs, Values, Power, and Public Definitions of Deviance." In F. J. Davis and R. Stivers (Eds.), *The Collective Definition of Deviance.* New York: Free Press, pp. 50–59.
DAVIS, G.
1978a   "Ripping Off The Company." *Financial Times of Canada* (July 17): 2–3.
1978b   "Corporate Theft." *Financial Times of Canada* (July 17): 2–3.
DAVIS, J.
1975   "Overview: Maintenance Therapy in Psychiatry: I. Schizophrenia." *American Journal of Psychiatry* 132: 1237–1245.
1976   "Overview: Maintenance Therapy in Psychiatry: II. Affective Disorders." *American Journal of Psychiatry* 133 (January): 1–13.
DAVIS, K.
1937   "The Sociology of Prostitution." *American Sociological Review* 2 (October): 744–755.
1971   "Prostitution." In R. K. Merton and R. Nisbet (Eds.), *Contemporary Social Problems*, 3rd Ed. New York: Harcourt Brace Jovanovich, pp. 341–351.
DAVIS, N. J.
1972   "Labeling Theory in Deviance Research: A Critique and Reconsideration." *The Sociological Quarterly* 13: 447–474.
1975   *Sociological Constructions of Deviance.* Dubuque: William C. Brown.
DAWE, A.
1970   "The Two Sociologies." *British Journal of Sociology* 21 (June): 207–218.
1971   "Review: A Sociology of Sociology." *Sociological Review* 19 (February): 140–147.
DENZIN, N. K.
1970   "Rules of Conduct and the Study of Deviant Behavior: Some Notes on the Social Relationship." In G. J. McCall et al. (Eds.), *Social Relationships.* Chicago: Aldine, pp. 62–94.
DICKSON, D. T.
1968   Bureaucracy and Morality: An Organizational Perspective on a Moral Crusade." *Social Problems* 16: 143–156.
DILLON, M., and D. LAHANE
1973   *Political Murder in North Ireland.* Middlesex: Penguin, p. 113.

DITTON, J.
1979   *Controlology: Beyond the New Criminology*. MacMillan: London.
DOUGLAS, J.
1967   *The Social Meaning of Suicide*. Princeton, N.J.: Princeton University Press.
1972   *Understanding Everyday Life*. Chicago: Aldine.
1977   "Watergate: Harbinger of the American Prince." In *Official Deviance: Readings in Malfeasance, Misfeasance, and Other Forms of Corruption*. Philadelphia: Lippincott, pp. 112–120.
DOWNES, D.
1979   "Praxis Makes Perfect: A Critique of Critical Criminology." In Downes and Rock (Eds.), *Deviant Interpretations*. Oxford: Martin Robertson.
DROPKIN, D., and S. BLUME
n.d.   "The Jewish Alcoholic: An Under-recognized Minority?" Duplicated paper.
DURKHEIM, E.
1951   *Suicide*. New York: Free Press.
1964a   *The Division of Labor in Society*. New York: Free Press. Originally published 1893.
1964b   *The Rules of Sociological Method*. New York: Free Press. Originally published 1895.
DUSTER, T.
1970   *The Legislation of Morality*. New York: Free Press.
ECKBERG, D. L., and L. HILL, JR.
1979   "The Paradigm Concept and Sociology: A Critical Review." *American Sociological Review* 44 (December): 925–937.
EDELHERTZ, H.
1970   *The Nature, Impact and Prosecution of White Collar Crime*. Washington, D.C.: U.S. Government Printing Office.
EDGERTON, R. B.
1973   "Deviant Behavior and Cultural Theory." Reading, Mass.: Addison-Wesley, Module in Anthropology, No. 37.
EGLIN, P.
1974   "Leaving out the interpreter's work: A methodological critique of ethnosemantics based on ethnomethodology." *Semiotica* 6: 23–33.
EITZEN, D. S.
1980   *Social Problems*. Boston: Allyn and Bacon.
EMERSON, J.
1970   "Nothing Unusual Is Happening." In T. Shibutani (Ed.), *Human Nature and Collective Behavior*. Englewood Cliffs, N.J.: Prentice-Hall.
EMPEY, L.
1978   *American Delinquency: Its Meaning and Construction*. Homewood, Ill.: Dorsey.

ENNIS, P. H.
 1967   "Criminal Victimization in the United States." Washington, D.C.:
        U.S. Government Printing Office.
ENVIRONMENTAL DEFENSE FUND, and R. H. BOYLE
 1980   *Malignant Neglect*. New York: Vintage.
ERICKSON, E.
 1950   *Childhood and Society*. New York: Norton.
ERICKSON, M. L., J. P. GIBBS, and G. F. JENSEN
 1977   "The Deterrence Doctrine and the Perceived Certainty of Legal Pun-
        ishments." *American Sociological Review* 42 (April): 305–317.
ERIKSON, K.
 1964   "Notes on the Sociology of Deviance." In H. S. Becker (Ed.), *The
        Other Side*. New York: Free Press, pp. 9–22.
 1966   *Wayward Puritans: A Study in the Sociology of Deviance*. New
        York: Wiley.
ERMANN, M. D., and R. J. LUNDMAN
 1978   *Corporate and Governmental Deviance: Problems of Organiza-
        tional Behavior in Contemporary Society*. New York: Oxford
        University Press.
ETZIONI, A.
 1968   "Shortcuts to Social Change." *The Public Interest* 12 (Summer):
        40–51.
FAGAN, R. W., JR., and A. L. MAUSS
 1978   "Padding the Revolving Door: An Initial Assessment of the Uni-
        form Alcoholism and Intoxication Treatment Act in Practice."
        Social Problems 26(2) (December): pp. 232–247.
FALLDING, H.
 1972   "Only One Sociology." *British Journal of Sociology* 23 (March):
        93–101.
FARIS, R. E. L., and H. W. DUNHAM
 1938   *Mental Disorders in Urban Areas: An Ecological Study of Schizo-
        phrenia and Other Disorders*. Chicago: University of Chicago Press.
FELLMETH, R. C.
 1973   "The Regulatory-Industrial Complex." In R. Nader (Ed.), *The
        Consumer and Corporate Accountability*. New York: Harcourt
        Brace Jovanovich, pp. 218–233.
FILIATREAU, J.
 1977   "The Louisville Mystery: Deadly Chemicals Clog a City's
        Sewers." *Washington Press* (April 25): A1, 6.
FISHMAN, M.
 1978   "Crime Waves as Ideology." *Social Problems* 25: 531–543.
FOSTER, J., S. DINITZ, and W. C. RECKLESS.
 1972   "Perceptions of Stigma Following Public Intervention for Delin-
        quent Behavior." *Social Problems* 20 (Fall): 202–209.
FOUCAULT, M.
 1973   *Madness and Civilization*. New York: Vintage.

1975   *The Birth of the Clinic.* New York: Vintage.

FOX, R. G.
1971   "The XYY Offender: A Modern Myth." *Journal of Criminal Law, Criminology and Police Science* 62: 59–73.

FREIDSON, E.
1966   "Disability as Social Deviance." In M. B. Sussman (Ed.), *Sociology and Rehabilitation.* Washington, D.C.: American Sociological Association.

1970   *The Profession of Medicine: A Study of the Sociology of Applied Knowledge.* New York: Dodd, Mead.

FULLER, L.
1968   *Anatomy of Law.* New York: New American Library, p. 17.

GALBRAITH, J. K., and N. SALINGER
1978   *Almost Everyone's Guide to Economics.* New York: Consumers Union.

GALLUP, G.
1975   *The Gallup Opinion Index.* Princeton, N.J.: The American Institute of Public Opinion.

GALTUNG, J.
1958   "The Social Functions of a Prison." *Social Problems* 6: 128–140.

GARBEDIAN, P.
1963   "Social Roles and Processes of Socialization in the Prison Community." *Social Problems* 11: 139–152.

1964   "Social Roles in a Correctional Community." *Journal of Criminal Law, Criminology and Police Science* 55: 338–347.

GARDINER, J.
1969   *Traffic and the Police: Variations in Law Enforcement Policy.* Cambridge, Mass.: Harvard University Press, pp. 118–123.

1970   *The Politics of Corruption.* New York: Russell Sage.

GARDNER, E.
1970   "Serving an Urban Ghetto through a Community Mental Health Center." In *Mental Health Program Reports No. 4.* Washington, D.C.: National Institute of Mental Health, pp. 69–106.

GARFINKEL, H.
1956   "Conditions of Successful Degradation Ceremonies." *American Journal of Sociology* 61: 420–424.

1963   "A Conception of and Experiments with 'Trust' as a Condition of Stable Concerted Actions." In O. J. Harvey (Ed.), *Motivation and Social Interaction.* New York: The Ronald Press, pp. 187–238.

1967   *Studies in Ethnomethodology.* Englewood Cliffs, N.J.: Prentice-Hall.

1974   "The Origins of the Term 'Ethnomethodology.' " In R. Turner (Ed.), *Ethnomethodology.* Middlesex, England: Penguin Education, pp. 15–18.

GARFINKEL, H. and H. SACKS
1970   "The Formal Properties of Practical Actions." In J. C. McKinney

and E. A. Tiryakian (Eds.), *Theoretical Sociology*. New York: Appleton-Century-Crofts.

GEERKEN, M., and W. GOVE
  1975   "Deterrence: Some Theoretical Considerations." *Law and Society Review* 9 (Spring): 497–513.
  1977   "Deterrence, Overload and Incapacitation: An Empirical Evaluation." *Social Forces* 56 (December): 424–447.

GEIS, G. (Ed.)
  1968   *White Collar Criminal: The Offender in Business and the Professions*. New York: Atherton.

GEIS, G.
  1974   "Deterring Corporate Crime." In C. E. Reasons (Ed.), *The Criminologist: Crime and the Criminal*. Pacific Palisades: Goodyear.
  1975   "Victimization Patterns in White Collar Crime." In I. Drapkin and E. Viana (Eds.), *Victimology: A New Focus, Volume V: Exploiters and Exploited: The Dynamics of Victimization*. Lexington, Mass.: Lexington Books.

GEIS, G., and R. F. MEIER
  1977   *White Collar Crime: Offenses in Business, Politics, and the Professions*. New York: Free Press.

GEIS, G., and E. STOTLAND
  1980   *White Collar Crime: Theory and Research*. Beverly Hills: Sage Publications.

GERSHON, E., W. BUNNEY, and J. LECKMAN
  1976   "The Inheritance of Affective Disorders: A Review of the Data and Hypotheses." *Behavioral Genetics* 6: 227–261.

GIBBS, J. P.
  1966   "Conceptions of Deviant Behavior: The Old and the New." *Pacific Sociological Review* 9: 9–14.
  1968   "Crime, Punishment, and Deterrence." *Southwestern Social Science Quarterly* 48 (March): 515–530.
  1972   "Issues in Defining Deviant Behavior." In R. A. Scott and J. D. Douglas (Eds.), *Theoretical Perspectives on Deviance*. New York: Basic Books, pp. 39–68.
  1975   *Crime, Punishment and Deterrence*. New York: Elsevier.

GIBSON, T.
  1970   "Towards a Libertarian Criminology." *Catalyst* 5 (Summer): 55–58.

GILKSMAN, J.
  1954   "Social Prophylaxis as a Form of Soviet Terror." In C. Friedrich (Ed.), *Totalitarianism*. Cambridge, Mass.: Harvard University Press, pp. 60–84.

GILLIS, H.
  1974   *Youth and History*. New York: Academic Press.

GLASBEEK, H. J., and S. ROWLAND
1979   "Are Injuring and Killing At Work Crimes?" *Osgoode Hall Law Journal* 17 (December): 507–594.

GLASER, D.
1974   "The Classification of Offenses and Offenders." In D. Glaser (Ed.), *Handbook of Criminology.* Chicago: Rand McNally, pp. 45–84.

GLASSNER, B.
1980a   *Essential Interactionism.* London: Routledge and Kegan Paul.
1980b   "Role Loss and Manic Depression." In H. Lopata (Ed.), *Research in the Interweave of Social Roles, Vol. 1.* Greenwich, Conn.: JAI Press, pp. 265–282.

GLASSNER, B., and B. BERG
1980   "How Jews Avoid Alcohol Problems." *American Sociological Review* 45: 647–664.

GLASSNER, B., and J. CORZINE
1978   "Can Labeling Theory Be Saved." *Symbolic Interaction* 1: 74–89.

GLASSNER, B., C. HALDIPUR, and J. DESSAUERSMITH
1979   "Role Loss and Working-Class Manic Depression." *Journal of Nervous and Mental Disease* 167: 530–541.

GLUCKMAN, M.
1965a   *The Ideas of Barotse Jurisprudence.* New Haven: Yale University Press, p. 175.
1965b   *Politics, Law and Ritual in Tribal Society.* New York: New American Library, p. 252.

GLUECK, S., and E. GLUECK
1937   *Later Criminal Careers.* New York: The Commonwealth Fund.
1956   *Physique and Delinquency.* New York: Harper & Row.

GOFF, C. H., and C. E. REASONS
1976   "Corporations in Canada: A Study of Crime and Punishment." *Criminal Law Quarterly* 18 (August): 468–498.
1978   *Corporate Crime In Canada: A Critical Analysis of Anti-Combines Legislations.* Scarborough: Prentice-Hall of Canada.

GOFFMAN, E.
1959a   *The Presentation of Self in Everyday Life.* Garden City, N.Y.: Doubleday/Anchor.
1959b   "The Moral Career of the Mental Patient." *Psychiatry* 22: 123–142.
1961   *Asylums.* Garden City, N.Y.: Doubleday.
1963   *Stigma.* Englewood Cliffs, N.J.: Prentice-Hall.
1967   *Interaction Ritual.* Chicago: Aldine.
1969   *Strategic Interaction.* Philadelphia: University of Pennsylvania Press.
1971   *Relations in Public.* New York: Basic Books.

GOLD, M., and J. WILLIAMS
  1969   "National Study of the Aftermath of Apprehension." *Prospectus*:
          3–12.
GONICK, C.
  1975   *Inflation or Depression*. Toronto: James Lorimer.
GOODE, E.
  1969   "Marijuana and the Politics of Reality." *Journal of Health and
          Social Behavior* 10 (June): 83–94.
  1970   *The Marihuana Smokers*. New York: Free Press.
GORDON, L.
  1980   "Where Do We Go From Here?" *Pacific Sociological Review* 23:
          251–270.
GORDON, L., and A. HUNTER
  1977   "Sex, Family and the New Right." *Radical America* 11(6): 8–25.
GORDON, M. M.
  1947   "The Concept of the Subculture and Its Application." *Social
          Forces* 26: 40–42.
GORING, C.
  1913   *The English Convict*. London: Her Majesty's Stationery Office.
GOTTFREDSON, M. R., M. J. HINDELANG, and N. PARISI
  1978   *Sourcebook of Criminal Justice Statistics—1977*. Washington,
          D.C.: Superintendent of Documents.
GOUGH, I.
  1979   *The Political Economy of the Welfare State*. London: Macmillan.
GOULDNER, A. W.
  1954   *Patterns of Industrial Bureaucracy*. New York: Free Press.
  1957   "Theoretical Requirements of the Applied Social Sciences."
          American Sociological Review 22 (February): 92–102.
  1968   "The Sociologist as Partisan: Sociology and the Welfare State."
          American Sociologist 3 (May): 103–116.
  1971   *The Coming Crisis of Western Sociology*. New York: Equinox.
GOVE, W. (Ed.)
  1975   *The Labelling of Deviance: Evaluating a Perspective*. New York:
          Sage/Halstead.
GOVE, W.
  1970   "Societal Reactions as an Explanation of Mental Illness: An Eval-
          uation." *American Sociological Review* 35: 873–884.
  1975   "Labelling and Mental Illness: A Critique." In W. R. Gove (Ed.),
          The Labelling of Deviance: Evaluating a Perspective. New York:
          Sage/Halstead, pp. 42–88.
GOVE, W., and H. COSTNER
  1969   "Organizing the Poor: An Evaluation of a Strategy." *Social Sci-
          ence Quarterly* 50 (December): 643–656.
GOVE, W., and J. LUBACH
  1969   "An Intensive Treatment Program for Psychiatric Inpatients: A

Description and Evaluation." *Journal of Health and Social Behavior* 10 (September): 225–236.

GRABINER, G.
1975   "The Situational Sociologies: A Theoretical Note." *Insurgent Sociologist* 5 (Summer): 80–81.

GRAHAM, H. D., and T. R. GURR
1969   *Violence in America: Historical and Comparative Perspectives.* New York: Bantam.

GRAY, L. N., and J. D. MARTIN
1969   "Punishment and Deterrence: Another Analysis of Gibbs's Data." *Social Science Quarterly* 50: 389–395.

GROB, G. N.
1966   *The State and the Mentally Ill: A History of the Worcester State Hospital in Massachusetts 1830–1920.* Chapel Hill: University of North Carolina Press.
1973   *Mental Institutions in America: Social Policy to 1875.* New York: Free Press.

GROSS, E.
1978   "Organizational Crime: A Theoretical Perspective." In N. Denzin (Ed.), *Studies in Symbolic Interaction, Vol. 1.* Greenwich, Conn.: JAI Press, pp. 55–85.
1980   "Organizational Structure and Organizational Crime." In G. Geis and E. Stotland (Eds.), *White Collar Crime: Theory and Research.* Beverly Hills: Sage Publications, pp. 52–76.

GRUSKY, O.
1959   "Organizational Goals and the Behavior of Informal Leaders." *American Journal of Sociology* 65: 59–67.

GUNNINGHAM, N.
1974   *Pollution, Social Interest and the Law.* London: Martin Robertson.

GURIN, G. J., J. VEROFF, and S. FELD
1960   *Americans View Their Mental Health: A Nationwide Interview Survey.* New York: Basic Books.

GUSFIELD, J. R.
1955   "Social Structure and Moral Reform: A Study of the Women's Christian Temperance Union." *American Journal of Sociology* 61 (November): 221–232.
1963   *Symbolic Crusade: Status Politics and the American Temperance Movement.* Urbana: University of Illinois Press.
1967   "Moral Passage: The Symbolic Process in Public Designations of Deviance." *Social Problems* 15 (Fall): 175–188.

GUSSOW, Z., and G. TRACY
1968   "Status, Ideology and Adaptation to Stigmatized Illness: A Study of Leprosy." *Human Organization* 17: 316–325. Reprinted in E. Sagarin (Ed.), *The Other Minorities.* New York: Wiley, 1971, pp. 242–262.

GUZZARDI, W., JR.
  1976   "An Unscandalized View of Those 'Bribes' Abroad." *Fortune*
          (July): 118+.
HABERMAS, J.
  1972   *Knowledge and Human Interests.* Boston: Beacon Press.
HACKER, A.
  1973   "Getting Used to Mugging." *The New York Review of Books* 20
          (April 16): 9–15.
HACKER, H. M.
  1971   "Homosexuals: Deviant or Minority Group." In E. Sagarin
          (Ed.), *The Other Minorities.* Waltham, Mass.: Ginn & Co., pp.
          65–92.
HAGAN, J., and L. JEFFREY
  1977   "Rediscovering Delinquency: Social History, Political Ideology
          and the Sociology of Law." *American Sociological Review* 42
          (August): 587–598.
HAKIM, S., A. OVADIA, and J. WEINBLATT
  1978   "Crime Attraction and Deterrence in Small Communities: Theory
          and Results." *International Regional Science Review* 3 (Winter):
          153–163.
HALL, P. M.
  1966   "Identification with the Delinquent Subculture and the Level of
          Self-Evaluation." *Sociometry* 29: 146–158.
HALL, S.
  1974   "Deviance, Politics and the Media." In P. Rock and M. McIntosh
          (Eds.), *Deviance and Social Control.* London: Tavistock; pp.
          261–305.
HALL, S., and T. JEFFERSON (Eds.)
  1975   *Resistance through Rituals: Youth Subcultures in Post-War Brit-
          ain.* London: Hutchinson.
HALL, S., C. CRICHTER, T. JEFFERSON, J. CLARKE, and B. ROBERTS
  1978   *Policing the Crisis: Mugging, the State and Law and Order.* Lon-
          don: Macmillan.
HALPERIN, M. H., J. BERMAN, R. BOROSAGE, and C. M. MARWICK
  1976   *The Lawless State: The Crimes of the U.S. Intelligence Agencies.*
          New York: Penguin.
HARRING, S. L.
  1977   "Class Conflict and the Suppression of Tramps in Buffalo, 1892–
          1894." *Law and Society Review* 11 (Summer): 873–911.
HASKELL, M. R., and L. YABLONSKY
  1978   *Criminology: Crime and the Criminal.* Chicago: Rand McNally.
HAWKES, R. K.
  1975   "Norms, Deviance, and Social Control: A Mathematical Elabora-
          tion of Concepts." *American Journal of Sociology* 80 (January):
          886–908.

HAWKINS, R., and G. TIEDEMAN
1975   *The Creation of Deviance: Interpersonal and Organizational Determinants.* Columbus, Ohio: Charles E. Merrill.
HAYNOR, N. S.
1943   "Washington State Correctional Institutions as Communities." *Social Forces* 21: 316–322.
HAYNOR, N. S., and E. ASCH
1939   "The Prison as a Social Group." *American Sociological Review* 5: 362–369.
1940   "The Prison as a Community." *American Sociological Review* 5: 577–583.
HEARN, F.
1973–74   "The Implications of Critical Theory for Critical Sociology." *Berkeley Journal of Sociology* 18: 127–158.
HEYDEBRAND, W. V.
1977   "The Context of Public Bureaucracies: An Organizational Analysis of Federal District Courts." *Law and Society Review* 5 (Summer): 759–821.
HEYL, B. S.
1977   "The Madam as Teacher: The Training of House Prostitutes." *Social Problems* 24(5) (June): 545–555.
Hill, D. G.
1978   *Human Rights In Canada: A Focus on Racism.* Ottawa: Canadian Labour Congress.
HILLS, S. L.
1980   *Demystifying Deviance.* New York: McGraw-Hill, Chapter II.
HIRSCHI, T.
1973   "Procedural Rules and the Study of Deviant Behavior." *Social Problems* 21: 159–173.
HIRSCHI, T., and H. C. SELVIN
1966   "False Criteria of Causality in Delinquency Research." *Social Problems* 13 (Winter): 254–268.
HOBBES, T.
1967   *Body, Man and Citizen.* New York: Collier.
1971   *Leviathan.* New York: Collier.
HOLLANDER, E. P.
1958   "Conformity, Status and Idiosyncracy Credit." *Psychological Review* 65: 117–127. Reprinted in E. Hollander and R. G. Hunt (Eds.), *Classic Contributions to Social Psychology.* New York: Oxford University Press, pp. 362–372.
HOLLINGSHEAD, A. B., and F. D. REDLICK
1958   *Social Class and Mental Illness.* New York: Wiley.
HOOTON, E. A.
1939   *The American Criminal.* Cambridge, Mass.: Harvard University Press.

HOPKINS, A.
    1980   "Controlling Corporate Deviance." *Criminology* 18 (August): 198–214.
HORKHEIMER, M.
    1972   *Critical Theory: Selected Essays.* New York: Seabury Press.
HORNING, D. M. N.
    1970   "Blue Collar Theft: Conceptions of Property Attitudes Toward Pilfering and Work Group Norms in a Modern Industrial Plant." In E. O. Smigel and H. L. Ross (Eds.), *Crimes Against Bureaucracy.* New York: Van Nostrand Reinhold, pp. 46–64.
HOROWITZ, I. L., and M. LIEBOWITZ
    1968   "Social Deviance and Political Marginality: Toward a Redefinition of the Relation between Sociology and Politics." *Social Problems* 15 (Winter): 280–296.
HOWELL, J. T.
    1973   *Hard Living on Clay Street: Portraits of Blue Collar Families.* New York: Anchor.
HUFFINE, C., and J. CLAUSEN
    1979   "Madness and Work: Short and Long Term Effects of Mental Illness on Occupation Careers." *Social Forces* 57: 1049–1063.
HUGHES, D. R., and E. KALLEN
    1974   *The Anatomy of Racism: Canadian Dimensions.* Montreal: Harvest House.
HUGHES, E. C.
    1958   *Men and Their Work.* New York: Free Press.
HUMPHREYS, L.
    1970   *Tearoom Trade.* Chicago: Aldine.
    1972   *Out of the Closets: The Sociology of Homosexual Liberation.* Englewood Cliffs, N.J.: Prentice-Hall.
HUMPHREYS, L., and B. MILLER
    1980   "Identities in the Emerging Gay Culture." In J. Marmor (Ed.), *Homosexual Behavior: A Modern Reappraisal.* New York: Basic Books, pp. 142–156.
HUSSERL, E.
    1962   *Ideas.* New York: Collier.
    1965   *Phenomenology and the Crisis of Philosophy.* New York: Harper & Row.
IANNI, F. A. J., and E. R. IANNI
    1972   *A Family Business: Kinship and Social Control in Organized Crime.* New York: Russell Sage Foundation.
INCIARDI, J. A.
    1980   *Radical Criminology: The Coming Crisis.* Beverly Hills: Sage Publications.
IRWIN, J.
    1980   *Prisons in Turmoil.* Boston: Little, Brown.

JACKSON, J. K.
    1954   "The Adjustment of the Family to the Crisis of Alcoholism."
            Quarterly Journal of Studies on Alcohol 15 (December): 562–
            586.
JACOBS, D., and D. BRITT
    1979   "Inequality and Police Use of Deadly Force: An Empirical As-
            sessment of a Conflict Hypothesis." *Social Problems* 26 (April):
            403–412.
JACOBSON, P., and J. BARNES
    1978   "£ 66m in Damages: The Car That Carried Death in the Boot."
            The Sunday Times (February 12): 4+.
JENSEN, G.
    1969   "Crime Doesn't Pay: Correlates of a Shared Misunderstanding."
            Social Problems 17 (Fall): 189–201.
JOEY, with D. FISHER
    1973   *Killer.* Chicago: Playboy Press.
JOHNSON, E.
    1961   "Sociology of Confinement: Assimilation of the Prison Rat." *Jour-
            nal of Criminal Law, Criminology and Police Science* 51: 528–533.
JOHNSON, J. M., and J. D. DOUGLAS
    1978   *Crime At The Top: Deviance In Business and the Professions.*
            Philadelphia: J. B. Lippincott.
JOINT COMMISSION ON MENTAL ILLNESS AND MENTAL HEALTH
    1961   *Action for Mental Health.* New York: Basic Books.
JONES, M.
    1953   *The Therapeutic Community.* New York: Basic Books.
KAMENY, F. E.
    1971   "Homosexuals as a Minority Group." In E. Sagarin (Ed.), *The
            Other Minorities.* Waltham, Mass.: Ginn & Co., pp. 50–65.
KANOWITZ, L.
    1969   *Women and the Law: The Unfinished Revolution.* Albuquerque:
            University of New Mexico Press.
KANTER, R. M.
    1979   "Effects of Proportions on Group Life: Tokenism, Not Sex Dis-
            crimination." *Sociological Inventory:* 5–9.
KARMEN, A.
    1974   "Agents Provocateurs in the Contemporary Leftist Movement."
            In C. E. Reasons (Ed.), *The Criminologist: Crime and the Crimi-
            nal.* Pacific Palisades, Calif.: Goodyear, pp. 209–226.
KAUFMAN, E.
    1979   "The Right to Treatment Suit as an Agent of Change." *American
            Journal of Psychiatry* 136 (November): 1428–1432.
KERLINS, M., and M. KNUDSEN
    1976   "State Hospital Review Boards in Minnesota." *Hospital and
            Community Psychiatry* 27: 641–643.

KETY, S., D. ROSENTHAL, P. WENDER, F. SCHULSINGER, and B. JACOBSON
1975   "Mental Illness in the Biological and Adoptive Families of Adopted Individuals Who Have Become Schizophrenic: A Preliminary Report Based on Psychiatric Interviews." In R. Fieve et al. (Eds.), *Genetic Research in Psychiatry*. Baltimore: Johns Hopkins University Press.

KITSUSE, J. I.
1972   "Deviance, Deviant Behavior and Deviants: Some Conceptual Issues." In W. Filstead (Ed.), *An Introduction to Deviance*. Chicago: Markham, p. 14.
1980   "Coming Out All Over: Deviants and the Politics of Social Problems." *Social Problems* 28(1) (October): 1–13.

KITSUSE, J. I., and A. CICOUREL
1963   "A Note on the Official Uses of Statistics." *Social Problems* II: 131–139.

KITSUSE, J. I., and D. C. DIETRICK
1959   "Delinquent Boys: A Critique." *American Sociological Review* 24 (April): 213–215.

KLEIN, J. F.
1974   "Professional Theft: The Utility of a Concept." *Canadian Journal of Criminology and Corrections* 16: 133–144.

KLERMAN, G., and G. SCHECHTER
1979   "The Impact of Psychopharmacology on the Mental Health Services System." Presented at the Conference on Human Behavior: A Bio-Psycho-Social Phenomenon, Vanderbilt University (April).

KNAPP COMMISSION
1972   "Masking Official Violence: Corporal Punishment in Public Schools." In J. M. Johnson and J. D. Douglas (Eds.), *Crime at the Top: Deviance in Business and the Professions*. Philadelphia: J. B. Lippincott, pp. 256–268.

KOTARBA, J. A.
1978   "Masking Official Violence." In J. M. Johnson and J. D. Douglas, *Crime at the Top: Deviance in Business and the Professions*. Philadelphia: Lippincott.

KREISMAN, D., and V. JOY
1974   "Family Response to the Mental Illness of a Relative: A Review of the Literature." *Schizophrenia Bulletin* 10: 34–57.

KUHN, T. S.
1970   *The Structure of Scientific Revolutions*. Chicago: University of Chicago Press.

KUMASAKA, Y., J. STOKES, and R. GUPTA
1972   "Criteria for Involuntary Hospitalization." *Archives of General Psychiatry* 26 (May): 399–404.

LAMB, H. R.
1969   "The New Asylums in the Community." *Archives of General Psychiatry* 36: 129–134.

LANDIS, C., and J. PAGE
1938   Modern Society and Mental Disease. New York: Farrar and Rinehart.
LEIGHTON, D. C., J. S. HARDING, and D. B. MACKLIN
1963   The Character of Danger. New York: Basic Books.
LEITER, K.
1969   Getting It Done. Unpublished master's thesis. Santa Barbara: University of California.
1974   "Ad Hocing in the Schools." In Cicourel et al. (Eds.), Language Use and School Performance. New York: Academic Press.
1976   "Teachers' Use of Background Knowledge to Interpret Test Scores." Sociology of Education Journal: 59–65.
1980   A Primer on Ethnomethodology. New York: Oxford University Press.
LEMERT, E. M.
1951   Social Pathology: A Systematic Approach to the Theory of Sociopathic Behavior. New York: McGraw-Hill.
1963   "Social Structure, Social Control and Deviation." In M. Clinard (Ed.), Anomie and Deviant Behavior. New York: Free Press, p. 59+.
1967   Human Deviance, Social Problems and Social Control. Englewood Cliffs, N.J.: Prentice-Hall.
1967a   "The Concept of Secondary Deviation." In E. Lemert (Ed.), Human Deviance, Social Problems and Social Control. Englewood Cliffs, N.J.: Prentice-Hall, pp. 62–92.
1967b   "Role Enactment, Self, and Identity in the Systematic Check Forger." In E. Lemert (Ed.), Human Deviance, Social Problems and Social Control. Englewood Cliffs, N.J.: Prentice-Hall, pp. 162–182.
1972   Human Deviance, Social Problems and Social Control, 2nd Ed. Englewood Cliffs, N.J.: Prentice-Hall.
1974   "Beyond Mead: the Societal Reaction to Deviance." Social Problems 21: 457–468.
1975   "Rules, Values and the Negotiation of Deviance." Presidential Address Pacific Sociological Association.
LESIEUR, H. R.
1977   The Chase: Career of the Compulsive Gambler. Garden City, N.Y.: Anchor/Doubleday.
LETKEMANN, P.
1973   Crime as Work. Englewood Cliffs, N.J.: Prentice-Hall.
LEVINE, J., A. VINSON, and D. WOOD
1973   "Subway Behavior." In A. Birenbaum and E. Sagarin (Eds.), People in Places: The Sociology of the Familiar. New York: Praeger, pp. 208–216.
LEYTON, E.
1975   Dying Hard: The Ravages of Industrial Carnage. Toronto: McClelland and Stewart.

LI, V.
1970   "The Role of Law in Communist China." China Quarterly 44: 86.
LIAZOS, A.
1972   "The Poverty of the Sociology of Deviance: Nuts, Sluts and Per-
        verts." Social Problems 20: 103–120.
1974   "Class Oppression: The Functions of Juvenile Justice." Insurgent
        Sociologist 5 (Fall): 2–24.
LIGHT, D.
1973   "Treating Suicide: The Illusions of a Professional Movement."
        International Social Science Journal 25(4): 475–488.
LINDESMITH, A.
1940   "Dope Fiend Mythology." Journal of Criminal Law, Criminology
        and Police Science 31: 199–208.
LINTON, R.
1952   "Universal Ethical Principles: An Anthropological View." In
        R. N. Anshen (Ed.), Moral Principles of Action. New York:
        Harpers.
LIZOTTE, A. J.
1978   "Extra Legal Factors in Chicago's Criminal Courts: Testing the
        Conflict Model of Criminal Justice." Social Problems 25 (June):
        564–580.
LLEWELLYN, K.
1973   "Letter to Hoebel." Cited in W. Twilling, Karl Llewellyn and the
        Realist Movement. London: Wiedenfield and Nicholson, p. 178.
LOFLAND, J.
1966   Doomsday Cult. Englewood Cliffs, N.J.: Prentice-Hall.
1969   Deviance and Identity. Englewood Cliffs, N.J.: Prentice-Hall.
LONEY, M.
1973   "Social Control in Cuba." In I. Taylor and L. Taylor (Eds.), Poli-
        tics and Deviance: Papers from the National Deviancy Confer-
        ence, Harmondsworth, England: Penguin, pp. 42–62.
LUBMAN, S.
1969   "Form and Function in Chinese Legal Process." Columbia Law
        Review 69: 558.
MAAS, P.
1973   Serpico. New York: Viking.
MACIVER, R.
1942   Social Causation. Boston: Ginn and Co., p. 375+.
MACKAY, A. W.
1978   "Human Rights in Canadian Society: Mechanisms For Raising
        the Issues and Providing Redress." Dalhousie Law Journal 4:
        739–779.
MACKAY, R.
1974   "Standardized Testing: Objective and Objectified Measures of
        Competence." In Cicourel et al. (Eds.), Language Use and School
        Performance. New York: Academic Press, pp. 218–247.

MANKOFF, M.
1971   "Societal Reaction and Career Deviance: A Critical Analysis."
       Sociology Quarterly 12: 204–218.
MANN, E., and J. A. LEE
1979   *RCMP vs. The People.* Don Mills: General Publishing Co.
MANNING, P. K.
1972   "Observing the Police: Deviants, Respectables, and the Law." In
       J. Douglas (Ed.), *Research on Deviance.* New York: Random
       House.
1975   "Deviance and Dogma: Some Comments on the Labelling Per-
       spective." *British Journal of Criminology* 15 (January): 1–20.
1977   *Police Work.* Cambridge, Mass.: M.I.T. Press.
MARMOR, J. (Ed.)
1980   *Homosexual Behavior: A Modern Reappraisal.* New York: Basic
       Books.
MARS, G.
1974   "Dock Pilferage: A Case Study in Occupational Theft." In
       P. Rock and M. McIntosh (Eds.), *Deviance and Social Control.*
       London: Tavistock, pp. 209–228.
MARTINDALE, D.
1981   *The Nature and Types of Sociological Theory*, 2nd Ed. Boston:
       Houghton Mifflin.
MARX, G. T.
1974   "Thoughts on a Neglected Category of Social Movement Partici-
       pants: The Agent Provocateur and the Informant." *American
       Journal of Sociology* 80: 404–442.
1980a "The New Police Undercover Work." *Urban Life* 8 (January):
       399–446.
1980b "Who Really Gets Stung? Further Thoughts on Recent Police
       Undercover Activities." Unpublished manuscript, Massachusetts
       Institute of Technology.
MATHIAS, P.
1977   "How Widespread Are (New Brunswick) Political Kickbacks?"
       Financial Post 71 (May 28): 1–4.
MATZA, D.
1964   *Delinquency and Drift.* New York: Wiley.
1969   *Becoming Deviant.* Englewood Cliffs, N.J.: Prentice-Hall, pp. 44–
       53.
MAURER, D. W.
1955   *Whiz Mob: A Correlation of the Technical Argot of Pickpockets
       with their Behavior Patterns.* University of Alabama Press.
1974   *The American Confidence Man.* Springfield, Ill.: Charles C. Thomas.
MCCAGHY, C. H.
1976   *Deviant Behaviour.* New York: Macmillan.
MCCLEERY, R.
1971   *One Life, One Physician: Ralph Nader's Study Group Report on*

the Medical Profession's Performance in Self-Regulation. Washington, D.C.: Public Affairs Press.

McCORKLE, L. W., and R. KORN
1954   "Resocialization Within Walls." The Annals of the American Academy of Political and Social Science 293 (May): 88–98.

McCORMICK, A. E.
1977   "Rule Enforcement and Moral Indignation: Some Observations of the Effects of Criminal Antitrust Convictions Upon Societal Reaction Processes." Social Problems 25 (October): 30–39.

McCORRY, C.
1972   Citizen Nader. New York: Saturday Review Press.

McCOY, A.
1972   The Politics of Heroin in Southeast Asia. New York: Harper Colophon Books.

McDONALD, L.
1976   The Sociology of Law and Order. Montreal: Book Centre.

McHUGH, P.
1970   "A Common-sense Perception of Deviance." In H. P. Dreitzel (Ed.), Recent Sociology. New York: Collier-Macmillan, pp. 152–179.

McLEERY, R. H.
1961a   "The Governmental Process and Informal Social Control." In D. R. Cressey (Ed.), The Prison: Studies in Institutional Organization and Change. New York: Holt, Rinehart and Winston, pp. 149–188.
1961b   "Authoritarianism and the Belief System of Incorrigibles." In D. R. Cressey (Ed.), The Prison: Studies in Institutional Organization and Change. New York: Holt, Rinehart and Winston, pp. 260–308.

McNALL, S. G., and J. C. M. JOHNSON
1975   "The New Conservatives: Ethnomethodologists, Phenomenologists, and Symbolic Interactionists." Insurgent Sociologist 5 (Summer): 49–65.

MEDVEDEV, Z., and R. MEDVEDEV
1971   A Question of Madness: Repression by Psychiatry in the Soviet Union. New York: Vintage.

MEHAN, H. B.
1974   "Accomplishing Classroom Lessons." In A. V. Cicourel et al., Language Use and School Performance. New York: Academic Press.

MEHAN, H., and H. WOOD
1975   The Reality of Ethnomethodology. New York: Wiley-Interscience.

MEIER, R., and W. JOHNSON
1977   "Deterrence as Social Control: The Legal and Extralegal Production of Conformity." American Sociological Review 42 (April): 292–304.

MEILE, R., and H. WHITT
  1980   "Cultural Consensus and Definitions of Mental Illness." Mimeo.
MELVILLE, K.
  1972   *Communes in the Counter Culture.* New York: Morrow.
MERTON, R. K.
  1938   "Social Structure and Anomie." *American Sociological Review* 3
          (October): 672–682.
  1957   *Social Theory and Social Structure.* New York: Free Press.
  1976   "The Sociology of Social Problems." In R. K. Merton and R. A.
          Nisbet (Eds.), *Contemporary Social Problems*, 4th Ed. New York:
          Harcourt, Brace, Jovanovich, 1976, pp. 5–43.
MERTON, R., and R. NISBET
  1971   *Contemporary Social Problems.* New York: Harcourt, Brace,
          Jovanovich.
MEYER, N.
  1974   "Legal Status of Inpatient Admissions to State and County Men-
          tal Hospitals 1972." Statistical Note 105, National Institute of
          Mental Health, Survey and Reports Branch.
MILLER, G.
  1978   *Odd Jobs: The World of Deviant Work.* Englewood Cliffs, N.J.:
          Prentice-Hall.
MILLMAN, M.
  1975   "She Did It All for Love: A Feminist View of the Sociology of
          Deviance." In M. Millman and R. Moss-Kanter (Eds.), *Another
          Voice: Feminist Perspectives on Social Life and Social Science.*
          Garden City, N.Y.: Anchor/Doubleday.
MILLS, C. W.
  1943   "The Professional Ideology of Social Pathologists." *American So-
          ciological Review* 49: 165–180.
  1971   *The Marxists.* Harmondsworth, England: Penguin.
MILLS, T. M.
  1959   "Equilibrium and Processes of Deviance and Control." *American
          Sociological Review* 24: 671–679.
MOLOTCH, H.
  1970   "Oil in Santa Barbara and Power in America." *Sociological In-
          quiry* 40(1) (Winter): 131–145.
MONTANINO, F.
  1977   "Directions in the Study of Deviance: A Bibliographic Essay,
          1960–1977." In E. Sagarin (Ed.), *Deviance and Social Change.*
          Beverly Hills: Sage Publications, pp. 277–304.
MONTANINO, F., and E. SAGARIN
  1977   "Deviants: Voluntarism and Responsibility." In E. Sagarin and F.
          Montanino (Eds.), *Deviants: Voluntary Actors in a Hostile
          World.* Morristown, N.J.: General Learning Press.

MOORE, M.
 1978   "The Pusher as a Rational Business Man." In L. D. Savitz and N.
         Johnston (Eds.), *Crime in Society*. New York: Wiley, pp. 716–
         748.
MORRIS, A.
 1935   *Criminology*. New York: Longmans, Green.
MORRISSEY, J.
 1979   "Keeping Patients Out: Organization and Policy Implications of
         Emergent State Hospital Deinstitutionalizing Practices." Pre-
         sented at the annual meeting of the Southern Sociological Soci-
         ety, Atlanta (April).
MOULEDOUX, J. C.
 1967   "Political Crime and the Negro Revolution." In *Criminal Behav-
         ior Systems: A Typology*. New York: Holt, Rinehart and Winston,
         pp. 217–231.
MOYNIHAN, P.
 1969   "Toward a National Urban Policy." *The Public Interest* (Fall): 8–9.
MURPHY, J. M.
 1976   "Psychiatric Labeling in Cross-Cultural Perspective." *Science*
         191: 1019–1027.
NASSI, A. J., and S. I. ABRAMOWITZ
 1976   "From Phrenology to Psychosurgery and Back Again: Biological
         Studies of Criminality." *American Journal of Orthopsychiatry*
         46: 591–607.
NATIONAL ADVISORY COMMISSION ON CIVIL DISORDERS
 1968   *A Report*. Washington, D.C.: U.S. Government Printing Office.
NATIONAL COMMISSION ON MARIHUANA AND DRUG ABUSE
 1972   *Marihuana: A Signal of Misunderstanding*. Washington, D.C.:
         U.S. Government Printing Office.
NETTLAR, G.
 1978   *Explaining Crime*. New York: McGraw-Hill.
NEWMAN, D. J.
 1958   "White Collar Crime." *Law and Contemporary Problems* (Au-
         tumn): 735–753.
NEWSDAY STAFF
 1973   *The Heroin Trail*. Long Island: Signet.
NEWTON, E.
 1972   *Mother Camp: Female Impersonators in America*. Englewood
         Cliffs, N.J.: Prentice-Hall.
NONET, P.
 1976   "For Jurisprudential Sociology." *Law and Society Review* 10
         (Summer): 525–545.
OAKE, G.
 1979   "Large Corporate Profits Enrage Labor." *The Calgary Herald*
         (February 8): 1.

O'CONNOR, J.
1975   *The Fiscal Crisis of the State.* New York: St. Martin's Press.
OFFE, C.
1972   "Advanced Capitalism and the Welfare State." *Politics and Society* 2 (Summer): 479–488.
1973   "The Abolition of Market Control and the Problem of Legitimacy (I)." *Kapitalistate* (1): 109–116.
1975   "The Theory of the Capitalist State and the Problem of Policy Formation." In L. N. Lindbert et al. (Eds.), *Stress and Contradiction in Modern Capitalism.* Lexington, Mass.: Lexington Books, pp. 125–144.
OFFICE DES PROFESSIONS DU QUÉBEC
1976   *Decisions Disciplinaries. Concernant Les Corporations Professionelles.* Québec: Editeur Officiel du Quebéc.
OHLIN, L.
1956   *Sociology in the Field of Correction.* New York: Russell Sage Foundation.
OLMSTEAD, D., and K. DURHAM
1976   "Stability of Mental Health Attitudes: A Semantic Differential Study," *Journal of Health and Social Behavior* 17: 35–44.
OLSHANSKY, S., S. BROB, and M. K. DAHL
1960   "Survey of Employment Experiences of Patients Discharged from Three State Mental Hospitals During the Period 1951–1953." *Mental Hygiene* 44: 510–521.
OWEN, D. R.
1972   "The 47, XYY Male: A Review." *Psychological Bulletin* 78: 209–233.
PALMORE, E., and F. WHITTINGTON
1970   "Differential Tends Toward Equality between Whites and Nonwhites." *Social Forces* 49 (September): 108–117.
PARSONS, T.
1951   *The Social System.* New York: Free Press.
1965   *Theories of Society.* New York: Free Press.
PARTRIDGE, W. L.
1973   *The Hippie Ghetto. The Natural History of a Subculture.* New York: Holt, Rinehart and Winston.
PEARCE, F.
1976   *Crimes of the Powerful: Marxism, Crime and Deviance.* London: Pluto Press.
PEARSON, J. S.
1978   "Organizational Response to Occupational Injury and Disease: The Case of the Uranium Industry." *Social Forces* 57 (September): 23–41.
PETERSILIA, J., P. W. GREENWOOD, and M. LAVIN
1978   *Criminal Careers of Habitual Felons.* Washington, D.C.: National

Institute of Law Enforcement and Criminal Justice, U.S. Department of Justice.

PETERSON, R. C.
1977   *Marihuana Research Findings 1976* (Research Monograph 14). Washington, D.C.: National Institute of Drug Abuse.

PFOHL, S. J.
1977   "The Discovery of Child Abuse." *Social Problems* 24 (February): 310–323.

PHILIPSON, M.
1972   "Phenomenological Philosophy and Sociology." In P. Filmer et al. (Eds.), *New Directions in Sociological Theory*. Cambridge, Mass.: M.I.T. Press.

PIERCE, R. E.
1972   "Aklyl Mercury Poisoning in Humans: Report of an Outbreak." *Journal of American Medical Association* 220: 1439–1442.

PILIAVIN, I., and S. BRIAR
1964   "Police Encounters with Juveniles." *American Journal of Sociology* 70 (September): 20–214.

PINKNEY, A.
1972   *The American Way of Violence*. New York: Vintage.

PLATT, A. M.
1975   "Prospects for a Radical Criminology in the USA." In I. Taylor, P. Walton, and J. Young (Eds.), *The New Criminology: For a Social Theory of Deviance*. Boston: Routledge and Kegan Paul, pp. 95–112.
1977   *The Child Savers: The Invention of Delinquency*. Chicago: University of Chicago Press.

PLATT, A. M., and P. TAKAGI
1979   "The American Society of Criminology: A Continuing Debate." *Crime and Social Justice* 12 (Winter): 52–56.

PLOSKIN, R.
1979   "Newfoundland B'ys Will Be B'ys." *Macleans Magazine* 91 (May): 28.

PLUMMER, K.
1975   *Sexual Stigma. An Interactionist Account*. London: Routledge and Kegan Paul.
1979   "Misunderstanding the Labelling Perspectives." In D. Downes and P. Rock (Eds.), *Deviant Interpretations*. Oxford: Martin Robertson.

POLLNER, M.
1974   "Sociological and Common-sense Models of the Labelling Process." In R. Turner (Ed.), *Ethnomethodology*. Middlesex, England: Penguin.
1978   "Constitutive and Mundane Versions of Labeling Theory." *Human Studies*: 269–288.

POLSKY, N.
  1969   Hustlers, Beats and Others. Garden City, N.Y.: Anchor/Double-
          day.
POPLAR, J. F.
  1969   "Characteristics of Nurse Addicts." American Journal of Nursing
          69 (January): 117–119.
PORTER, J.
  1965   The Vertical Mosaic. Toronto: University of Toronto Press.
PREWITT, K., and S. VERBA
  1979   An Introduction to American Government. New York: Harper &
          Row.
QUINNEY, E. R.
  1964   "The Study of White Collar Crime: Toward a Reorientation in
          Theory and Research." Journal of Criminology, Criminal Law
          and Police Science 55: 208–214.
QUINNEY, R.
  1970   The Social Reality of Crime. Boston: Little, Brown.
  1974   Critique of Legal Order. Boston: Little, Brown.
  1975   "Crime Control in Capitalist Society: A Critical Philosophy of the
          Legal Order." In I. Taylor, P. Walton, and J. Young (Eds.), The
          New Criminology: For a Social Theory of Deviance. Boston:
          Routledge and Kegan Paul, pp. 181–222.
  1977   Class State and Crime: On the Theory and Practice of Criminal
          Justice. New York: Longman.
  1979   Criminology: Analysis and Critique of Crime in America, 2nd
          Ed. Boston: Little, Brown.
RABKIN, J.
  1974   "Public Attitudes Toward Mental Illness: A Review of the Litera-
          ture." Schizophrenia Bulletin 19: 9–33.
  1979   "Who Is Called Mentally Ill: Public and Professional Views."
          Journal of Community Psychiatry 7: 253–258.
RAINS, P. M.
  1971   Becoming an Unwed Mother: A Sociological Account. Chicago:
          Aldine-Atherton.
  1975   "The Imputation of Deviance: A Retrospective Essay on the La-
          belling Perspective." Social Problems 23: 1–11.
REASONS, C. E.
  1975   "Social Thought and Social Structure: Competing Paradigms in
          Criminology." Criminology 13 (November): 332–365.
  1980   "Crime and the Abuse of Power: Offences and Offenders Beyond
          the Reach of the Law." Paper presented to the International Con-
          ference on Economic and White Collar Crime. Potsdam, New
          York (February).
REASONS, C. E., and C. H. GOFF
  1980   "Corporate Crime: A Cross-National Analysis." In White Collar

Crime: Theory and Research. Beverly Hills: Sage Publications, pp. 126–141.

REASONS, C. E., and W. D. PERDUE
1981   *The Ideology of Social Problems.* Sherman Oaks, Calif.: Alfred Publishing Company.

REASONS, C. E., and R. M. RICH
1978   *The Sociology of Law: A Conflict Perspective.* Toronto: Butterworth.

REASONS, C. E., L. ROSS, and C. PATERSON
1981   *Assault on the Worker: Occupational Health and Safety in Canada.* Toronto: Butterworth.

RECKLESS, W.
1969   *Vice in Chicago.* Montclair, N.J.: Patterson Smith. Reprint of 1933 edition originally published by University of Chicago Press.

REGIER, D., I. D. GOLDBERG, and C. A. TAUBE
1978   "The de facto U.S. Mental Health Service: A Public Health Perspective." *Archives of General Psychiatry* 35: 685–693.

REIDER, R., and E. GERSHON
1978   "Genetic Strategies in Biological Psychiatry." *Archives of General Psychiatry* 35: 866–873.

REIMAN, J. H.
1979   *The Rich Get Richer and the Poor Get Prison.* New York: Wiley.

REISS, A.
1970   "Putting Sociology into Policy." *Social Problems* 17 (Winter): 289–294.

REPORT OF THE ROYAL COMMISSION ON CORPORATE CONCENTRATION
1978   Ottawa: Minister of Supply and Services Canada.

REPORT OF THE SENATE SELECT COMMITTEE ON INTELLIGENCE
1978   In M. D. Ermann and R. J. Lundman (Eds.), *Corporate and Governmental Deviance: Problems of Organizational Behavior in Contemporary Society.* New York: Oxford University Press.

REX, J.
1973   *Key Problems in Sociological Theory.* London: Routledge and Kegan Paul.

RIST, R. C.
1973   "Policy, Politics and Social Research: A Study in the Relationship of Federal Commissions and Social Science." *Social Problems* 21 (Summer): 113–128.

RITZER, G.
1975   "Sociology: A Multiple Paradigm Science." *American Sociologist* 10 (August): 156–167.

ROBY, P. A.
1969   "Politics and Criminal Law: Revision of the New York State Penal Law on Prostitution." *Social Problems* 17 (Summer): 83–109.

ROCK, P.
1973   *Deviant Behavior.* London: Hutchinson University Library.

1979   "The Sociology of Crime, Symbolic Interactionism, and Some Problematic Qualities of Radical Criminology." In D. Downes and P. Rock (Eds.), *Deviant Interpretations*. Oxford: Martin Robinson.

ROGERS, J., and M. D. BUFFALO
1974   "Fighting Back: Nine Modes of Adaptation to a Deviant Label." *Social Problems* 22: 101–118.

ROMAN, P. M.
1974   "Settings for Successful Deviance: Drinking and Deviant Drinking Among Middle and Upper-Level Employees." In D. Bryant (Ed.), *Deviant Behavior: Occupational and Organizational Bases*. Chicago: Rand McNally, pp. 109–128.

ROSE, V. M.
1977   "Rape as a Social Problem: A Byproduct of the Feminist Movement." *Social Problems* 25 (October): 75–89.

ROSENHAN, D. L.
1973   "On Being Sane in Insane Places." *Science* 179: 250–258.

ROSS, E. A.
1907   *Sin and Society*. Boston: Houghton Mifflin.

ROSS, H. L.
1970   *Crimes Against Bureaucracy*. New York: Litton Educational Publishing.

ROSS, H. L., and D. CAMPBELL
1968   "The Connecticut Speed Crackdown: A Study of the Effectiveness of Legal Change." In H. L. Ross (Ed.), *Perspectives on the Social Order*. New York: McGraw-Hill, pp. 30–35.

ROSS, I.
1980   "How Lawless Are Big Companies?" *Fortune* (December 1): 56–64.

ROTH, D.
1974   "Intelligence Testing as Social Activity." In A. V. Cicourel (Ed.), *Language Use and School Performance*. New York: Academic Press, pp. 143–217.

RUBINGTON, E.
1967   "Drug Addiction as a Deviant Career." *International Journal of the Addictions* 2 (Spring): 3–20.

1968   "The Bottle Gang." *Quarterly Journal of Studies on Alcohol* 29 (December): 943–955.

1975   "Top and Bottom: How Police Administrators and Public Inebriates View Decriminalization." *Journal of Drug Issues* 5 (Fall): 412–425.

RUSHING, W.
1978   "Status Resources, Societal Reactions and Type of Mental Hospitalization." *American Sociological Review* 43 (August): 521–533.

SACKS, H.
1963   "Sociological Description." *Berkeley Journal of Sociology* VIII: 1–16.

SAGARIN, E.
1969   *Odd Man In.* Chicago: Quadrangle Books.
1975   *Deviants and Deviance: An Introduction to the Study of Disvalued People and Behaviour.* New York: Praeger-Holt.
SAGARIN, E., and D. E. J. MACNAMARA
1970   "The Problem of Entrapment." *Crime and Delinquency* 16: 363–378.
SAMPSON, A.
1973   *The Sovereign State of ITT.* Greenwich, Conn.: Fawcett Crest.
SANDERS, W. B.
1977   *Detective Work.* New York: Free Press.
SANDERS, W. B., and H. DAUDISTEL
1976   *The Criminal Justice Process.* New York: Praeger.
SATA, L., and E. GOLDENBERG
1977   "A Study of Involuntary Patients in Seattle." *Hospital and Community Psychiatry* 28: 834–840.
SCHEFF, T. J.
1966   *Being Mentally Ill.* Chicago: AVC.
1974   "The Labelling Theory of Mental Illness." *American Sociological Review* 39 (June): 444–452.
1975   *The Labelling Theory of Mental Illness.* Englewood Cliffs, N.J.: Prentice-Hall, p. 22.
SCHRAG, P., and D. DIVOKY
1975   *The Myth of the Hyperactive Child and Other Means of Child Control.* New York: Dell (Laurel Editions).
SCHRAGER, L. S., and J. F. SHORT, JR.
1978   "Toward a Sociology of Organizational Crime." *Social Problems* (June): 407–419.
1980   "How Serious a Crime? Perceptions of Organizational and Common Crimes." In G. Geis and E. Stotland (Eds.), *White Collar Crime: Theory and Research.* Beverly Hills: Sage Publications.
SCHRAGG, C.
1944   "Social Types in a Prison Community." Unpublished master's thesis, Department of Sociology, University of Washington, Seattle.
1954   "Leadership Among Prison Inmates." *American Sociological Review* 19: 37–42.
SCHUCK, P.
1972   "The Curious Case of the Indicted Meat Inspectors." *Harper's* (September): 81–88.
SCHUR, E. M.
1965   *Crimes Without Victims.* Englewood Cliffs, N.J.: Prentice-Hall.
1969a   *Our Criminal Society: The Social and Legal Sources of Crime in America.* Englewood Cliffs, N.J.: Prentice-Hall.
1969b   "Reaction to Deviance: A Critical Assessment." *American Journal of Sociology* 75: 309–322.

1975   "Comments " in W. Gove (Ed.), The Labelling of Deviance. New York: Halstead/Sage.

1971   Labeling Deviant Behavior. New York: Harper & Row.

1980   The Politics of Deviance: Stigma Contests and the Uses of Power. Englewood Cliffs, N.J.: Prentice-Hall.

SCHUTZ, A.

1962   Collected Papers I: The Problem of Social Reality. The Hague: Martinus Nujhoff.

1964   Collected Papers II. The Hague: Martinus Nujhoff.

SCHWENDINGER, H., and J. SCHWENDINGER

1970   "Defenders of Order or Guardians of Human Rights?" Issues in Criminology 5 (Summer): 123–157.

1974   The Sociologists of the Chair: Radical Analysis of the Formative Years of North American Sociology: 1883–1922. New York: Basic Books.

1975   "Defenders of Order or Guardians of Human Rights?" In I. Taylor, P. Walton, and J. Young (Eds.), Critical Criminology. Boston: Routledge and Kegan Paul, pp. 113–146.

1976a   "Delinquency and the Collective Varieties of Youth." Crime and Social Justice 5 (Spring–Summer): 7–25.

1976b   "Marginal Youth and Social Policy." Social Problems 24(2) (December): pp. 184–191.

1977   "Social Class and the Definition of Crime." Crime and Social Justice 7 (Spring–Summer): 4–14.

SCOTT, R. A.

1969   The Making of Blind Men. New York: Russell Sage.

SCULL, A. T.

1977   "Madness and Segregative Control: The Rise of the Insane Asylum," Social Problems 24 (February): 337–351.

SEGAL, S.

1974   "Life in Board and Care: Its Political and Social Context." In S. Plog and S. Weiner (Eds.), Where Is My Home: Proceedings of a Conference on the Closing of State Mental Hospitals. Menlo Park, Calif.: Stanford Research Institute.

SEGAL, S. P., and V. AVIRAM

1978   The Mentally Ill in Community-Based Sheltered Care. New York: Wiley.

SELBY, H. A.

1974   Zapotec Deviance. Austin: University of Texas Press.

SELLIN, T.

1979   "The Conflict of Conduct Norms." In D. H. Kelly (Ed.), Deviant Behavior: Readings in the Sociology of Deviance. New York: St. Martin's, pp. 70–74.

SHAW, C. R.

1930   The Jack Roller. Chicago: University of Chicago Press.

SHAW, C. R., and H. D. McKAY
  1931   Social Factors in Juvenile Delinquency. Washington, D.C.: U.S. Government Printing Office.
  1972   Juvenile Delinquency and Urban Areas. Chicago: University of Chicago. Revised edition of 1942 original publication.
SHAW, C. R., with the assistance of H. D. McKAY and J. F. McDONALD
  1938   Brothers in Crime. Chicago: University of Chicago Press.
SHAW, C. R., in collaboration with M. E. MOORE
  1931   Natural History of a Delinquent Career. Chicago: University of Chicago Press.
SHAW, M.
  1972   "The Coming Crisis of Radical Sociology." In R. Blackburn (Ed.), Ideology in Social Science: Readings in Critical Social Theory. Fontana: Great Britain.
  1975   Marxism and Social Science. London: Pluto Press.
SHELDON, W. H.
  1949   Varieties of Delinquent Youth. New York: Harper Bros.
SHEPPARD, N., JR.
  1978   "A Tavern Precipitates Latest Chicago Corruption Scandal." New York Times (January 23): A12.
SHORT, J. F., JR., and F. L. STRODTBECK
  1965   Group Process and Gang Delinquency. Chicago: University of Chicago Press.
SILLS, D. L.
  1957   The Volunteers: Means and Ends in a National Organization. New York: Free Press.
SIMMEL, G.
  1955   Conflict and the Web of Group-Affiliations. New York: Free Press.
SIMPSON, R.
  1976   From the Closet to the Courts. New York: Viking.
SINGER, G., and B. RODGERS
  1975   "Mercury: The Hidden Poison in the Northern Rivers." Saturday Night (October): 15–22.
SLATER, P.
  1970   Pursuit of Loneliness: American Culture at the Breaking Point. Boston: Beacon.
SMART, C.
  1977   Women, Crime and Criminology: A Feminist Critique. London: Routledge and Kegan Paul.
SMIGEL, E. O., and H. L. ROSS
  1970   Crime Against Bureaucracy. New York: Van Nostrand Reinhold.
SNIDER, D. L.
  1978   "Corporate Crime in Canada: A Preliminary Report." Canadian Journal of Criminology 20 (April): 142–168.

SOLOMON, H.
    1977   "The Economists' Perspective of Economic Crime." *American Criminal Law Review* 14: 64–69.
SOLZHENITSYN, A.
    1973   *The Gulag Archipelago.* New York: Harper & Row.
SPECTOR, M., and J. KITSUSE
    1977   *Constructing Social Problems.* Menlo Park, Calif.: Cummings.
SPILERMAN, S.
    1970   "The Causes of Racial Disturbance: A Comparison of Alternative Explanations." *American Sociological Review* 35 (August): 627–649.
SPITZER, S.
    1975   "Toward a Marxian Theory of Deviance." *Social Problems* 22 (June): 638–651.
    1977   "On the Marxian Theory of Social Control: A Reply to Horowitz." *Social Problems* 24 (February): 364–366.
    1981   "The Dialectics of Formal and Informal Control." In R. L. Abel (Ed.), *The Politics of Informal Justice. Vol. 1: The American Experience.* New York: Academic Press.
SPRADLEY, J. P.
    1970   *You Owe Yourself a Drunk.* Boston: Little, Brown.
SROLE, L., T. S. LANGNON, and S. T. MICHAEL
    1962   *Mental Health in the Metropolis: The Midtown Manhattan Study, Vol. 1.* New York: McGraw-Hill.
STEADMAN, H.
    1979   *Beating a Rap? Defendants Found Incompetent to Stand Trial.* Chicago: University of Chicago Press.
STEBBINS, R. A.
    1971   *Commitment to Deviance: The Nonprofessional Criminal in the Community.* Westport, Conn.: Greenwood.
    1980   "Tolerable Deviance: The Study of Unthreatening Aberrant Behavior." Paper presented at the Annual Meeting of the Canadian Sociology and Anthropology Association, Montreal (June).
STENT, G. S.
    1978   *Paradoxes of Progress.* San Francisco: W. H. Freeman.
STEPHENSON, R. M.
    1973   "Involvement in Deviance: An Example and Some Theoretical Implications." *Social Problems* 21(2) (Fall): 173–190.
STIMSON, G. V.
    1973   *Heroin and Behavior.* New York: Wiley.
STINCHCOMBE, A. L.
    1963   "Institutions of Privacy in the Determination of Police Administrative Practice." *American Journal of Sociology* 69 (September): 150–160.

STONE, C. D.
 1975   Where the Law Ends: The Social Control of Corporate Behavior.
         New York: Harper Colophon Books.
STOUFFER, S. A., A. A. LUMSDAIME, and M. H. LUMSDAIME
 1949   The American Soldier: Combat and Its Aftermath, Vol. 2. Prince-
         ton, N.J.: Princeton University Press.
STREET, D., R. D. VINTNER, and C. PERROW
 1966   Organization for Treatment. New York: Free Press.
STUDT, E., S. MESSINGER, and T. P. WILSON
 1968   C-Unit: Search for Community in Prison. New York: Russell Sage
         Foundation.
SUBCOMMITTEE ON CRIME OF THE COMMITTEE ON THE JUDICIARY, U.S. HOUSE
OF REPRESENTATIVES
 1980   Corporate Crime. Ninety-Sixth Congress, Second Session. Wash-
         ington, D.C.: U.S. Government Printing Office.
SUDNOW, D.
 1975   "Normal Crimes: Sociological Features of the Penal Code in a
         Public Defender Office." In F. Scarpitti and P. McFarlane (Eds.),
         Deviance, Action/Reaction/Interaction. Reading, Mass.: Addison-
         Wesley.
SUTHERLAND, E. H.
 1924   Principles of Criminology. New York: J.B. Lippincott.
 1937   The Professional Thief. Chicago: University of Chicago Press.
 1939   Principles of Criminology, 3rd Ed. New York: J. B. Lippincott.
 1940   "White-Collar Criminality." American Sociological Review 5: 1–
         12.
 1949   White Collar Crime. New York: Holt, Rinehart and Winston.
SYKES, G. M.
 1956   "Men, Merchants, and Toughs: A Study of Reactions to Impris-
         onment." Social Problems 4: 130–138.
 1958   The Society of Captives. Princeton, N.J.: Princeton University
         Press.
 1978   Criminology. New York: Harcourt, Brace, Jovanovich.
SYKES, G. M., and S. MESSINGER
 1960   "The Inmate Social System." In R. Cloward et al. (Eds.), Theo-
         retical Studies in Social Organization of the Prison. New York:
         Social Science Research Council, pp. 5–19.
SZASZ, T.
 1961   The Myth of Mental Illness. New York: Heuber-Harper.
 1970   The Manufacture of Madness: A Comparative Study of the Inqui-
         sition and the Mental Health Movement. New York: Harper &
         Row.
TANNENBAUM, F.
 1938   Crime and the Community. New York: Columbia University Press.
TATARYN, L.
 1979   Dying for a Living. Ottawa: Deneau and Greenberg Publishers.

TAYLOR, I.
1980a *Crime at the End of the Welfare State.* London: Macmillan.
1980b "The Law and Order Campaigns in Britain and Canada." *Canadian Journal of Sociology* (forthcoming).
1980c "Some Theoretical Observations on *Homicide in Canada.*" In P. Reed (Ed.), *Homicide in Canada: An Anthology* (forthcoming).
TAYLOR, I., and L. TAYLOR
1973 *Politics and Deviance: Papers from the National Deviancy Conference.* Harmondsworth, England: Penguin.
TAYLOR, I., P. WALTON, and J. YOUNG
1973 *The New Criminology: For a Social Theory of Deviance.* Boston: Routledge and Kegan Paul.
1975 *Critical Criminology.* Boston: Routledge and Kegal Paul.
TAYLOR, L.
1970 "The Criminologist and the Criminal." *Catalyst* 5 (Summer): 48–54.
1971 *Deviance and Society.* London: Michael Joseph.
TAYLOR, L., and I. TAYLOR
1968 "We Are All Deviants Now—Some Comments on Crime." *International Sociology* 8: 29–32.
TAUBE, C., and R. REDICK
1977 "Provisional Data on Patient Care Episodes in Mental Health Facilities, 1975." *Mental Health Statistical Note* 139, National Institute of Mental Health, Survey and Reports Branch.
THE PRESIDENT'S REPORT ON OCCUPATIONAL SAFETY AND HEALTH
1972 Washington, D.C.: U.S. Government Printing Office.
THERBORN, G.
1980 *What Does the Ruling Class Do When It Rules?* London: Verso.
THIO, A.
1973 "Class Bias in the Sociology of Deviance." *American Sociologist* 8 (February): 1–12.
THIRD SPECIAL REPORT TO THE U.S. CONGRESS ON ALCOHOL AND HEALTH FROM THE SECRETARY OF HEALTH, EDUCATION AND WELFARE
1978 Washington, D.C.: U.S. Government Printing Office (June).
THOMAS, J.
1980 *The Relationship of Federal Sponsorship of Criminology and Policing Research in the Social Sciences,* Ph.D. Dissertation, Michigan State University, University Microfilms, Ann Arbor.
1981a "Class Struggle and Racial Hegemony in Prison Existence." Paper presented at the Western Criminology Association, San Diego (February).
1981b "Street Gangs and Marxian Delinquency Theory: Toward the Resolution of a Crisis." Paper presented at North Central Sociology Association, Cleveland (April).
Forthcoming "Delinquency and Marxian Theory: The Fabrication of a Crisis."

THOMAS, J. et al.
1980   "The Ideology of Prison Research: A Critical View of *Stateville: The Penitentiary in Mass Society.*" *Crime and Social Justice* 14: 45–50.

THOMPSON, H. S.
1966   *Hell's Angels.* New York: Random House.

THRASHER, F.
1963   *The Gang: A Study of 1,313 Gangs in Chicago.* Chicago: University of Chicago Press. Originally published in 1926.

TITLE, M. M.
1978   "Canadian Wiretaps Legislation: Protection or Erosion of Privacy." *Chitty's Law Journal* 26: 47–49.

TITTLE, C. R.
1969   "Crime Rates and Legal Sanctions." *Social Problems* 16 (Spring): 409–423.

1972   *Society of Subordinates.* Bloomington: Indiana University Press.

1975   "Labelling and Crime: An Empirical Evaluation." In W. Gove (Ed.), *Labelling of Deviance.* New York: Sage/Halstead, p. 176.

TITTLE, C. R., and D. P. TITTLE
1964   "Social Organization of Prisoners: An Empirical Test." *Social Forces* 43: 216–221.

TOULMIN, S.
1970   "Reasons and Causes." In R. Berger and F. Cioffi (Eds.), *Explanations in the Behavioral Sciences.* Cambridge: Cambridge University Press, p. 2.

TOWNSEND, J. M.
1976   "Self Concept and the Institutionalization of Mental Patients: An Overview and Critique." *Journal of Health and Social Behavior* 17: 263–271.

TRICE, H. M.
1957   "A Study of the Process of Affiliation with Alcoholics Anonymous." *Quarterly Journal of Studies on Alcohol* 18 (March): 39–54.

1966   *Alcoholism in America.* New York: McGraw-Hill.

TRIPP, C. A.
1975   *The Homosexual Matrix.* New York: New American Library.

TRUMAN, D.
1965   "Disillusion and Regeneration: The Quest for a Discipline." *American Political Science Review* 59 (December): 865–873.

TURK, A. T.
1969   *Criminality and the Legal Order.* Chicago: Rand McNally.

TURNER, S. H., and L. ROSEN
1967   "An Evaluation of the Lander Approach to Ecology of Delinquency." *Social Problems* 15 (Fall): 189–200.

ULC, O.
1972   The Judge in a Communist State. Athens, Ohio: Ohio University
        Press, p. 97.
URMER, A. H.
1978   "As Assessment of California's Mental Health Program: Implica-
        tions for Mental Health Delivery Systems." In C. J. Frederick
        (Ed.), Dangerous Behavior: A Problem in Law and Mental
        Health. Rockville, Md.: Center for Studies of Crime and Delin-
        quency, National Institute of Mental Health, pp. 137–152.
URQUHART, I.
1976   "The Skyshops Five." Macleans Magazine (May 3): 19–21.
1978   "The Bucks Start Here—Behind Every Great Leader is an Equally
        Great Bagman." Macleans Magazine 91 (May 15): 44+.
USEEM, M.
1976   "Government Influence on the Social Science Paradigm." Socio-
        logical Quarterly 19 (Spring): 146–61.
VAUGHAN, D.
1980   "Crime Between Organizations: Implications For Victimology."
        In G. Geis and E. Stotland (Eds.), White-Collar Crime: Theory
        and Research. Beverly Hills: Sage Publications, pp. 77–97.
VOLD, G. B.
1958   Theoretical Criminology. New York: Oxford University Press.
VOLD, G. B., and T. J. BERNARD
1979   Theoretical Criminology, 2nd Ed. New York: Oxford University
        Press.
VOLKMAN, R., and D. R. CRESSEY
1963   "Differential Association and the Rehabilitation of Drug Ad-
        dicts." American Journal of Sociology 69 (September): 129–142.
WALDORF, D.
1973   Careers in Dope. Englewood Cliffs, N.J.: Prentice-Hall.
WALKER, N.
1974   "Lost Causes in Criminology." In R. Hood (Ed.), Crime, Criminol-
        ogy and Public Policy. New York: Free Press, p. 58+.
WALLACE, S. E.
1968   "The Road to Skid Row." Social Problems 16 (Summer): 96–102.
WALTON, P.
1973   "The Case of the Weathermen: Social Reaction and Radical Com-
        mitment." In I. Taylor and L. Taylor (Eds.), Politics and Devi-
        ance: Papers from the National Deviancy Conference. Harmonds-
        worth, England: Penguin, pp. 157–181.
WARD, D., and G. KASSEBAUM
1965   Women's Prison. Chicago: Aldine.
WARREN, C. A. B., and J. JOHNSON
1972   "A Critique of Labeling Theory from the Phenomenological Per-

spective." In R. Scott and J. Douglas (Eds.), *Theoretical Perspectives on Deviance* New York: Basic Books.

WEINBERG, G.
1972   *Society and the Healthy Homosexual.* New York: St. Martin's.

WEINBERG, M. S.
1978   "Becoming a Nudist," and "The Nudist Management of Respectability." In E. Rubington and M. S. Weinberg (Eds.), *Deviance: The Interactionist Perspective*, 3rd Ed. New York: Macmillan, pp. 305–318 and pp. 342–351.

WEINBERG, M. S., and C. J. WILLIAMS
1974   *Male Homosexuals.* New York: Oxford University Press.

WEINBERG, S. K.
1942   "Aspects of Prison Social Structure." *American Journal of Sociology* 47: 717–726.

WEISSMAN, M., and G. KLERMAN
1978   "Epidemiology of Mental Disorders: Emerging Trends in the United States." *Archives of General Psychiatry* 35 (June): 705–712.

WENGER, M. G., and T. A. BONOMO
1978   "Crime, Crisis, and Social Revolution: An Examination of the Progressive Thesis in Marxist Criminology." *Transforming Sociology Series.* Red Feather Institute, Red Feather, Colorado.

WHEELER, S.
1961   "Socialization in Correctional Communities." *American Sociological Review* 26: 699–712.

WHITT, H., R. MEILE, and L. LAVSON
1979   "Illness Role Theory, the Labelling Perspective and the Social Meanings of Mental Illness: An Empirical Test." *Social Science and Medicine* 13A: 655–666.

WHYTE, W. F.
1943   *Street Corner Society.* Chicago: University of Chicago Press.

WIEDER, D.
1970   "On Meaning by Rule." In J. Douglas (Ed.), *Understanding Everyday Life.* Chicago: Aldine.
1974   *Language and Social Reality.* The Hague: Mouton.

WIEDER, D. L., and D. ZIMMERMAN
1976   "Regeln im Erklarungsprozess: Wissenschaftliche und Ethnowissenschaftliche Soziologie." In Weingarten, Sack, and Schenkhein (Hrsg.), *Ethnomethodologie.* Frankfurt: Suhrkamp.

WILEY, E. D.
1965   "Legislation Affecting Psychiatry and Mental Health." *New York State Journal of Medicine* 65 (November): 2718–2728.

WILKINS, L. T.
1964   *Social Deviance*, Englewood Cliffs, N.J.: Prentice-Hall.

WILMER, H. A.
1965   "The Role of the 'Rat' in Prison." *Federal Probation* 29: 44–29

WILSON, J. Q.
   1968   "The Police and the Delinquent in Two Cities." In S. Wheeler
           (Ed.), Controlling Delinquents. New York: Wiley & Son.
WILSON, T. P.
   1970   "Conceptions of Interaction and Forms of Sociological Explana-
           tion." American Sociological Review 35: 697–710.
WINICK, C.
   1961   "Physician Narcotic Addicts." Social Problems 9 (Fall): 174–
           186.
WIRTH, L.
   1928   The Ghetto. Chicago: University of Chicago Press.
WISE, D.
   1973   The Politics of Lying: Government Deception, Secrecy, and
           Power. New York: Vintage.
WISEMAN, J. P.
   1970   Stations of the Lost. The Treatment of Skid Row Alcoholics.
           Englewood Cliffs, N.J.: Prentice-Hall.
WOLFENSBERGER, W.
   1975   The Origin and Nature of Our Institutional Models. Syracuse,
           N.Y.: Human Policy Press.
WOLFF, M.
   1973   "Notes on the Behavior of Pedestrians." In A. Birenbaum and E.
           Sagarin (Eds.), People in Places: The Sociology of the Familiar.
           New York: Praeger, pp. 35–48.
WOODWARD, B., and BERNSTEIN, C.
   1974   All the President's Men. New York: Simon & Schuster.
WRIGHT, C., and S. RANDALL
   1978   "Contrasting Conceptions of Deviance in Sociology: Functional-
           ism and Labeling Theory." British Journal of Criminology 18:
           217–231.
WRIGHT, E. O.
   1973   The Politics of Punishment. New York: Harper Colophon Books.
   1979   Class, Crisis and the State. London: Verso.
WRONG, D.
   1961   "The Oversocialized Conception of Man in Modern Sociology."
           American Sociological Review 26: 183–193.
YABLONSKY, L.
   1959   "The Delinquent Gang as a Near-Group." Social Problems 7
           (Fall): 108–117.
   1968   The Hippie Trip. New York: Pegasus.
YARROW, M. R., C. G. SCHWARTZ, H. S. MURPHY, and L. C. DEASY
   1955   "The Psychological Meaning of Mental Illness in the Family."
           Journal of Social Issues 11: 12–24.
YOUNG, J.
   1970   The Drugtakers: The Social Meaning of Drug Use. London: Mac-
           Gibbon and Kee.

1973   "The Hippie Solution: An Essay in the Politics of Leisure." In I. Taylor and L. Taylor (Eds.), *Politcs and Deviance: Papers from the National Deviancy Conference*. Harmondsworth, England: Penguin, pp. 182–208.
1974   "Mass Media, Drugs and Deviance." In P. Rock and M. McIntosh (Eds.), *Deviance and Social Control*. London: Tavistock.

YOUNG, T. R.
1971   "The Politics of Sociology: Gouldner, Goffman and Garfinkel." *American Sociologist* 6 (November): 276–281.
1978   "Crime and Capitalism." Red Feather Institute, Red Feather, Colorado.
1980   "Corporate Crime: A Critique of the Clinard Report." No. 55 in *Transforming Sociology Series*. Red Feather Institute, Red Feather, Colorado.

ZABLOCKI, B.
1971   *The Joyful Community*. Baltimore: Penguin.

ZIMMERMAN, D. H.
1970   "The Practicalities of Rule Use." In J. Douglas (Ed.), *Understanding Everyday Life*. Chicago: Aldine.
1978   "Normen in Alltag." *Materialien zur Sociologie des Altags. Kolner Zeitschrift fur Sociologie und Sozialpsychologie*. Sonderheft 20: 86–99.

ZIMMERMAN, D. H., and M. POLLNER
1970   "The Everday World as a Phenomenon." In J. Douglas (Ed.), *Understanding Everyday Life*. Chicago: Aldine.

ZIMMERMAN, D. H., and D. L. WIEDER
1970   "Ethnomethodology and the Problem of Order: Comment on Denzin." In J. Douglas (Ed.), *Understanding Everyday Life*. Chicago: Aldine.

ZINBURG, N., and A. WEIL
1969   "Cannabis: The First Controlled Experiment." *New Society* 16 (January).

ZNANIECKI, F.
1952   *Cultural Sciences*. Urbana: University of Illinois Press.

ZORBAUGH, H. W.
1929   *The Gold Coast and the Slum*. Chicago: University of Chicago Press.

ZURCHER, L. A., and W. KEY
1968   "The Overlap Model: A Comparison of Strategies for Social Change." *Sociological Quarterly* 10 (Winter): 85–96.

ZURCHER, L. A., R. G. KIRKPATRICK, R. G. CUSHING, and C. K. BOWMAN
1971–72   "The Anti-Pornography Crusade: A Symbolic Crusade." *Social Problems* 19: 217–239.

INDEX